Multi-Perspective Modelling
for Knowledge Management
and Knowledge Engineering:
Practical Applications of
Artificial Intelligence

John K.C. Kingston

Ph.D.
University of Edinburgh
2007

About the Author

Dr John K.C. Kingston's interest in artificial intelligence first sprang out of his undergraduate studies in cognitive psychology, from where the AI programming concepts of "production rules" and "frames/objects" originate, and in game theory. He spent sixteen years in the Artificial Intelligence Applications Institute at the University of Edinburgh; AIAI's brief was to transfer AI technology from the university into the world of government, commerce and industry. He developed or supervised the development of prototype knowledge-based AI systems in fields ranging from air campaign planning to assessment of mortgage applications. The most successful of these systems was developed for the RAF Logistics Command (now the Joint Forces Logistics Command); it helped 'range managers' to recognise special circumstances that altered the number of spare parts they needed to order. It is saving an estimated £30 million per year.

He then became the Director of an interdisciplinary research centre in forensic statistics and legal reasoning. After leaving Edinburgh, he studied law for two years and then spent six years in the Civil Service and private industry. He is now a Senior Lecturer in Information Systems and Business Computing at the University of Brighton.

John holds degree level qualifications in psychology (B.Sc., Durham University); artificial intelligence (M.Sc. and Ph.D., University of Edinburgh); and law (Graduate Diploma in Law, University of Huddersfield and Diploma in Legal Practice, BPP Law School).

Abstract

It seems almost self-evident that "knowledge management" and "knowledge engineering" should be related disciplines that may share techniques and methods between them. However, attempts by knowledge engineers to apply their techniques to knowledge management have been praised by some and derided by others, who claim that knowledge engineers have a fundamentally wrong concept of what "knowledge management" is. The critics point to specific weaknesses of knowledge engineering, notably that the captured knowledge often lacks any description of its context.

Knowledge engineering has suffered some criticism from within its own ranks, too, particularly of the "rapid prototyping" approach, in which acquired knowledge was encoded directly into an iteratively developed computer system. This approach was indeed rapid, but when used to deliver a final system, it became nearly impossible to verify and validate the system or to maintain it. A solution to this has come in the form of knowledge engineering methodology, particularly from the CommonKADS methodology which proposes developing a number of models of the knowledge from different viewpoints at different levels of detail. CommonKADS also offers a library of generic models for the "inference structures" – the steps by which certain types of knowledge-based task are tackled. CommonKADS is now the most widely used non-proprietary knowledge engineering methodology.

The purpose of this book is to show how an analytical framework originally intended for information systems architecture can underlie knowledge management, knowledge engineering and the closely related discipline of ontology engineering. The framework suggests analysing information or knowledge from six perspectives (Who, What, How, When, Where and Why) at up to six levels of detail (ranging from "scoping" the problem to an implemented solution). The way that each of CommonKADS' models fit into this framework is discussed, in the context of several practical applications of artificial intelligence. Strengths and weaknesses in the models that are highlighted by the applications are analysed to show where CommonKADS is currently useful and where it could be extended.

The same framework is also applied to knowledge management; it is established that "knowledge management" is in fact a wide collection of different approaches and techniques, and the framework can support and extend every approach to some extent, as well as helping decide which approach is best for a particular case. Specific applications of using the framework to model medical knowledge and to resolve common problems in ontology development are presented.

The book also includes research on mapping knowledge acquisition techniques to CommonKADS' models; proposing some extensions to CommonKADS' library of generic inference structures; and it concludes with a suggestion for a "pragmatic" KADS for use on small projects. The appendices include extensive guidance on how to apply CommonKADS to a knowledge engineering project.

Acknowledgements

Thanks to all those who commented on drafts of papers in this book, especially Gail Anderson, Ruth Aylett, Jim Doheny, Brian Drabble, Ian Filby, John Levine, Ann Macintosh, Robert Rae, Dave Robertson and Austin Tate.

Thanks also to (most of) the anonymous referees of the papers included in this book.

Thanks to Robert Inder for regular creative ideas and suggestions during his time at AIAI, including identifying the value of Kline & Dolins' work on "probing questions", and proposing the "negative truth maintenance" approach outlined in section 13.3.3.

Thanks to all those who acted as domain experts for the projects described in this book.

Thanks to Jim Howe and Peter Ross for authorising the purchase of the laptop on which I wrote or re-wrote much of the material that turned this from a collection of papers into a Ph.D. thesis. I have been grateful to AIAI management for their support and flexibility over the years.

Thanks to Julian Smart for developing and regularly augmenting the HARDY tool with which I drew many of the diagrams that appear in this book.

Thanks to my parents for supporting my education and (repeatedly) encouraging me to finish this book.

I would especially like to thank Ian Filby, with whom I shared an office for many years, for many helpful discussions regarding CommonKADS; parts of this book would not have been written without Ian's suggestions, corrections, and "but what if..."s.

Declaration

I hereby declare that I composed this book entirely myself, with the exceptions described below, and that it describes my own research.

Chapters 2 through to 13 consist of previously published papers. The remaining chapters constitute new work written for this book.

- Chapter 2 is an extended version of a paper published in the proceedings of AI-METH 05, Gliwice, Poland, Nov 2005
- Chapter 3 was originally published in *Expert Systems with Applications*, 34, 1, 541-550, Jan 2008
- Chapter 4 was published in proceedings of ES '02, the annual conference of the British Computer Society's Specialist Group on Artificial Intelligence, Peterhouse College, Cambridge, 10-12 Dec 2002.
- Chapter 5 is an extended version of "Multi-Perspective Modelling of the Air Campaign Planning Process", a paper presented at IJCAI-97, Nagoya, Japan, 26-29 July 1997.
- Chapter 6 was originally published as "Modelling Agents and Communication using CommonKADS" in *Research and Development in Expert Systems XVII*, Proceedings of Expert Systems 00, the annual conference of the British Computer Society's Specialist Group on Expert Systems, Peterhouse College, Cambridge, Dec 2000.
- Chapter 7 originally appeared as "KBS Methodology as a framework for Co-operative Working" in *Research and Development in Expert Systems IX*, Proceedings of Expert Systems 92, the annual conference of the British Computer Society's Specialist Group on Expert Systems, Brighton, Dec 15-17 1992.
- Chapter 8 was published as "Re-engineering IMPRESS and X-MATE using CommonKADS" in *Research and Development in Expert Systems X*, Proceedings of Expert Systems 93, the annual conference of the British Computer Society's Specialist Group on Expert Systems, St. John's College, Cambridge, Dec 15-17 1993.
- Chapter 9 was published in the proceedings of AAAI-96, the Nineteenth Annual Conference of the American Association for Artificial Intelligence, Portland, Oregon, July 1996, under the title "CommonKADS Models for Knowledge Based Planning."

- Chapter 10 has not been published. It was released as "Design by Exploration: A Proposed CommonKADS Inference Structure", AIAI Technical Report, number AIAI-PR-62.
- Chapter 11 first appeared as "Linking Knowledge Acquisition with CommonKADS Knowledge Analysis" in *Research and Development in Expert Systems XI*, Proceedings of Expert Systems 94, the annual conference of the British Computer Society's Specialist Group on Expert Systems, St. John's College, Cambridge, December 15-17 1994.
- Chapter 12 was originally published as "Designing Knowledge Based Systems: The CommonKADS Design Model" in *Research and Development in Expert Systems XIV*, Proceedings of Expert Systems 97, the annual conference of the British Computer Society's Specialist Group on Expert Systems, St. John's College, Cambridge, December 15-17 1997. It was also published in a special double issue of the *Knowledge Based Systems Journal* containing the twelve best papers from ES '97: Elsevier, May/June 1998.
- Chapter 13 was originally published as "Pragmatic KADS: A methodological approach to a small expert systems project" in *Research and Development in Expert Systems VIII*, Proceedings of Expert Systems 91, the annual conference of the British Computer Society's Specialist Group on Expert Systems, St. John's College, Cambridge, December 15-17 1991.
- Appendix D was originally available as: AIAI Internal Report IR-6, August 1993. Section D.9 originally appeared in the first edition of the newsletter of the BCS SGES Methodologies Interest Group in the spring of 1992.

The contributions of those named as co-authors of original papers were as follows:
- Chapter 5: Terri Lydiard of the University of Edinburgh's Artificial Intelligence Applications Institute (AIAI) wrote the material on IDEF modelling in section 5.5.2. Anna Griffith of ISX Corporation, as custodian of the models developed on the project, made several changes and corrections.

• Chapter 9: Austin Tate of AIAI provided much of the information and some of the text for section 9.3. Nigel Shadbolt was also named as a co-author.

The following acknowledgements appeared on the original papers:

• Chapter 8: Much of the analysis carried out for this project was performed using KADS Tool from ILOG. AIAI wishes to thank ILOG for its support in this project.

• Chapter 9: The work described in this paper was carried out for a project commissioned by the Defence Research Agency Flight Systems Division, Farnborough. The project was entitled "Acquiring and Using Planning Knowledge for Search and Rescue". Thanks are due to the RAF Rescue Co-ordination Centre, Edinburgh for their co-operation and support, in particular Squadron Leader W. Gault. The contributions of the other staff on this project – H. Cottam (University of Nottingham), H. Beck and T. Duncan (AIAI) – are gratefully acknowledged.

One of the authors was sponsored by the Advanced Projects Research Agency (ARPA) and Rome Laboratory, Air Force Materiel Command, USAF, under grant number F30602-95-1-0022. The U.S. Government is authorised to reproduce and distribute reprints for governmental purposes notwithstanding any copyright notation hereon.

The views and conclusions contained herein are those of the author and should not be interpreted as necessarily representing the official policies or endorsements, either expressed or implied, of ARPA, Rome Laboratory or the U.S. Government.

All other contributions from others' work are identified in the text. The largest contributions are as follows:
• Chapter 18 and elsewhere: descriptions of CommonKADS models have been largely drawn from "the CommonKADS book" [147]
• Chapter 18: The capability descriptors for problem solving methods were almost entirely researched and proposed by Stuart Aitken.

- Chapter 15: an extended quotation is used from [58].
- Appendix D: the guidance questions in section D.7 are the work of Andreas Krueger, a student supervised by Ian Filby from AIAI [108] while the questions in Appendix C are the work of Colin Macnee, a student supervised by me [98] [120].

John K C Kingston
Edinburgh
August 27, 2007

Contents

1   Introduction

The subjects of this book are knowledge management, knowledge engineering, and ontological engineering. It has become increasingly clear that these subjects are interrelated. The goals of this book are to propose an underlying framework for all three of these subjects; to discuss the application of this framework and its potential advantages; and to illustrate this with detailed worked examples.

1.1   Overview

This book spans several years' worth of applied research. The research began by applying the CommonKADS methodology to a number of knowledge engineering projects, identifying strengths and weaknesses of the method, and proposing improvements to it. The projects required knowledge acquisition and/or knowledge based system development to a commercially acceptable standard. Typically, each project involved doing some knowledge acquisition, deciding which CommonKADS model(s) to develop, and then working with the "official" definition of the model and the acquired knowledge to produce an instantiated version of that model that represented the acquired knowledge. Depending on the results of these efforts, the next stage might include further knowledge acquisition and model instantiation; identifying weaknesses in the model definition that made it difficult or impossible to represent features of the task, and adapting the model accordingly; or even partially discarding the models recommended by CommonKADS in favour of another modelling technique. Each task therefore constituted an empirical test of the adequacy and applicability of CommonKADS models to real-world knowledge modelling.

After a while, the various projects described above spawned broader research into a consideration of the principles underlying CommonKADS. Experience has suggested that applying CommonKADS is not as straightforward as it seems (see for example the results of the Sisyphus project [68], in which four research groups using

CommonKADS to solve the same problem produced four very different knowledge models), and the goal of the research was to consider the basis on which CommonKADS was built in order to understand how to use it most effectively. Why were some knowledge models recommended and others not? How did the models relate to each other? This was coupled with an ongoing interest in which models were most useful in practice and which might not be needed in typical knowledge engineering projects.

The primary observation from this research was that CommonKADS is based on modelling knowledge and information using multiple perspectives at multiple levels of detail, and that as detail is added, an organisational goal is gradually refined into domain-specific or task-specific knowledge which is then transformed into a design specification for a knowledge based system. Given that CommonKADS begins by modelling organisational knowledge, it can be seen that the research described in this book will touch on principles of knowledge management as well as knowledge engineering.

Chapters 2 to 5 of this book focus on ontology development and knowledge management. Chapter 2 describes the multi-perspective modelling approach used throughout this book, and considers its implications and benefits for the selection and use of the various approaches and techniques that are collectively referred to as "knowledge management". Chapters 3 and 4 look at the implications of the multi-perspective framework for ontology development. Chapter 5 then begins the examination of the CommonKADS methodology by considering an application of CommonKADS' organisation level models, using a range of modelling formats.

The remaining chapters (chapter 6 onwards) discuss how CommonKADS was applied to various practical applications of artificial intelligence. The chapters include discussion of knowledge acquisition, generic knowledge models, ontology, and other issues. The chapters are ordered according to the recommended order of model development within CommonKADS: chapter 6 deals with the Agent and Communication Models (which are seen as representing part of the organisational context within which a knowledge based system can be developed); chapters 7 through to 11 discuss the Expertise Model; chapter 12 discusses the Design Model; and chapter 13 serves as a summary by proposing "Pragmatic KADS" i.e. identifying a minimal set of CommonKADS models for use on small KBS development projects.

1.2   Definitions

1.2.1 Knowledge Management

The exact definition of knowledge management has been, and is, a matter of considerable debate. Definitions range from "a method for gathering information and making it available to others" [1] through "capturing, organizing, and storing knowledge and experiences of individual workers and groups within an organization and making this information available to others in the organization"[2] to "the strategic use of information and knowledge resources to an organizations best advantage" [3] . Perhaps the most widely known definition (though arguably one that only describes some aspects of knowledge management) is that of Nonaka and Takeuchi [132], who argue that a successful KM program needs to "convert internalised tacit knowledge into explicit codified knowledge in order to share it, but also on the other hand for individuals and groups to internalise and make personally meaningful codified knowledge once it is retrieved from the KM system."

It's clear that the common theme is the application of knowledge throughout an organisation. The disagreements that arise are often connected with the focus of the definition ... is it on the knowledge itself, the process of distributing that knowledge, or the people who give/receive the knowledge? These disagreements are partly based on fundamentally different views on the nature of knowledge; those holding constructivist views of knowledge tend to favour approaches that focus on people, while those with a more cognitive view of knowledge are more inclined to focus on the knowledge itself. These views are discussed further in the review chapters of this book (chapters 14 to 20), but for now, it will simply be noted that a 'spectrum' of definitions exists, ranging from knowledge engineering solutions ('transactional' knowledge management) to community-based approaches ('innovation' knowledge management). This 'KM spectrum'

[1] www.qualishealth.org/qi/collaboratives/glossary.cfm

[2] library.ahima.org/xpedio/groups/public/documents/ahima/pub_bok1 025042.

[3] www.gov.bc.ca/prem/popt/service_plans/srv pln/pssg/appen_a.htm

was first proposed in [39] and was further discussed and developed in [78].

1.2.2 Knowledge Engineering

Knowledge engineering is the science/practice of developing knowledge based systems. It is directly analogous to software engineering of more conventional computer programs. It requires:

- identifying a human expert or another source of valuable knowledge;
- acquiring that knowledge in a systematic form;
- encoding that knowledge in a knowledge based computer program.

Typically, the resulting "knowledge based system" will ask users of the system for information and then process that information according to the knowledge that it possesses, in order to produce a reasoned conclusion. Many systems can also provide explanations of their reasoning.

1.2.3 CommonKADS: A   Knowledge   Engineering methodology

CommonKADS (and its predecessor, KADS – the acronym stood for either "Knowledge Acquisition and Design System" or "Knowledge Analysis and Design System") views knowledge engineering as a modelling activity, where each model is "a purposeful abstraction of some part of reality" (i.e. an "intermediate representation" between reality and some application of that model e.g. implementation in a knowledge based system). Each model focuses on certain aspects of the knowledge and ignores others. A knowledge engineering project entails the construction of a set of models that together constitute the knowledge that is being engineered. Knowledge models typically consist of one or more diagrams containing nodes (boxes, ellipses, or other icons) representing knowledge items, and arcs (arrows) between nodes representing input/output, flow of control, or other relationships. CommonKADS proposes a suite of six knowledge models that could be developed; if all are developed, they should gradually transform knowledge from a set of organisational needs & requirements to a high level design specification for a knowledge based system. The six models are:

• An Organisational model that represents the processes, structure and resources within an organisation, with the aim of identifying fruitful areas for better application of knowledge;

• A Task model to show the activities carried out in the course of a particular organisational process;

• An Agent model to represent the capabilities required of the agents who perform a process, and constraints on their performance;

• A Communication model to show the communication required between agents during a process;

• An Expertise[4] model which is a model of the expertise required to perform a particular task;

• A Design model which culminates in a design specification for a knowledge based system to perform all or part of the process under consideration.

1.2.4 Ontology

Like "knowledge management", the term "ontology" has been defined in various ways. Guarino & Giaretta [77] have identified no fewer than eight different meanings of it in the relevant literature:

1. Ontology as a philosophical discipline
2. Ontology as an informal conceptual system
3. Ontology as a formal semantic account
4. Ontology as a specification of a "conceptualization"
5. Ontology as a representation of a conceptual system via a logical theory
    a. characterized by specific formal properties
    b. characterized only by its specific purposes
6. Ontology as the vocabulary used by a logical theory
7. Ontology as a (meta-level) specification of a logical theory

There are three main themes in the above list. Definition 1 is quite different from all the others, and reflects the original meaning of the word 'ontology', before it became a widely used term in the knowledge

---

[4] The "CommonKADS book" [147] refers to this model as the "Knowledge Model". While the original label of "Expertise Model" was sometimes inaccurate, because the knowledge needed to carry out tasks is not always expert knowledge, "knowledge model" is a very general term that could encompass any or all of the CommonKADS models. I have chosen to use the original name to avoid confusion with multiple other uses of the terms 'knowledge' and "knowledge model" within this book.

management community ... ontology is a philosophical discipline is "the study of the nature of being, reality and substance". Definitions 2 and 3 conceive an ontology as a conceptual "semantic" entity, either formal or informal, while according to the interpretations 5-7 an ontology is a specific "syntactic" object ... or rather, a syntactic descriptive scheme that can be used to label other objects and to describe their interrelationships.

For the purposes of this book, a pragmatic definition will be used that follows the latter theme. The definition is based on that of Gruber [75], who stated (*inter alia*) that "an ontology is an explicit specification of a conceptualisation." To this, I will add the following: "In knowledge engineering practice, an 'ontology' often equates to the definition of what can be represented within a computer program."

1.2.5 Knowledge Engineering Methods: A Brief History

Early approaches and reusability

When expert systems initially emerged from the research laboratory into the commercial world with systems such as MYCIN [154] and PROSPECTOR [25], they were typically developed by "rapid prototyping". This was a recognised technique in software engineering, where a "quick and dirty" version of the final system was developed in order to test out certain programming approaches, and to show to the end users as an aid to requirements capture. Since the acquisition of expert knowledge has many similarities to requirements capture, knowledge engineers seized on this method as a way of quickly developing an impressive-looking system. The method employed was typically to obtain some knowledge from the expert, to program this into an "expert system shell" usually in the form of IF-THEN rules, and then to show the resulting program to the expert both to verify that the system correctly reflected the expert's knowledge to date and also as an *aide memoire* to the acquisition of further knowledge.

The method was very effective in triggering expert's memories and in developing small systems with impressive speed. However, in software engineering, rapidly prototyped systems are normally considered to be "throwaway prototypes", whereas early expert system developers often developed the prototype to the point where it included sufficient expert knowledge to be considered an adequate expert system, and then delivered it to the users. This led to considerable problems when the knowledge needed updating or the system needed future maintenance, because there was often little or no documentation describing the system's structure, nor was there any "intermediate representation" of the expert's knowledge. In one case (reported in [80]), even the original designer and programmer of an expert system was unable to understand its code six months after the system was initially delivered.

Rapid prototyping led to some other problems, too. In some cases, the expert's knowledge was not necessarily suitable for encoding as IF-THEN rules, but the constraints of the programming environment led to knowledge engineers trying to squeeze the knowledge into that format [5] . Another problem was that knowledge engineers who developed several systems, particularly in the same domain, began to notice certain patterns emerging but had no way of recording thos patterns for re-use in future systems. Eventually, it was realised that the patterns recurred across domains as long as the same type of task was being tackled (see e.g. [95]). It was this observation coupled with a desire to introduce some good practice from software engineering into the development of expert systems that led to the development of KADS.

Software engineering and the development of CommonKADS
Software engineering methods were largely ignored by early expert system developers. The reasons are not clear; it may be that most of these developers came from research laboratories where such methods were not part of the culture, or that the methods themselves were considered inadequate for a system that encoded expert knowledge. If the latter is true, it may be that expert system developers were actually criticising the wrong target – the "waterfall model", first identified by Royce [143]. In the waterfall model, the various phases of software engineering (requirements, design, implementation, verification and maintenance) proceed in a purely sequential manner; once a stage has been completed, and its outputs handed on to the next stage, it is never revisited. This model has certain advantages; getting the early stages 100% right saves considerable time in later stages, and

---

[5] For an illustration of a task where the same system was programmed using three different "expert system shells" offering different programming environments, and the advantages of having object-oriented programming available to complement IF-THEN rules, see [84].

also facilitates the distribution of a project between departments. But it has been heavily criticised for its lack of iteration; in fact, Royce himself only identified it in order to make this criticism and to recommend a more iterative model. Since rapid prototyping of expert systems is perhaps the ultimate iterative system development technique, it is hardly surprising that a "culture gap" existed between expert system developers and software engineering methods that were perceived to be based on the waterfall model.

Yet software engineering methods offer far more than just a lifecycle process. They also offer recommended documents that are needed for describing the outputs of each stage; notations for modelling the flow of information and other processes within the planned software system; and design and testing techniques. The original KADS methodology was largely focused on its library of "interpretation models" (i.e. attempts to capture some of the patterns that recurred across different knowledge-based tasks), but CommonKADS was explicitly designed to incorporate aspects of other software engineering methods. Its notation drew on methods such as PRINCE [133], Rumbaugh's and Yourdon's object-oriented state diagrams [144] [32], and Jackson's structured programming methods [54], especially in the notation for its diagrams. It also extended its libraries (it started to build a library of "problem solving methods" – more detailed process control descriptions for knowledge based tasks) and created a conceptual modelling language (CML) into which instantiated knowledge models could be translated. There was even a formal modelling language (FML, later $(ML)^2$) into which CML could be transformed for logical verification purposes; this language was highly regarded in the knowledge engineering community [181]. When the CommonKADS book was published in 1999 [147], a number of documents were recommended to accompany (or in some cases embody) some of the knowledge models.

Today, most software engineering methods prefer a "spiral lifecycle" model (see [11]) in which (in general terms) several iterations of the entire 'waterfall' are carried out, with risk assessments performed before each new iteration is begun; and many of the software engineering notations that CommonKADS drew on have been superseded by, or incorporated into, the Unified Modelling Language (UML) [137]. CommonKADS' notation, as defined in the CommonKADS book, has many similarities with UML notation.

Other knowledge engineering methods and knowledge engineering workbenches

KADS and CommonKADS were not the only knowledge engineering methods developed in late 1980s and early 1990s, but they were easily the most influential. At least one project funded under the ESPRIT programme, VITAL (see e.g. [51]), aimed to provide a competing methodology and an associated workbench [6]; however, while the resulting method was considerably stronger than CommonKADS on the development and inclusion of knowledge acquisition tools, its library of generic tasks was largely copied from KADS. A number of management consultancies also developed their own proprietary methods, but significantly, Touche Ross chose to use KADS and CommonKADS, and used them with considerable commercial success.

Following a different thread, Chandrasekaran's Generic Tasks approach [27] and Steels' Components of Expertise [161] provided patterns that represented generic knowledge based tasks, but in smaller components than KADS did. One of the goals of developing CommonKADS was to incorporate these approaches into KADS, or at least to make them usable in parallel. This is discussed in more detail in chapter 8.

Three different workbenches were developed to support KADS: ILOG's KADSTool, a well-designed commercial product; Bull's OpenKADSTool which attempted to support a methodology derived from the original KADS and developed in parallel with CommonKADS; and the CommonKADS workbench developed as part of the KADS-II project which had the most functionality (it allowed output into CommonKADS' Conceptual Modelling Language, for example, and even promised a CML to FML converter) but was based on software that was perceived not to be commercially robust (SICStus Prolog). For a comparison of these three workbenches, see [101].

Today, the three KADS workbenches are no longer available. The knowledge acquisition tools from the VITAL workbench survive in the PC Pack tool from Epistemics Ltd.

---

[6] A 'workbench' is a software system supporting the use of a method. In software engineering they are often known as CASE (Computer-Aided Software Engineering) tools. The obvious correlate for knowledge engineers would be CAKE tools; however, this acronym struggled to find widespread acceptance, and 'workbench' is the preferred term in this book.

1.2.6 Overview of the book

The key contributions of this book to the field of knowledge engineering are:

• The smooth integration of knowledge management with knowledge engineering. Knowledge based systems (or other outputs of the knowledge engineering process) are seen as one possible method of implementing knowledge management for a particular organisational task; further, it is argued that the analyses carried out to determine what knowledge management technique is appropriate for a task can or should be based on knowledge engineering methods;

• A step-by-step guide is given to using the CommonKADS methodology, from organisational analysis through to knowledge based system design and implementation;

• Some proposals are made for additions to CommonKADS' library of inference structures (see Chapters 9 and 10) and problem solving methods (see Chapter 8);

• Each aspect of CommonKADS is analysed for its contribution to a typical knowledge engineering task, and a list of the models that are absolutely necessary is proposed for knowledge engineers carrying out small KBS projects.

Part I: Multi-Perspective Modelling

Part I: Multi-Perspective Modelling

2 Multi-Perspective Modelling for Knowledge Management

2.1 Introduction

The subject of this chapter is the modelling of organisational knowledge for the purpose of knowledge management. Modelling expresses concepts that allow each part of an organisation to understand and contribute to its own development. A good model can communicate much of a company's purpose to stakeholders in the business, whether they are employees, shareholders, or customers. Modelling can be applied to all stages of business and systems development, whether at the higher levels of considering business structure and business processes, or looking at particular tasks or knowledge assets in more detail.

Many readers will be familiar with modelling of information and of information systems. The basic approach to modelling knowledge is similar; models typically consist of annotated box-and-arrow diagrams, representing processes, taxonomic classification, or other relationships. This is possible because the relationship between knowledge and information is similar to the relationship between information and data; information consists of data that are linked or applied in some way to provide relevance or purpose, while knowledge consists of pieces of information that are linked or applied, usually in order to make decisions. To give an example, a car driver may possess the following data: the price of petrol, the fuel level in his car, the fuel consumption rate of his car, the distance to his destination, and the amount of cash in his wallet. Information can be obtained from these data by calculation (how much it would cost to fill the tank; how much petrol the driver can afford; whether either of these amounts of petrol will be sufficient to get to the destination). Decisions can then be made based on this information; e.g. that it's necessary for the driver to drive home to collect his credit card, or that he must drive slowly in order to reduce the fuel consumption rate of the car. There is some debate whether the knowledge resides in the set of possible decisions, in the justification for those decisions, or in the deductive process itself; this chapter considers that any of these may constitute knowledge.

The key to the use of knowledge models within knowledge management is that models only become meaningful to an enterprise when they cause action and provoke thought. Since knowledge management typically focuses on knowledge already within the organisation that is at present being under-used, then understanding the organisation, provoking thought and supporting action are all crucial aspects of knowledge management. Models also promote understanding across different business groups in an organisation. However, some knowledge management researchers have suggested that modelling's greatest strength - the elimination of irrelevant information - is also its greatest weakness, especially in cases where there are many interacting patterns of information and knowledge which must all be taken into account in order to understand the real world fully. While this criticism is primarily based on fundamentally differing views of the nature of knowledge and hence of knowledge management (a claim which is discussed more fully in [78]), limitations caused by such elimination do exist, and those who wish to model knowledge must either accept these limitations or try to overcome them.

A possible solution to this problem can be found in the use of *multi-perspective modelling* - the creation of a number of different models of the same artefact, from different viewpoints. The term "multi-perspective modelling" has been used in multiple ways by previous authors (see discussion below); in this paper, multi-perspective modelling refers to building a number of models of the same knowledge but with different emphases. For example, one model might focus on processes, another on agents, another on communication, and another on concepts or resources.

The multi-perspective approach proposed in this chapter is based on the Zachman framework for Information Systems Architecture which provides a framework for categorizing different information perspectives, at different levels of detail. This chapter describes the Zachman framework and the derived multi-perspective modelling approach in some detail, then shows how the models from an existing information modelling method (UML, the Unified Modelling Language) and an existing knowledge modelling method (CommonKADS) map onto this framework. The chapter then extends the framework by applying its principles at a meta level, and validates the usefulness of the framework by showing how a couple of well-known software development techniques can be derived from this meta-analysis.

2.2 The Zachman framework

The Information Systems Architecture framework proposed by Sowa & Zachman [197] [159] is intended to provide a framework for creating all the models necessary to create an overall model of an organisation or enterprise. John Zachman describes it as "a simple, logical structure of descriptive representations for identifying models that are the basis for designing the enterprise and for building the enterprise's systems" [197]. It is also a good framework for characterizing the role, function and purpose of information systems within an organisation. The framework consists of a 6x6 matrix (see Tables 2.1(a) and (b)), whose two dimensions represent the perspective being taken on information and the level of detail at which this information is being represented. It turns out that the level of detail corresponds closely with progress in a software development project. So, if the result of knowledge management is to propose a software development project (or any other project that requires development of some artefact by progressive refinement of a specification) then the Zachman framework should provide a structure for that project.

2.2.1 Perspectives in the Zachman framework

The "perspectives" dimension of the Zachman framework proposes that six perspectives on information (and, by extension, knowledge) are necessary, characterised by the phrases *who, what, how, when, where* and *why*. A multi perspective approach to knowledge modelling will create models that represent only the knowledge relevant to that perspective: for example, the "who" perspective will focus on agents, representing their capabilities and responsibilities, while the "how" perspective will focus on tasks or processes that need to be performed. A full description of the expected contents of each perspective can be found in Table 2.2 which is taken from [197].

	What	How	Who
Objectives/ Scope "contextual"	List of things important to the business	List of business processes	List of business locations
Enterprise "conceptual"	Enterprise Entity e.g. Semantic Model	Enterprise process e.g. Business process Model	Enterprise Location e.g. Business Legacy Systems
System "logical"	Entity Type e.g. Logical data model	System Process e.g. Application Architecture	Site e.g. Distributed Systems Architecture
Technology constrained "physical"	Data Structure e.g. Physical Data Model	Application e.g. System Design	Connection Port e.g. System Architecture
Detailed representations "out of context"	Data Container e.g. Data description	Module/ Object e.g. Programs	Address/ protocol e.g. Network Architecture
Functioning enterprise	Information e.g. Data	Procedure e.g. Function	Client/ Server e.g. Network

Table 2.1a: The Zachman framework (part 1)

	When	Where	Why
Objectives/ Scope "contextual"	List of important organisations	List of events	List of Business goals & strategies
Enterprise "conceptual"	Organisation e.g. Workflow model	Organisation e.g. Master Schedule	Objective e.g. Business Plan
System "logical"	Role e.g. Human Interface Architecture	System Event e.g. Processing Structure	Criterion e.g. Business Rule Model
Technology constrained "physical"	User e.g. Presentation Architecture	Technical Event e.g. Control Structure	Condit-ion e.g. Rule Design
Detailed representations "out of context"	Individual transaction e.g. Security Architecture	Component Event e.g. Timing Description	Sub-condition e.g. Rule Specification
Functioning enterprise	Worker e.g. Organisation	Operating Event e.g. Schedule	Target e.g. Strategy

Table 2.1b: The Zachman framework (part 2)

Why is this approach useful? Well, let us assume that a specialised, experienced department, whose task is to diagnose unusual faults with products and recommend solutions, has been identified as a "knowledge asset" during a knowledge management feasibility exercise. The different perspectives can be thought of as different managers' views on the department. For example, an operations manager might view the department as a user of external resources and a solver of specialised problems; a personnel manager might view the department as a network of interactions between agents (i.e. people with defined roles); and the CEO might view it as a producer of reports and a necessary contributor to the company's overall vision to supply high quality products to the market. In other words, the operations manager is concerned with "what" the department consumes, "where" these resources come from and "how" the department contributes to the overall process; the personnel manager is concerned with "who" is involved; and the CEO is concerned with "why" that department exists as well as with "what" its outputs are. So by modelling each manager's view separately, while referring to the same concepts and relationships, it is possible to obtain a more complete view of the department than any of the managers hold, whilst enabling each of them to see (and to verify and approve) a specific model representing their perspective.

2.2.2 Levels of detail in the Zachman framework

As mentioned above, the Zachman framework proposes six levels of detail for models. Starting from the most general, these are labelled as "scope", "enterprise", "system", "technology", "detail", and "functioning enterprise"[7]. These are described further in Table 2.3 which is partly drawn from [34].

These levels can be seen as the concerns of different *professions* [159], whereas the previous section proposed that the perspectives can be considered to be the views of different *managers*. So if the overall task is the design and construction of a building, then the architect is concerned with the broad view of gross sizing, shape and spatial relationships, as well as the overall structure of the building; the owner

---

[7] Strictly speaking, the Zachman framework proposes five levels of models, plus the implementation of those models. As a result, the functioning enterprise level, also called the "implementation" level, does not appear in some versions of the Zachman framework.

Perspective	Description
What	Declarative knowledge about things as opposed to procedural knowledge about actions. "What" knowledge encompasses concepts, physical objects and states. It also includes knowledge about classification or categorisation of those states.
How	Knowledge about actions or events. It includes knowledge about which actions are required if certain events occur; which actions will achieve certain states; and the required or preferred ordering of actions.
When	When actions or events happen, or should happen, it is knowledge about the time at which events happen and of controls needed on timing and ordering of events
Who	The agents (human or automated) who carry out each action and their capabilities and authority to carry out particular actions.
Where	Where knowledge is needed and where it comes from – communication and input/output knowledge.
Why	Rationale, reasons, arguments, empirical studies and justifications for actions and how they are done.

Table 2.2: Description of perspectives

Level of detail	Description
Scoping (Contextual)	Defines high level business needs and business functions at a global enterprise level. Identifies key enterprise functions that run the business.
Enterprise (Conceptual)	Defines in more detail the business functions and needs of the enterprise, concentrating on one business function at a time.
System (Logical)	Defines the steps taken and resources needed to carry out a single business process.
Technology (Physical)	A high level design specification for an implementation that will represent everything that appeared at the system level
Detailed representation (Out-of-context)	A more detailed specification, targeted at a particular situation.
Functioning enterprise (Implementation)	An implementation of the design: a software program, a building, or another constructed artefact.

Table 2.3: Description of levels of detail in the Zachman framework

relationships, as well as the overall structure of the building; the owner is concerned with floor plans and facilities; the designer must consider strength, support and stability of each floor; the builder is concerned with beams, junctions, and concrete; the subcontractor is concerned with a single aspect of the builder's job (delivering beams, welding junctions, etc); and the bricklayer and the carpenter are the ones who do most of the actual building. So each profession must look at the same building at a different level of detail in order to understand the design fully enough to carry out their particular job.

It's worth noting that the six levels of detail require two rather different types of model. The first three levels - scope, enterprise and system - are increasingly detailed models of existing processes and related information/knowledge, while the remaining levels - technology, detailed representation and implementation - are increasingly detailed representations of a design that meets the requirements of representing a particular business process. In the language of the CommonKADS methodology (which is discussed further below), the transformation from one level to the next is usually a *refinement* task - describing something in greater detail – but in the case of the transformation from the system level to the technology level, it is more of a *selection* task - choosing design techniques that are suitable for the modelled knowledge. This implies that this transformation is likely to be knowledge-intensive compared with the other transformations.

2.2.3 The multi-perspective matrix: the Zachman framework

Having established the need for representing different perspectives, and different levels of detail, the most important remaining question for practical purposes is whether all six perspectives need to be modelled at all six levels of detail. To answer this, let's return to the example above where an entire department was considered to be a knowledge asset. Now let's consider a collection of help desk reports compiled by this department to be a knowledge asset at a lower level of detail (the "system level", in Zachman's terms). Note that a similar pattern emerges: the departmental librarian treats the reports as a resource to be managed ("what"), newly recruited technicians may treat them as a step by step guide to problem solving ("how"), the designer of the company intranet might link them together as interdependent knowledge sources ("where" and, if they are linked to their authors for the purposes of establishing trust, also "who"), while the quality manager may be mostly concerned that the reports provide sufficient evidence of good practice ("why") to show that the departmental quality system is working. For good measure, let's extend the example to the design of a help desk decision support system (i.e. the "technology level"); the designer needs to consider the static objects ("what"), the process flows and inferences ("how), the user interface and other interfaces ("who" and "where"), and flow of control ("when"). In other words, most of the perspectives do seem to be needed at each level of detail. The Zachman framework is therefore taken to be a reasonably complete specification of the models needed to represent an organisation or enterprise fully.

2.2.4 Different meanings of multi-perspective modelling

Before continuing with discussion of perspectives and levels of detail in the context of the Zachman framework, a diversion is necessary to discuss the use of the term "multi-perspective modelling" in software engineering literature. The reason for this is that two or three distinct uses of the term have emerged, but have not been clearly distinguished. These uses are characterised below as the *negotiation* approach, the *crystallography* approach and the *stereoscopy* approach.

Negotiation approach: This approach uses the term "multi-perspective modelling" to refer to the representation of conflicting views of different agents about the same artefact or concept. Each agent involved in a development process has its own view on the artefact or system it is trying to describe or model, and these views may contain conflicting information. The goal of multi-perspective modelling is therefore a negotiated settlement of conflicting views, and the two critical issues are the choice of viewpoints to represent an artefact fully, and the management of inconsistencies between views [160]. At least one workshop has been held that brought together researchers in this area [56]; other publications in this area include [66] and [29].

Crystallography approach: Researchers on the Tropos project [107] consider a software development project from different angles (e.g. in terms of actors and their capabilities; in terms of goals and intentions; or in terms of processes or in terms of constituent objects). To them, the purpose of "multi-perspective modelling" is for an individual to understand the structure of a project by assembling several partial views of the structure into a single conception. Similarly, another project which used multiple modelling techniques for an interface design problem was "not looking at widely different techniques to see which one of them is best, but ... argue[d] that the impact from a collection of techniques is greater than the sum of their individual contributions" [196] - in other words, these researchers also considered that multiple consistent perspectives may be held by a single individual, but extended the idea to claim that the interaction of the multiple perspectives provides additional information. This view of multi-perspective modelling as being "examination of a single artefact from many angles by an individual" is taken in this chapter.

Stereoscopy approach: A project on image rendering of Chinese landscape paintings [30] is concerned with perspectives in the literal sense - visual angles on a physical object (in this case, a Chinese painting). This approach is akin to stereoscopy which gives an impression of three dimensions by using multiple two-dimensional images of the same objects, taken from slightly different angles. This use of the term "multi-perspective modelling" is rare in the software engineering literature, but is noted for completeness.

The reason why this analysis is needed is that without it, very different understandings of the Zachman framework can arise. For the "crystallography" approach, the perspectives are represented by the columns of the Zachman framework, while the rows represent levels of detail. But for the "negotiation" approach, the perspectives could be represented by the columns or the rows, depending on whether the conflicting opinions were held by different managers or different professions (or both!). And for the stereoscopy approach, the Zachman framework has little relevance. It's also worth noting that the term "viewpoints" is highly ambiguous; while the term has been used extensively by researchers following the "negotiation" approach to represent conflicting opinions, it could equally be used in its more literal sense by the other two approaches.

For simplicity, the term "viewpoints" is avoided in this book.

2.3   Worked example: Medical diagnosis and treatment

At this point, a worked example of multi-perspective modelling would be helpful. The example below is taken from [100], and consists of a number of models of a medical process: the diagnosis and treatment of tumours on the parotid gland (which is in the neck). The models are considered to be at the second (enterprise) level of detail.

2.3.1   "How": Clinical protocol

Figure 2.1 shows a portion of a clinical protocol (i.e. recommended procedure) for diagnosis and treatment of parotid tumours. This portion of the protocol is concerned with diagnosis and treatment selection for a progressive lump (i.e. a lump on or near the parotid gland that is growing progressively larger). The model of the full clinical protocol consists of about 10 diagrams of similar size; see [155] for details. This diagram which is drawn using a diagramming technique known as ProFORMA [64], shows that the first stage of investigating a progressive lump is to carry out fine needle aspiration cytology (FNAC) which draws some fluid out from the lump and then to send it away for analysis. Once the results of this enquiry have been returned, two decisions are needed; what type of scan is required (CT scan, ultrasound and MRI are the usual options) and what treatment is required. The remaining boxes represent links to other process diagrams.

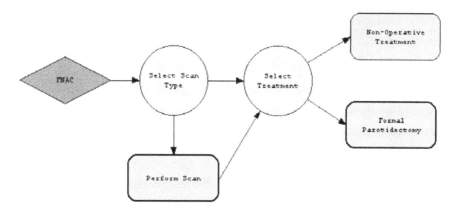

Figure 2.1: Protocol for diagnosing a progressive lump

2.3.2   "Where": Inter-Department Communication

The "where" perspective shows communication that is needed during a procedure. At the enterprise level of abstraction, communication is generally concerned with the transfer of information or artefacts between individuals or departments. In this example, the clinician must communicate with the laboratory that performs the FNAC tests, with the radiology department that performs scans, and with the surgical unit that arranges operations. This information can be represented in a Role Activity Diagram (RAD) [135] which shows which departments (or, more generally which roles) perform which activities; by including the sequence of activities, the needs for communication become obvious. An example of a RAD can be seen in Figure 2.2.

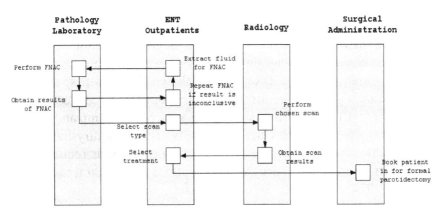

Figure 2.2: The "where" perspective – Role Activity Diagram

2.3.3   "Who": Agent Modelling

In addition to the information captured in a Role Activity diagram, there is a need for the "who" perspective to represent the capability of agents, departments, or other role-players to perform certain actions and the authority that certain agents have to perform those actions or to use, consume or modify resources (Figure 2.3). At an enterprise level of abstraction, capability and authority may be expressed by defining the rights and responsibilities of an agent. For example, a doctor may have rights to add to a patient's medical record, implying both authority to change an artefact and the capability to do so, as well as responsibilities such as making sure a patient's medical record is kept up to date.

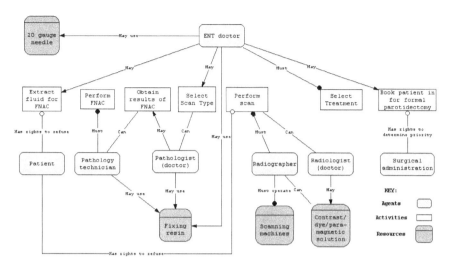

Figure 2.3: Capabilities, authorities, rights and responsibilities of agents

The modelling technique used here is loosely based on the ORDIT method for requirements definition [50] and the CommonKADS Agent Model [186]. Capability, authority, rights and responsibilities are represented by four different types of arc: these arcs are labelled "can", "may", "has rights to" and "must" respectively.

2.3.4   "What": Data, Information and Resources

The "what" perspective considers the data and information that are referred to and the resources that are used, consumed, modified, manipulated or otherwise involved in the overall process. Cook (op.cit.) argues that "the data architecture is more critical than the process architecture because most business processes exist to manage the assets, not the other way around". She proposes that the enterprise level of the "what" perspective should contain data classes which are subclasses of global data classes; the relationships between classes can be defined using entity relationship diagrams. In practice, these data classes often subsume information such as summations or categorisations as well as data. In this example, data classes might include clinical tests and patients; information represented in data classes might include results of tests; and resources include the machines required for scanning, the chemical solutions required as "markers" for scanning, and the needles required for extracting fluid for an FNAC. The resources may have associated constraints; for example that use of a scanning machine requires several weeks' notice, or that patients might be allergic to the iodine-based "contrast" that is injected as a marker for CT scans. At the system level of abstraction, where resources, constraints, and information artefacts are identified individually, there are several ways in which resources might need to be modelled. If the resources can be grouped into classes, then a taxonomic hierarchy might be advantageous; for example, it might be helpful to know if scanning machines belong to a class of machines that uses X-rays, and if so, whether they belong to the sub-class of machines that includes automatic cut-outs to prevent overdoses. If a detailed representation of relationships between resources was needed, then a semantic network could be drawn. However, at the enterprise level of abstraction, a more general representation is more appropriate; an entity-relationship diagram could be used, but we have chosen to use a UML class diagram, to represent constraints more clearly. Figure 2.4 therefore shows a UML class diagram representing a simple hierarchy of resources and a simple hierarchy of test results.

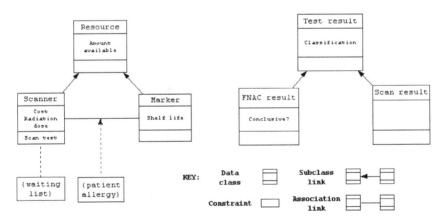

Figure 2.4: UML class diagram: resources and test results

2.3.5 "When": Schedules

Information about timing of activities and actions is very important in a planning problem; for other tasks, such as this diagnostic task, there is less need for such information. It is, nevertheless, advisable to draw a PERT chart, GANTT chart, or simple timeline of activities and any necessary inter-activity delay (such as the waiting list for scanning appointments) in order to highlight any time-related issues (such as the fact that the chemicals used for marker solutions have a limited shelf life) or bottlenecks.

Figure 2.5 shows a PERT chart of activities and inter-activity delays; the durations (which appear at the bottom of the activity nodes) are in hours. It shows the two bottlenecks in the process (waiting lists for scanning and for operations) clearly. N.B. For illustrative purposes, it has been assumed that the "select scan type" activity can be carried out in parallel with awaiting the results of the FNAC.

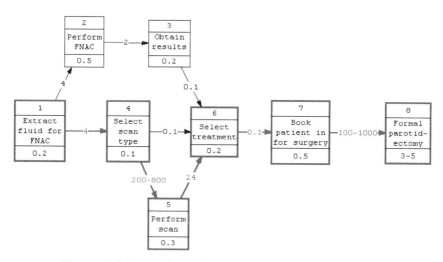

Figure 2.5: A timeline of activities in diagnosing progressive lumps

2.3.6 "Why": Published Clinical Evidence

The "why" knowledge for a clinical protocol consists of clinical evidence - published results of clinical trials, meta-studies, and expert opinions. The relative importance of different types of clinical evidence has been discussed in [122].

For the small part of the clinical process that we are considering, the "why" knowledge consists of all known articles published to date; at the time when this protocol was prepared, there were eight relevant published articles. Five of them argue for or against particular types of scan, the others argue for or (primarily) against formal parotidectomy. These justifications can be represented in a rationale diagram; Figure

2.6 uses and extends the QOC (Questions, Options & Criteria) notation [119] to represent rationale for the "Select Scan Type" decision.

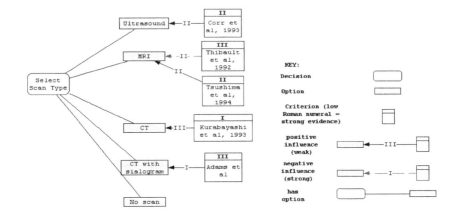

Figure 2.6: Extended QOC diagram showing the rationale for a decision

2.4   Multi-perspective Knowledge Management

In this section, we look at two approaches to characterizing knowledge management activities: Derek Binney's KM spectrum and Boisot's knowledge asset description characteristics. Both are considered from the viewpoint of multi-perspective modelling to show the advantages this brings.

2.4.1 Binney's Knowledge Management Spectrum

The KM spectrum proposed by Derek Binney [39] (Table 2.4) identifies six [8] ways in which knowledge management is typically carried out within organisations:

- Transactional knowledge management
- Analytic knowledge management
- Asset management
- Process management
- Development & training
- Innovation & creation

---

[8] A seventh category, Asset Improvement, is needed for completeness, to deal with applications that optimize existing assets; this should appear between Analytic KM and Asset management. See [78] for a more detailed discussion of this point.

Note that the spectrum focuses on highly codified knowledge at the top and highly tacit knowledge at the bottom. Binney also identifies technologies or methods that are associated with each of these approaches to knowledge management, and typical applications that address these.

From a multi-perspective viewpoint, Binney has classified knowledge management activities according to a *why* dimension (i.e. according to the organisational goal), and has proposed that this is correlated with a *what* dimension (applications) and therefore also a *how* dimension (technologies/methods appropriate for each application). A brief consideration of the remaining three perspectives suggests that correlations may also exist on the *who* perspective with professions (ranging from software/knowledge engineers to ethnographers/psychologists via librarians and operations researchers), and on the *when* perspective with organisational maturity (older, larger organisations will focus on best practice and standardisation while newer organisations may focus on innovation and creativity). Correlations with the *where* perspective may occur, but there is no hard and fast rule; indeed, it may be profitable for an organisation to investigate why a branch in one country is focusing heavily on innovation and creation while another focuses on best practice.

2.4.2 Boisot's knowledge asset description

The concept of an I-Space which measures knowledge assets on three dimensions, is proposed in [12]. *Codification* represents the degree to which knowledge has been encoded, ranging from zero (it resides in an expert's head and is so intuitive that he cannot explain it even to himself) to maximum (it is written down in a concise logical format). *Abstraction* represents the level to which the knowledge has been generalized, ranging from zero (individual and independent specific cases are recorded) through to very high (a set of generally applicable principles). And *Diffusion* is similar to scarcity, in that it reflects the number of people who have access to the knowledge. These dimensions make it possible to establish how far a particular group of knowledge assets are structured and shared within a given population. They also make it possible to draw up a value map for the analysis of knowledge assets.

Transactional	Analytical	Asset Management
Case Based Reasoning (CBR) Help Desk Applications Customer Service Applications Order Entry Applications Service Agent Support Applications	Data Warehousing Data Mining Business Intelligence Management Information Systems Decision Support Systems Customer Relationship Management Competitive Intelligence	Intellectual Property Document Management Knowledge Valuation Knowledge Repositories Content Management
Expert Systems Cognitive Technologies Semantic Networks Probability Networks Rule Induction Decision Trees Geographic Information Systems	Intelligent Agents Web Crawlers Relational and Object DBMS Neural Computing Push technologies Data Analysis and Reporting Tools	Document Management Tools Search Engines Knowledge Maps Library Systems

Table 2.4(a): Binney's KM Spectrum with associated applications and technologies, part 1

Process	Developmental	Innovation and Creation
Total Quality Management Best Practices Quality Management Business Process (Re) Engineering Process Automation Lessons Learned Methodology: Capability Maturity Model, ISO 9xx, Six Sigma	Skills Development Staff Conpetencies Learning Teaching Training	Communities Collaboration Discussion Forums Networking Virtual teams Research and Development Multi-Disciplined Teams
Workflow Management Process Modelling Tools	Computer-based Training Online Training	Groupware e-mail Chat rooms Video Conferencing Search Engines Voice Mail Bulletin Boards Simulation technologies

Table 2.4(b): Binney's KM Spectrum, part 2

It is clear that the value of knowledge is increased by abstraction (for abstract knowledge has wider utility) and decreased by diffusion (because diffusion is inversely proportional to scarcity). Codification can be a two-edged sword, for increased codification increases the utility of knowledge by making it more comprehensible, but only for those who do not possess it in the first place (thus implying increasing diffusion). The swiftness of diffusion with modern technology sharpens both edges of the sword; knowledge can be made widely available to those who need it more quickly, but by definition also becomes diffused more quickly. The maximum value of an information good in the space is therefore achieved when its degree of codification and abstraction are at a maximum; but at this point, entropy level is high because of swift diffusion. Conversely the minimum value of such good is reached either when diffusion is at a maximum or when codification and abstraction are at a minimum. Boisot uses this analysis to suggest a tripartite classification of knowledge assets:

- *Base* technologies are well codified and have a large diffusion across industries;
- *Key* technologies are codified and usually abstracted, but not yet diffused and can be a source of competitive advantage. These technologies are the highest value technologies. However, the paradox of value is that the more competitive value is derived from a key technology, the more precarious is its status as a key technology on account of the diffusion of know how that using the technology sets in motion.
- *Emergent* technologies are not yet codified, abstracted or diffused. It's necessary to develop these technologies for them to become a source of competitive advantage.

From the viewpoint of multi-perspective modelling, Boisot's characteristics can be viewed as follows:

- Abstraction is concerned with where the knowledge is applicable;
- Diffusion is concerned with who possesses the knowledge;
- Codification is concerned with how the knowledge is stored or presented.

A brief analysis of the remaining three perspectives suggests that knowledge assets have no value at all unless they are available when needed, their content (what) is actually useful, and they contribute to the goals of the process or the organisation (why). So we can conclude that:

- a knowledge asset has virtually no value unless it meets criteria of content, availability at the point of need, and purpose (what, when and why);
- its value is modified by applicability, form and uniqueness (where, how and who).

2.5 Software & knowledge engineering: UML and CommonKADS

In this section, the relationship between an information modelling method (UML), a knowledge modelling method (CommonKADS) and the Zachman framework will be discussed.

2.5.1 UML and the Zachman framework

UML (the Unified Modelling Language) prescribes a standard set of diagrams and notations for modelling object-oriented systems, and describes the underlying semantics of what these diagrams and symbols mean. It's a consolidation of many of the most used object-oriented notations and concepts, especially the work of Grady Booch, James Rumbaugh, and Ivar Jacobson. It has become widely accepted as a *de facto* standard for modelling information related to software systems, hardware systems, and real-world organisations.

UML offers nine diagrams with which to model systems:

- Use Case diagram for modelling the business processes;
- Sequence diagram for modelling message passing between objects;
- Collaboration diagram for modelling object interactions;
- State diagram for modelling the behaviour of objects in the system;
- Activity diagram for modelling the behaviour of Use Cases, objects, or operations;
- Class diagram for modelling the static structure of classes in the system;
- Object diagram for modelling the static structure of objects in the system;
- Component diagram for modelling components;
- Deployment diagram for modelling distribution of the system.

These diagrams represent different perspectives. The Activity diagram represents "how" (processes); the Sequence diagram represents "when" (ordering); the Collaboration diagram represents "where" (interactions); the State, Class and Object diagrams represent "what" (concepts and states, static or dynamic); and the Use Case diagram, despite claiming to model business processes, actually models the links between business processes and their agents, and therefore represents "who" rather than "how". As for the Component and Deployment diagrams, these represent the same perspective ("what", in the sense of "what parts are required") but at different levels of detail; it can also be seen that the Class and Object diagrams represent two different levels of detail of the "what" perspective.

The Zachman framework therefore implies that UML is a reasonable complete modelling method in terms of the perspectives that it covers, except that there is no specific facility for modelling rationale and justifications ("why"). However, UML only explicitly covers two or three different levels of detail, and so it is likely that a full set of UML diagrams to support organisational analysis and software development would require extensive decomposition, or repeated use of the same UML diagrams to capture information at each level of detail. It's also worth noting that UML separates static taxonomic information (classes/objects), dynamic information (states), and parts (components) under the "what" perspective, a distinction that is not made clearly by the Zachman framework.

2.5.2 CommonKADS and the Zachman Framework

CommonKADS [147] is a collection of structured methods for building knowledge based systems, analogous to structured methods for software engineering; as such, it provides an enabling technology for the analysis of acquired knowledge and the design of knowledge based systems. It was developed between 1983 and 1994 on two projects funded by the European Community's ESPRIT program. CommonKADS proposes that up to six models (some with several subcomponents) should be developed in order to represent the knowledge management and knowledge engineering process from application selection through to developing a design specification for a knowledge-based system.

These models are:

• An Organisation model which represent the processes, structure and resources within an organisation, with the aim of identifying fruitful areas for better application of knowledge. The organisation model has various suggested subcomponents: these include a diagram of the organisation's structure, a diagram of its important business functions, a "power and authority" diagram (recognizing that such relationships are not always defined by the organisation structure), and diagrams of various resources [45].

• A Task model to show the activities carried out in the course of a particular organisational process;

• An Agent model to represent the capabilities required of the agents who perform a process, and constraints on their performance;

• A Communication model to show the communication required between agents during a process;

• An Expertise model which is a model of the expertise required to perform a particular task. This has three major subcomponents: domain models which represent concepts and their relationships; an inference structure which records the inference processes required during problem solving; and a task structure which accompanies the inference structure to describe ordering of the inference processes and other control features.

• A Design model which culminates in a design specification for a knowledge based system to perform all or part of the process under consideration.

The way the models relate to each other as shown in Figure 2.7[9]. It can be seen that the models are considered to represent four different stages in the knowledge management/knowledge engineering process:

1. The Organisation model is used for identifying organisational strengths, weakness, opportunities and threats;

2. The Task and Agent models are used to analyse a key business process and to select a task within that process that would benefit from being supported by a knowledge based system or another knowledge based artefact (e.g. a good manual or an interactive training program);

---

[9] N.B. The distinction between "within a task" and "between tasks" for the Agent and Communication models is an extension to CommonKADS proposed in [100]

3.The Expertise model captures, records and structures the knowledge that is used to carry out that knowledge based task, while the Communication model records the interactions that take place during the task;

4.The Design model records decisions made about how each function and concept in the Expertise model can be implemented, and draws on the Communication model as well for interface design. It then brings these recommendations together into a structured design specification.

These models can therefore be seen to cover the top four levels of the Zachman framework. The Organisational model represents the Scoping level, and its various sub-diagrams cover the "who", "how", and "what" perspectives. The Task, Agent and Communication models represent individual perspectives (how, who and where) at the Enterprise level. The three components of the Expertise model represent the "what", "how" and "when" perspectives at the System level; these can be coupled with "within task" versions of the Agent and Communication models to model the "who" and "where" perspectives as well. Finally, the Design model represents the transformation of the Expertise and Communication models into a high level design specification at the Technology level.

Comparing this analysis against the Zachman framework, it can be seen that CommonKADS provides more comprehensive coverage of the cells of the Zachman framework than UML does. However, neither UML nor CommonKADS provide an explicit representation of the "why" perspective; and neither method represents the lowest two levels of the Zachman framework. With these exceptions, however, CommonKADS seems to be capable of representing almost everything that the Zachman framework recommends. It's also worth noting that the Expertise model carries the responsibility of representing the transformation from the System level to the Technology level which was identified above as a knowledge-intensive selection operation rather than a refinement operation, and that the Expertise model is usually the model that is developed in most detail by CommonKADS users, with its three subcomponents (domain, inference and task) each represented by a number of diagrams.

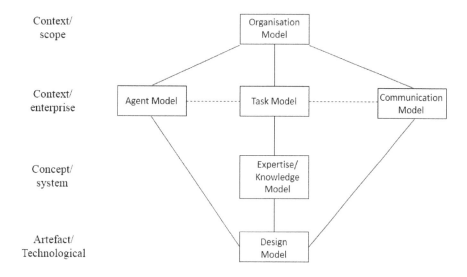

Figure 2.7: Relationship between the various CommonKADS models

2.6 Meta-analysis of the Zachman framework

2.6.1 Meta-analysis of Zachman's perspectives

It's obvious that the Zachman framework is a 2-dimensional categorisation of information and knowledge. If it is assumed that each of the six "who, what, how, when, where and why" perspectives can be represented on an ordinal or categorical scale, then the 2-dimensional nature of the Zachman framework implies that it only represents two out of six perspectives. Since the columns of the Zachman framework describe different categories of knowledge while the rows bear a strong resemblance to a design process, the Zachman framework seems to represent the "what" and "how" of knowledge representation.

If the Zachman framework was extended to six dimensions, what should appear on the four new axes? Here are some suggestions, with specific reference to the representation of knowledge assets:

- Where: Knowledge sources, such as: experts, protocols, text, machine learning/data mining. In this case, the "where" perspective would be a nominal dimension (like the perspectives) rather than an ordinal dimension (like the levels of detail). It might be beneficial to introduce some ordering criterion, such as "perspicacity of knowledge" (high for experts, low for machine learning) or "can be automated" (low for experts, high for data mining).

• Who: Involved agents - expert users, lay users, funding sources, project managers, experts, programmers, senior management. Zachman's examples of the framework assume that these professions are correlated with the columns of the framework, but this is not always going to be entirely accurate, and so provisions should be made for modelling the interests and involvement of various professions. Again, this is a nominal categorisation rather than an ordinal or cardinal dimension. An obvious ordering criterion is the level of detail they are likely to be concerned with, so senior managers and strategists would appear at one end of the scale while programmers or bricklayers appear at the other end. Other ordering criteria might include "importance to the project" or "degree of involvement with the project" which could be used to assess project risks.

• When: The "when" perspective represents both time constraints (schedule, timing description) and also other constraints that control processing of the steps described in the "how" perspective (processing structure, control structure). Since the meta-how dimension is represented by the rows of the Zachman framework, the meta-when perspective must represent constraints and criteria for moving from one level to the next. These might include achieving agreed criteria in describing a level, completing enough to achieve the required functionality at the next level, or simply reaching the point in a schedule where the handover must take place.

• Why: reasons that knowledge must be represented. These might include knowledge archiving (a key expert is leaving the company); standardisation of practice; knowledge discovery (e.g. identifying connections between two knowledge sources that had never been noticed before); knowledge distribution (getting knowledge gained from many years' experience to practitioners who lack that experience); or simply knowledge organisation (e.g. a taxonomy or ontology is required to facilitate future operations). A possible ordering criterion would be a financial one, based on the opportunity cost of not gathering the knowledge; this would be company-specific to some extent, but knowledge archiving is likely to score highly in many cases while knowledge organisation will be more difficult to quantify.

This six-dimensional framework is capable of representing multiple views of the same artefact (meta-what), at multiple levels of details (meta-how), according to different agents' possibly conflicting perceptions (meta-who), drawing on various knowledge sources (meta-where), under various constraints (meta-when), and for various purposes (meta-why). It is, of course, unlikely that all six dimensions will be represented fully in any single project because of the effort involved in representing a framework with 6^6 cells, but this is often not necessary. Assuming that the two dimensions of the "normal" Zachman framework are always required, a problem requiring negotiation of conflicting opinions (as discussed in section 2.2.4), for example, will require the meta-who dimension to represent the different views of the different agents alongside one (or both?) of the original two dimensions. A problem concerning organisational priorities, on the other hand, might require a meta-why dimension, to describe the effect on the knowledge, resources and processes of the company of various organisational emphases. And a problem concerning resource allocation might use the meta-when dimension to consider different views of the workloads that can be allocated to particular tasks. Only the most intractable problems - for example, differences of opinion that are actually based on different views of organisational priorities - are likely to require four or more dimensions.

Applying this analysis to knowledge management (as illustrated in Figure 2.8), it is possible to derive a large part of the information that is needed for initiating a successful knowledge management project:

• The need for knowledge management in a particular area is usually determined by the desires or requirements of various agents - senior managers or funding agencies who want to see certain knowledge made more widely available, or users and programmers who need knowledge that is not available to them.

• The best way of implementing knowledge management can be derived from the meta-where perspective (i.e. where the knowledge resides at present) and the meta-why perspective (what is this exercise trying to achieve?). If the purpose of the knowledge management exercise is to standardize on best practice or to archive knowledge, then a knowledge engineering approach is a good idea; if the main purpose is knowledge discovery or innovation, then there are strong arguments for an approach that uses data mining rather than knowledge engineering, or even for an approach that does not "capture" knowledge at all, but merely facilitates communication (possibly via an intranet) in order to allow new knowledge to emerge from interactions among key individuals. See [78] for further discussion of the mapping of knowledge management approaches to goals.

• Feasibility and risk assessment can be derived by comparison with past projects with similar features. Also, available skills within the organisation and activities that need to be carried out for successful knowledge management can be mapped to identify organisational strengths and weaknesses.

Figure 2.8: A meta-perspective view of the Zachman framework (with an emphasis on knowledge management issues)

2.6.2   Meta-Analysis of Zachman's levels of detail

There is one more meta-level of knowledge modelling to consider. We have considered whether the Zachman framework itself represents a full range of perspectives - the columns of the original Zachman framework – and suggested that a six-dimensional framework might be required rather than a mere two-dimensional framework. So we now need to consider whether the Zachman framework itself should be subject to multiple levels of detail. In other words, is this Zachman framework only one framework in a set of six, each of which is a specialisation, refinement or realisation of another?

In principle, the answer is "yes", but the sheer number of cells in meta-frameworks (up to 6^7, allowing for meta-perspectives) makes this concept overwhelming both to analyse and to use. To make this discussion tractable, we will focus on only one of the six perspectives - the "how" perspective.

Meta-analysis of levels of abstraction: the "how" perspective

This chapter has claimed that the levels of detail in the original Zachman framework actually represent a design process; when considering knowledge assets, this might begin with a "knowledge management" task (is the development of this knowledge asset feasible?) through a "system" level (exactly what will be developed?) and a "technological" level (design specification) to a "functioning enterprise" (i.e. some kind of implementation). Yet the output of each of these stages is itself a knowledge asset of some description: a feasibility study, a set of knowledge models, a design specification, or an efficient and robust implementation. It therefore seems that each of the key stages (feasibility; analysis; design; and implementation) can be decomposed into a series of sub-tasks.

Let's assume that the knowledge asset to be represented is diagnostic expertise for personal computers, in the context of a help desk. This knowledge asset will probably appear at the System level in a "normal" Zachman framework, with the following instantiations of the different System level perspectives:

- "Who": the technicians, the help desk operators, the knowledge engineers and the management in the help centre;
- "Where": technicians' experience, previous call logs, and system manuals;
- "What": PC components, common faults, and known solutions;
- "How": probably a combination of gathering routine information and asking questions to narrow down the fault, a technique known as "cover-and-differentiate";

- "When": determined by the organisation's requirements on the help desk - an example requirement might be "If you can't solve it in 5 minutes, refer it upwards";
- "Why": to make the technicians' expertise available to help desk operators.

The tasks that must be carried out to turn this knowledge asset into a working knowledge based system include knowledge acquisition, knowledge representation & analysis, KBS design, and KBS implementation. Each of these requires three or four subtasks to be carried out by knowledge engineers. Knowledge acquisition requires determining the feasibility of acquiring knowledge from various sources; determining which KA technique(s) to use; designing a knowledge acquisition schedule; and carrying it out. Knowledge representation & analysis requires determining the feasibility and utility of using various knowledge modelling techniques; deciding how particular items of knowledge should be represented; and producing knowledge models. KBS design starts by determining whether it's advisable to use a recognized AI paradigm (e.g. model-based reasoning) throughout the design; continues by choosing a design approach (e.g. object-oriented design); and produces a design specification. And implementation of the system is essentially a software engineering task, and implementers must consider the feasibility of using different programming approaches to implement the design specification; do some prototyping to determine if these programming approaches are efficient (or even possible) in the chosen programming language; produce a detailed design specification (or at least, add comments to their code); and generate usable code (by compiling, testing, or whatever).

If the form of the knowledge asset was something quite different - case histories stored in a database, perhaps - then the stages followed would be different, but would still decompose in the same way, In this case, KBS development might be replaced by data mining. Knowledge acquisition, representation, analysis and design would be replaced by selection of a suitable data mining algorithm, pre-processing of the data, selecting algorithm parameters, and applying the algorithm, plus additional steps needed for creating and applying a test suite to the results. All of these tasks decompose into subtasks; for example, any selection task breaks down into at least three stages (collecting data about the target and the selection set, matching that data against each member of the selection set, and choosing the one with the optimal match results), while pre-processing of data requires one or more of data cleaning (removing or reducing noise, inconsistencies, and incompleteness), data integration (merging data from a number of sources), data transformation (into forms more suitable for the algorithm in question) and data reduction (to manageable volumes).

So it can be seen that each stage of development of the "how" perspective in a normal Zachman framework can be decomposed into a sub-process. Further, we can see that each series of subtasks follows a pattern that more or less corresponds to feasibility-analysis-design-implementation which (roughly) corresponds with the six levels of detail in a Zachman framework. So we can claim that the Zachman framework can always be decomposed into lower levels of abstraction. This concept is illustrated in Figure 2.9.

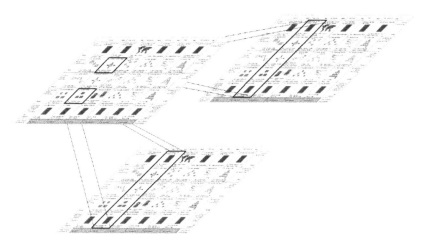

Figure 2.9: Decomposing different stages of the "how" perspective in a Zachman framework

Supertasks of the "how" perspective

Having seen that the Zachman framework decomposes downwards, does it also 'compose' upwards? It has been claimed that the supertask of the "how" perspective of a typical Zachman framework could be "knowledge engineering" or "data mining". In practice, however, it's rare for any software system to be developed once and to be declared complete; instead, systems are developed in increments of functional capability (progressing from a "proof of concept" system to a "prototype", "alpha test", "beta test", and eventually to "version 1.0").

It can therefore be considered that the development of each incremental version of the system is a supertask of the "typical" Zachman framework. That is, for each version of the system, the entire feasibility-analysis-design-implementation process must be followed. Moreover, the "proof of concept" can be viewed as a way of determining the feasibility of the system, while the prototype can be seen as an aid to analysis, and so on; so the task of "developing a functioning software system" can be seen as a further level up the meta-Zachman framework.

Deriving project lifecycle models

So it has been demonstrated (for the "how" perspective) that the Zachman framework itself can be usefully considered to have at least four levels of abstraction. Since we derived a number of knowledge management considerations from our meta-analysis of perspectives, can we derive anything useful from this analysis?

I will claim that at least two different approaches to managing project lifecycles can be derived from this. The first is the "waterfall" project lifecycle. The "waterfall" (Figure 2.10) assumes a sequence of activities with defined inputs and outputs and no iteration; i.e. feasibility, analysis, design and implementation are performed once, in sequence. This can be considered to correspond to the "how" perspective of the "typical" Zachman framework. However, this approach has been criticized for its inflexibility, and other approaches have been suggested.

One of these other approaches is Boehm's spiral lifecycle model [11] (Figure 2.11), in which a series of activities (under the four general categories of review, risk, plan and monitor) are carried out, and the end result is a new incremental development of the system; the stages in the lifecycle are then repeated for the next incremental stage. This approach can be derived from the meta-analyses of the Zachman framework; the concept of incremental development and the four overall stages can be derived from the multiple levels of abstraction of the "how" perspective of the Zachman framework, whilst the specific activities that are carried out on each iteration can be derived from the meta-analysis of the perspectives.

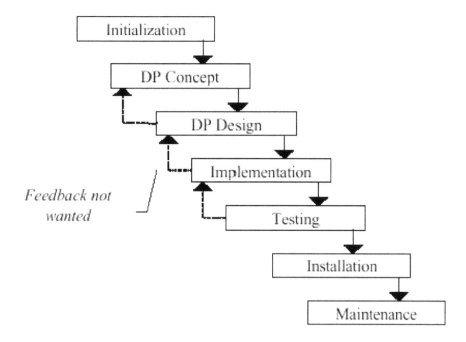

Figure 2.10: The waterfall lifecycle model

So it can be shown that recognized project management lifecycles can be derived from this meta-analysis of the levels of detail in the Zachman framework. This supports the contention that the Zachman framework is indeed a good structure for representing both knowledge in general, and knowledge about software development in particular.

2.7 Discussion

The thesis of this chapter was that the perspectives and levels of the Zachman framework can represent any knowledge asset. We have seen that the framework (when understood from a "crystallography" viewpoint) can represent all the knowledge (and more) required by a major software engineering method (UML) and a major knowledge engineering method (CommonKADS). This implies that, for practical purposes (i.e. representing a knowledge asset in order to develop or distribute it), multi-perspective modelling based on the Zachman framework is indeed capable of representing all the knowledge required about a knowledge asset.

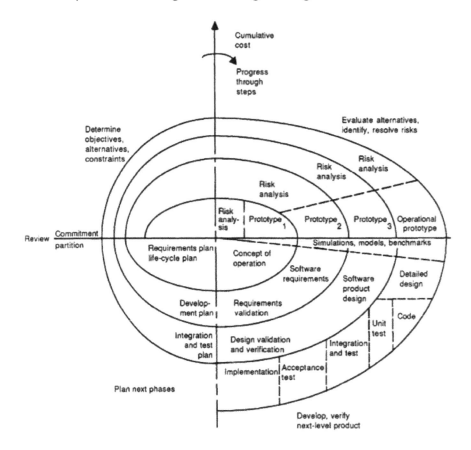

Figure 2.11: Boehm's spiral lifecycle model

In terms of guidance provided to developers of knowledge systems, the development of several knowledge models covering different perspectives provides an excellent basis both for analysis (has all the relevant knowledge been acquired?) and for design (by preserving the structure of the models which in turn should reflect the experts' way of thinking). While modelling clearly eliminates some information that is considered irrelevant, multi-perspective models run far less risk of eliminating information that might be important. KM researchers who claim that any elimination of information is potentially fatal to obtaining a holistic understanding of shared knowledge should note that Binney's KM spectrum demonstrates that the term "knowledge management" actually covers a range of applications, and probably of different types of knowledge, and Multi-Perspective

Modelling that "holistic views of shared knowledge" are probably only necessary for applications that fall into the Innovation & Creation category in the spectrum.

The Zachman framework is also shown to be a robust framework for software development because meta-analysis of it is able to derive common software engineering approaches. Further work on meta-analysis of perspectives other than "what" and "how" also shows how key considerations can be modelled as needed.

One issue that was raised by the analysis of UML and CommonKADS was the absence of any facilities to model "why" knowledge. The main reason seems to be that there are always at least two answers to the question "why are you doing this?" - one that justifies the process being used and the other that describes the goal that is being sought. In the former case, modelling the 'why' perspective is beneficial, though is often only conducted in situations when the validity of rules or laws are under discussion. In the latter case, the answer to most 'why' questions within the context of the Zachman framework is "in order to achieve the next level up in the framework". For example, the goal of a house designer is to provide the owner with the desired floor space at sufficient strength. In such cases, there is no need for explicit models of 'why' knowledge; all that is needed is some pointers to levels above. Further work on methods and applications of 'why' knowledge is suggested.

This chapter has shown how the Zachman framework can be used as an overall structure to support knowledge management and knowledge engineering. The next chapter will look at whether this structure can be used in conjunction with an ontology to provide a rich description of knowledge.

Part II: Ontology Development & Issues

3 Multi-perspective Ontologies: Solving Common Ontology Issues

3.1 Introduction

Ontology - the theory of objects and their relationships - has become a hot topic in recent years. One reason is that organisations that have entered into knowledge management have discovered the need to classify their knowledge in a manner that is both accessible to users and robust enough to represent different types of knowledge in a coherent manner and have developed taxonomies (ontologies that use only the IS-A relation) to address this need. Another reason is that object-oriented software development which is a widely used approach to producing software, requires an understanding of ontological principles: authors in the field have claimed that "a clear understanding of ontology helps to avoid the introduction of accidental, as opposed to essential, objects", and "the exploding interest, both theoretical and practical, in the development of object-oriented languages ... has led computer science squarely into the business of doing research in ontology. This is an unavoidable conclusion of taking a serious look at practice" [74] [157].

However, attempts to develop taxonomies for classification purposes have run into various difficulties, and it has been recognised that taxonomies, and ontologies in general, suffer from a number of problems in practical situations. These problems do not prevent usable ontologies from being developed, but they do make it difficult to develop ontologies in a standardised manner; this reduces the extensibility and reusability of ontologies, and makes it particularly difficult to merge ontologies created separately, even if they address the same areas. This chapter outlines an approach to ontology development based on multi-perspective modelling that is able to resolve some of the common problems that arise in ontology development.

3.2 Multi-level Ontologies

The working definition of an ontology being used in this book is that defined by Gruber [75]: an ontology is an explicit specification of a conceptualisation which, in knowledge engineering practice, equates to the definition of what can be represented within a computer program.

However, there is considerable debate about the exact definition of ontology and ontologies. Guarino and Giaretta [77] present 8 definitions that are in use in the literature today:

1. Ontology as a philosophical discipline;
2. Ontology as an informal conceptual system;
3. Ontology as a formal semantic account;
4. Ontology as a specification of a conceptualisation;
5. Ontology as a representation of a conceptual system via a logical theory
6. characterized by specific formal properties;
7. characterized only by its specific purposes;
8. Ontology as the vocabulary used by a logical theory;
9. Ontology as a (meta-level) specification of a logical theory.

Guarino and Giaretta favour interpretation 5a - an ontology is a logical theory, characterized by specific formal properties. This is because this definition fits with three common technical uses of the term "ontology": meaning an ontological theory; a specification of an ontological commitment; or a conceptualisation. However, they also give some credence to the other interpretations, because ontologies typically exist at different levels. For example, definition 1 tries to answer the question "What are the features common to all beings?" and results in a generic ontology that is common to all domains but describes very little that is specific to any domain.

The practical implications of this (heavily abbreviated) discussion are that ontologies can be separated into core ontologies (meta-descriptions of ontological terms), general ontologies (definitions of common sense concepts) and domain-specific or company-specific ontologies. The remainder of this chapter is concerned with domain or company-specific ontologies, unless stated otherwise, for these are the ontologies that are most obviously useful for knowledge management.

3.3 Problems with Ontologies

So what are the main problems that arise with such ontologies? A selection of problems is outlined below, drawn from [35] and other sources.

3.3.1 IS-A overloading

"IS-A overloading" [128] is the use of the IS-A relation to carry multiple meanings in a single taxonomy. Guarino identifies five such misuses from a survey of popular ontologies: confusion of senses (for example, in Mikrokosmos, a window is both an artefact and a place); reduction of sense (e.g. in Pangloss, a person is both a physical object and a living thing); overgeneralisation (a place is a physical object in both Mikrokosmos and WordNet); suspect type-to-role links (in WordNet, a person is both a living thing and a causal agent); and confusion of taxonomic roles (both Pangloss and Penman offer a taxonomy of qualities, but qualities are better represented as properties only rather than as concepts). While these misuses may reflect accepted practice in natural language (for example, the term 'window' can refer either to a single window pane, a connected set of multiple panes, or the space that pane occupies), they can cause great difficulties in accurate ontological classification, and they make logical inference across multiple ontologies very difficult.

3.3.2 Inaccurate expert responses

Another problem that arises from loose use of natural language is that ontological questions supplied to knowledge experts may be answered incorrectly, either through the experts misunderstanding the question or misunderstanding the ontological implications of their answer. For example, experts who are asked, "Please give a subclass of X i.e. tell me something that is a X" may answer with a superclass of X; they may provide a member of the class X rather than a subclass; or they may supply a concept that is related to X by some relation apart from IS-A, such as naming subparts of an object (e.g. giving "engine" as a subclass of "car"). These faults are multiplied when developing ontologies other than taxonomies; for example, asking experts "what causes A" sometimes elicits a response of the form "A causes B", while asking experts "how do I do C" (aiming to elicit subtasks of C) may bring the response "Well, first you do D and then E, and then you can do C". So the difficulty for the ontology engineer lies in transforming the answers provided by experts into a valid taxonomy or other type of ontology.

3.3.3 Levels of detail and inferencing bias

Inferencing bias occurs because it's not practical to define all ontologies at a universally accepted "primitive" level - which, most people would agree, corresponds to an atomic or molecular level. However, the level of detail that is appropriate is usually determined by the problem being tackled rather than the domain. So different ontologies of the same domain may be incompatible because they were developed to solve different problems. As an example, let's consider ontological definitions of colour. In this case, there is probably general agreement that a 'primitive' definition of colour should consist of the intensity of light of different wavelengths that is reflected or emitted by the 'coloured' objects. However, while an ontology for physicists may require this level of detail, photographers and artists only need an ontology that specifies colour as a concept with properties such as hue, brightness and intensity, and a car salesman probably views colour merely as a property of the cars he sells.

These varying levels of detail would be less of a problem if there was agreement on how to combine 'primitive' definitions into higher level concepts. This is definitely not the case for colour, however; in a project to build an ontology of art objects for Interpol [193] [172], the researchers discovered that colour terms used to describe paintings are entirely different to the colour terms used to describe ceramics [Wielinga, personal communication]. In practice, colour is an exceptionally hard concept to define, because its 'categories' are actually composed of arbitrarily defined points on three continuous dimensions (red, green and blue light); the philosophical term for this is that colours are *determinable* concepts as opposed to *determinate* concepts. So perhaps the problem of inferencing bias is more acute for colour and other determinable concepts (such as geographical location or price) than for determinate concepts such as physical objects. For ontological engineers, inferencing bias is an inescapable fact that should, at least, be identified when building an ontology.

3.3.4 Dependence relations

As stated above, experts who are asked to give subclasses of concept X will often answer with concept Y which is related to X in some other way. Typically, the reason is that concept Y depends on X in some fashion. Corazzon [35] identifies many kinds of dependence relations, including dependencies between levels of reality, between wholes and their parts, between parts, between wholes and their environments, between wholes, and between particulars and determinations. However, it is difficult to model these relationships clearly in any ontology, and well-nigh impossible in a taxonomy.

3.3.5 Particulars

Taxonomies often represent particulars (i.e. individuals, or individual objects) well, but struggle with other types of concept, such as Processes, Groups, or Stuff (substances described as "an amount of" rather than "a collection of" - water is a good example). But the need to represent these concepts in ontologies has been clearly identified (see e.g. [113]). So what is to be done about these issues? In the next section I will describe an approach to ontology development that can address at least some of these problems.

3.4 Multi perspective ontologies

Imagine that you have been asked to rent a DVD to watch that will be appropriate for yourself and five friends. When asked for their preferences, the first friend wants to see action, horror or science fiction; the second wants innovative special effects; the third wants something that wasn't filmed in the USA; the fourth asks for a film made fairly recently - "not a classic oldie"; and the fifth wants a film that features her favourite actor, who turns out to be Keanu Reeves. You may not realise it, but you have been given a multi-perspective classification problem. Each of your friends classifies films in a different way (or at least, prioritises their classification of films in a different way); one cares *what* genre of film it is, another *how* the film was made, another *where* it was made, the fourth *when* it was made, and the fifth *who* is in it. As you stroll away from the shop with a copy of The Matrix in your hand, it occurs to you that these different classifications map neatly to the different perspectives on information and knowledge proposed in another matrix - the Zachman framework for Information Systems Architecture.

The Zachman framework suggests that multiple perspectives and multiple levels of detail are needed for full-scale knowledge representation. Since organisational ontologies already exist at multiple levels of detail (domain, general, and core ontologies), the main message of the Zachman framework for developers of organisational ontologies is the need to develop ontologies from different perspectives. Continuing the cinematic example, ontologies of film genres can be obtained from Yahoo (www.yahoo.com) and from the Internet Movie Database (www.imdb.com). It can be seen that these ontologies attempt to address the multi-perspective problem by providing a range of ways of searching for films; the Internet Movie Database (see Table 3.1) allows searching for films by genre, co-stars, location, or release date, thus covering the 'what', 'who', 'where' and 'when' perspectives proposed by the Zachman framework, while Yahoo (Table 3.2) offers a broad range of categories that cover not just films themselves but also related information (reviews, spoilers, fan fiction, cinemas, etc.). In fact, a detailed examination shows that both ontologies provide indexing on all six perspectives suggested by the Zachman framework; the Internet Movie Database offers a keyword search facility that can be used to browse the 'how' or 'why' perspectives, while Yahoo offers a particularly rich indexing of the 'why' perspective, by offering categories such as 'Made-for-TV movies' 'Theory and Criticism', 'History' and 'Cultures and Groups'. Both ontologies also offer an additional domain-specific perspective of identifying the 'best' films, according to box office ratings, critics' choices, or votes by users of the website.

What this discussion highlights is that, in practical ontology building, there will almost always be a need - or at least, a demand from users – to represent non-taxonomic methods of classification. This chapter proposes that the best way to clarify these various classification methods is to build separate ontologies based on separate relationships. The need for separate ontologies can be identified according to the relations that need to be represented. Relations that are typically associated with each of Zachman's six perspectives are suggested below:

- WHAT perspective: *is-a* (taxonomy), *part-of* (mereonomy)
- HOW perspective: *achieves* (goal), *transforms, creates/destroys*, any term reflecting a specific action (*selects, matches*, etc);
- WHO perspective: *plays-the-role-of, responsible-for, has-rights-to*;
- WHEN perspective: *precedes/follows* (possibly with time intervals specified);

Top Titles	On our Top Movies page you can find links to all sorts of "tops" lists. Whether it's top grossers at the box-office, top renters at video stores, or top films in genres & decades based on user votes, you can find it here.
Search by Ratings	Our User Ratings Browser duplicates some of the tops/bottoms lists from the Top Movies page plus it allows you to search for movies that fall within a certain user ratings range. You can also specify a genre and year or range of years... or not.
Titles by Year	Find titles and other information categorized by year from 1892 to the present and beyond.
Titles by Country	Find titles based on the country of origin for a title. This is not based on the filming locations but on the country that produced it.
Titles by Language	Find titles based on the language in which they were filmed.
Titles by Genre	Find titles based on their genre.
Titles by Location	Using the Search and Browse By Level features in our Filming Locations Browser allows you to find films based on their filming locations.
Titles by Business Information	Find titles based on release dates, copyright holder, etc.
Titles by Awards	Use our database of over 300 awards ceremonies and film festivals to find the titles that have been nominated, selected or honored by each event.
Titles by Keywords	A keyword can describe a plot theme (e.g. a beach) or a more esoteric notion (e.g. a sequel). Our keywords browser will allow you to peruse a list of keywords in use as well as searching for titles whose keywords match one or more that you select.
Titles by Co-Stars	Our complex name search allows you to enter the names of two or more people and finds all the titles where they're both listed.

Table 3.1: Classification of films, as provided by the Internet Movie Database

By Region
Actors & Actresses
Awards
Box Office Reports
Cultures and Groups
Genres
Independent
Made-for-TV movies
Organisations
People
Ratings
Reviews
Screenplays
Studios and Production Companies
Theory and Criticism
Titles

Table 3.2: Classifications of films provided by Yahoo

- WHERE perspective: *location, connected-to,* or terms reflecting geographical relationships (*close-to, south-of,* etc);
- WHY perspective: *causes, justifies.*

Note that the suggestions above are intentionally limited to those that relate two items of the same type[10] – for while there are many relationships between items of different types (e.g. relationships between agents and the tasks they are responsible for), it is usually unproductive to use these as a basis for classification, since these relationships are typically temporary assignments rather than inherent characteristics. Further examples of existing ontologies are given in the next section, showing how multiple perspectives can enrich the representation of each of them.

---

[10] with the possible exception of the HOW perspective - for example, *matches* relates 3 items, 2 of the same type and one Boolean value

3.5 Multi-perspective ontologies – Examples

3.5.1 Example 1: Scientific Knowledge Management
A worked example of multi-perspective ontologies is drawn from a top level ontology of "Scientific Knowledge Management" (i.e. academics, their projects and publications), whose development was discussed in [87]. The ontology in its current form is shown in Figure 3.1. This ontology was designed based on several principles, but the main ones were to fit in with two existing upper level ontologies: one from the Open University, whose top level categories were *Tangible Thing, Intangible Thing*, and *Temporal Thing*, and one from the Ontoclean ontology, the top level of which consisted of six categories: *Abstraction, Quality, Aggregate, Feature, Object*, and *Event*. It was decided that the OU's three categories should represent the top level of the ontology and the Ontoclean categories should represent the second level. The concepts that had to be classified, and their classifications in the above scheme, are as follows:

- Documents, publications, etc. - Objects (Tangible Thing);
- Conferences, workshops, seminars - Events (Temporal Thing);
- Research groups, universities, funding bodies - Organisations (Tangible Thing);
- Students, professors, supervisors - People (Tangible Thing);
- Research areas (Generic Areas of Interest) - Abstractions (Intangible Thing);
- Projects, grants - Tasks (Temporal Thing).

These top level categories are reasonably well separated from a multi-perspective viewpoint. Objects address the WHAT perspective, People and Organisations address the WHO perspective, and Tasks (which are a subcategory of Event, not shown in Figure 3.1) address the HOW perspective. The WHEN and WHERE perspectives are also addressed to some extent, by the categories of "Temporal Things" and "Aggregates", respectively.

However, this ontology is not perfect, because it attempts to use taxonomic links to represent relationships that are not truly taxonomic. For example, Kingston [99] pointed out that Publications are not really a subclass (i.e. in a taxonomic WHAT relationship) to Documents but

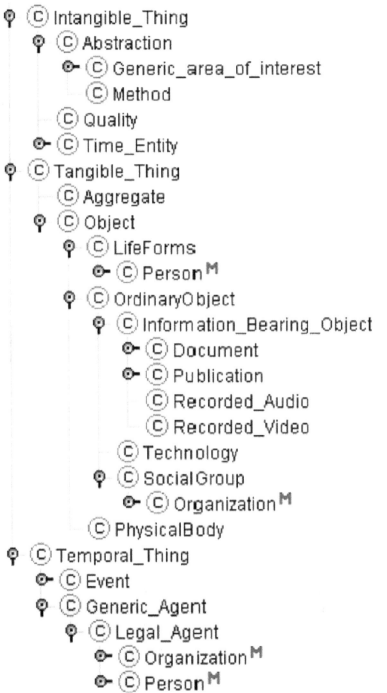

Figure 3.1: Current ontology of Scientific Knowledge Management

are dependent on (the existence of) a document. This can be resolved using multi-perspective ontologies by stating that publications express WHERE a document can be found in the public domain. This allows the dependence to be expressed, as well as correctly allowing more than one publication of a single document.

Similarly, Methods are taxonomically classified as Abstractions but are more commonly thought of in terms of the goal that they can achieve, and this can be captured in an ontology for the HOW perspective. And People and Organisations may be classified taxonomically as Legal Agents, but as Guarino highlighted in his discussion on IS-A overloading, they actually *play the role of* agents (a WHO link) rather than being *a kind of* agent (a WHAT link).

3.5.2 Example 2: the ACM classification scheme

The top level of the ACM classification scheme for computer-related topics is shown in Table 3.3. An extension to the Artificial Intelligence classification has been designed by Scientific Datalink [40], and part of this extended classification is shown in Table 3.4.

A	General literature
B	Hardware
C	Computer system organisation
D	Software
E	Data
F	Theory of computation
G	Mathematics of computing
H	Computing methodologies
I	Computer applications
J	Computer milieux (philosophy, legislation, administration)

Table 3.3: Top level of the 1998 ACM classification scheme

The ACM classification covers several of the multiple perspectives. The perspectives covered include WHAT is needed for a computer system (hardware and software), HOW to build a computer system (techniques), and WHY systems are built (computing milieux). The categories also cover different levels of abstraction: some categories consider the contents of the computer itself (hardware,

I.2.1. Applications and Expert Systems

1.0 Cartography	
1.1 Games	Chess, Checkers, Backgammon, Bidding Games, Wagering Games, War Games, Other
1,2 Industrial Applications	Automatic Assembly, Parts Handling, Inspection, Welding, Planning for Production, Inventory
1.3 Law	
1.4 Medicine	Medical Applications, Chemical Applications, Biological Applications, Geological Applications
1.5 Natural Language Interfaces	
1.6 Office Automation	
1.7 Military Applications	Autonomous Vehicles, Integration of Information, Decisions Aids, Target Tracking, Communication
1.8 Business and Financial	Tax experts, Investment, Financial Planning, Information Storage and Retrieval
1.9 Natural Language Processing Applications	
1.10 Mathematical Aids	
1.11 Education	Tutoring systems, Intelligent Computer-aided Instruction, Aids to learning Programming, Curriculum Design
1.12 Library Applications	
1.13 Engineering Automation	Computer System Design, VLSI Design Aids, CAD/CAM, Programming Aids
1.14 System Troubleshooting	
1.15 Expert Systems	Expert System Languages and Aids for Building Expert Systems, Acquisition of Expert Knowledge, Plausible Reasoning, Representation of Expert Knowledge, Generation of Explanations, Expert Systems based on Simulation and Deep Models, User Interfaces for Expert Systems, Validation of Expert Systems
1.16 Prosthetics	
1.17 Aviation Applications	
1.18 Applications, Other	

I.2.4 Knowledge Representation	
4.0 Frames and Scripts	Defaults, Stereotypes and Prototypes, Generation of Expectations, Frame Languages, Frame-Driven Systems, Inheritance Hierarchy
4.1 Predicate Logic	First Order Predicate Calculus, Skolem Functions, Second Order Logic, Modal Logics, Fuzzy Logic
4.2 Relational Systems	Relational Data Bases, Associative Memory
4.3 Representation Languages	
4.4 Representations (Procedural & Rule-Based)	Production Rule Systems, Knowledge Bases
4.5 Semantic Networks	
4.6 Connectionist Systems	
4.7 Multi Agent/ Actor Systems	
4.8 Constraints	
4.9 Discrimination Trees & Networks	
4.10 Belief Models	
4.11 Representing the Physical World	
4.12 Representing Natural Language Semantics	

Table 3.4: Part of the Scientific Datalink AI classification scheme

software, computer systems organisation, data, information systems) while other categories consider the computer as a single concept in the context of applications (computing methodologies, computer applications, computing milieux). There's also a third level of detail to be found in the two theoretical categories (Theory of Computation and Mathematics of Computing) which provide the foundational techniques for computer systems organisation, data and information systems.

The Scientific Datalink extension also uses a formula where formalisms/resources (WHAT knowledge) are mixed with methods/techniques ("how" knowledge) to generate subcategories. For example, most of the subcategories of Knowledge Representation are concerned with different knowledge representation formalisms - the WHAT of knowledge representation – but two (Representation of the Physical World and Representation of Natural Language Semantics) are primarily concerned with knowledge representation as a task rather than a formalism – i.e. with HOW rather than WHAT.[11] Similarly, most of the subcategories of Applications and Expert Systems are concerned with different domains in which expert systems have been applied (similar to the ACM's taxonomic breakdown of Computer Systems Applications into different disciplines), but I.2.1.15 ("Expert Systems") and I.2.1.5 ("Natural Language Interfaces") are more concerned with techniques for expert system construction, and I.2.1.14 ("System Troubleshooting") focuses on a particular task rather than on a domain.

In short, the ACM classification scheme and the Scientific Datalink extension would be better structured if they were split into at least two ontologies, one reflecting the "what" perspective (i.e. a taxonomy) and the other representing the "how" perspective (i.e. methods and techniques). This would allow more complete representation of (e.g.) goals for knowledge representation, techniques for expert system construction, and task-focused categories. Further perspectives might also prove beneficial.

This example is discussed in more detail in chapter 4.

3.5.3 Example 3: Struts example

Swartout et al [165] highlight a problem with ontological classification in which the concept "strut" can be linked to the top level concept "Thing" in two different ways. In one way, "strut" is a subclass of "support" which is a subclass of "decomposable object" which is a subclass of "Thing"; in the other, "strut" is a subclass of both "durable good" and "load bearing member" which are both subclasses of "physical object" which is a subclass of "Thing".

From a multi-perspective viewpoint, there are several difficulties with this apparently simple ontology. Webster's dictionary defines 'strut' as "a structural piece designed to resist pressure in the direction of its length", while a 'support' is simply "something that carries out the act of supporting". So 'strut' is indeed a subclass of 'support', since they

---

[11] Some may argue that knowledge representation formalisms such as predicate logic or semantic networks are methods and therefore belong under the HOW perspective, while "representation of the physical world" describes WHAT is to be represented, thus reversing the perspectives proposed in this chapter. Strictly speaking, most of the subcategories of Knowledge Representation are methods while the categories 4.11 and 4.12 are goals to be achieved. From a knowledge engineer's viewpoint, methods constitute the resources available (WHAT) while goals represent a problem to be solved (HOW).

are both playing a similar role, but the latter subsumes the former - and, in fact, 'load bearing member' is a superclass of 'strut' (since buildings include not only struts but also rafters, purlins and other load bearing members) and a subclass of 'support' (since something can be a 'support' without necessarily being a 'member' of a building - indeed, it need not be a physical object at all, for gravity or magnetism can act as supports).

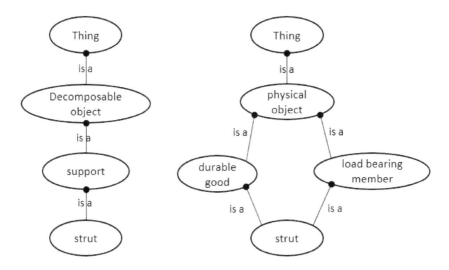

Figure 3.2: Two alternative ontologies for 'strut'

Yet we can also see that a strut will in fact be a beam (of wood or metal, usually) that plays the role of a structural component in a building. Furthermore, the link between beams and durable goods is another *plays the role of* link, for beams are only goods (Webster: "something that has economic utility or satisfies an economic want" or "something manufactured and produced for sale") as long as they are in demand, or as long as they are offered for sale. And finally, the concept of "decomposable object" is one that is criticised by Guarino & Giaretta under the heading of confusion of senses; they believe that this should only ever be a property rather than a concept in a taxonomy.

In short, these two apparently contradictory taxonomies can be sorted out by rewriting them using both taxonomic links and a "who" ontology based on the relation "plays the role of". Figure 3.3 shows four ontology components written in this fashion.

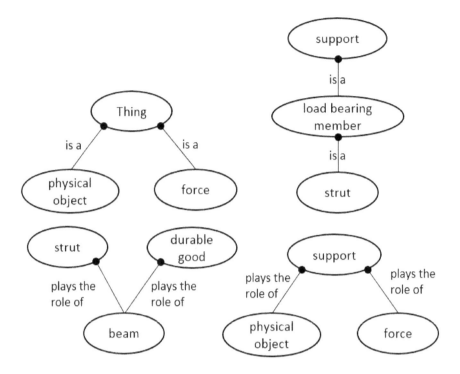

Figure 3.3: Representing "strut" with multi-perspective ontologies

3.6   Dealing with ontology issues

In this section, the ontology problems listed above will be considered in turn, with indications on how or whether multi-perspective ontologies can resolve the problem.

3.6.1 IS-A overloading

Five types of ontology problem due to IS-A overloading were identified by Guarino et al. Multi-perspective ontologies can deal with two of these directly: suspect type-to-role links should be eliminated if an ontology based on the relation *plays the role of* is developed; and confusion of taxonomic roles should also be eliminated (since qualities and decomposable objects don't appear as one of the recommended perspectives, it is unlikely that a taxonomy of them will be developed). The remaining problems are due to weak consideration by knowledge engineers of the ontological links that can be introduced into an ontology; multi-perspective ontologies don't deal with this directly, but by breaking down ontologies into a number of single-perspective ontologies, they should make it easier to identify the implications of making certain links.

3.6.2 Inaccurate expert responses

Multi-perspective ontologies can be of great help in dealing with inaccurate expert responses, particularly if they are combined with a software tool that allows swift representation and display of acquired knowledge. If, for example, a knowledge engineer asks "what causes A?" and the expert inaccurately replies "B" when in fact A causes B, an ontology based on the 'causes' relation can be created or opened, the relationship can be entered, and the results displayed to the expert. The expert can then immediately see their statement in the context of other knowledge, and should recognise their mistake.

3.6.3 Levels of detail and inferencing bias

The Zachman framework clearly suggests that knowledge or information assets need to be represented not only from different perspectives but also at different levels of detail, as discussed in chapter 2. It's clear that the concept of agreed levels of detail of ontologies is needed, but it's far from clear that the levels proposed by the Zachman framework map well to levels for ontology representations - not least because the six levels of the Zachman framework do not in fact represent six increasing levels of detail, but rather three levels of detail of models of the world (scoping, enterprise, system) followed by three levels of detail of models of a system (technology, details representation, functioning enterprise). The subject of appropriate levels of detail for an ontology is therefore a subject for future work. Interested readers might want to look at the nine ontology levels proposed by Guarino [128].

Another suggestion, made by Corazzon [35], is that a Standard Template Library or a Pattern for ontological categories and constructs should be developed, akin to the templates used by the software patterns movement. These templates would be used to classify "fragments of reality", and would implicitly allocate those fragments to an appropriate level of detail. However, as Corazzon points out, there is no general consensus on the general features of an ontology, never mind an appropriate standardised format for them.

3.6.4 Dependence relations

The problem of representing dependence relations is greatly simplified by using multi-perspective ontologies. The reason is that the most common dependence relationships can actually be expressed as other relations that fit into the multi-perspective framework. One example appears in the worked example of scientific knowledge management: the existence of a Publication depends on the existence of a Document, but can be re-expressed by saying that a Publication gives a (public) location of a document - a relation that can be found in an ontology based on the WHERE perspective. Similarly, the existence of a car can be said to depend on the continued existence of (most of) its parts which can be modelled using part-of relationships; and the continued existence of a procedure depends (or ought to depend) on there being continued justification for it being performed which can be modelled in a WHY ontology.

3.6.5 Particulars

The representation of processes and groups also fits very well with the philosophy of multi-perspective modelling. It is to be expected that the majority of concepts in a HOW ontology will be processes or events rather than individuals. And a WHO ontology, showing capability, authority, rights and responsibilities as well as organisational structures, can represent links between individuals and groups. The distinction between "stuff" and discrete objects is a high level concept better represented using definitional properties in general ontologies rather than with relations in domain-specific ontologies.

3.7 Discussion

It seems that the ability to search for a concept or category by more than one route is highly prized by users, and multi-perspective ontologies are ideal for supporting this. We have seen that the creation of multi-perspective ontologies is capable of resolving several of the most common problems that arise in ontology development. Some issues remain to be resolved, such as defining agreed "levels of detail" for ontologies, and determining the most appropriate set of definitional properties for ontological concepts. Readers interested in these concepts are directed to discussions in [99] and [128] respectively.

Some may argue that multi-perspective ontologies introduce multiple inheritance onto ontologies and that this is unacceptable. While multiple inheritance clearly is introduced, this is not so much unacceptable as inevitable for real world ontologies. Indeed, multiple inheritance already appears in existing ontologies such as the ontology of Scientific Knowledge Management shown in Figure 3.1 (where Person and Organisation have multiple superclasses). If the argument against multiple inheritance is based on the (common) inability of certain knowledge management software tools to support multiple inheritance, the message of this chapter is that it's time for a new version of that software tool to be developed.

This chapter has shown how the perspectives of the Zachman framework can be used to tackle common ontology problems. The next chapter looks at a detailed example of this: the framework is applied to the ACM classification scheme to see if it has any of the common ontology problems, and to determine if a multi-perspective analysis could help to solve them.

4 Ontology Issues: Correct Classification

4.1 Introduction

Much work is being carried out these days on the classification of objects or concepts in a standardised manner; such a classification is often referred to as an *ontology*. Various researchers are promoting different ontologies, approaches to building ontologies, standards for ontologies, and so on. Such work is valuable and worthy of respect, but often a single ontology cannot describe an object or concept fully. It is proposed in chapter 2 (with a case study in [103]) that representing an object or concept completely may require up to six ontologies, covering *who, what, how, where, when and why* perspectives, and furthermore that these perspectives may recur at different levels of abstraction, from an "organisational" level right down to a "system implementation" level. This is referred to as a *multi-perspective modelling* approach.

The purpose of this paper is to test the theory of multiple perspectives being necessary for completeness in ontologies by applying it to the task of placing "knowledge management" and "knowledge engineering" within the ACM classification scheme. This task arose from a request by the librarian of the Artificial Intelligence library at the University of Edinburgh. For several years, the AI library has been classifying its collection according to the ACM classification scheme, along with an extension to the Artificial Intelligence section of the scheme that was published in the AI magazine in 1985 [40]. However, recent interest in knowledge management from commercial and research organisations, along with a grant from EPSRC to develop a Master's Training Package in Knowledge Management and Knowledge Engineering, has led to an influx of books and other materials on these topics. There is no entry in the current ACM scheme for knowledge management, and although there is an existing category for knowledge engineering in the extended version of the scheme (as a subclass of

Learning), the librarian had noticed that books on knowledge engineering were being classified in four different places.

The thesis of this paper is that a multi-perspective analysis of the ACM classification scheme and the AI extension should demonstrate some of the principles on which the classification is based, and therefore help in deciding where knowledge management and knowledge engineering should appear in the classification.

4.2   The ACM Classification Scheme and extension

The ACM classification scheme [127] was first published in 1964, with seven top level topics. In its third revision, produced in 1998, the number of top level categories had increased to 11 (see Table 4.1), along with major extensions of lower level categories.[12]

A	General literature
B	Hardware
C	Computer systems organisation
D	Software
E	Data
F	Theory of computation
G	Mathematics of computing
H	Information systems
I	Computing methodologies
J	Computer applications
K	Computer milieux (philosophy, legislation, administration)

Table 4.1: Top level of the 1998 ACM classification scheme

---

[12] The report accompanying the 1998 classification suggests that another major revision is needed, but because deletion of categories would render historical indexes inaccurate, it was decided that a major revision would be delayed; and in addition, categories that were considered redundant would be "retired" rather than being deleted from the hierarchy.

Artificial Intelligence appears in the ACM classification scheme as a subcategory of one of the newer top level categories, "Computing Methodologies", alongside "symbolic and algebraic manipulation", "computer graphics", "simulation and modelling", "document and text processing", and others.

The subcategories of AI (apart from General and Miscellaneous which appear in every list of subcategories) are Applications and Expert Systems; Automatic Programming; Deduction and Theorem Proving; Knowledge Representation Formalisms and Methods; Programming Languages and Software; Learning; Natural Language Processing; Problem Solving, Control methods and Search; Robotics; Vision and Scene Understanding; and Distributed Artificial Intelligence. Each of these has some suggested interest areas (i.e. a partial list of possible subcategories); for Applications and Expert Systems, for example, the current list of interests includes (among others) cartography, games, industrial automation, law, medicine and science, natural language interfaces, mathematical aids and prosthetics. It's immediately clear to readers familiar with the Artificial Intelligence field that, however valid this classification was when it was developed, it does not reflect the current levels of interest in the field very well: an obvious example is cartography which is listed as a fourth level classification here, but nowadays would probably not even make it to the fifth level – it might be regarded as a subclass of "Geographical applications" which in turn would be a subclass of "Medicine and Science". Similarly, it's hard to believe that a new classification would grant "Distributed Artificial Intelligence" the same level of prominence as "Applications and Expert Systems". The original classification may have been based on what was known at the time, on the political preferences of the ACM committee[13], or on some other basis. However, this highlights the need to understand the principles on which ontological decisions are based to be noted.

---

[13] To illustrate "political preferences", AIAI helped to carry out a project to merge four ontologies of "scientific knowledge management" (i.e. academics and their publications) prepared by different universities into one "reference ontology" [99]. When the four original ontologies were compared it was noted that there were many similarities, but if a research group's own special interest area appeared in the ontology, it was classified at a higher level in its own ontology than in the others' ontologies.

In 1985, David Waltz was invited by Scientific Datalink, a division of Comtex Scientific Corporation to extend the AI classification to account for some of the subdivisions of AI, to aid Comtex in indexing the series of AI memos and reports that they had been gathering. The resulting classification which has been published by Waltz in AI Magazine [40], retains all of the above top level categories except for "Distributed Artificial Intelligence" which is replaced by "Specialized AI Architectures". Two new categories are also added: "Cognitive Modelling and Psychological Studies of Intelligence", and "Social and Philosophical issues". The contents of most categories have been significantly expanded: continuing the earlier example, "Applications and Expert Systems" now has 19 subcategories, including the 7 proposed as "interests" by the ACM, and these 19 subcategories have up to 11 sub-sub-categories or even sub-sub-sub-categories. Space prevents the replication of the entire classification here, but four of the nineteen categories are described in detail in Table 4.2.

4.3   Dimensions of classification

The ACM classification scheme is considered to be a four-level, hierarchical taxonomy. A "taxonomy" is defined in Merriam-Webster's dictionary as "a classification, especially an orderly classification of plants and animals according to their presumed natural relationships". Taxonomies are typically used to represent one class of objects or concepts and its sub-types; that is, objects/concepts that possess all the defining features[14] of the higher level object/concept plus a couple of extra features. A 'true' taxonomy therefore includes only one relationship between objects or concepts; one object/concept is a subclass (or "a kind of") the other.[15]

---

[14] There is much debate in psychological circles about what constitutes a "defining feature". Interested readers might look at the work of Rosch on "typicality" [142].

[15] There is also a variant of 'subclass' – 'instance-of' – that allows for individual members of classes; so an object can be an instance of a class. Strictly speaking, therefore, a taxonomy allows two types of relationship between objects and concepts.

I.2.1. Applications and Expert Systems

1.0 Cartography	
1.1 Games	Chess, Checkers, Backgammon, Bidding Games, Wagering Games, War Games, Other
1,2 Industrial Applications	Automatic Assembly, Parts Handling, Inspection, Welding, Planning for Production, Inventory
1.3 Law	
1.4 Medicine	Medical Applications, Chemical Applications, Biological Applications, Geological Applications
1.5 Natural Language Interfaces	
1.6 Office Automation	
1.7 Military Applications	Autonomous Vehicles, Integration of Information, Decisions Aids, Target Tracking, Communication
1.8 Business and Financial	Tax experts, Investment, Financial Planning, Information Storage and Retrieval
1.9 Natural Language Processing Applications	
1.10 Mathematical Aids	
1.11 Education	Tutoring systems, Intelligent Computer-aided Instruction, Aids to learning Programming, Curriculum Design
1.12 Library Applications	
1.13 Engineering Automation	Computer System Design, VLSI Design Aids, CAD/CAM, Programming Aids
1.14 System Troubleshooting	
1.15 Expert Systems	Expert System Languages and Aids for Building Expert Systems, Acquisition of Expert Knowledge, Plausible Reasoning, Representation of Expert Knowledge, Generation of Explanations, Expert Systems based on Simulation and Deep Models, User Interfaces for Expert Systems, Validation of Expert Systems
1.16 Prosthetics	
1.17 Aviation Applications	
1.18 Applications, Other	

I.2.4 Knowledge Representation

4.0 Frames and Scripts	Defaults, Stereotypes and Prototypes, Generation of Expectations, Frame Languages, Frame-Driven Systems, Inheritance Hierarchy
4.1 Predicate Logic	First Order Predicate Calculus, Skolem Functions, Second Order Logic, Modal Logics, Fuzzy Logic
4.2 Relational Systems	Relational Data Bases, Associative Memory
4.3 Representation Languages	
4.4 Representations (Procedural & Rule-Based)	Production Rule Systems, Knowledge Bases
4.5 Semantic Networks	
4.6 Connectionist Systems	
4.7 Multi Agent/ Actor Systems	
4.8 Constraints	
4.9 Discrimination Trees & Networks	
4.10 Belief Models	
4.11 Representing the Physical World	
4.12 Representing Natural Language Semantics	

I.2.6 Learning

6.0 Analogies	Geometric Analogies, Natural Language Analogies, Structural Analogies, Functional Analogies
6.1 Concept learning	Near-Miss Analysis, Version Spaces, Schema Acquisition & Generalising, Learning of Heuristics, Credit & Blame Assignment, Conceptual Clustering
6.2 Induction	Statistical Methods, Inductive Inference
6.3 Knowledge Acquisition	Advice Taking and Learning by Being Told, Learning from Examples, Learning by Observation, Learning from Experience, Learning by Discovery
6.4 Knowledge Engineering	Dialogues with Experts, Knowledge Base Stability, Knowledge Base Consistency
6.5 Language Acquisition	Acquisition of Grammar, Learning of Concepts through Language
6.6 Parameter Learning	
6.7 Associative Learning	
6.8 Learning of Skills	
6.9 Developmental and Incremental Learning	
6.10 Evolutionary Learning	

I.2.8 Problem Solving, Control methods and Search	
8.0 Backtracking	
8.1 Dynamic Programming	
8.2 Graph and Tree Search Strategies	Depth first, Breadth first, Best first, Branch & Bound, Hill Climbing, Minimax, Alpha-Beta, A*, Beam, Dependency-Directed Backtracking, Constraint Propagation, Relaxation Methods, Marker Passing, Bidirectional, Data-Driven/Top-Down
8.3 Heuristic Methods	Nature of Heuristics, Heuristic Control of Search, Strategies, Default Reasoning, Closed World Heuristics, Induction and Evaluation of Heuristics, Qualitative Reasoning and Envisionment
8.4 Plan Execution, Formation, Generation	Means-End Analysis, Forward Chaining, Backward Chaining, Weak methods, Generate and Test, Hierarchical Planning, Meta-planning and Multiple Goals, Plan Verification, Plan Modification
8.5 Matching	

Table 4.2: Part of the Scientific Datalink AI classification

However, when ontologies are built to represent the relationships between tasks, activities, philosophies, or other conceptual entities, it's often difficult to connect them all using only subclass relationships; maybe there are no obvious taxonomic groupings, or maybe there is a more obvious grouping according to function, form, role or relevance. An example of a "more obvious" grouping can be found in vegetable classification; while it might possibly be helpful to know that the Linnaean classification of (most) tomatoes places them alongside aubergines and potatoes in the Nightshade genus of the Potato family, many gardeners would probably prefer to see tomatoes classified alongside other vegetables that grow on vines, vegetables that grow in greenhouses, or even vegetables that are served in salads. An example of "no obvious groupings" can be found by looking at cars. Possible classifications include "saloon", "hatchback", "sports car", etc. (based largely on form, but also on role) or "petrol engine cars", "diesel engine cars" and "alternative fuel engine cars" (based on function), but such subdivisions seem less "natural" than the higher level classes – and yet taxonomies are supposed to be based on "presumed natural relationships".

In fact, the whole issue of "natural" versus "artificial" classification has been a major subject of academic debate. A good summary is produced by Wilkins [194] who argues that "all classifications are artificial, but some have a degree of naturalness about them" and quotes R.G. Millikan who proposes that a "natural" concept can be determined by making a historical investigation of how an object and its name came about, and then determining what the name refers to today in most cases.[16] The practical result of these "artificial" distinctions is that taxonomies are sometimes based on relationships other than 'subclass'. Common ones are 'part of', 'causes/produces', and 'has property'[17]. In the next section, an analysis of the ACM classification will be carried out to determine what relationships are actually used.

4.4 The ACM Classification scheme: analysis

The ACM classification covers several of the multiple perspectives. The perspectives covered include "what" is needed for a computer system (hardware and software), "how" to build a computer system (techniques), and "why" systems are built (computing milieux). The categories also cover different levels of abstraction: some categories consider the contents of the computer itself (hardware, software, computer systems organisation, data, information systems) while other categories consider the computer as a single concept in the context of applications (computing methodologies, computer applications, computing milieux). There's also a third level of detail to

---

[16] This is a highly simplified summary; there is an entire journal devoted to classification. Wilkins' complete summary quotation is: "All classifications are artificial, but some have a degree of naturalness about them. Natural classifications are the result of a refinement of the intension of terms based on a very broad and generally culture-neutral set of observations. Species names, indeed all taxa names, are terms with a proper function assigned by the history of their use, and which may change as new evidence is arrived at."

[17] Each of these relationships can be broken down into a number of distinct relationships, but this level of detail is beyond the scope of this paper. For an example, see [1] on the breakdown of 'part of'.

be found in the two theoretical categories (*Theory of Computation* and *Mathematics of Computing*) which provide the foundational techniques for computer systems organisation, data and information systems. See Table 4.3 for a summary.

This organisation is broadly mirrored in the organisation of some of the second level categories in the ACM classification scheme. For example, the subclasses of *Computer Systems Organisation* are *Processor Architectures* and *Computer-Communication Networks* (two disjoint components that are necessary for a functioning hardware system, aka *Hardware* and *Software* at the top level); while *Special Purpose and Application Based Systems* and *Computer systems implementation* look at the "what" and "how" perspectives on hardware construction "applications". There's also a subcategory for *Performance of systems* which probably falls under the "when" perspective.

The subclasses of Information Systems, Data and Software all use a similar multi-perspective classification scheme. Not all of the second level categories and their decompositions fit neatly into this multi-perspective framework, however. The subdivisions of *Computer Applications* appear to be closer to a taxonomy, in that their second level breakdown consists of different areas of study or different disciplines which reads like a list of university faculties (*Administrative data processing, Physical sciences and engineering, Life and medical sciences, Social and behavioural sciences, Arts and Humanities).* While disciplines are not strictly speaking subclasses of "computer applications", they do (or should) form a single coherent subclass of a (hypothetical) taxonomy of knowledge. [18] The two top-level categories with a theoretical leaning also have sub-categories that reflect different areas of study in the disciplines of (applied) mathematics and (applied) logic.

A third approach is found in the *Hardware* category; its subcategories name different areas of hardware design (*Control structures, Arithmetic and logic structures, Memory structures, Input/Output and Data Communications, Register-transfer-level implementation, Logic Design* and *Integrated Circuits*), each of which includes the same small set of sub-sub-categories: *Design Styles, Design Aids*, and (until it became a separate category in the 1998 classification),

---

[18] If the subcategories were relabelled "Applications in <Discipline>" rather than just <Discipline>", the taxonomic connection would be much clearer.

	Applications	What goes inside a computer	Theoretical level
What	Computer Applications	Hardware Software	
How	Computing Methodologies	Computer Systems Organisation, Data Information Systems	Theory of Computation Mathematics of Computing
Why	Computer milieux		
Who			
When			
Where			

Table 4.3: Top level categories from the ACM scheme, classified according to multi-perspective modelling

Performance and reliability. It seems, therefore that the Hardware category is decomposed into its second level using the 'part of' relation instead of the 'subclass' relation (i.e. each subcategory is a "part of" the hardware of a computer system rather than a subclass) while a multi-perspective approach is used at the third level which explains the recurrence of the same subcategories at this level.

4.5 The Scientific Datalink AI extension: analysis

As with the ACM classification, each of the four categories of the Scientific Datalink AI classification (as reproduced in Table 4.2) can be broken down into subgroups.

• *Applications and Expert Systems* has nineteen subcategories, seven of which are drawn from the "interests" in the ACM classification scheme. Most of these are concerned with different domains in which expert systems have been applied (similar to the ACM's taxonomic breakdown of Computer Systems Applications into different disciplines), but I.2.1.15 ("Expert Systems") and I.2.1.5 ("Natural Language Interfaces") are more concerned with techniques for expert system construction, and I.2.1.14 ("System Troubleshooting") focuses on a particular task rather than on a domain. The distinction between tasks and domains which is a key tenet of the CommonKADS methodology for knowledge engineering [147], corresponds to the distinction between "how" and "what" in multi-perspective modelling.

• Most of the subcategories of *Knowledge Representation* are concerned with different knowledge representation formalisms – the "what" of knowledge representation. Frames and Scripts, Predicate Logic, Procedural & Rule-based Representations, Semantic Networks, Constraints and Connectionist Systems all fall into this category. The odd ones out are Representation of the Physical World and Representation of Natural Language Semantics; while these have some correlation with representation formalisms (e.g. simulation models with Representation of the Physical World), these two categories are primarily concerned with knowledge representation as a task rather than a formalism – i.e. with "how" rather than "what".

• Several subcategories of *Learning* deal with different methods of learning (by analogy; induction; associative learning), others deal with subjects to be learned (Concept learning; Language Acquisition; Learning of Skills). So here there is a multi-perspective decomposition; some subclasses represent "what" subcategories while others represent "how". And then there's Knowledge Acquisition and Knowledge Engineering. Knowledge Acquisition is apparently categorised under "learning" because its subcategories include learning from examples (i.e. induction), learning by observation, learning from experience and learning by discovery. Yet several popular knowledge acquisition techniques are not covered here at all – and while there is a category named "Acquisition of Expert Knowledge" (I.2.1.15.1) two levels down from "Applications and Expert Systems", the popular techniques are classified in various different places rather than being collected together in I.2.1.15.1. Protocol analysis, for example, is categorised under I.2.11 Cognitive Modelling and Psychological Studies of Intelligence, while the analysis of interview transcripts is most closely covered under Dialogues with Experts which is considered to be one of only three subcategories of Knowledge Engineering. The reader is left with a strong feeling that Knowledge Acquisition and Knowledge Engineering are underspecified, incomplete, and (possibly as a result) misclassified.

• The final category considered here, *Problem Solving, Control Methods and Search* seems to be something of a catch-all category for methods of controlling inference in AI programs. It has six subcategories, two of which are (unsurprisingly) *Heuristic Methods* and *Graph and Tree Search Strategies*. It also has categories for *Backtracking, Dynamic Programming* and *Matching* which are concerned with the implementation of rule-based systems, and finally a category for *Plan Execution, Formation and Generation*. Control knowledge is slightly difficult to categorise within a multi-perspective framework. In theory, it should be "meta-how" knowledge (i.e. knowledge about the process of controlling processes); in practice, it often includes information about the ordering or processes and the timing of key inputs and outputs to a process, and thus consists of "when" knowledge. This is particularly true of knowledge about planning.

To summarise: Scientific Datalink's AI extension to the ACM classification seems to stick with a formula where formalisms/resources ("what" knowledge) are mixed with methods/techniques ("how" knowledge) to generate subcategories. A taxonomic breakdown is also used (for Applications).

4.6   Correct   classification   of   knowledge-related disciplines

Having carried out this detailed analysis, it is time to use the principles identified to meet the original goal of this paper: to determine where Knowledge Management and Knowledge Engineering should be classified. Knowledge Acquisition will be considered too.

4.6.1   Correct classification of Knowledge Engineering

Knowledge Engineering has been variously classified as "the design and development of knowledge based systems"; "application of logic and ontology to the task of building computable models of some domain for some purpose"; "[the study of] the development of information systems in which knowledge and reasoning play pivotal roles"; and "[a] scientific methodology to analyse and engineer knowledge". Using the classifications identified earlier, it's clear that knowledge engineering is primarily application-focused (as opposed to concerned with the internal function of knowledge based systems or theoretical principles of knowledge); and that it focuses on the task of system development (i.e., "how" knowledge). From this analysis, the following classifications of *Knowledge Engineering* are possible:

• Knowledge Engineering could be a subclass of *I.2.1 Applications and Expert Systems*. Unfortunately, *Applications and Expert Systems* uses a largely taxonomic breakdown; but there are two subcategories of *Applications and Expert Systems* that are concerned with techniques for expert system construction. These do not fit well with in the taxonomic breakdown of I.2.1, but would be appropriate siblings for Knowledge Engineering.

• Knowledge Engineering could sit alongside Software Engineering as a subcategory of *D. Software* in the ACM classification. The primary objections to this are the "political" ones – there's much more interest and activity in Software Engineering than in Knowledge Engineering which makes it difficult to place them at the same level.

• Knowledge Engineering could be a subcategory of *D.2 Software Engineering*. This is probably the most "principled" place to put it, since knowledge engineering is indeed a subcategory of software engineering – it is software engineering for a specialised type of software system. However, this conflicts with the current basis of decomposition of Software Engineering which is by subtasks rather than a "taxonomy" of types of software.

• Knowledge Engineering could appear alongside *Representation of the Physical World* and *Representation of Natural Language Semantics* as a "how" category under *I.2.4 Knowledge Representation* in the AI extension. The difficulty with this is that the focus of Knowledge Representation is very much on the internals of a knowledge based system, whereas the focus of Knowledge Engineering is on applications, so there is a clash in levels of abstraction.

• Finally, Knowledge Engineering could be left in its current location as a subcategory of *I.2.6 Learning*. This is probably the worst option of all, since knowledge engineering techniques (with accompanying knowledge models) are only appropriate for software that *doesn't* rely on learning as its primary input method, since it's hard to analyse knowledge that has not yet been learned.

In summary, there is no ideal location for Knowledge Engineering in the ACM or Scientific Datalink hierarchies. Since a proposal is needed, a "tie-breaker" can be found in the current subcategory *I.2.1.15 Expert Systems* of *I.2.1.Applications and Expert Systems*. This subcategory actually has a number of knowledge engineering subtasks as its subcategories already. For the sake of backward compatibility, therefore, I.2.1.15 should be left in its current position in the hierarchy, but be renamed to "Expert Systems and Knowledge Engineering".

4.6.2   Correct classification of Knowledge Acquisition

Once the classification of Knowledge Engineering has been decided, the correct classification of Knowledge Acquisition is fairly easy to determine, for Knowledge Acquisition is a subtask of Knowledge Engineering. Indeed, there is already a category I.2.15.1 named "Acquisition of Expert Knowledge". The only difficulty lies in determining where to classify those topics that are currently subclasses of *I.2.6.3 Learning: Knowledge Acquisition*. Since the Learning section needs to revised anyway to take account of (a) the removal of Knowledge Engineering and (b) the presence of Induction but the absence of two related technologies, Case Based Reasoning and Neural

Networks[19], it is proposed that the subcategories of I.2.6.3 are either transferred to other categories under Learning (for example, *I.2.6.3.1, Learning from Examples*, would be appropriate for this) or moved to *I.2.1.15.1, Acquisition of Expert Knowledge.*

4.6.3   Correct Classification of Knowledge Management

Deciding where to classify knowledge management is difficult because there is considerable disagreement about the best approach to knowledge management. A good working definition of knowledge management would be "the deliberate design of artefacts with the intent to improve the use of knowledge within an organisation", but a range of artefacts have been suggested, from knowledge based systems (thus considering knowledge management as an early stage in knowledge engineering) through to communication forums (considering knowledge management as a process of community interaction in which knowledge-based technology has no part to play). A good survey is given by Binney [39] in which he identifies a "KM spectrum" where knowledge management activities are classified according to their overall goal. Applications that embed knowledge in organisational transactions lie at the "technology-focused" end of the spectrum whereas applications that support innovation and creation of new knowledge lie at the "community-focused" end of the spectrum. Between these two extremes can be found "analytical KM" (the use of knowledge to interpret vast amounts of material); "asset management" KM; "process-based" KM (the codification and improvement of organisational processes); and "developmental" KM (increasing the competencies or capabilities of an organisation's knowledge workers).

KM is therefore generally application-focused; it can be focused on "what", "how", "who" or even "why" depending on the KM approach that is taken; and Binney's decomposition of KM is focused on "how" a particular goal should be achieved. From this analysis, options for classification of Knowledge Management would be:

---

[19] There are existing Scientific Datalink categories for Connectionist systems under Knowledge Representation, and Connectionist Architectures under *I.2.12 Specialised AI Architectures*, but there is no explicit category for "how" to build neural networks. There is so much work on neural networks these days that it probably deserves its own separate category.

• As a subclass of *I.2.1.15 Applications and Expert Systems*, alongside Knowledge Engineering;

• As a subclass of *I.2.4 Knowledge Representation*; however, the arguments against this are the same ones that applied to Knowledge Engineering;

• As a subclass of *I.2.13 Social and Philosophical Issues [in Artificial Intelligence].* This, however, is more of a theoretical perspective while Knowledge Management is more focused on applications;

• As a subclass of *H.4 Information Systems* in the ACM classification scheme. This removes the commitment that a KM system must be knowledge-based in some fashion, and thus encompasses more of the various KM approaches than would otherwise be the case, but it's debatable whether or not Knowledge Management should appear at the same level as Database Management – for despite the similarity in terminology, these are really quite different tasks;

• As a subclass of *H.4.1 Office Automation* underneath *H.4 Information Systems.* H.4.1 already contains a category for Workflow management which is a key enabling technology for process-based KM, and a category for Groupware;

• As a subclass of *H.4.2 Types of Systems* underneath *H.4 Information Systems.* This category currently includes "Decision support systems (e.g. MIS)" and "Logistics", both of which are reasonably application-focused and also focus on "how" tasks are done.

It seems that there are advantages in taking "Knowledge Management" outside the Artificial Intelligence classification and using the Information Systems classification instead, since some knowledge management approaches are based on software that is not knowledge based. The final recommendation is that Knowledge Management should be a subclass of *H.4.2 Types of [Information] Systems*, since it fits better alongside other types of systems (decision support systems and logistics) than alongside its own enabling technologies (workflow systems and groupware). A new category is therefore proposed, to be labelled *H.4.2.3 Knowledge Management.*

4.7 Discussion

It has been shown that the ACM classification, and Scientific Datalink's extension, are based on two or three different structuring principles: sometimes taxonomic, sometimes based on "what" knowledge, (which implies that the subcategory is something that is used for, or produced by the top level category; it is a resource in the most general sense of the word), and sometimes based on "how" knowledge – i.e. techniques for, or methods to achieve the top level category. In addition, the Hardware category has a 'part of' decomposition, and some political considerations come into play as well.

What does this tell us about the ACM classification, about multi-perspective modelling, and about ontologies in general? It tells us that if an ontology tries to use "natural" categories, then it will almost certainly be developed using multiple perspectives; so the original thesis of this paper that multiple ontologies from different perspectives are needed for completeness, is borne out. However, the "what" and "how" perspectives are much more common than the "who", "when", "where" and "why", so it seems that while six ontologies from different perspectives may be necessary, two – with appropriate attention to whether the ontology is focused on theoretical principles, system internals, or applications – will often be sufficient.

It also tells us that "political" considerations – the level of interest in a subject – have considerable weight when determining the level of various categories in the ontology. The underlying message of this is that there is no canonical way of determining when a set of subcategories is complete – or at least, no way that is sufficiently widely accepted to override political concerns. Some guidance on category completeness may be available from other research; to give an example, "System Troubleshooting" has been identified as the only subcategory of *I.2.1.15 Applications and Expert Systems* that represents an application-focused task. However, a set of "knowledge based tasks" has been proposed by the CommonKADS methodology [20], and one of them (diagnosis) can be instantiated to "troubleshooting". This implies that all the other knowledge based tasks should be eligible, or even expected to make an appearance in I.2.1.15; examples might be "artefact design", "system monitoring", and "selection/ assessment". But this set of tasks is not theoretically proven to be complete; in fact, the original author of this set of tasks has since revised his opinions and proposed that the tasks above are actually composed from a smaller set of five or six "primitive" tasks [18]. So while published sets of categories such as this can be pragmatically useful to ontology developers, they rarely actually solve the problem of canonically determining all possible members of a category.

The ACM classification scheme itself, along with its AI extension, is detailed, widely accepted, and reasonably principled, and so should continue to be used. Some revisions are needed, though (especially under I.2.6 Learning in the AI extension), and it is worth questioning why *Hardware* uses a different decomposition principle from the rest of the scheme: is this an artefact of political lobbying, or is there a "natural" principle here that could be extended to other areas of the classification?

Finally, the new classifications proposed by this paper have classified Knowledge Engineering and Knowledge Management very differently. This raises the issue of the purpose of a classification: should it be carried out according to ontological principles for robustness, or should it be organised to place relevant subjects close to others, to facilitate serendipitous browsing? The case of knowledge management is a difficult one because there are different opinions about it – some books on knowledge management will draw heavily on techniques from knowledge engineering and will serve as useful precursors to knowledge engineering projects, while other books will have little or no relevance to knowledge engineering. An intriguing alternative to the ontological approach would be to use learning techniques to create an entirely new classification scheme based on cluster analysis (using references, keywords, or other criteria); an examination of this approach is suggested for future research.

Having shown that the perspectives of the Zachman framework have value in both knowledge management and ontology analysis, the next chapter of this thesis turns to the topic of the applicability of the Zachman framework to knowledge engineering.

Part III: The CommonKADS Methodology

5 Knowledge Engineering: the CommonKADS Methodology

5.1 Introduction

In previous chapters, the value of a multi-perspective modelling approach in knowledge management and in ontology development has been discussed. The purpose of this chapter is to show how this concept can be applied to knowledge engineering: the acquisition and representation of knowledge, and the implementation of that knowledge in a knowledge-based reasoning system. Specifically, the chapter introduces the CommonKADS approach to knowledge management and knowledge engineering, and considers how well it supports a multi-perspective approach to knowledge modelling.

In the early days of the development of expert systems, the construction of these systems was often carried out by "rapid prototyping"; that is, acquiring some knowledge from the expert, and immediately implementing this knowledge in software. Future knowledge acquisition sessions were then used to increment the functionality of the software. While rapid prototyping has some benefits in swiftly proving the usefulness of the software, it proved to have numerous disadvantages in maintainability of the systems, not least because there was no representation of the knowledge independent of its implementation. It was perhaps a growing desire for such an independent representation, backed by Newell's "knowledge level" principle [130] which proposes that knowledge should be represented at a conceptual level that is independent from specific computational constructs that led to the first proposals for knowledge modelling - that is, representing knowledge as a set of diagrams and accompanying text.

As knowledge based systems became increasingly of interest to the commercial world, a desire began to grow for knowledge based systems to be developed in traceable and reliable manner. Software engineering methodologies such as SSADM, Prince, or the emerging object oriented analysis and design methods viewed the development of software as a sequential process, with some loopbacks permitted (since it had been discovered that a pure "waterfall" approach, with no loopbacks to earlier stages allowed, caused some expensive mistakes due to late detection of early errors). Broadly speaking, these stages were the gathering of system requirements from users; analysis of these requirements; design of a system that would meet the requirements; implementation of the system; and testing the system against requirements. To companies and industries for whom accuracy, reliability and maintainability were far more important that speed of development or trying out new technical approaches, this type of structured methodology was much more acceptable than rapid prototyping.

It was in this environment that the CommonKADS methodology was developed. CommonKADS started life as KADS, a methodology developed by a European Union-funded collaborative project between 1983 and 1987. The acronym either stood for Knowledge Acquisition Documentation System or Knowledge Analysis and Design System; it seems that the project was originally motivated by a desire to represent acquired knowledge at the "knowledge level" which is referred to frequently in early documentation, but was later transformed into something more closely resembling a software engineering methodology.

KADS focused on the transformation of expert knowledge into a system design for a knowledge based system. It introduced (or popularised) two key concepts to the knowledge engineering process: the separation of analysis into different but related layers, and the use of template models to guide both knowledge acquisition and system structuring. The "layer" approach encouraged knowledge engineers to model the static domain knowledge (concepts, instances, relationships) separately from the inference knowledge (inference steps, and the role that knowledge played in reasoning), with further layers for the task knowledge (control of the ordering of inference steps, and of inputs and outputs) and the problem solving knowledge (deciding what strategy to take in solving a problem). These layers were clearly interrelated, and the separation proved to be a useful support to knowledge acquisition, for if knowledge was required by one layer but did not exist in another layer, there was a clear requirement for further knowledge acquisition.

The second key innovation of KADS was the provision of generic template models for problem solving. These models were intended to support the inference layer of reasoning (some support for the task layer was also provided) by suggesting the types of knowledge and of inference steps that were required in various problem solving tasks. The development of an inference layer then switched from being a model creation task to a model instantiation task. Inspired by Clancey's generic model of heuristic classification tasks [31], generic template models were developed for a variety of analytic tasks (diagnosis, assessment, monitoring, etc.), synthetic tasks (design, planning, configuration) and modification tasks (repair, control). These templates, known as "interpretation models", proved to be KADS' most popular innovation, since they provide an easy route to choosing an adequate system design.

KADS was criticised, however, from two main camps: those who criticised its modelling for not taking into account other modelling approaches (such as Chandrasekaran's Generic Tasks approach [27] and Steels' Components of Expertise approach [161]), and those who criticised it for being too narrowly focused on the transformation of expert knowledge into a system design without consideration of the organisational context in which a system will operate (i.e. without sufficient attention to the requirements and system analysis stages of KBS development). The result was CommonKADS, developed on a second EU-funded project (KADS-II, 1989-1994) which extended KADS to take in many of these components. Some revisions were made to the model of expertise (principally moving problem solving knowledge from being a layer of the expertise model to being a separate library of problem solving methods), but the biggest change came in the introduction of five new models:[20] models of the organisation, task, agents involved, communication, and system design. These embodied an approach that allowed for development of a knowledge based system by progressive transformation of models from a model of the organisation through increasingly specific models until an implementable system design is produced. The "CommonKADS book" [147] presents these models as being at three levels of detail: an organisational level, an expertise level and a design level. From my own practical experience with CommonKADS, I have revised this into a four-level model, as shown in Figure 5.1.

---

[20] KADS did propose a model of "modality" which formed the foundation of the Agent and Communication models, so perhaps CommonKADS only introduced three or four 'new' models.

By introducing these new models, and encouraging knowledge engineers to work top-down through them, CommonKADS became a knowledge engineering methodology that is analogous to software engineering methodologies. This was quite deliberate; indeed, CommonKADS chose to use (early) UML diagramming conventions for its models. However, CommonKADS' use of multiple models at multiple levels of detail also fits well with the philosophy of the Zachman framework for Information Systems Architecture [197]. This chapter therefore has two purposes: to describe the upper level CommonKADS models briefly, and to discuss the mapping between CommonKADS and the Zachman framework.

5.2 The CommonKADS Organisation Model

CommonKADS' concept of a model includes a range of features: content (elements and relations), rationale, and possible model states. Model states are considered in some detail, and are considered to have quality criteria, land mark and transition types, and internal and external dependencies (see figure 1.1 in [44]). The concept of model states is considered in some detail throughout the publications of the KADS-II project, and while it has not been taken up in detail by many knowledge engineers, it fits well into the concept of CommonKADS as a software engineering methodology.

The Organisation model of CommonKADS was designed to represent the different aspects of an organisation that might be relevant for decision making in a knowledge based systems project. Its sub-goals are to support the identification of knowledge based systems applications within the organisation; to facilitate assessing the impact that a knowledge based system might have when it is introduced into the organisation; and to familiarise knowledge engineers with the culture (the 'feeling') of the organisation. It can be represented as a number of sub-diagrams. The first (published) proposal [44] was that the sub-diagrams should consider organisational structure, organisational functions, organisational processes, organisational resources (knowledge, computing and other), people (i.e. roles and responsibilities), and power/authority relationships that crossed over organisational structure. A case study was published by the KADS-II project [43] which demonstrated how these aspects were used to represent the Dutch social security organisation. The structure, process, and power/authority diagrams are reproduced in Figures 5.1,

5.2 and 5.3 below (note that the process diagram incorporates all the identified organisational functions). It can be seen that the social security organisation had all its computing functions outsourced to an external computing centre (Figure 5.1); it can also be seen that a number of unofficial power/authority relationships did exist, including the tester's power to demand time of low level branch staff (to carry out tests) and a relationship between the secretary of one head of unit and the head of another unit (they were married to each other).

But the real benefits of this approach become obvious in the "cross product" diagram that is reproduced in Figure 5.4 which maps functions to structure. The initial concept behind developing this model was to support the Decision Making function with a knowledge-based system; but from Figure 5.4 it is obvious that the Decision Making function is actually distributed over a number of departments, making the implementation of a knowledge based system difficult in practice. Furthermore, the appearance of the "Archiving" function in no less than three locations in the diagram led the researchers to develop another cross product, of functions against resources; in other words, they investigated how much time was spent on each function. They found that Decision Making took up relatively little time of the processing of a social security application while Archiving took up around 30% of the total time. So not only would a KBS be complex to put into practice, but also there was little to be gained from automating the decision making function!

The Organisation model has undergone some changes in the CommonKADS book: to summarise them, the recommended set of perspectives has changed ('functions' are no longer recommended since they appear in the process perspective anyway), and knowledge engineers are encouraged to represent the perspectives using a number of worksheets rather than as diagrams. However, the general principle of representing the organisation from a number of different perspectives remains.

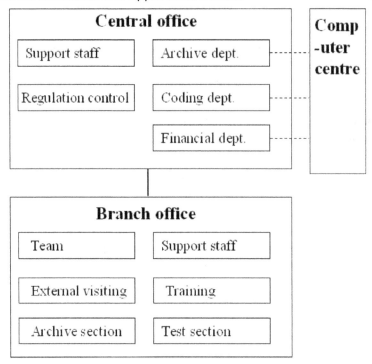

Figure 5.1: Social Security department: organisational structure

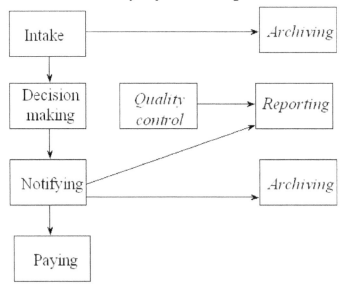

Figure 5.2: Social Security department: organisational processes

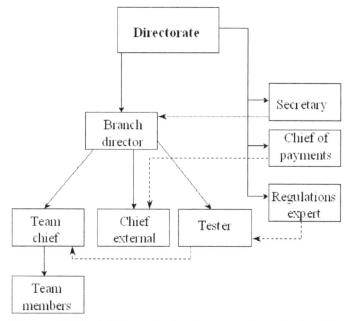

Figure 5.3 Social Security dept: power & authority links

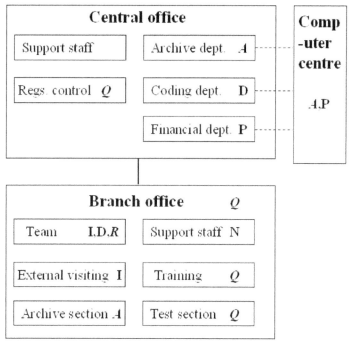

Figure 5.4: Cross product between structure & process

5.4 The CommonKADS Task Model

The CommonKADS Task Model examines a single business function in more detail, focusing on the functions and process(es) that make up that top-level business function. For example, if the top level function was "Archiving", the sub-functions might include "assessing required level of confidentiality", "indexing", and "transferring to storage". It also includes more detail about the inputs and outputs of the process. Various aspects of the task may be represented, including:

- The goal of the task and the degree to which it generally can be achieved;
- The preconditions of a task (either inputs or completion of other tasks);
- Control over sub-tasks;
- Knowledge or skills required to complete the task;
- Whether the task decomposes according to time, sub-goals or ingredients;
- How the tasks will differ in the required situation from the current situation.

The end result can be represented as structured text (as recommended by the original Task model definition report [55]), or as a set of worksheets (as recommended by the CommonKADS book). However, since all other CommonKADS models have a diagram format recommended, it is useful to be able to represent the Task model as a diagram too - perhaps a UML Activity diagram, or using some other process diagramming format.

The purpose of the Task model is to mitigate certain risks attendant to knowledge management and knowledge engineering. Duursma [55] identifies the following:

- A system is constructed that does not benefit the organisation;
- A system is constructed that performs tasks that are not part of the problem;
- Task actors are not clearly specified;
- The organisation model cannot be completed;
- No expertise model can be developed;
- Tasks appear in the design model that were not previously specified;

- Inter-task communication is not understood.

In other words, the Task model is an integral part of the CommonKADS model suite, and it may be difficult to develop any of the other models without having developed a task model.

5.5   Worked   Example: Air   Campaign Planning

This section describes how the CommonKADS Organisation, Task and Agent models were used to model the top level process of USAF air campaign planning. This example is based on work carried out to support a consortium of researchers who were developing knowledge-based software and techniques to support the task of air campaign planning.

5.5.1   Knowledge acquisition

Knowledge acquisition was initially carried out using interviewing techniques. These interviews provided much useful knowledge, and also highlighted the existence of a number of relevant documents, from which much further knowledge was acquired. Two other knowledge acquisition techniques were also used; protocol analysis of a sample planning scenario provided useful information about the priorities, ordering, and necessary information for the planning process; and the repertory grid knowledge elicitation technique was used at a later stage to determine which activities within the planning process were difficult or had highest impact, to determine which activities might benefit from knowledge based system support.

The knowledge that was acquired showed that air campaign planning is hierarchically organised. When a crisis occurs, the Commander in Chief (CinC) provides planning guidance to the Joint Forces Commander (JFC). This guidance is communicated to the component commanders (e.g. the Air Component commander), who will in turn communicate the guidance to the air campaign planners. Based on the guidance, the planning staff will take between 3 days and 1 week to build a plan that may be executed. The acquired knowledge also showed that certain documents (such as the Master Attack Plan and the Air Tasking Order) form the outputs of key activities, and constitute a major method of communication within the planning process.

5.5.2   Knowledge modelling
The acquired knowledge was then classified into appropriate CommonKADS models.

Organisation model
A number of organisation model perspectives were developed, including organisational structure, resources, and process. The representation of power/authority relationships was considered superfluous by the experts because power/authority maps closely to structure within a military organisation, and so this perspective was not developed.

The resulting organisation model consisted of diagrams of activities (such as Figure 5.5), agents within an organisational structure, and resources. These were then combined to produce "cross products". Figure 5.6 shows an early version of the cross product between activities and resources. In this diagram, solid links between activities imply that the first activity *precedes* the second; dashed links show an information flow.

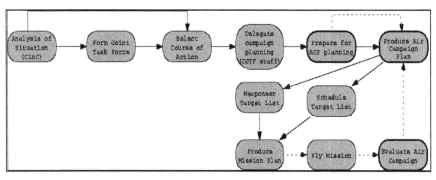

Figure 5.5: Air Campaign Planning: Top Level Activities

The Organisation model helps to identify the following information:
- The air campaign planning process is divided into three or four major phases which each have their own outputs: the Commander in Chief's Objectives, the Master Air Attack Plan, the Air Targets Plan, and finally the Air Tasking Order.
- The total time for development of a plan, even under war conditions, is between 1.5 and 3 days;

- The key decisions are made by small hand-picked "planning cells" for reasons of experience, efficiency and security.

It therefore seems that there is considerable scope for technological support to improve the air campaign planning process; and furthermore that this technological support should identify clearly which of the four main outputs it is using and which it is helping to produce.

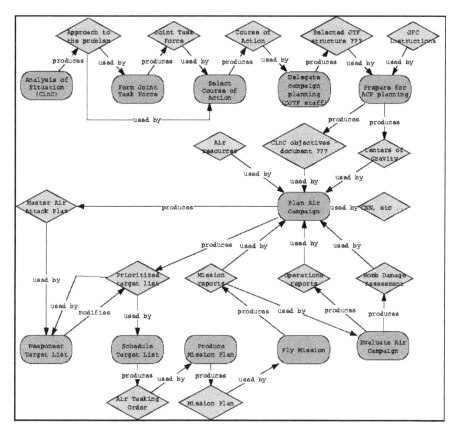

Figure 5.6: Air Campaign Planning: Activities/Resources Cross Product

Task Model

For this project, it was decided that the IDEF3 technique for process representation [92] would be used to represent the Task model.

IDEF3 is a process capture technique which was designed to be tolerant of incomplete and inconsistent descriptions, and to be flexible enough to deal with the incremental nature of the information acquisition process. It provides both a process-centred view of a system, via the *Process Flow Network*, and an object-centred view of a system via the *Object State Transition Network*.

A process flow network displays a sequence of *Units of Behaviour* (UOB) which represent activities, actions, processes or operations. These are linked together by precedence arcs. Where the process flow diverges (fan-out) or converges (fan-in) junction boxes are used. Junctions are of the AND, OR or Exclusive OR type and can be synchronous or asynchronous. This notation may impose timing constraints on the process flow. For example, a synchronous fan-in junction indicates that the incoming processes must complete simultaneously before the next UOB can begin.

In addition to UOBs and junctions, process flow networks can include referents, elaboration forms and UOB decompositions. Referents are used to indicate context-sensitive information and may refer to any other type of UOB such as an elaboration form, another process flow network, an object state transition network, an entirely different scenario, a note, or act as a GO-TO within the network. In some cases referents may impose timing constraints on the process so there is the option to be synchronous or asynchronous as needed. An elaboration form holds specific textual information for each UOB such as the object used by it, constraints acting on it, facts about it and a description of it. Decompositions enable each step of the process to be broken down into more detailed process descriptions, allowing descriptions to be held at varying levels of abstraction. This is indicated on the diagrams by a shadow on the parent UOB box.

The Task Model consisted of a series of IDEF3 diagrams, representing high level processes and their subtasks. An example of one component of the Task model can be seen in Figure 5.7. From this model we can learn that certain tasks can be carried out in parallel and others form potential bottlenecks in the process; this helps decide which tasks need supporting most urgently. It also provides information about other prerequisites of tasks.

Communication Model

The CommonKADS Agent and Communication models support the Task model by identifying other information about the sub-processes being modelled. They are discussed in more detail in the next chapter, so are only briefly covered here. The Agent model represents the capabilities and skills of the agents (staff, clients, or computer programs) who perform each activity within a sub-process, while the Communication model represents all communication that must take place between agents in order for a process to be completed.

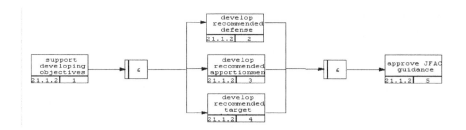

Figure 5.7: An IDEF3 Process Flow Network diagram

One or the primary uses of the Agent model is to determine which roles can be performed by a human which by a computer, and which by a human and computer working together. As this was not a major purpose of this modelling exercise, it was decided that an Agent model was not required. A Communication model was required, however, because effective transfer of information from one person or working group to the next is an important factor in the completion and efficiency of the planning process.

The diagram format used for the Communication Models was that of Role Activity Diagrams [135] which actually differs little from the recommended format for the CommonKADS Communication Model. Part of the Role Activity Diagram that was developed for Air Campaign Planning can be seen in Figure 5.8; each shaded box represents a person or group of people.

This model tells us which planning cells are actually responsible for which decision making tasks; for example, it shows us that the "JFACC Guidance letter" is not actually written by the JFACC (the Joint Forces Air Component Commander) but by the Air Strategy planning cell, and is then approved and signed by the JFACC. This therefore provides us with a better idea of which tasks can be supported and, importantly, of the tasks' inputs and outputs.

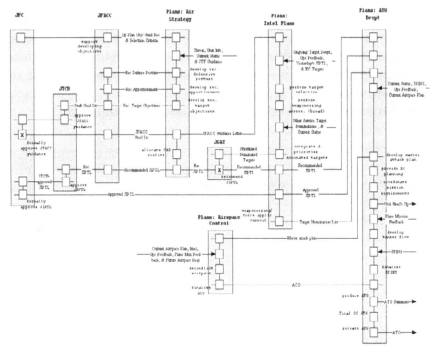

Figure 5.8: Role Activity Diagram showing initial communication in the air campaign planning process

5.6   Discussion: Multi   perspective modelling and CommonKADS

Having seen how some of CommonKADS' top level models are applied, let us return to the key claim of this chapter: that CommonKADS is based on a multi-perspective modelling approach. To do this, we must consider whether CommonKADS' models map well to the Zachman framework. If each CommonKADS model (or sub-model) maps to a single cell of the Zachman framework, and most of the cells are covered, then the claim that CommonKADS supports multi-perspective modelling is supported; if the models do not map well, then the claim must be rejected.

5.6.1   The Organisation model

The CommonKADS Organisation model seems to map well to the uppermost ("scoping") level of the Zachman framework. The brief of the scoping level is to consider "a number of organisational processes" [34], and this is clearly the role of the Organisation model. Furthermore, the different sub-models of the Organisation model correspond to the perspectives of the Zachman framework as follows:

- Function/Process sub-model: HOW perspective;
- Structure sub-model and Power/authority sub-model: WHO perspective;
- Resources sub-model: WHAT perspective (and possibly WHERE resources are located).

The WHEN perspective can be considered to be covered by the Process sub-model (showing the order in which functions are carried out) or by a "time per task" analysis such as that carried out by de Hoog et al. for the Dutch social security department. The WHY perspective does not map to any sub-model well, but should be covered in text accompanying the Organisation model discussing the reasons for its development.

5.6.2   The Task, Agent and Communication models

The Task, Agent and Communication models are considered together because they each constitute different perspectives at the second ("enterprise") level of the Zachman framework. According to Cook [op. cit.], the enterprise level is concerned with a single business process, and since the brief of the Task model is to expand the sub-tasks within a single business process identified from the Organisation model, this is clearly the most appropriate level for the Task model. The Task model therefore constitutes the HOW perspective of the Enterprise level. The WHO and WHERE perspectives are covered by the Agent and Communication models respectively (N.B. the CommonKADS book considers the Communication model to belong to the "system" level rather than the "enterprise" level of abstraction, but the next chapter will argue that both Agent and Communication models are needed at both these levels of abstraction in order to provide a more complete multi-perspective modelling approach). Again, the WHEN perspective may be considered to be inherent in the control of tasks in the task model - certainly, the use of IDEF3 makes ordering constraints very clear. The WHAT perspective only appears as a property of individual tasks, however, and perhaps it may be advisable to develop models of resources using either the modelling techniques recommended for the Organisation model or another modelling format such as UML class diagrams - the appropriateness of UML class diagrams for representing the WHAT perspective is illustrated in [103].

In short, the CommonKADS Organisation model does seem to map well to the uppermost level of the Zachman framework, and hence to a multi-perspective modelling approach; three of the perspectives at the second level of the framework are also covered by the Task, Agent and Communication models. Furthermore, it can be seen that where CommonKADS does not recommend a model, or where a model exists but CommonKADS' diagramming format is less favoured, it is possible to substitute models from other modelling approaches to "fill in the gaps". However, two principles are identified that will recur throughout the discussion of mapping CommonKADS to the Zachman framework: firstly, there is ambiguity over whether the WHEN perspective concerns the time taken to carry out activities (as may be represented in a PERT chart) or the control over processes (i.e. as an addendum to the HOW perspective); and secondly, the WHY perspective is not supported as well as the other perspectives.

It seems that the perspectives of the Zachman framework map well to the various models and sub-models suggested by CommonKADS for organisational analysis. The next chapter continues examination of CommonKADS, looking at two models that bridge the gap between organisational and task-specific modelling: the Agent and Communication Models.

6   The Agent and Communication Models

6.1 Introduction

Knowledge based systems (KBS) have been a commercially viable technology for over a decade now. As a result of their growing use, users and managers have demanded that KBS be verifiable, maintainable and repeatable. This has led to the development of a number of systematic methods which formalise and direct the knowledge engineering process. A survey of methods can be found in [85].

One such method is the CommonKADS methodology which recommends that knowledge engineers develop a suite of models that both represent knowledge from different perspectives and gradually transform knowledge from the real world, via a conceptual representation, to a system design. Models are typically represented as one or more node-and-arc diagrams, but may also include tables or other textual representations of knowledge. This paper examines two of these six models: the Agent model and the Communication model which focus on the capability, role, requirements and outputs of various agents in a knowledge-based process.

The Agent and Communication models are responsible for modelling "roles" and "cooperation" within CommonKADS. The Agent model majors on *who* has the capability to carry out each task and what role they play in the process, while the Communication model highlights *where* information is needed within the process and how information is transmitted between agents during the process. In conjunction with a third model, the Task model (which specifies *how* tasks need to be carried out in order to achieve a particular goal), these models provide a rich process description that can be used for a range of purposes, from process re-engineering to intranet development.

6.1.1 The Agent Model

The purpose of the CommonKADS Agent Model is to determine the roles and competences that the various actors in the organisation bring with them to perform a shared task ([147], p.48). Tasks are carried out by agents, each of whom must have authority to perform the task, may be responsible for performing that task, ought to be capable of performing that task, and should have rights to resources needed to perform that task. The degree of truth of each of these four statements will determine the competences of the agents which in turn will help to define the roles of agents.

CommonKADS recommends that the Agent model is represented by a table defining the key features of agents ([147], p.50). CommonKADS recommends the use-case diagrams of UML [137] as a graphical representation of Agent models.

6.1.2 The Communication Model

A task that is carried out by one agent may produce results in the form of information objects that need to be communicated to other agents. The purpose of the Communication model is to identify the information exchange procedures that realise the knowledge transfer between agents [147]. Each knowledge transfer will have information content, a sender, one or more receivers, and an initiator; it may also have internal structure, and/or constraints and preconditions. The Communication model is intended to capture and represent these features of transfers of information or knowledge.

In the Communication model, each information object that is communicated is described as a *transaction*. CommonKADS recommends that a communication model should include:

- A dialogue diagram: a high level description of which tasks send or receive information.
- A transaction control plan, showing ordering and dependencies of communications. This is also usually represented as a diagram.
- Specification of individual transactions: a collection of attributes of each information exchange. These attributes include the information object(s), the sending and receiving agent, and any constraints on the transaction occurring. This is represented in a table.
- A detailed description of the information exchanged, including the structure of the transaction, the role of the information object

(whether it is the 'core' of the transaction or supporting information), the proposed medium of interaction, and the "illocutionary force" of the communication (e.g. 'request', 'demand' or 'warning'). These details also appear in a table.

6.1.3 Thesis of this chapter

KADS which was the predecessor to CommonKADS, did not separate the Agent and Communication models; both were incorporated into its "model of co-operation" [42] which could be used to identify the actors carrying out tasks as well as the inputs and outputs of those tasks. It therefore seems natural that an Agent model should be accompanied by a Communication model at the same level of abstraction i.e. containing the same tasks. Yet CommonKADS proposes that an Agent model represents agents' roles and capabilities for the various tasks in a particular business process, but the Communication model should represent communication between subtasks within a single "business process task" model. This is probably due to the clear need for communication features to form an input to the Design model; but it seems that much useful detail is lost if agents' roles are only assigned at a between-task level of abstraction, whilst communication is only detailed at a within-task level. The resulting proposed model suite is shown in Figure 6.1.

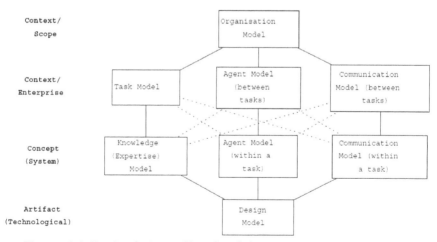

Figure 6.1: Revised view of levels of abstraction of CommonKADS models

This paper will propose that both the Agent and Communication model can usefully be developed at both between-task and within-task levels of detail. The rest of this paper will work through an example in which both models are used to represent knowledge at both the between-task ("enterprise") level and the within-task ("system") level. The example concerns the design of small scale industrial buildings.[21]

6.2 Example: design of industrial buildings

Any task which involves designing something is a task that requires knowledge – and considerable amounts of it. It's necessary to understand how well the artefact being designed fulfils its performance requirements; which components of the design are compatible with other components; whether the final design will be robust enough to withstand the pressures it must face in normal use and in extreme circumstances; whether components are easy to manufacture; whether the design is feasible to assemble; and so on. As a result, many design companies employ strategies to reduce the difficulty of the design task. They may offer a number of "standard" designs which can be adapted to specific requirements; they may generate several design prototypes which can be critiqued and improved; or they may subdivide the different aspects of the design work so that one person or group of people is responsible for high level design, another for low level design, another for checking against requirements and constraints, and so on. They may also take different approaches to generating the design (transformational design, propose-and-revise design, etc.) – comparison of these approaches is beyond the scope of this paper, but interested readers should look at [19] among other references.

The example that will be used in this paper will be a (fictional) small company, referred to as ABC Holdings Ltd., whose task is to design small-scale industrial buildings. They specialise in a particular structural technique known as "portal frame" design which is commonly used for buildings such as DIY stores. Their strategy is to subdivide design work between different groups of people, and it is this subdivision which is captured and represented in the Agent and Communication models below.

---

[21] This example is based on a tutorial exercise originally developed with funding from the SERC Computing Facilities Committee Support for Engineers programme. A proof-of-concept system for checking standards in portal frame designs was implemented.

Before building the Agent and Communication models, however, it's necessary to determine what tasks are actually carried out in portal frame design. This is represented in the CommonKADS Task model. The Task model for designing of portal frame buildings is shown in figure 6.2. The upper layer represents the top level tasks, and the lower layer shows subtasks of "Design building" and "Check building meets specification".

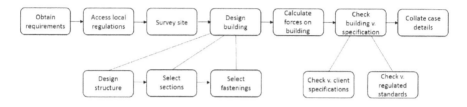

Figure 6.2: Task model for designing a portal frame building

The tasks identified in the Task model serve as the starting point for developing the Agent and Communication models at the enterprise level.

6.2.1 Agent model for portal frame design

When ABC Holdings design a portal frame building, the client's requirements are gathered by the partners, who then pass the actual design task to one of their engineers. The engineer creates a design, assisted by technicians (who do the low level design – literally, the "nuts and bolts" of the design), a CAD package that generates a numerical description of the design, and a program (written in FORTRAN) that calculates the effects of wind and snow forces on the building from that numerical description. The resulting design is then checked against legislation, company standards, and the client's requirements before being passed to the partners for approval. There are therefore at least six agents involved in the design process: the partners, the engineer, the technician, the two computer programs, and the client. Some would argue that the legislator constitutes a seventh agent; other would omit him or her because the legislator does not have any dynamic input to the design process.

CommonKADS recommends that a set of attributes are identified for each agent and presented in a table. These attributes are:

- The name of the agent.

- The agent's position in the organisation. This information should be obtainable from the Organisational model. This attribute should also define the type of the agent (typically either 'human' or "information system").
- The tasks that the agent is involved in.
- The agents that this agent communicates with.
- The knowledge items possessed by this agent.
- Other required or present competences of the agent.
- Responsibilities of the agent in task execution, and restrictions in this respect. This item is also intended to include constraints such as limitations on authority or responsibility to legal or professional norms.

Many values for these attributes can be derived from other CommonKADS models. The last two attributes, however, are unique to the Agent model. CommonKADS doesn't give much guidance on which "other competences" should be considered, or what "responsibilities and constraints" might arise. In order to make things a little clearer, I have drawn on the ORDIT framework for requirements engineering [49] which defines four roles for an agent with respect to a task: capability (the agent CAN do the task), authority (the agent MAY do the task), responsibility (the agent MUST do the task), and rights (the agent HAS RIGHTS TO use certain resources in order to perform the task). This definition encompasses three levels of agent-to-task mapping; CAN is the weakest, MAY is stronger because it (hopefully) implies CAN, and MUST is stronger still because it implies both CAN and MAY. It also identifies resources that are needed for a task, providing a useful link to the domain knowledge as well as the task knowledge.

Table 6.1 below represents a CommonKADS Agent Model. It has been extended with the four attributes derived from ORDIT, plus a catch-all "other constraints" column.

In order to represent the agent model diagramatically, CommonKADS recommends the use of UML use case diagrams, in which each "use case" represents one task from the Task Model. An example is given in Figure 6.3. While use case diagrams are well understood and widely accepted, they are intended to show which agents are involved in which use cases; there is no mechanism for representing capability, authority, roles and responsibilities of agents. As a result, an extended diagram format is proposed in which the use cases are labelled; this can be seen in Figure 6.4.

Agent	Capability	Authority	Rights	Responsibility	Other Constraints
Partner	Obtain client's requirements		View clients' requirements View legislation View case records View previous designs	Collate details of case	Insufficient time to do all tasks properly
Engineer	Can perform all necessary tasks		Access to site, etc.		
CAD package					
Technician					
FORTRAN program					
Legislator					
Client					

Table 6.1: A CommonKADS Agent Model

6.2.2 Communication model: Portal Frame building design

Each time a new agent takes on a task where the previous task was carried out by a different agent, communication is required. The Communication model represents the communications that occur between tasks. If a Communication model is to represent the same level of abstraction as the Agent model, then it must represent the same tasks that appear in the Agent model. The reader should therefore refer back to the Task model in Figure 6.2 for the source of the tasks that appear in this model.

Dialogue diagram

The first component of a communication model is a *dialogue diagram* which shows which tasks are carried out by which agents, and where communication is needed between agents. Figure 6.5 shows a dialogue diagram for portal frame design, using the format recommended by CommonKADS (p.225 of [147]) which is derived from UML's Use Case diagrams [137]. Columns headed **Dialogue** show communication transactions; each other column represents an agent, with the darker ellipses representing tasks carried out by that agent.

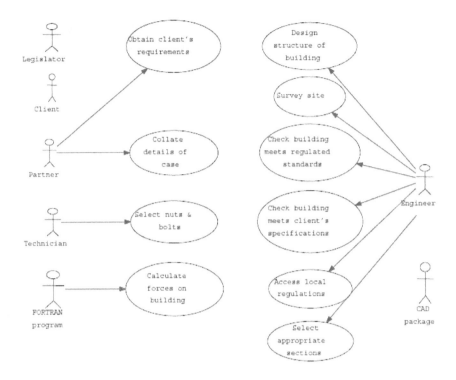

Figure 6.3: Agent model for designing a portal frame building

Note that there are links in the dialogue diagram between tasks performed by the same agent (e.g. from *Survey Site* to *Design Structure of Building*). These links do not represent communication between agents, but rather dependencies between tasks (usually inputs/outputs); this can be thought of as communication "within" an agent. These are worth describing because they may be required as input to more detailed models of individual tasks.

Control of transaction

The second component of the Communication Model is the transaction control diagram which describes the sequence of transactions. The diagram format used for these is the state diagram notation taken from UML. Transaction control diagrams may not always need to be developed, but can be very useful when flow of control is complex e.g. when external events conditionally trigger tasks or transactions. These diagrams also represent, and maybe introduce, certain design decisions regarding communication; a common design decision involves determining who takes the initiative in a transaction. Figure 6.6 shows the transaction control diagram associated with Figure 6.5.

It can be seen that the flow of control is assumed to be largely sequential, unless a design fails its checks (against legislation and user requirements), in which case looping occurs.

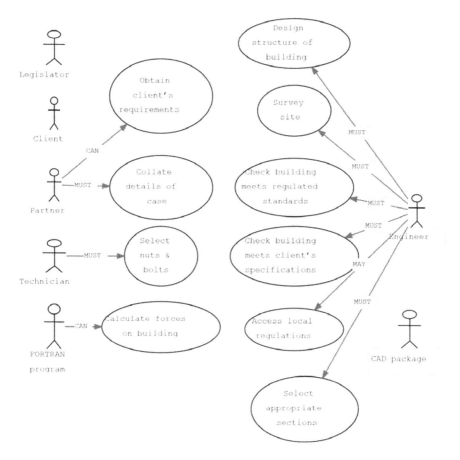

Figure 6.4: Agent model for designing a portal frame building: extended format

Transactions

CommonKADS proposes that a number of properties are identified for each transaction that appears in a Communication Model. These properties are identified below (from p.228 of [147]):

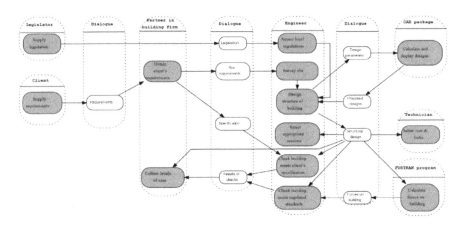

Figure 6.5: Dialogue diagram for designing a portal frame
building

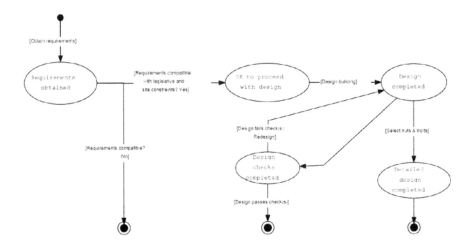

Figure 6.6: Transaction control diagram for designing a
portal frame building

Transactions

CommonKADS proposes that a number of properties are identified for each transaction that appears in a Communication Model. These properties are identified below (from p.228 of [147]):

• **Transaction Identifier/Name**: A transaction is to be defined for each information object that is output from some leaf task in the Task Model or in the Knowledge/Expertise Model (i.e. a transfer function), and that must be communicated to another agent for use in its own tasks. The name must reflect, in a user-understandable way, what is done with the information object by the transaction. In addition to the name, give a brief explanation here of the purpose of the transaction.

• **Information object:** Indicate the (core) information object, and between which two tasks it is to be transmitted.

• **Agents involved:** Indicate the agent that is sender of the information object, and the agent that is receiving it

• **Communication plan:** Indicate the communication plan of which this transaction is a component

• **Constraints:** Specify the requirements and (pre)conditions that must be fulfilled so the transaction can be carried out. Sometimes, it is also useful to state post-conditions that are assumed to be valid after the transaction.

• **Information Exchange Specification:** Transactions can have an internal structure, in that they consist of several messages of different types, and/or handle additional supporting information objects such as explanation or help items.

For the transactions in Figure 6.5, the relevant information is given in Table 6.2, omitting the "communication plan" attribute (which is the same for all transactions) and the "information exchange specification".

Information Exchange

The information exchange specification constitutes the third layer of the CommonKADS Communication Model. It refines the description of transactions in two ways: by giving the internal message typing and structure of the transaction, and by giving information about the syntactic form and medium of the messages.

The information that could appear in an information exchange specification is shown below (taken from p. 230 of [147]). A representative example of an information exchange specification for one transaction is shown in Table 6.3.

Trans-action Name	Information object	Agents involved	Constraints
Require-ments	Features of the building	Client Partner	A meeting takes place; Contract agreed/ signed
Legis-lation	Permitted/ prohibited features of the building Permitted/ prohibited working practices and equipment	Legislator Engineer	Legislation is available At least one agent knows all legislation that is relevant Legislation is understandable
Site Require-ments	Load bearing potential etc.	Partner engineer	Surveying equipment is adequate
Specific-ation	Features of the building	Partner engineer	Specification is understandable
Results of checks	Success/ failures/ warnings	Engineer partner	Checks can be carried out
Design para-meters	Features of design	Engineer CAD package	CAD package is able to represent desired features Engineer is able to use CAD package
Proposed designs	Design diagrams and tables	CAD package engineer	All info. for calculations is entered correctly
Struct-ural design	Structural description of design	Engineer technician FORTRAN program	
Forces on building	Calculations of wind & snow forces on walls & both sides of roof	FORTRAN program engineer	

Table 6.2: CommonKADS Communication Model

- **Transaction Name:** Transaction name and identifier of which this information exchange specification is a part
- **Agents involved:** The **sender** (the agent sending the information item/items) and the **receiver** (the agent receiving the information item/items)
- **Information Items:** List all information items that are to be transmitted in this transaction. This includes the ('core') information object, the transfer of which is the purpose of this transaction. However, it may contain other, supporting information items that provide help or explanation, for example. For each information item, describe the following:

Attribute	Value
Transaction Name	Requirements
Agents involved	Client & Partner
Information Items	Features of the building Role: Core object Form: Requirements Specification Document Medium: Negotiation Meetings
Message Specifications	Communication type: Request-Propose Content: Client's requirements on the design – as agreed by the designer Reference: It may be deemed necessary to refer to specific laws of contracting here
Control over Messages	The document is iterated between client and partner until both agree on its contents and sign the final version.

Table 6.3: Transactions

- **Role:** whether it is a *core* object or a *support* item;
- **Form**: the syntactic form in which it is transmitted to another agent e.g. data string, canned text, a certain type of diagram, 2D or 3D plot;
  – **Medium**: the medium through which it is handled in the agent-agent interaction e.g. a pop-up window, navigation and selection within a menu, command-line interface, human intervention

• **Message specifications:** Describe all messages that make up the transaction. For each message, describe:
  – **Communication type**: the communication type of the message, describing its intention ("illocutionary force", in speech-act terminology). Some predefined intentions are suggested in [147].
  – **Content**: the statement or proposition contained in the message.
  – **Reference**: in certain cases it may be useful to add a reference, for example to what domain knowledge model or

agent capability is required to be able to send or process the message.

• **Control over messages:** Give, if necessary, a control specification over the messages within the transaction. This can be done in pseudocode format or in a state-transition diagram, similar to the transaction control diagram described above. I have chosen to use plain text.

6.3   Concept/System level Models: Design Checking

The Concept or System level (the 3rd level identified in Figure 6.1) deals with the problem solving steps that comprise *one* of the tasks that were identified in the Task Model. This reflects the typical knowledge engineering process of examining tasks within a business process, and deciding which one(s) would benefit from being supported with a KBS or other automated system. In this example, the task that has been chosen for further decomposition is "Check building meets regulated standards". The knowledge that is required to perform this particular subtask – the steps involved, the resources and information required, and the order in which the steps are carried out – is expanded in detail in the Knowledge/ Expertise model.

At this level of abstraction, the tasks that provide the source for the Agent and Communication models are drawn from the "task structure" component of the Knowledge/Expertise model. This component can be represented in a diagram (similar in format to Figure 6.2) or in a semi-formal language (CommonKADS' Conceptual Modelling Language, or CML) - see Figure 6.7.

6.3.1 Agent Model: checking a design against standards

The Agent model for checking a design against standards, in "extended use case" format, is shown in Figure 6.8. It includes a number of information sources (such as manufacturer's tables) which are considered too specific to include in the higher level model. Drawing on ORDIT again, these information sources are treated as resources. Since resources are static objects, the extended agent model diagram uses the notation of the UML class diagram.

If a particular subtask is carried out by one or at the most two agents, it is not necessary to prepare an Agent model at this level of detail. However, when the ORDIT-based constraints of CAN, MAY, MUST and HAS RIGHTS TO are introduced, then the value of developing an Agent model at this level of detail can be seen.

6.3.2   Communication model: Design checking
Dialogue diagram

The dialogue diagram derived from this task structure is shown in Figure 6.9. In this diagram, as in the Agent model, I have chosen to represent information sources. These join with the links representing information flow between tasks and transactions to provide a data flow diagram for the task of checking a design against standards.

Transaction control diagram

Much of the transaction control at the system level is represented in the (CML) task structure, so there is little need for a transaction control diagram at the system level.

> **task** assessing-building-against-British-standards
> **goal** check a building design conforms to British standards
> **task structure**
>   assessing-building-against-British-standards
>   (check results)
>   *obtain* (numerical description of building)
>   **transform** (numerical description → model of
>   the building)
>   *loop until* all checks are completed
>   **select**(a check to perform)
>   *obtain*(any further information required)
>   **match**(model of building + standards
>   relevant to the chosen check → check result)
>   *report*(check results)

> Figure 6.7: Task structure for checking a
> design against standards in CML

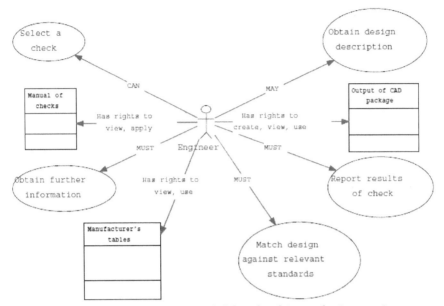

Figure 6.8: Agent model for checking a design against
regulated standards

The only remaining feature of control on transactions that needs
to be noted is that the engineer takes the initiative in consulting
information sources. This may seem an obvious statement, but if the
reverse was true (such as might occur with an information source that
supplied stock market prices, for example) then there are many
important issues raised for any resulting implementation connected
with asynchronous inputs and real-time processing. This information
can be captured in the Information Exchange Specification tables,
however.

Transactions
The transactions for this communication model are represented
in Table 7. The most noteworthy column of this table is the Constraints
column, where constraints that might otherwise be glossed over as
being too obvious (e.g. that all relevant checks must actually be in the
manual of checks) are identified.

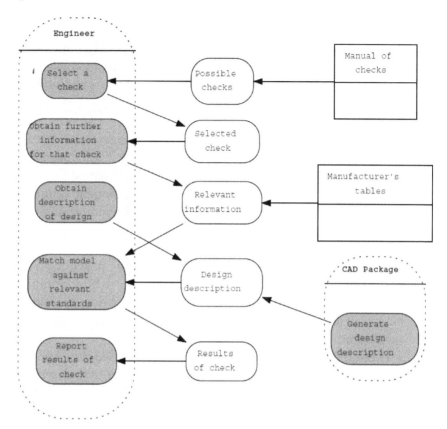

Figure 6.9: Dialogue diagram for checking a design against regulated standards

Information exchange specification

As stated above, the information exchange specification gives details of initiative in transactions. It also plays a similar role to the Transactions table in that it makes sure that apparently obvious assumptions, such as that checks are performed one at a time, are identified.

6.4 Discussion

6.4.1 Benefits

The main benefits of building these models are as follows:

• They serve as an *aide memoire*; that is, they help raise issues that may have been overlooked but which are important in understanding the business process or in system design. For example, the "Transactions" table of the system level communication model specifies that the CAD package must be in working order. Being forced to specify this leads to considering alternatives to the process when the CAD package is not working, as well as considering the adequacy of backup procedures for the data stored in the CAD package.

• The models are also helpful when they identify key competences that are necessary; for example, highlighting that the engineer must be able to understand the manual of design checks might suggest that an explanation component should be included in the final system for the use of more junior engineers who have trouble understanding the manual.

• When they are used to describe an existing system or process, they organise the knowledge well, thus both providing clear descriptions of the process and making it easier to build complete models of all relevant knowledge – for when knowledge is laid out clearly in separate categories, it becomes easier to identify gaps in that knowledge.

• These models are arguably most beneficial when they are used to prescribe future roles and co-operation, rather than describing an existing situation. In this instance, the models can be used to analyse the situation, and to support decisions about the allocation of roles. Such decisions can have an enormous impact on the resulting business process (for enterprise level models) or system design (for system level models).

6.4.2 Drawbacks
The most obvious drawback of developing all these models is the time required to produce all the tables and diagrams. In some circumstances (e.g. safety critical applications, or applications where there is a high turnover of staff), the effort of developing all these models is paid back by reduced risk or higher maintainability of the resulting system. However, many KBS developers will find the development of a full suite of agent and communication models to be more effort than it's worth.

Because of this, a shorthand version of the Agent and Communication models is suggested:

• Agent model: draw the extended use case diagram (i.e. the one with labelled arcs and "resources");

• Communication model: draw the dialogue diagram. This diagram is very similar to Role Activity Diagrams [135] which have been proposed as a shorthand format for both the Agent and Communication models in previous publications (e.g. [102]).

• Communication model: produce a table of communications that combines the Transactions table and the Information Exchange specification table.

6.4.3 Summary

In summary, the Agent and Communication models represent the roles and capabilities of agents and the transactions that occur during a particular process. They are a valuable component of the overall CommonKADS suite of models, and can be used to support organising acquired knowledge, re-organising a business process, or designing a knowledge based system. They organise knowledge clearly (if not concisely), and are particularly useful if used at two different levels of detail, capturing both the agents and communications at the level of tasks within a particular business process, and at the level of subtasks within a single (knowledge-based) task.

Having moved from examining the modelling of organisational knowledge to the examination of task-specific knowledge, the next chapter begins a series of four chapters that look at the 'heart' of CommonKADS: the Expertise Model that is designed for modelling the knowledge used in a particular task. Chapter 7 describes an application which will be used as an example in later chapters.

7 The Expertise Model: manufacturing diagnostics example

7.1 Introduction

In January 1992, a small Scottish manufacturing company obtained funding from Scottish Enterprise to help them in the development of a knowledge based system (KBS) for fault diagnosis. The company manufactured precision plastic mouldings, such as casings for PCs, or control panels for video recorders. They have a reputation for high quality which they want to maintain. However, from time to time, problems with their injection moulding machines mean that substandard mouldings are produced, and these have to be scrapped to maintain the reputation for quality. While the company have technicians who are very competent at solving these problems, these technicians have a variety of roles to perform. If a technician is working on an urgent task, or is absent through holidays or illness, it may take some hours before diagnostic expertise is available. Shift leaders are able to provide some backup to technicians, but they have even more demands on their time than the technicians do. As a result, there are times when no-one with diagnostic knowledge is available, particularly during some night shifts.

After attending a seminar organised by AIAI and the Scottish Office in the summer of 1991, the idea of building a KBS to help with the diagnostic process was born. The project was set up in January 1992 with the company releasing one member of staff to work on the project for two days per week. This member of staff [JM] was a newly recruited graduate in Polymer Technology with knowledge of the process of injection moulding, but very little computing experience. AIAI were engaged to provide JM with initial training in KBS programming, knowledge elicitation and knowledge engineering (a total of 7 days' training) and then to provide 15 man days' consultancy spread over the 4-month duration of the project. The intention was that by the end of the project, JM would be fully conversant with the techniques used to develop the KBS, and would therefore be able to maintain the system if any changes were needed after installation.

AIAI decided to use a methodological approach to this project. The need for a methodological approach to KBS development was not widely acknowledged when this system was developed, but AIAI were sufficiently convinced of the benefits of methods to use parts of the KADS methodology on this project. However, in this project, the methods were used not only to formalise and guide the development of the KBS itself, but also to act as a framework for the division of labour and transfer of KBS expertise. This paper describes the benefits and drawbacks of using a methodology in this way.

Before any development could take place, however, a number of factors needed to be established to ensure that the KBS project stood a good chance of success. These included:

• Economic considerations. The company do have a genuine problem with quality control - they scrap around 2% of their production each month. The KBS is likely to make a significant improvement to the availability of diagnostic expertise, and to the early detection of faults, thus reducing scrap rates.

• Technical considerations. Diagnosis is known to be a task type which KBS are well suited for; also, the technicians currently take between several minutes and a few hours to solve problems, so there are unlikely to be any stringent requirements for real-time problem solving.

• Personnel considerations. The project was initiated by the company's General Manager, so management support was assured. The users - the machine operators - are likely to appreciate any help their shift leaders can give them in diagnosing faults. However, the commitment of the shift leaders and technicians themselves was unclear, so the AIAI consultant [JK] made a presentation to these people which included a demonstration of a very simple KBS which diagnosed three different faults in the plastic moulding process. While the underlying structure of this demonstration system was very shallow in its reasoning, and drew knowledge from just one day of knowledge acquisition, it was sufficient to convey the concept of a KBS to the shift leaders and technicians, and to excite their curiosity so that they began to ask questions about the capabilities of the system. This was deemed to be sufficient commitment for the project to proceed.

The project was named IMPRESS (the Injection Moulding PRocess Expert SyStem project).

7.2 The framework of the IMPRESS project

The KADS methodology divides the process of KBS development into three phases: knowledge elicitation and analysis, KBS design and KBS implementation. The IMPRESS project was set up with a number of intermediate milestones accompanied by deliverables; these milestones were based around the phases specified by KADS. The phases specified in the project plan were:

- Knowledge elicitation and analysis - 6 weeks.
- KBS design - 4.5 weeks
- KBS implementation - 4.5 weeks
- Testing and installation - 2 weeks

The workload was divided between JM and JK in a manner which was intended to get the project completed within the deadline, but also to give JM a sufficient awareness of KBS development and the contents of the IMPRESS system to enable him to update it. The policy pursued was for both JK and JM to attend knowledge elicitation sessions; then for JK to perform the knowledge analysis and KBS design while JM undertook background reading on KADS so that he understood the deliverables which JK produced; and finally for JM to undertake the lion's share of the implementation, and to carry out user acceptance testing, any consequent alterations, and installation. The plan was adhered to fairly closely, and JM was indeed able to make alterations to the KBS himself in response to comments from the users.

7.3 Progress of the project
7.3.1 Knowledge Elicitation

Knowledge elicitation for the IMPRESS system was carried out at the company's premises. The first interview was with one of the shift leaders, who was asked to provide a general overview of the problems which arise in the plastic moulding process. The interview was guided using the "laddered grid" knowledge elicitation technique [152]. This technique supplies a number of template questions which are designed to prompt experts to supply further information about a taxonomic hierarchy - for example, the question "Can you give me some examples of *Class*" will supply information about instances or subclasses of the class *Class*. The technique can also be used to elicit procedural information. In the interview with the shift leader, the resulting grid comprised both a detailed description of some of the faults which arise in the plastic moulding process, including descriptions of different symptoms and associated faults, and also explanations and corrective action for some faults. While it is not desirable for analysis purposes for the expert to be allowed to mix taxonomic and procedural information (i.e. descriptions of faults and descriptions of actions) in his replies, this interview nevertheless provided a concise introduction to the domain and the diagnostic task.

The next interview was with the Quality Manager, who provided a breakdown of the five main categories of fault. These categories are

- Contamination - dirty marks of some kind on the final moulding
- Shorts - certain parts of the mould do not fill with plastic
- Burns - discolouration due to plastic being overheated
- Degate - human error when trimming with a knife
- Others

The Quality Manager keeps detailed statistics of the number of times each fault has occurred, and how long it takes to solve. From examination of these statistics, it became obvious that contamination was the most frequently occurring problem, and that contamination problems took an average of almost 2.5 hours to solve. Based on this information, it was decided that the KBS would initially be limited to diagnosing contamination problems only.

All other knowledge elicitation interviews were conducted with technicians, who are the day to day diagnostic experts. Most of these interviews used a "20 questions" knowledge elicitation technique [24]. This technique is normally used after several knowledge elicitation sessions, because it requires the knowledge engineer to be fairly familiar with the task. The knowledge engineer selects a potential fault which the expert is required to diagnose; the expert does this by asking questions which the knowledge engineer answers. As JM had some knowledge of the injection moulding process and of the company's machinery, it was possible to use this technique from a very early stage.

A typical "20 Questions" session is shown below. The hypothesised fault was dust entering the machine via the drier which dries the raw material. The technician was told that there were "black specks on the moulding". JM's answers to the technician's questions are shown in brackets.

```
What's the tool? [155]
Where   are   the   marks?   [Back
face, sides - all over] How long
has the job been running? [2 days]
```
Has the problem been present since start up? [Yes]
```
Is the problem getting worse? [Yes]
Have you cleaned the shims? [Yes, it caused a
little improvement, but the problem recurred]
Is the temperature unstable, or too high? [No]
Check the thermocouplings [OK]
Check the condition of the screw, and look for
black specks on the screw [OK]
```
On being told the answer, the technician commented that dust from the drier was almost never a problem because of the reliability of the drier's filtration system. This was a surprise to both JK and JM, and thus provided some unexpected further knowledge acquisition.

The technician was then asked to explain his reasons for asking each question. The information which was extracted from the conversation described above and the subsequent explanation included:

• Possible faults include dirty shims, incorrect temperature settings, loose thermocouplings, and dirt on the screw.

• Some faults are more prevalent on certain machine tools - usually tools which produce large mouldings.

• If the marks had appeared only on the bottom edges of the moulding, this would have been a very strong indicator of one particular fault.

• Certain faults only occur shortly after the machine has been started up. Many of these are due to the machine not being cleaned properly before being shut down.

• If the problem only occurs for a short time, then the fault is likely to be contamination in a single batch of raw material.

• If the problem is getting worse, then it is likely to be due to some material which is trapped in the machine and slowly degrading

• Dust in the drier hardly ever causes a problem because it is filtered out

The "20 Questions" technique proved to be very helpful for eliciting diagnostic information, with a lot of useful information obtained in a concise format in a short period of time.

7.3.2 Knowledge Analysis

The technicians' knowledge divides into three main categories:

• Declarative knowledge - the workings of the machine, and knowledge of all faults which may occur.

• Procedural knowledge - knowing how to test for and how to fix faults.

• Control knowledge - performing tests in a sensible order.

The declarative and procedural knowledge was relatively straightforward to extract from the results of the "20 Questions" sessions, but the control knowledge required a little more thought. It was eventually determined that the likelihood of a fault occurring, and the time required to perform a particular test, were the most important factors in deciding the order in which tests should be performed. For example, in the "20 Questions" session quoted above, the technician asked about the condition of the screw last, because it takes a couple of hours to dismantle the machine sufficiently to expose the screw, and he did not ask about dust in the drier at all, because it is such a rare fault.

It turned out that there are quite a number of rare faults. However, as JM spent much of his time on the shop floor when he was not working on the KBS, it was decided that JK would press ahead with the analysis phase while JM completed the elicitation of all possible faults from the experts. The final KBS contains about 40 faults (broken down into five subclasses) and a similar number of tests.

7.3.3 KBS design, implementation, testing & installation

The analysed knowledge was transformed into a KBS design using techniques based on the KADS methodology (these techniques are outlined in section 7.4). The KBS was then implemented in KAPPA-PC version 1.2 on an Apricot 486 PC. The resulting design suggested that faults, tests, and test results should be represented using individual objects, while inference should be implemented primarily using a mixture of rules and functions, with a little use of object-oriented methods and demons. However, it transpired that some of the desired rule functionality was unavailable in KAPPA-PC; it also became clear that the time taken to execute a rule which matched on a set of objects was similar to the time taken for a function to iterate over the same objects.

As a result, it was decided that rules would not be used at all, and so much of the inference in the IMPRESS system was implemented using functions.

The KBS was subjected to testing by developers concurrently with the implementation of the user interface, and was installed in the first week of August 1992. At the time of writing, few firm results were available, because there have been relatively few occasions since the installation of the KBS when there has been no technical expert available to answer questions. However, the fact that the system can be used "off-line" has been appreciated, and the KBS has been used several times for training purposes by interested machine operators.

7.4 Using KADS for the IMPRESS project

The KADS methodology for KBS development [82] is intended both to guide and to formalise KBS development. To this end, it provides guidance on obtaining knowledge, analysing it, and transforming it into a detailed design for an implemented KBS. The IMPRESS project focussed on the construction of the Expertise model recommended by the KADS methodology.[22]

7.4.1 Knowledge analysis: generic inference structures

Once some knowledge has been acquired, the KADS methodology recommends selection of a *generic inference structure*[23] from a library.

---

[22] KADS was the forerunner of CommonKADS. For the sake of consistency with other papers, I have altered the terminology used in this paper where it differs between KADS and CommonKADS. Footnotes are used to describe these instances.

[23] KADS used the term "interpretation models" instead of "generic inference structures". Interpretation models differed slightly from generic inference structures, because they were permitted to contain some control information (task structure) as well as a generic inference structure. However, this feature was hardly ever made use of. The successor in CommonKADS to these "generic task structures" are *problem solving methods* which are described in chapter XX.

Generic inference structures are task-specific breakdowns of the inferences and items of knowledge required in a typical task of that type. These models are intended both to formalise acquired knowledge and to guide further knowledge acquisition. For the IMPRESS system, it was obvious from the start that the task type was diagnosis; however, KADS offers several different generic inference structures for different methods of performing diagnosis. Eventually, it was decided that the generic inference structure for *systematic diagnosis* was the most appropriate. This model is shown in Figure 7.1 below; the ellipses are known as "inference steps",[24] and the boxes as "knowledge roles".

This model represents the inference which is expected to be performed when a task involving systematic diagnosis is executed. For example, if a user reports a problem with a machine, it is expected that a particular system model representing the correct operation of that machine will be selected, and a number of faults will be suggested. Based on a 'focussed' subset of these faults, a number of characteristics of the machine will be measured and compared with their expected values in the system model.

This model was then adapted to the domain of the IMPRESS system, as shown in Figures 7.2 and 7.4.1 below (Figure 7.4.1 is an expansion of the **select-1** inference step in Figure 7.2), to produce a problem-specific inference structure. This inference structure indicates that the IMPRESS system will identify a set of possible faults (hypotheses) based on the reported contamination problem. A test is then recommended, based on the likelihood of the hypotheses, the time required to perform a test and the time required to alter the state of the machine so that the test can be performed. Once it has been decided which test will actually be performed, the test is carried out, and the actual result is compared against a set of expected results (see below) in order to update the set of hypotheses.

It can be seen that the adaptation from the generic inference structure to the problem-specific inference structure involved a number of changes. Most of these changes are relatively minor, such as the removal of the focussing of the set of hypotheses into a smaller set; it was felt that the set of hypotheses was sufficiently small that such a

---

[24] In KADS, these were referred to as "inference functions"

step was not necessary. However, one of the changes implies a fundamental change to the approach taken to reasoning. This change involved replacing the generic inference structure's suggestion of comparing values against a system model which is a *model-based* approach to KBS construction, with a set of faults and expected test results which is a *classification-based* approach.[25] While a model-based approach would have worked adequately for the IMPRESS system, it was felt that explicitly representing injection moulding processes was not worth the effort, primarily because all the company's machines operate in the same manner, and so only one "system model" would be required. Instead, it was decided that for every known fault, the expected results of each test would be represented. For example, if the fault was "Contamination of raw material due to the box of material being left open", then a check on the material currently being fed into the machine should produce the result *Contamination present*, while a check on a fresh box of material should produce the result *Contamination absent*. These values were explicitly represented, and compared against the actual results of tests, as shown at the bottom of Figure 7.2.

7.4.2 Further guidance provided by KADS

The remaining stages of the KADS analysis and design phases gradually extend and transform the knowledge which is represented in the inference structure into a detailed KBS design, with any design decisions being explicitly recorded. These stages are:

Knowledge analysis:

Flow of control: The *task structure* which is a component of the Expertise model, identifies the flow of control between inference functions, and also identifies any inputs and outputs of the KBS.

Task assignment: It's important to make rational decisions about which agents carry out which tasks in the final KBS, since this can have a big effect on the required development time. The tasks include both the inference steps and dealing with inputs to the system; for example, of data is required from a manual, should the user be asked to look up that data, or should the system auto-

---

[25] For more on the distinction between these two approaches, see section 18.2.1.

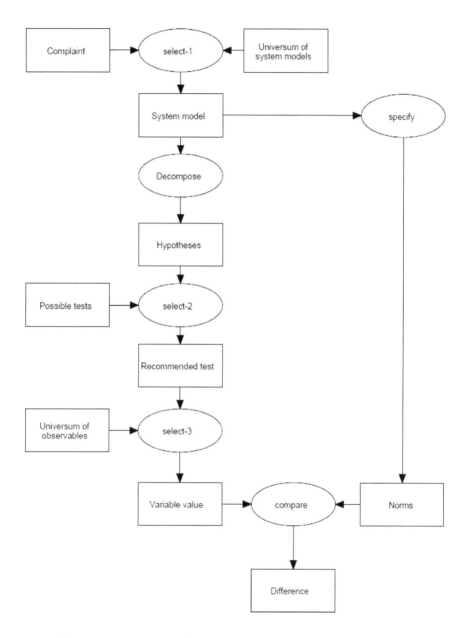

Figure 7.1: Generic inference structure for systematic diagnosis

-matically access a version of that manual stored in a spreadsheet? In CommonKADS, this would be represented within the Agent and Communication models; for this project, a *model of interaction* was developed [26] which is used to determine which of the inference steps should be performed by the system which by the user, and which by the two working together. It also explicitly identifies every input and output within the system.

The main decision made when developing the model of interaction for the IMPRESS system was that the selection of a test to perform would be done by the KBS and user in conjunction, rather than by the KBS alone; in other words, the KBS would recommend a test to perform, but the user would be free to reject the recommendation.

KBS design:

Application design[27] involves laying out the inference functions, knowledge roles and inputs/outputs in a single diagram, and identifying the data flow between them.

Architectural design [28] involves the selection of AI "design methods", such as best-first search, blackboard reasoning, or truth maintenance, to implement each function in the application design. AIAI have developed a set of *probing questions*, based on the work of Kline & Dolins [104], to recommend design methods; see appendix D for more details.

Physical design involves the selection of rules, objects, or other low-level design techniques to implement the chosen design methods. This proved to be the most difficult of all the analysis and design stages, partly because the architectural design stage did not produce many strong recommendations for particular design methods.

KADS recommends that the selection of a KBS implementation tool should be based on the results of this stage; however, an implementation tool has often been chosen by the time this stage of the

---

[26] The model of interaction is a locally-developed variant of KADS' model of co-operation, the forerunner of the Agent and Communication models. See Chapter 13 and appendix D.

[27] In KADS, the only approach recommended for application design was functional decomposition. I have found it convenient to retain this approach wherever possible. For more on other approaches, see chapter 12.

[28] This was called "behavioural design" in KADS.

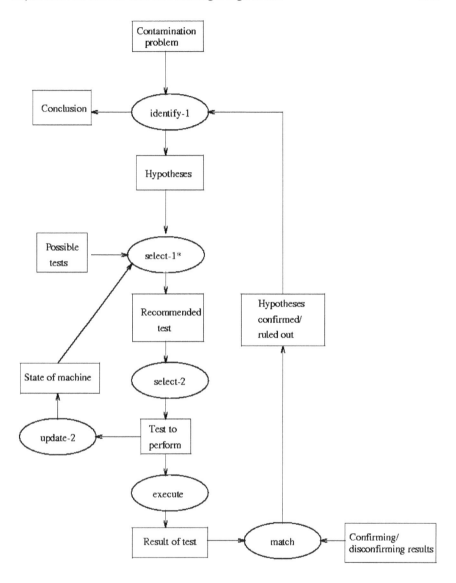

Figure 7.2: Inference structure for IMPRESS system

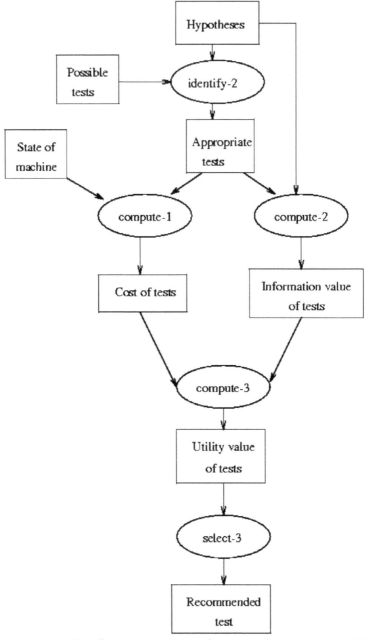

Figure 7.3: Inference structure for test selection in IMPRESS system

project is reached, and so it is sensible if the capabilities of the KBS tool are borne in mind when performing physical design.

Once the physical design is complete, KADS suggests using conventional software engineering methods. While these methods are likely to work for implementation, they may not be adequate for verification and validation which may differ significantly between a KBS and conventional computer programs [175].

7.4.3 Technology transfer using KADS

During the stages of knowledge analysis and KBS design, technology transfer was accomplished by introducing JM to KADS. This was achieved during JM's initial training. JM was also asked to read sections of the best available book on KADS [82]. With this background, JM was able to understand the deliverables from the analysis and design phases at a detailed level, and to use these deliverables as a basis for the implementation of the IMPRESS system.

The aim of using KADS for technology transfer was that JM would understand the KADS models sufficiently well that, should the occasion arise, he would be able to make a change to the inference structure and propagate the change through all the remaining stages in order to produce a revised physical design. This change would then be implemented in the KBS, and the revised set of models would serve as up to date documentation for the system. This purpose appears to have been achieved.

7.5   Benefits and weaknesses of KADS for the IMPRESS project

The use of KADS for the IMPRESS project provided a number of benefits, but also had some weaknesses. These are outlined below.

Benefits: The major advantage of KADS from the point of view of technology transfer is the large number of models which are produced during the development of the KBS. These models represent the KBS from a number of different viewpoints, so a novice stands a much greater chance of understanding the workings of the KBS from these models than from any single document describing the KBS. The variety of models also helps greatly when a new piece of knowledge or a new procedure must be added to the KBS, and it is difficult to decide where this new information fits into the previous structure. These models also force the KBS developer to document design decisions explicitly which is almost essential for successful long-term maintenance, and can constitute a set of deliverables from each stage of the project for the management or project monitoring officer.

KADS itself has some particular advantages. The library of generic inference structures is widely thought to be the most useful contribution of KADS to knowledge engineering, and it certainly provided a lot of assistance for the IMPRESS project. There is also some reasonably comprehensible background reading available on KADS which helps introduce novices to the methodology.

Weaknesses: Perhaps the biggest disadvantage of using KADS, when compared with a "rapid prototyping" approach to KBS development, is that implementation does not begin until relatively late in the project. While the preparation of a design which has been thought out and documented well provides plenty of justification for KADS' approach, late implementation carries disadvantages both for technical development and for technology transfer.

From the viewpoint of technical development, KADS' approach loses the advantages of iterative prototyping for knowledge acquisition and investigating possible implementation techniques. KADS does not rule out the use of prototyping as a knowledge acquisition technique, but it is time-consuming to build a prototype based on an uncertain system design which will eventually be thrown away, and it was decided that this approach was not worthwhile for a small-scale project such as the IMPRESS project. Iterative prototyping is also very useful for identifying omissions or misunderstandings in knowledge acquisition and analysis, and the fact that most of KADS' models are based on the analysed knowledge (directly or indirectly) means that errors in knowledge acquisition and analysis are costly, because they require almost all the models to be updated. A CAKE (computer aided knowledge engineering) tool which supported the construction of CommonKADS models would go a long way towards alleviating this difficulty.

From the viewpoint of technology transfer, KADS' approach means that a novice KBS programmer (JM in this project) is thrown into programming at the deep end, rather than being gradually introduced to implementation techniques as the prototype is built. While JM was given some training and programming exercises in KAPPA-PC while the analysis and design phases were being conducted, it is received wisdom that the only way to understand a KBS implementation tool fully is to use it to develop a full-scale KBS, and this project reinforced that belief. This unfamiliarity was a major contributor to the fact that the implementation phase overran by about 3 weeks, the only phase to show a significant deviation from the initial plan.

Two other features of KADS were noted which were minor disadvantages in the IMPRESS project:

- KADS provides little guidance on user interface design which is something of a disadvantage since the development of user interfaces may take up a large proportion of the code and the development time for a KBS. For the sake of simplicity, the IMPRESS project used KAPPA-PC's built-in user interface facilities (menus, message boxes and text windows) to develop its user interface.

- The physical design stage should take into account the features of the chosen KBS implementation tool. KADS recommends that a tool should be chosen based on the results of the physical design stage, but in practice a tool has almost always been chosen before this stage. For example, the physical design for the IMPRESS system recommended the use of a series of demons on the slots of the **State of the machine** object to calculate the total time required for the machine to be put into a particular state. However, demons in KAPPA-PC do not return a value, so instead of using a return value, the technique had to be implemented using a global variable to accumulate the total time.

7.6 Conclusion

On the whole, the use of a methodology as a framework for technology transfer worked well on the IMPRESS project, and is recommended for other projects. However, a number of factors must be considered carefully when doing so:

- Considerable effort is required to make sure that knowledge analysis is done properly, because of the effort required to correct errors at a later stage. In larger projects, or other projects where the knowledge to be acquired is particularly complex, it may well be worth developing a prototype to assist in knowledge acquisition.
- The implementation stage should be given at least as much time as the analysis stage, if not more, unless the chief programmer is **fully** conversant with the KBS implementation tool before the implementation stage is reached.
- Documentation should be prepared in a format which is fairly easy to update, since it is expected that the documentation will change over time.
- The features of the chosen implementation tool should be taken into account at the physical design stage (or equivalent stage in the chosen methodology).

IMPRESS was built before the CommonKADS methodology was published. The next chapter looks at how CommonKADS updated KADS, and how this would have affected the IMPRESS project and another project.

8 Knowledge Engineering: The Expertise Model

8.1 Introduction

It was decided that two KBS projects which had been originally developed with the aid of KADS, or a variant of KADS, would be re-engineered using CommonKADS in order to obtain first-hand experience of the advantages and disadvantages of CommonKADS over KADS. The projects chosen were the X-MATE project which developed a KBS for deciding whether mortgages should be granted [95], and the IMPRESS project which produced a KBS for diagnosing faults in plastic moulding machinery [94].

This paper will describe the re-engineering of the domain, inference and task levels of expertise in IMPRESS and X-MATE.

8.1.1 How to Build the CommonKADS Expertise Model

In KADS, modelling of expertise was usually performed by selecting a generic inference structure from the appropriate library, modelling the domain sufficiently to instantiate the inference structure to the current application, and then proceeding with task modelling and design. CommonKADS suggests a number of approaches to modelling ([191]), including:
- bottom-up assembly of models from data;
- model assembly around a problem solving method (e.g. for a constraint satisfaction problem);
- model assembly from generic components (as in KADS);
- model specification based on top-down task decomposition;
- adapting models by knowledge differentiation (introducing new knowledge roles to circumvent computational or pragmatic constraints);
- model generation by structure mapping.

In the project described in this paper, the primary modelling method used was model assembly from generic components. However, occasional use of other approaches was found to be useful - bottom-up assembly was used in domain modelling, and a form of knowledge differentiation was used to ensure that all relevant domain categories were represented in the inference structure.

8.1.2 Overview of this Chapter

This chapter looks at the three levels of expertise modelling in CommonKADS in turn. For each level, a brief introduction is given, followed by description and results of the re-engineering of X-MATE and IMPRESS. Finally, an evaluation of the CommonKADS techniques for that level is provided.

Currently, CommonKADS' main guidance on generic components is at the inference level, and so the first step in the re-engineering process was to develop an inference structure. For this reason, the inference level of CommonKADS is described before the domain level. In practice, however, it was found that these two levels tended to be developed simultaneously, with modelling at one level helping to guide and refine the other. The task level was not developed until the other levels were complete, and so it is described last. The conclusion to the paper highlights the perceived strengths and weaknesses of expertise modelling in CommonKADS.

8.2   Configurable Inference Structures

When developing an expertise model in KADS, one of the first actions which a knowledge engineer performed was to identify the task type of the KBS application (examples of task types include heuristic classification, assessment, and configuration). On the basis of this decision, an inference structure was selected from KADS' library of task-related models. The next step was to instantiate the knowledge roles and inference actions in the inference structure to terms from the domain. However, it was commonly found that this process required alterations to the structure of the generic model, rather than merely instantiating its nodes; both the X-MATE and the IMPRESS projects demonstrated this. At the time of writing, CommonKADS' proposed solution to this problem is to decompose the inference structures in the library into components, and to provide guidance on configuring an inference structure to a particular application. The guidance is provided by a set of questions which the knowledge engineer must ask himself about the project.

Configurable inference structure components were defined for the Assessment task type (see [116]). X-MATE's task of deciding whether to grant mortgages was identified as an assessment task, while the IMPRESS project classified the diagnosis faults in plastic moulding machinery as a systematic diagnosis task. The X-MATE project will therefore be used to provide the worked example for this section.

8.2.1   Using KADS on the X-MATE Project

The main contribution of KADS to the X-MATE project was the inference structure for assessment tasks. This inference structure is shown in Figure 8.1. When the XMATE project was carried out, it was found that this structure needed to be changed in at least one respect in order to reflect the task of mortgage application assessment: the "ideal system model" in the top right-hand corner had to be changed to "several typical non-ideal cases". The reason for this change was that mortgage application assessment is carried out by trying to identify danger signals in mortgage applications, rather than identifying aspects of the application which match the profile of an ideal applicant. See [95] for more details.

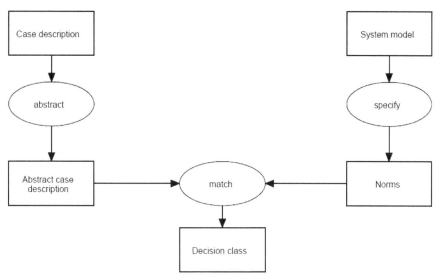

Figure 8.1: Generic inference structure for Assessment tasks in KADS

8.2.2   Configurable Inference Structures for X-MATE

In CommonKADS, however, the basic model for Assessment tasks is simply the matching of a case description with a system model to produce a decision (Figure 8.2). This model is then extended by asking a series of questions about the application.[29] These questions ask the knowledge engineer about each knowledge role. Depending on the answer to each question, inference functions and knowledge roles may be inserted into the inference structure. For example, if the question:

- Is the case description already abstract enough to be matched?

was answered NO, then an **abstract** inference function and an **abstract case description** knowledge role would be added between the **case description** knowledge role and **match case** inference function.

For the X-MATE project, the questions were answered as follows:
- Is the case description already abstract enough to be matched?

    YES. A mortgage application form contains all the requisite information in an accessible form.
- Is the system model already specific enough to be matched?

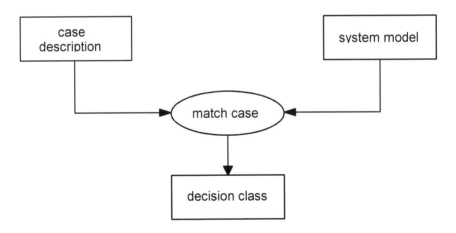

Figure 8.2: Basic inference structure for Assessment tasks in
CommonKADS

---

[29] The full set of questions, and of consequent model components, can be found in [116].

NO. As a result of this answer, a **specify** inference function is added to the inference structure, and further questions are asked about the specification process.

- Is the system model suitable for use in the specification process (or does it need to be focused because there is more than one type of system?) It needs to be FOCUSED since there are 3 "system models" which correspond to the 3 main reasons for defaulting on mortgages. A **focus** inference function is therefore added.
- Is the specification of the measurement system independent from the case description?

YES. Therefore, the **case description** should provide input to the **focus** inference function, not the **specify** inference function.

- Is the decision class the direct result of matching the case against the measurement system (i.e. measuring the case)?

NO. The decision class depends on the sum of several matches of the case against the measurement system.

- Is the decision class the result of a computation?

YES. As a result, a **compute** inference function and another **specify** inference function are included.

The resulting inference structure is shown in Figure 8.3, and its instantiation to the domain of mortgage application assessment is shown in Figure 8.4. Note that the knowledge role that is outlined in bold lines represents **static** knowledge – that is, the knowledge in this knowledge role is not changed during the inference process. The distinction between static and dynamic knowledge roles is another innovation in CommonKADS.

8.2.3 Evaluation of Configurable Inference Structures

The inference structure in Figure 8.3 and the instantiated inference structure in Figure 8.4 reflect the process of mortgage application assessment much more accurately than the structure shown in Figure 8.1. The configuration process takes little time, and can be done even by novice knowledge engineers (see [141] or [178]). On the basis of these observations, configurable inference structures are judged to be a valuable tool for knowledge modelling.

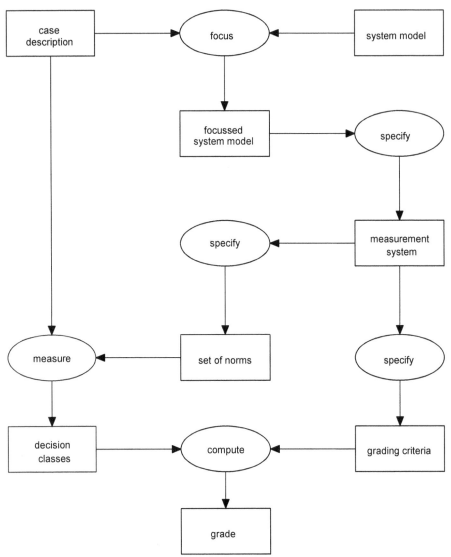

Figure 8.3: Inference structure for Assessment tasks, configured
to the task of mortgage application assessment

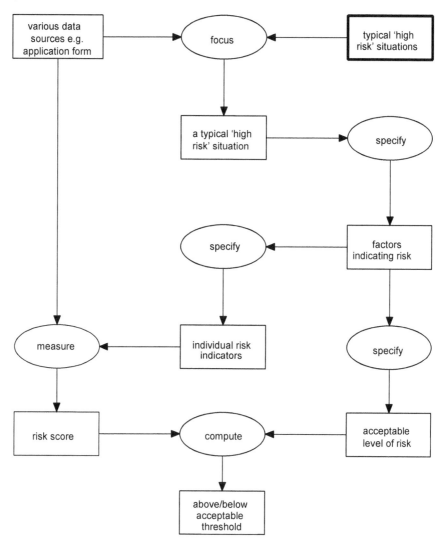

Figure 8.4: Configured inference structure for Assessment tasks, instantiated to the domain of mortgage application assessment

8.3   The Domain Level in CommonKADS: Domain Models

Having configured an appropriate inference structure, the domain level of the expertise model can be completed. While domain modelling was recommended in the KADS methodology, the only real guidance given was on the analysis of transcripts from interviews; it was suggested that the knowledge engineer should identify domain *concepts* from the transcript, and if possible, structure these in a hierarchy. CommonKADS has taken this idea and extended it to suggest the construction of:

- a *domain ontology* which broadly corresponds to defining a number of dictionaries of domain terms. It is suggested that the knowledge engineer defines 'dictionaries' of
  - concepts;
  - properties;
  - relations;
  - expressions (one or more statements of the form *property = value* which can be conjoined to produce rules).
- a number of *domain models*. Typically, there will be one domain model for each relation identified: for example, if the relation **causes(A,B)** has been identified then a causal domain model will be defined which displays all the terms which are related by the **causes** relation.

In addition, CommonKADS suggests that a *model ontology* and *model schema* are defined. These represent the domain models at a more abstract level. The purpose of these models is to provide an explicit link between the domain models and the inference structure, and also to produce a representation which can be re-used in other KBS applications which perform the same task type. The model ontology represents the domain ontology at a more abstract level (for example, the relation **subsystem-of** in the domain ontology might be represented as **part-of** in the model ontology); the model schema represents all the domain models, with one node for each domain model, using the terms defined in the model ontology.

8.3.1 Domain Modelling for the IMPRESS System

Domain ontology: A transcript from an IMPRESS knowledge elicitation session was used as the basis for the re-engineering exercise. Concepts, properties, relations and expressions were identified, created in appropriate dictionaries and linked to the transcript. KADS Tool also supports the identification of *inferences* and *tasks* in a transcript; a number of tasks were identified in the IMPRESS transcript. A portion of the transcript, with its associated dictionaries (i.e. domain ontology), is shown in Figure 8.5 and Table 8.1.

The analyses below were carried out using KADS Tool which provides good support for building domain ontologies and defining domain models. See [97] for further details.

Technician: Here's a <u>faulty part</u> – as you can see, the <u>fault</u> is *black* <u>specks</u>, on the back face of the moulding, on the sides of the moulding – *all over*, in fact. [**He scratches a speck with his pocket knife**]. They're quite *deeply embedded* – not *surface* specks. That means that the problem is being CAUSED by <u>something in the material</u> or <u>in the process</u>, rather than <u>external dust</u>, or dripping water. [He speaks to the machine operator]. *How long* has **the job been running**?

Figure 8.5: Part of a transcript describing diagnosis of plastic moulding machinery

Concepts (underlined)	Properties and values (in *italic font*)
concept faulty part;	
concept fault;	property colour of specks
concept specks;	value-set black, etc
concept contaminated material;	property location of specks
	value-set: all over, etc;
concept process fault;	property depth of specks
concept external dust;	value-set: deep, surface, etc;
concept dripping water;	property duration of job
	value-set: value-set: 2 days, etc;
Relations (in SMALL CAPS) relation causes;	Tasks (in **bold font**) task scratch specks with pocket knife; task ask duration of job;

Table 8.1: Domain ontology elicited from the transcript shown in Figure 8.5

Domain models: When the identification of concepts etc. in the acquired knowledge is complete, the next step is to build one or more domain models. The experience gained on this project suggests that it is wise to use the inference structure as a guide in deciding which domain models to build. The configured inference structure for the IMPRESS system (Figure 8.6 [30]) which is derived from the generic inference structure for systematic diagnosis tasks, suggests that the domain models might include the following:

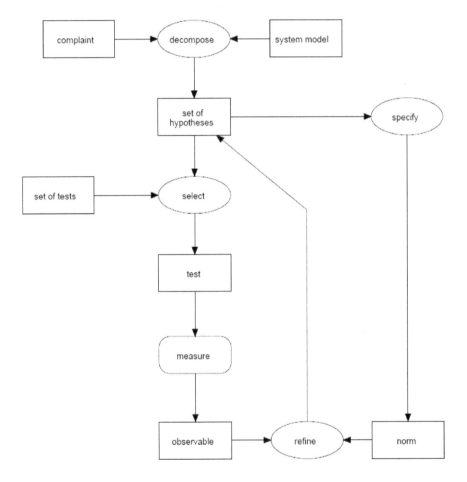

Figure 8.6: Configured inference structure for IMPRESS

---

[30] The rounded rectangle around *measure* indicates that "measure" is not, strictly speaking, an inference function; instead, it is a transfer task, (see section 8.3.3). This syntax is another innovation in CommonKADS.

- a link between complaints (symptoms) and hypothesised faults (based on the **decompose** inference function);
- a link between tests and observable properties (based on the **select** inference function);
- a link between observable properties and hypothesised faults (based on the **refine** inference function);
- a decomposition of a plastic moulding machine into its subcomponents (based on the **system model** knowledge role).

All of these suggested relationships are supported by the domain ontology:

- The link between complaints and hypothesised faults is represented by the relation **causes**;
- The link between tests and observable properties is represented by the relation **observes**;
- The link between observable properties and hypothesised faults is represented by the relation **indicates**;
- The decomposition of a plastic moulding machine into its subcomponents is represented by the relation **part of**.

Four domain models were therefore constructed to represent each of these relationships. Part of the behavioural model (which represents the **indicates** relation) is shown in Figure 8.7.[31]

In addition, there are some concepts which have been identified, but are not yet found in any domain model. This discovery requires a decision from the knowledge engineer: do these concepts need to be represented in a domain model, or can they safely be ignored? In the case of the IMPRESS system, the extra concepts included several concepts which referred to various states of the machine; from the transcript, it became obvious that a number of tests required the machine to be in a certain state. As a result, a new relation – **requires** – was created, and a domain model of preconditions was built to represent the requirements of tests for certain states of the machine.

---

[31] Note that Figure 8.7 uses the semantic net representation which is usually used within KADSTool to represent domain models. The CommonKADS book [147] recommends using UML object notation for domain model diagrams.

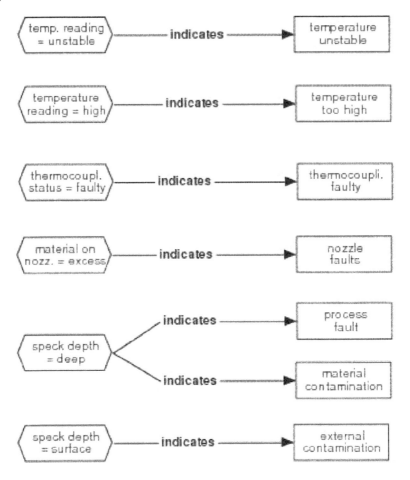

Figure 8.7: Part of the behavioural domain model for IMPRESS

Model ontology and model schema: The model schema for IMPRESS is shown in Figure 8.8. The terms used (i.e. the model ontology) can readily be seen to map each node to one domain model, with the exception of *manifestations* which are defined as expressions on observable properties. The relations from the domain ontology are considered to be sufficiently abstract to be used without alteration.

It can be seen from the model schema that the domain model of machine components which represents the decomposition of a plastic moulding machine, has no links with the remainder of the domain model. This suggests that the use of an explicit decomposition of the machine is not essential for the process of diagnosis – which was actually the case in the original IMPRESS project. The model schema can therefore be used to identify concepts which do not need to be built into the final KBS.

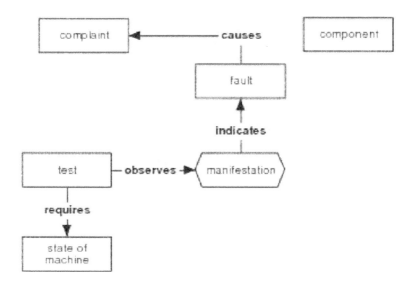

Figure 8.8: Model schema for IMPRESS

The nodes and relations in the model schema should map directly to knowledge roles and inference functions in the inference structure. The addition of the domain model of preconditions therefore necessitated a change in the inference structure. The final top level inference structure for IMPRESS is shown in Figure 8.9. (The double ellipse for the **select** inference function indicates that this inference function is expanded into a more detailed structure at a lower level in the analysis).

8.3.2 Domain Modelling for the X-MATE Project

The domain model for the X-MATE project turned out to be surprisingly simple. The domain ontology contained many rules but hardly any relations. As a result, only two domain models were identified: a hierarchy of professions (since certain categories of professions are more prone to income fluctuations than others), and a hierarchy of risks (where the top level nodes in the hierarchy represent the "typical non-ideal cases" identified in the original X-MATE project). The development of the model ontology proved useful, because it helped highlight the fact that different properties had to be acquired from different sources – a factor which was a key to the design of the X-MATE system, because the different sources required widely different

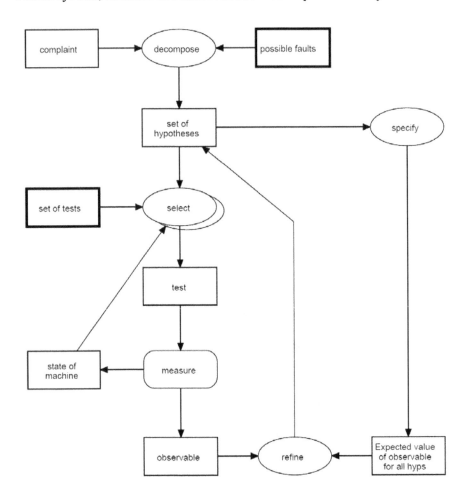

Figure 8.9: Final instantiated inference structure for IMPRESS

amounts of effort from the user of X-MATE. This necessitated a change to the inference structure: a *select* inference action and a **selected data source** knowledge role were added between the *various data sources* knowledge role and the *measure* transfer task.

The final inference structure for X-MATE is shown in Figure 8.10 which follows the discussion of the task level below. This is because the development of the task level for X-MATE resulted in some knowledge roles being identified as static knowledge roles rather than as dynamic knowledge roles. Discussion of this transformation can be found in section 8.4.

8.3.3 Evaluation of Domain Modelling

Performing the task of domain modelling was an enlightening exercise. The elicitation of a domain ontology and the subsequent construction of domain models was found to be a valuable exercise for the following reasons:

• It provided models of various aspects of the domain. This dissection of the domain, and the "cross-checking" effect of using the same concepts in more than one domain model, is an effective way of checking that all the necessary knowledge has been acquired.

• It provides a "theory" of the domain which is consistent, (hopefully) complete, and which has inter-relationships explicitly represented.

• It provides a structured approach to making alterations to an inference structure (over and above those made during the configuration process) when instantiating the inference structure to the domain.

• It provides (and possibly uses) re-usable models of the domain.

During domain modelling, however, some difficulties arose which are worthy of comment. The first difficulty was simply the sheer number of concepts which can be found in a transcript. The domain modelling exercise was carried out using one transcript of a protocol analysis session which contained only 600 words, and yet it produced 50 concepts and 25 other items in the domain ontology. Since an average human being can speak at about 10,000 words per hour (see [115]), the time required to identify concepts in a single transcript could potentially be very large indeed[32]. The use of KADS Tool (as opposed to using a highlighter pen and paper) makes this task feasible, but it can still be onerous. A possible solution to this problem would be to use structured knowledge acquisition techniques such as the laddered grid, the repertory grid, or card sorting ([47]), but none of

---

[32] This is acceptable if all these concepts are to be used in the final KBS, but at this stage of the modelling process bottom-up assembly is being employed, and so it is not known which concepts will ultimately be used.

these are likely to acquire *all* the necessary knowledge ([23]), and none are currently supported by KADS Tool.

The second difficulty affects the process of domain modelling itself. The development of an inference structure provides guidance to a knowledge engineer on which concepts and relations can be expected in the domain, but this is not always sufficient guidance on determining the ontological type of a fragment of acquired knowledge. For example, if the transcript indicated that the complaint may be due to a fault in the thermocouplings of the plastic moulding machine, the choices for representation in the domain ontology might include any of the following four options:

concept thermocouplings-faulty;

concept thermocouplings
  property faulty
    value-set yes, no;

concept thermocouplings
  property status
    value-set OK, faulty;

property thermocouplings-status
  expression thermocouplings-status = faulty;

An attempt has been made to develop heuristics to help in ontological assignment (e.g. "If the item can have properties of its own, then it is a concept; if it cannot have properties of its own, it is a property"), but these heuristics have proved difficult to apply, largely because different domain models present different views on the knowledge base ([141]).

For the domain modelling of IMPRESS, the inference structure provided sufficient guidance to make most ontological decisions. However, the ontological assignment of tests presented considerable difficulties. In the sample application provided with KADS Tool (diagnosis of faults in a printer), tests are considered to be **transfer tasks** (tasks in which the user or another external information source transfers knowledge to the knowledge base). This is also true of the IMPRESS project – tests obtain data about the plastic moulding machine, and this data is reported to the KBS. However, CommonKADS does not allow tasks to have properties – and yet a key part of the reasoning in IMPRESS is to decide which test to perform next, on the basis of the time required for that test and the explanatory power of the properties which are measured by the test. In order to represent this, tests had to be described both as tasks **and** as concepts which is far from ideal.

A less serious version of this problem can be seen from the above example of representation of thermocouplings. It was decided that the information about faulty thermocouplings would be represented as a concept, since **thermocouplings-faulty** is a fault, and also as a property, because **thermocouplings-status** can be checked by the technician).

A final difficulty is that domain modelling is only intended to represent semantic relationships, hence the use of semantic nets in KADS Tool to represent domain models. Semantic networks only allow a given node to appear once in any one model. This is a problem when using CommonKADS to model non-semantic relationships. An example can be found in [178], where modelling of molecular structures using KADS Tool proved difficult because organic molecules may contain many carbon atoms, and KADS Tool insisted that each atom was represented using a different concept.

On balance, the construction of domain models and a model schema is deemed to be a useful activity when constructing a KBS. The knowledge engineer should, however, be aware of the potential difficulties.

8.4 The Task Level in CommonKADS: Problem Solving Methods

The third level of expertise modelling in CommonKADS is the task level. CommonKADS requires a task *definition* to be written which is then instantiated into a task *body* using one of a number of *problem solving methods*. For example, if the task was diagnosing faults in a car engine, the problem solving method chosen might be "generate (all possible faults) and test (each one)". The task specification can be derived from the inference structure (or rather, from the CML description of the inference functions – see the appendix of [97] for a worked example); the major decision at this stage is which problem solving method to use.

Problem solving methods are a prescription of the way in which a certain class of task definitions can be satisfied. They specify the relation between a task definition and a task body [191] using CML and first order logic. It follows that the choice of the most appropriate problem solving method is made by comparing the task definition with the method description of each problem solving method.

8.4.1   Choosing a Problem Solving Method for IMPRESS

The task specification states that fault f is a solution if:
- f covers (i.e. is capable of causing) the observed complaint;
- all the observed properties indicate that f could be true;
- there is no other fault that covers and is indicated.

If there are still two or more faults under suspicion, a test should be performed to investigate one of those faults.

Task definition for IMPRESS:
        task machine-fault-diagnosis(c, f)
        goal: Find a fault f that explains a given symptom c
        $\wedge$ all manifestations observed indicate f
        $\wedge$ no other fault is indicated by all the manifestations
            roles:
            case-initial-input: c: complaint
            case-user-input: M: set of manifestations
            solution: f: fault
            task-specification:
            covers(f, c)
            $\wedge$ ($\forall$ m:manifestation indicates(m,f))
            $\wedge\neg(\exists$ f2:fault $\wedge$ covers(f2,c)
                $\wedge$ ($\forall$ m:manifestation indicates(m,f2)))
            $\vdash$ solution(f);
            covers(f, c)
            $\wedge$ ($\forall$ m:manifestation indicates(m,f))
            $\wedge$ ($\exists$ f2:fault $\wedge$ covers(f2,c)
            $\wedge$ ($\forall$ m:manifestation indicates(m,f2)))
            $\wedge$ ($\exists$ t:test observes(t,m) $\wedge$ indicates(m,f))
            $\vdash$ perform(t);

Figure 8.10: Task definition for IMPRESS

The knowledge engineer's task now is to choose a problem solving method. In this example, the choice has been narrowed down to two options: *generate and test* or *confirmation by exclusion*. (Figures 8.11 and 8.12). It is clear that these two method definitions are very similar. Both can be applied if the task specification can be interpreted as a conjunction of two criteria, and both involve generating and repeatedly testing hypotheses. However, the task characterisation of the method for confirmation by exclusion indicates that the method is dependent on the **non-existence** of the second criterion which is a key feature of the task specification. Further examination of the task reveals that it fulfils all the statements of the method definition, and so confirmation by exclusion is chosen as the problem solving method for IMPRESS. The resulting 'task body' appears in Figure 8.13.

Problem solving method: generate and test:
   problem solving method *generate and test*
   goal: G: find(s:solution)
   task-characterisation:
            criterion1(s) ∧ criterion2(s) ⊢ solution(s)
            control-roles: *c*: complaint *h*: hypothesis
      → solution
         sub-tasks:
         generate(complaint, hypothesis)
         test(hypothesis)
         method-definition:
          A1: ∀ x solution(x) ⊢ generate(x)
          A2: ∀ x generate(x) ∧ test(x) ⊢ solution(x)
          A3: ∀ x generate(x) ⊢ criterion1(x)
          A4: ∀ x test(x) ⊢ criterion2(x)
         A1 ∧ A2 ∧ A3 ∧ A4 ⊢<P1>∃ s solution(s)
         task-expression-schema P1
          repeat
          generate(c,h) until test(h)
          result(h)

Figure 8.11: Problem solving method - generate and test

Problem solving method: confirmation by exclusion:
problem solving method *confirmation by*
exclusion

  goal: G: find(s:solution)
  task-characterisation:

      criterion1(s) ∧¬∃ criterion2(s) ⊢ solution(s)
      control-roles:
      c: complaint
      h: hypothesis → solution
      H: set of hypotheses
      M: set of manifestations
      n: number of hypotheses in H
    sub-tasks:
      generate(complaint, set of hypotheses)
      test(hypothesis)
      refine(set of hypotheses)
      compute(number of hypotheses in set)
    method-definition:
      A1: ∀x solution(x) ⊢ generate(x)
      A2: ∀x generate(x) ∧ set(manifestations) ⊢
    solution(x)
      A3: ∀x generate(x) ∧ set(manifestations) ⊢
    criterion1(x)
      A4: ∀x generate(x) ∧ set(manifestations) ⊢
    criterion2(x)
      A1 ∧ A2 ∧ A3 ∧ A4 ⊢<P2>∃ s solution(s)
    task-expression-
  schema P2 generate(c,H)
      repeat
        test(h) → M
        refine(M, H)
      until
      n <= 1

Figure 8.12: Problem solving method – confirmation by
exclusion

IMPRESS task body:

    task body sub-goals:

      G1: find all fault states h with covers(h,c)

      G2: test a manifestation m such that h ∈ H

        ∧ indicates(m, h)

    G3: refine the set of hypotheses by removing all h
  for which indicates(¬m, h)

    sub-tasks:

      G1: generate(c,H) *G2*: test(h → m)

      G3: refine(m, H)

    control-roles:

      hypothesis h: fault

      manifestation m: manifestation

      number of hypotheses in H n: positive
  integer

    task-expression

      generate(c,H)

      repeat

        test(h) → m refine(m, H)

      until

      n <= 1

Figure 8.13: Task body for IMPRESS

8.4.2   Choosing a Problem Solving Method for X-MATE

The task modelling for X-MATE produced a very simple task structure. The reason for this is that much of the knowledge required for mortgage application assessment – the specification of a measurement system, the specification of risk indicators, and so on – has been **compiled** into a set of rules. In CommonKADS terminology, much of the inference has been done in advance, producing knowledge roles which are now static knowledge roles, from the viewpoint of the KBS. Figure 8.14 shows an inference structure which indicates the processing which is actually performed by X-MATE. The obvious problem solving method for a problem in which matching is the critical inference step is to use rule-based pattern matching. CommonKADS does not yet provide any guidance on choosing an appropriate rule-based paradigm (e.g. forward chaining vs backward chaining); some heuristic guidance can be found in appendix C.

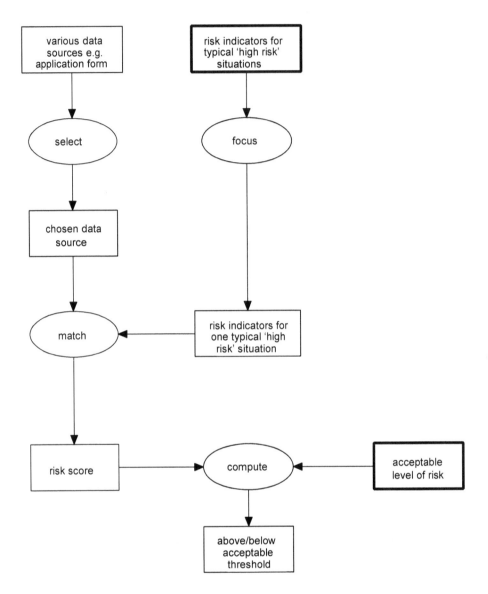

Figure 8.14: The actual inferences performed by X-MATE

8.4.3 Evaluation of Task Modelling

It can be seen that the task body for IMPRESS shown above provides a much more detailed prescription for the design phase of CommonKADS than the task structure in the KADS methodology. The use of problem solving methods is therefore recommended. The main difficulty is that the library of problem solving methods currently contains just one method (generate and test, specified in [191]) – the method for confirmation by exclusion was defined in the course of this project, thus doubling the current size of the library! It is therefore unsurprising that little is known about techniques for choosing between similar problem solving methods. It is hoped that such techniques will be developed in due course. (For guidance on development on problem solving methods, and a theoretical underpinning of them, see [4]).

8.5 Conclusion

The process of re-engineering two existing KBS applications into CommonKADS has shown that the refinements introduced to expertise modelling by CommonKADS are all useful techniques, and are recommended for future KBS projects. However, both the guidance on configuring inference structures and the library of problem solving methods are currently very sparse, and need to be expanded greatly for CommonKADS techniques to be widely usable. Domain modelling in CommonKADS has undergone the greatest transformation of all from KADS; it encourages greater understanding of the domain, provides explicit links with (and justification for adaptations to) the inference level, and aids in the development of re-usable domain models. Domain modelling can be a big task, however; it would be made easier by the provision of some guidance on ontological classification.

9 Inference Structure for Issue-based Planning

Having reviewed the Expertise model in detail, the next two chapters of this book look at research that I have carried out to extend the library of generic inference structures that is available to assist with developing the Expertise model. The first chapter looks at a model for planning tasks, and the second at a model for design tasks.

9.1 Introduction

The key element in the success of CommonKADS is the library of generic inference models which can be applied to tasks of specified types. These models suggest the inference steps which take place in a typical task of that type, and the roles which are played by domain knowledge in the problem solving process. For example, the generic model for a systematic diagnostic task (e.g. [97]) includes inference steps such as **decomposing** a set of possible faults, and **matching** observed values against expected values. This model also shows that the set of possible faults plays two roles in the diagnostic process; firstly as a part of a model of the behaviour of a faulty system, and secondly as hypothesised causes of the symptom(s) currently being observed. These generic models can either be used in a top-down manner, as frameworks for knowledge acquisition (e.g. [95]), or they can be used to verify the completeness of models developed bottom-up by analysis of the domain (e.g. [37]).

CommonKADS' generic model for diagnostic tasks is well-developed and well-understood. However, the generic models for some task types are not as well developed. This is true for tasks involving knowledge-based planning; while CommonKADS does give some guidance in this area [177], this guidance focuses on domain models, rather than inference models. Since knowledge-based planning is an important commercial application of Artificial Intelligence, there is a clear need for the development of generic models for planning tasks.

Many of the generic models which currently exist have been derived from existing AI systems, whose operation has been modelled and purged of their domain content. These models have the strength of proven applicability. There are a number of well-known and well-tried AI planning systems in existence; one of the best known is the Open Planning Architecture (O-Plan) [170]. O-Plan which was developed by AIAI's Knowledge Based Planning and Scheduling Group, provides a generic domain independent computational architecture suitable for command, planning and execution applications. O-Plan makes use of a variety of AI planning techniques, including a hierarchical planning system which can produce plans as partial orders on actions (cf. [145]); an agenda-based control architecture; incremental development of "plan states"; temporal and resource constraint handling (cf. [184]); and a number of data structures used in Nonlin [167] which was the forerunner of O-Plan. It therefore seemed that there would be considerable benefit in using O-Plan as a basis for generating a CommonKADS generic model for planning tasks.

The purpose of this paper is to describe the CommonKADS models which were developed from O-Plan. The paper also briefly describes the verification of these models in the context of a real-life planning task: the assignment and management of Search and Rescue operations by the Royal Air Force.

The format of the paper is:
• A brief description of the CommonKADS methodology;
• A brief description of O-Plan, and how its components relate to the CommonKADS view of knowledge representation;
• A description of the key planning models which were derived from O-Plan;
• A description of how these generic models were verified during the development of a KBS which supported Search and Rescue planning.

9.2 Knowledge   Representation   in CommonKADS

CommonKADS is the name of the methodology developed by the KADS-II project which was funded under the CEC ESPRIT programme [149]. It is a collection of structured methods for building knowledge based systems, analogous to methods such as SSADM for software engineering. CommonKADS views the construction of KBS as a modelling activity, and so these methods require a number of models to be constructed which represent different views on problem solving behaviour, in its organisational and application context. CommonKADS recommends the construction of six models:

- A model of the organisational function and structure. The key elements of this model are *business processes*, *structural units*, *business resources* and the various *relationships* between them.
- A model of the tasks required to perform a particular operation. The key elements in this model are the *tasks* required for a single business process, and the *assignment* of tasks to various agents.
- A model of the capabilities required of the agents who perform that operation. The key elements of this model are *agents* (human or automated) and their *capabilities*.
- A model of the communication required between agents during the operation. The key elements of this model are *transactions*.
- A model of the expertise required to perform the operation (see below).
- a model of the design of a KBS to perform all or part of this operation. The key step in a CommonKADS design model is (usually) a *functional decomposition* of a knowledge-based process into its component *functional units*.

The key model – the *expertise model* – is divided into three "levels" representing different viewpoints on the expert knowledge:

- The **domain knowledge** which represents the declarative knowledge in the knowledge base. The key elements in domain knowledge are *concepts*, *properties* of concepts, and *relations*. *Tasks* can also be considered to be part of the domain knowledge in some circumstances.
- The **inference knowledge** which represents the knowledge-based inferences which are performed during problem solving. Inference knowledge is represented using *inference functions* (inferences which must be made in the course of problem solving) and *knowledge roles* (domain knowledge which forms the input and output of the inference functions).
- The **task knowledge** which defines a procedural ordering on the inferences. The key elements at this level are *tasks* and their decomposition; in this respect, this level is very similar to the CommonKADS *task model*.

The contents of these three levels can be defined graphically, or using CML [19] [46] [148]. For a worked example of the development of each of these three levels, see [97].

CommonKADS models are typically developed concurrently with the acquisition of knowledge; initial knowledge acquisition is used to populate higher level models (e.g. the organisational or task models) and then these models may be used to document, structure, or guide knowledge acquisition. Partially completed models and/or generic models may even be presented to the experts to allow them to comment on the appropriateness of the models; this technique is similar to the "rapid prototyping" (iterative refinement) approach which was popular in the early days of KBS development. The key difference is that the CommonKADS models are being iteratively refined, rather than an implemented system; this removes many of the problems which were associated with "rapid prototyping" of a KBS, such as lack of documentation, and difficulties in identifying and justifying design decisions.

For more details on the contents of all the models described above, see [46].

9.3 O-Plan: The Open Planning Architecture

The development of open planning and scheduling systems seeks to support incremental extension and change, and to facilitate communication between processing agents (both automated and human). The need to support inter-process communication has become apparent from practical experience; unforeseen events or consequences of concurrent activities can have a major effect on planning, and so the role of the human system operator is crucially important. O-Plan has therefore been designed with an agent-oriented architecture in which job assignment, planning and execution are separated [170], and communication between agents is conducted using the same representations that the planner uses. This separation not only introduces flexibility into the planning process, but also fits well with CommonKADS' multi-viewpoint approach to knowledge representation.

O-Plan is a multi-faceted system, and much has been written about its different features (e.g. [169] [38] [53]). The main components of O-Plan are:

- Domain information;
- Plan/schedule states;
- Knowledge sources;

- Controller;
- Several support modules, including constraint managers.

The remainder of this section describes how these components relate to the different models proposed by CommonKADS.

9.3.1 Domain information

The best model in CommonKADS for representing domain information is the domain level of the expertise model. This model normally contains declarative information about physical objects, states which objects can be in, and relationships between objects; objects and states are represented using *concepts* and *properties*, while relationships are represented by *relations*. However, domain information in O-Plan includes a description of the *activities* which can be undertaken to achieve various planning tasks, as well as information on physical resources available to the planning process (e.g. helicopters, lifeboats, hospitals), and possible states of those resources. The need to represent activities in the domain information implies that the corresponding CommonKADS domain knowledge will include many *tasks* - procedures which can or must be carried out as part of a plan to achieve an objective.[33] From this, it becomes clear that a key factor in knowledge-based planning is the ability to represent activities in a declarative form, so that these activities can be reasoned about. Using this paradigm, the constraints between activities can be represented as relationships between tasks in the CommonKADS domain model.

9.3.2 Plan states

Plan states have three components: a plan agenda, the planning entities, and plan constraints. The agenda consists of *issues* to be resolved, such as getting a resource into a particular state; planning entities typically consist of planned activities which change the state of resources; and plan constraints provide detailed domain information which constrains further planning, such as the availability of resources. If the Search and Rescue planning task (which is described in section 9.5) is taken as an example, then an issue might be "a helicopter must

---

[33] CommonKADS and O-Plan ascribe different meanings to the term *task*. For the purposes of this paper, O-Plan "activities" and CommonKADS "tasks" can be considered to be broadly equivalent.

be present at the site of the operation"; a planning entity might be "scramble helicopter no. 007 immediately"; and a plan constraint might be "helicopter no. 007 only has enough fuel for 2 hours' flying". [34]This tripartite breakdown of plans corresponds to the <I-N-OVA> (issues, nodes and constraints) model described in [168].

All these components map to *knowledge roles* in the inference level of CommonKADS' expertise model; in other words, they consist of domain knowledge which plays a particular role in problem solving. As a reminder, domain knowledge consists of possible activities, physical resources, possible states of those resources, and relationships between resources and states. At the inference level:

- **Issues** consist of one or more resource states (which need to be achieved), and form an input to a particular planning cycle;
- **Planning entities** in the plan consist of activities, and form the output of a planning cycle;
- **Plan constraints** consist of both the states of physical resources, and of relationships between planned activities. They provide an intermediate input to a planning cycle.

9.3.3 Knowledge sources

The knowledge sources in O-Plan address specific planning requirements through the application of plan state modification operators. These include expanding an activity into sub-activities; choosing activities to achieve desired domain states; and selecting resources to perform activities.

These knowledge sources map to *inference steps* (in the inference knowledge of the Expertise model) in the CommonKADS framework. The knowledge sources transform the components of the plan state into other components; for example, an issue from the agenda which is expanded is likely to produce new issues. Since the components of the plan state have been identified as CommonKADS knowledge roles, the knowledge sources must correspond to CommonKADS inference steps.

---

[34] It is convenient to consider these three components separately when making the comparison with CommonKADS, even though all of these components can be thought of as constraints on future planning.

9.3.4 Controller

Throughout the plan generation process, O-Plan identifies outstanding issues to address; these issues are then posted on an agenda list. The controller computes the context-dependent priority of the agenda items and selects an item for processing. This provides the fundamental opportunism which is inherent in any planning task.

The knowledge used by the controller could be represented in CommonKADS at the *task level* of the Expertise model (with a few extensions to represent opportunism). The task level specifies ordering on the inference level, and also identifies input and output. For O-Plan, the task knowledge performs reasoning which dynamically determines an ordering on the inference knowledge; this is eminently sensible for any task which involves reacting to a dynamically changing situation, such as planning, scheduling, or control tasks.

9.3.5 Support modules

Support modules, such as database management facilities or context-layered access to the plan state, do not map into CommonKADS knowledge representation; they are either considered as external agents or extra requirements which have to be considered when the CommonKADS Design model is produced. However, some support modules in O-Plan, such as the constraint managers (which track the availability of resources, the temporal constraints on activities, and the relational constraints on objects), have a considerable effect on the planning cycle. The constraints themselves can be represented as *knowledge roles* in the inference knowledge of the Expertise model.

9.4 Generic CommonKADS models for Planning

It can be seen from the section above that the knowledge representation structure used in O-Plan corresponds fairly closely with the knowledge representation framework used by CommonKADS; specifically, by the CommonKADS Expertise Model. This made it possible to subdivide the next task in this project which was to derive generic CommonKADS models for planning from the architecture of O-Plan. It was decided to focus on deriving generic inference models ("inference structures") for the inference level of the CommonKADS

Expertise model, since, as noted in section 9.1, these models often provide most assistance to a KBS developer.[35]

The derived inference structure can be seen in Figure 9.1. A typical "run" through the inference structure would see the following operations taking place:

- The **current plan state** is notionally decomposed into three components: the **agenda** of issues which are to be resolved, the **current plan entities** and the **availability of resources**. This decomposition does not alter any of these structures; it simply makes explicit the role which each component of the plan state plays in the problem solving process. These roles are described in [169].

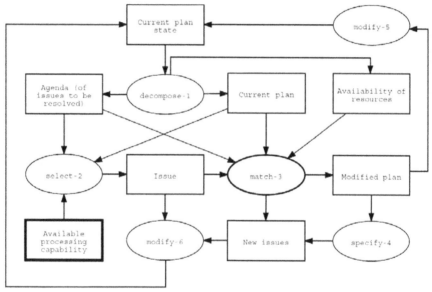

Figure 9.1: Top level inference structure for the O-Plan planner

- From the agenda of issues, at least one **issue** is selected for resolution. The choice of an issue depends on a number of factors

---

[35] O-Plan can be used for a variety of tasks, including but not limited to planning. For the sake of the current project, it is useful to specify an inference structure which represents the operation of O-Plan as a planner. This inference structure is designed to make explicit the processes which O-Plan goes through when performing planning tasks.

monitored by the **controller**, such as the available processing capabilities, the knock-on effect on other issues, etc.

• Pattern matching between issues and possible activities is used to find a way of resolving the current issue, perhaps by adding activities to the plan, or by creating new issues. Three ways of resolving issues are shown in Figures 9.2 to 9.4 below.

• The plan is updated with the modified plan state and any new issues that have arisen.

Figures 9.2 to 9.4 show three of O-Plan's "knowledge sources", represented as CommonKADS inference structures. These knowledge sources are each capable of resolving an outstanding issue, but in different ways. The methods used are:

• Adding a new activity, or further constraints on currently planned activities, in order to resolve the issue (Figure 9.2);

• "Backward chaining": adding new issues to the plan which, if resolved, will allow the current issue to be resolved (Figure 9.3);

• Expanding the issue into a number of sub-issues (Figure 9.4). [36]

In CommonKADS terms, these three knowledge sources constitute different possible decompositions of the **match-3** inference step. The three decompositions are described in more detail in the following paragraphs.

Figure 9.2 represents the resolution of an issue by **condition satisfaction**: i.e. the conditions for an activity that is capable of fulfilling the outstanding issue, are found to be matched. Conditions typically consist of one or more resources being in one or more states. For example, if an issue in the plan was to arrange transport for a mountain rescue team from Kinloss to Ben Nevis, then one possible activity (discovered by **match-3.1.7**) might be to transport the team by helicopter. The conditions of this activity might be that the mountain rescue team is present at a helicopter landing site, and an airworthy

---

[36] The numbering system used for inference steps in these inference structure diagrams is based on the numbering scheme used in the IDEF3 method for process modelling. In the top level diagram, every inference step is given a single unique number. At lower levels, inferences are numbered $x.y.z$, where:

-    x is the unique number of the "parent" inference step;
-    y is the number of the decomposition. An inference usually only has one decomposition, but if there are alternative ways of achieving an inference step then there may be multiple decompositions;
-    z is the unique number of this inference step.

helicopter is also present at that site; constraints determined by the availability of resources and currently planned activities will determine if these conditions can be fulfilled (**match-3.1.14**). If the conditions of an activity can be fulfilled, and that activity is selected as the best method of transporting the team (**select-3.1.8**), then the plan is modified and the issue is removed from the agenda.

It is possible that there may be more than one way of matching the conditions of an activity; for example, there may be more than one helicopter available. In that case, O-Plan automatically selects one option which is used for further depth-first reasoning, and maintains the other *Possible modified plans* as choice points in case backtracking is required.

Figure 9.3 represents the resolution of an issue for which there is no matching activity whose conditions are currently satisfied (as determined by **match-3.2.9**). The approach taken by O-Plan in this case is a form of "backward chaining"; a search is made for other activities which, if added to the plan, will create the right conditions for an activity to be added that fulfils the current issue (**specify-3.2.15**). If a suitable activity is found, then the performing of this activity is added to the agenda of issues (**specify-3.2.10**). This is known as **achieving** in O-Plan.

Figure 9.4 represents the resolution of an issue by **expansion**. If the current issue matches with an activity (**match-3.3.11**) which can be decomposed into sub-activities, then the current issue is removed from the agenda and appropriate sub-issues are created and added to the agenda (**decompose-3.3.16**. For example, if "move mountain rescue team to pickup point" was an issue, then this might be expanded into "contact team", "instruct team", and "confirm team have arrived at pickup point".

In summary, these inference structures represent the core activities of the O-Plan planning process. The system-independence of these inference structures allows them to be used as generic models of the inference processes required for knowledge-based planning.[37]

---

[37] There are also many controls on efficiency and processing capability implemented within the O-Plan Controller; these are not considered here.

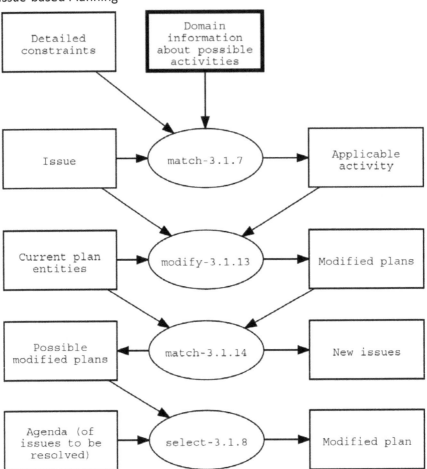

Figure 9.2: Inference structure for resolving an issue by introducing new activities or constraints into the plan

9.5   Verifying the planning models: Search and Rescue

In the previous section, a set of inference structures were derived from the O-Plan approach to planning, and were proposed as generic inference models for knowledge-based planning tasks.

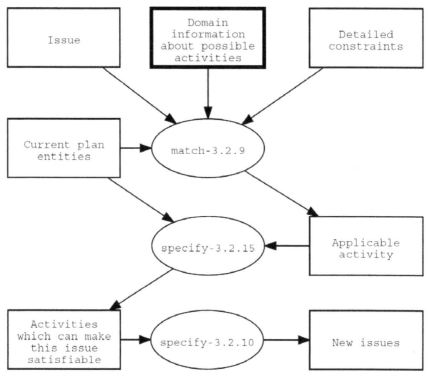

Figure 9.3: Inference structure for resolving an issue by "backward chaining"

Despite the fact that O-Plan is intended to be a generic architecture for implementing different types of knowledge-based planning systems, this proposition is a strong one, because there is a wide variation in task types which fall under the category of knowledge-based planning, this proposition is a string one, because there is a wide variation in task types which fall under the category of knowledge-based planning. Knowledge-based planning tasks may vary in the type of feedback data which is available to the planner[38] [176]; in the depth of search required; and in the type of support which a human user needs (fully automated planning vs. monitoring and support of human planning).

---

[38] Valente classifies planners as *linear*, *non-linear*, *reflective* or *skeletal* according to the use which they make of state change data and plan assessment knowledge.

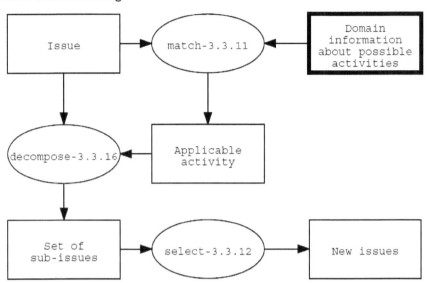

Figure 9.4: Inference structure for resolving an issue by
expanding it into sub-issues

9.5.1 Inference modelling for Search and Rescue planning

In order to verify the claim that the inference structure presented in the previous section can act as a generic inference model for planning tasks, it is therefore important that these models should be seen to be appropriate for real-life planning tasks. One such task is that of planning the use of resources in a Search and Rescue incident. A project entitled "Acquiring and Using Planning Knowledge for Search and Rescue" [37] was carried out jointly by the University of Nottingham and AIAI, and produced a prototype KBS for supporting Royal Air Force (RAF) personnel in their allocation and management of resources such as Search and Rescue helicopters, RAF mountain rescue teams, and RAF Nimrod aircraft. The responsibilities of the Rescue Co-ordination Centres of the RAF include support and co-ordination of civilian emergencies; this includes direct responsibility for the allocation, application and co-ordination of military resources, as well as co-ordination with a number of civilian emergency authorities such as fire, police, ambulance, coastguard and civilian mountain rescue teams. A rescue incident can vary in scale from retrieving a walker with a sprained ankle to handling a large air crash; the Rescue Co-ordination Centres may have to manage several incidents simultaneously, each requiring one or two aircraft as well as one or more other search teams or emergency services.

Knowledge acquisition and high-level task modelling for this system are described in [37]; the result of these activities was to design and develop a system which supported RAF personnel in making planning decisions, in remembering all the tasks which needed to be undertaken, in deciding what to do next, and in logging actions taken. The system was *not* designed to be a 'closed-loop' planner which would generate a complete plan with little user consultation; during knowledge acquisition, it was noted that the users always maintained control over the planning process, to the extent that planning is sometimes deliberately delayed until more domain information has been obtained. If the generic inference models which were derived from O-Plan can be shown to be applicable to a system which, unlike O-Plan, is not a closed-loop planner, then the generic models should be applicable to a wide range of knowledge-based planning tasks.

The approach which was taken to the design of the KBS for search and rescue support was to develop a domain-specific inference structure in a bottom-up fashion based on structured interviews, video tape analysis, protocol analysis, incident documentation and structured analysis of specific incident cases [37]. This inference structure can be seen in Figure 9.5. Although Figure 9.5 looks very different from Figures 9.1 to 9.4 at first sight (partly because it uses the terms "goal" and "action" instead of "issue" and "activity"), there are some common components between the two. Figure 9.5 shows that planning for Search and Rescue operations takes place by choosing an appropriate "template plan" which contains a list of goals (issues) to be satisfied; selecting one of these goals; either matching the goal to an action, or expanding it into a set of sub-goals which are then individually matched against actions; and then adding all the actions into the current plan. Both Figures 9.1 to 9.4 and Figure 9.5 represent the matching of issues against possible activities (**match-3** in Figure 9.1 and **match-1** in Figure 9.5); both allow issues to be decomposed as part of the planning process (**decompose-3.3.16** in Figure 9.4 and **decompose** in Figure 9.5); and both identify selection of the next issue as an important inference step in the planning process (**select-2** in Figure 9.1 and **select** in Figure 9.5).

The generic inference structure was then used to critique the domain-specific inference structure. The result of the comparison showed that the inference structure derived from O-Plan:

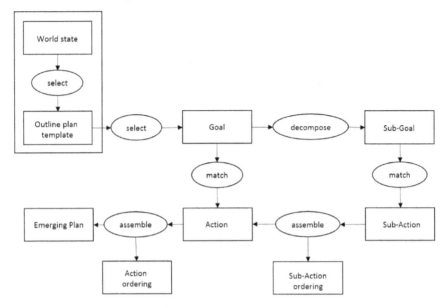

Figure 9.5: Inference structure derived from knowledge
acquisition and domain analysis

- had a richer representation of techniques for matching issues to activities (**match1** in Figure 9.5 is replaced by the whole of Figure 9.2; **decompose** and **match-2** in Figure 9.5 are replaced by Figure 9.4; and there is no representation in Figure 9.5 of the "achieving" represented in Figure 9.3);
- identified some important knowledge roles (resource constraints, and the library of possible activities) which were not explicitly represented in the domain-driven inference structure.

while the domain-derived inference structure highlighted knowledge which is particularly important in the Search and Rescue domain. This primarily consisted of the use of an outline plan template as a framework for planning.

The next stage of modelling is to determine whether the model components which are present in the generic model but do not appear in the domain-derived model are in fact applicable to this planning task. It was easy to determine that the task of Search and Rescue planning is sometimes constrained by available resources (there are only a few helicopters and aircraft available to them), and that the planners select from a library of possible activities when deciding how to fulfil an issue (this is most noticeable when different ways of transporting a casualty to safety are considered). Further investigation also determined that there was (occasionally) a requirement to "achieve" a state of affairs by introducing other activities earlier in the plan. This often occurs when the planners want to use facilities controlled by other authorities, such as lifeboats; in these situations, the facilities cannot be used until permission has been granted by the controlling authority. The activity of "scramble lifeboats" therefore requires the activity of "obtain permission" to be performed before its conditions can be fulfilled.

The conclusion which can be drawn is that the generic inference models specified in Figures 9.1 to 9.4 are adequate for representing the task of Search and Rescue planning, once a few domain-specific adaptations have been made[39]; more importantly, the use of a generic inference model acts as a completeness check on acquired procedural knowledge, by prompting a knowledge engineer to consider possible aspects of the planning process which may not have been identified during initial knowledge acquisition.

9.5.2 Implementation

In the course of developing the Design Model, it became apparent that there were two options for implementing the planner, using the CLIPS KBS development package. The first option was to implement the acquired issue/activity matching rules directly in CLIPS; the second option was to encode these acquired rules and their conditions as possible activities, as is done in the domain knowledge of O-Plan. These possible activities would effectively be declarative rules (i.e. concepts stating that if this activity was added to the plan which could only occur IF certain pre-conditions were fulfilled, THEN certain changes would be made to the plan state) which would then be activated by a set of meta-rules. In the former approach, planning is achieved by running any or all rules which are applicable; in the latter approach, planning consists of running rules which compare the conditions of possible activities with the current state of the world. If the conditions of an activity are matched, then that activity may be introduced into the plan; if the conditions are not matched, the system can reason about what is required in order to permit that activity to be introduced to the plan.

---

[39] Such adaptations are a common feature of KBS projects which use CommonKADS (see [116], for example).

The second approach was chosen. A set of meta-rules were written in CLIPS which match a set of possible activities (encoded as instance objects within CLIPS' object-oriented language) against data about the Search and Rescue incident and the availability of resources (also represented as instance objects). This meta-rule approach enables a virtual planning architecture to be implemented within the CLIPS language. The identification of this approach was a direct consequence of the use of generic inference models as a basis for system design, and the structure of the implemented system reflects the structure of the inference models which were developed.

The system which was constructed was therefore based on an inference structure which incorporated the best of both worlds; it had all the matching capabilities and inputs of the generic inference structure, as well as the selection of a "template plan" specified by the domain-derived inference structure. The structure of the system was based on the inference structure (with additional transformations and design decisions made using the CommonKADS Design Model); the reasoning component of the system consisted of a number of objects representing possible activities, another set of objects representing issues on the agenda, and a set of rules which matched issues against possible activities. The system also used objects to represent resources (helicopters, mountain rescue teams, etc), and to represent the plan itself, with relations between objects specifying the order of planned activities. User interfaces included a PERT chart-style viewer of the planned activities, a TO DO list showing issues on the agenda, and a "status board" showing the current commitments of resources. For further details, see [37].

9.6 Future work

We have showed that a set of CommonKADS inference models can be derived to represent the workings of the O-Plan system. We have also seen that these models can be beneficially applied to the modelling of a real-life planning task, identifying important aspects of the task which were not immediately obvious from acquired knowledge. We can therefore argue that the consideration of these generic models will be beneficial to anyone constructing a planning system, for these models may highlight aspects of the problem which should have been considered.

However, this paper does not claim that the generic inference models highlight *every* aspect that needs to be considered in any planning task. Knowledge-based planning is a wide-ranging field, using a number of different approaches. While O-Plan can perform a wide range of planning tasks (and some other tasks as well), it is based on a particular approach to planning; the inference models derived from O-Plan inevitably reflect the approach. If the generic models shown in Figures 9.1 to 9.4 included control information, then the relationship between O-Plan and the generic models would be the same as the relationship between MYCIN and the expert system 'shell' derived from it, E-MYCIN. The deliberate exclusion of control information from CommonKADS inference models helps to lift the generic models to a slightly higher level of abstraction than E-MYCIN, but these models cannot be considered to be a generic model for all planning tasks.

What is needed is a top-down approach to classifying planning tasks which identifies the important characteristics of different approaches to planning, and suggests the types of knowledge which are considered by each type of planning. Since this paper was originally submitted, a paper has been published [8] which takes such an approach, using the CommonKADS framework to produce a high-level description of different planning systems and the approaches which they use. From this perspective, the models produced by Barros *et al* are the "generic" models, specifying the types of operation which a planner is expected to perform (e.g. *select goal* or *critique plan*), whereas the models described in Figures 9.1 to 9.4 are the "domain-derived" models, representing the actual operation of a particular planning system. By applying the same technique of comparing and combining "generic" models with "domain-derived" models, the models described in Figures 9.1 to 9.4 can be verified for completeness, and correctly classified according to the types of planning task for which they are most appropriate, while the models described by Barros *et al* can be enriched. Furthermore, this technique could be used to incorporate a number of other "generic planning models" which have been proposed (such as that of [22], and possibly even case-based models such as that used by [71]) into a common framework, thus permitting rational selection of the "best" generic planning model for a particular planning task.

10 Inference Structure for Propose-and-Revise Design

10.1 Introduction

The original KADS methodology classified task types into a taxonomy [20]. The principal distinction in this taxonomy is between *system analysis* tasks and *system synthesis* tasks. Analytic tasks, such as diagnosis and assessment, have as their ultimate goal the establishment of unknown properties or behaviour of the system; synthetic tasks, such as configuration and planning, aim to define a structural description of a system in terms of some given set of elements. Certain tasks, such as repair or control, are considered to involve aspects of both analytic and synthetic tasks; these are known as *system modification* tasks. The majority of successful KBS systems have dealt with analytic tasks, such as diagnosis or selection, although several successful KBS have been developed for synthetic tasks, either using KADS or CommonKADS (see e.g. chapter 13) or without such methods (e.g. [124] [169]). There are very few successful KBS systems which successfully handle modification tasks.

Design problems are classified in the taxonomy as synthetic tasks, and are classified into three subtypes: design by hierarchical decomposition, design by gradual refinement, and design by transformation. Each of these subtypes has its own inference structure. The thesis of this paper is that the repertoire of inference structures for design tasks is incomplete. At least one more model needs to be added: a model which supports the process of *propose-and-revise* design (also known as *propose-critique-modify* design). This paper contains a justification for the addition of this model, a suggested framework for the model, and a discussion of knowledge acquisition techniques suitable for propose-and-revise design.

10.2 The design process

10.2.1 KADS modelling of the design process

There is considerable debate about the way in which design is, or should be, carried out. The underlying reason for this debate is that designers not only work in different ways, but actually think in different ways. Many textbooks on design encourage designers to think divergently, deliberately **not** restricting themselves to a fixed "design process", in order to stimulate the emergence of "creativity" which is seen as the key to many successful designs. Others argue that a design process should be used because, in some situations, creativity is less important than productivity, reusability, or ensuring that a design meets safety standards.

While the arguments continue, attempts have been made to categorise the ways in which design is actually performed (e.g. [121]). KADS offered the following categorisation [20]:

1. **Hierarchical design**. In this process, a design task is broken down into a number of smaller design tasks which are tackled separately, and then the results are recombined. Ideally, each subtask would be further decomposed until it reaches the stage where there is a well-understood solution: for example, in software design, a low-level subtask might be to design an ordered set of elements. This task could be solved by writing a sorting algorithm and applying it to the elements.

    Hierarchical design is used in cases where independent sub-problems can be defined, such as software design, where modules only interact via their inputs and outputs. However, such independence is often impossible to achieve in design tasks; for example, the construction of a house cannot be broken down into an independent consideration of the design of each room in the house, because the chosen shape and the location of utilities in each room affects the design of the other rooms.

    An example of the use of hierarchical design can be found in [109] which records an empirical study which aimed to identify the approaches taken by industrial designers to designing a garbage disposal system for a train.

2. **Transformational design**. This is a version of design in which a full specification of the artefact is available at an early stage of the design process, but is formulated in a different

manner from the elements of the solution domain. A good example is VLSI design in which an algorithm is input to the design process (a formal specification) and the layout of the actual chip is the required output [20]. It is likely that the main knowledge-based components of transformational design will be problem-specific.

      3. **Incremental design**. This occurs when there is no straightforward transformation of the conceptual design to a detailed design model; instead, the conceptual model is separated into design elements and constraints. Both of these are then transformed (perhaps in several stages) to a form where they can be amalgamated into a final design model.

In order to understand the above categorisation, it is important to note two points:

1.The categories above represent *generic* frameworks for performing a design task. These frameworks need to be instantiated to particular design tasks which may involve the addition or removal of some inference steps in order to reflect the actual inferences which are performed for a particular task. The knowledge engineer is therefore asked to determine the most appropriate generic inference structure, rather than the only appropriate inference structure.

2.The modelling of expert tasks may require more than one level of decomposition or refinement: taking hierarchical design as an example, each sub-part of the overall design may need to be modelled individually in order to produce a fully detailed model of the design. It is important to note that tasks specified at a more detailed level will not necessarily use the same approach to problem solving (and hence the same generic inference structure) as the top level task; to continue the example, an approach which uses hierarchical design as the overall approach to problem solving level may use transformational design or incremental design to produce certain sub-parts of the design.

10.2.2   Higher level frameworks: data flow vs iteration

The different approaches to design suggested by KADS provide a fairly comprehensive classification of approaches to design – *if* it is assumed that design is a sequential, non-iterative process. This can be seen in the KADS "generic design model" (reproduced in Figure 10.1), in which an informal problem statement is transformed into a detailed design with no significant iteration between the various stages of transformation. The different approaches to design suggested by KADS are essentially special cases of the generic design model, with emphasis on different inference steps; for example, incremental design emphasises the **transform/expand/refine** inference step [166].

This sequential approach to design has been recommended by several sources (e.g. [7] [83]), including the influential Royal Institution of British Architects ([140]). It has been proposed as a suitable model for software engineering, where it corresponds to the 'waterfall' model of software development (see [143]). However, more recent writers have criticised the sequential approach to design. It has been claimed that this approach over-emphasises the need for the communication of data and underemphasises the need to integrate the knowledge and information used in design [158]; that the development of sequential models fails to represent the true nature of the design process [185]; and that the sequential approach has more to do with the job of managing the people employed in design, rather than with what designers actually do (cf. pp. 25-26 of [111]). The second and third criticisms certainly seem to be valid in software design, for very few software projects actually adhere to a strict waterfall model of development.

So, if designers do not work according to a sequential model of design, how do they operate? The alternative to a sequential approach is an iterative approach. In such an approach, designers do not work through a problem step by step, first analysing and then synthesising. Instead, designers propose a solution at an early stage, and then iterate towards a final solution by presenting the early solution for criticism; this may involve elicitation of further constraints. In software engineering, this approach to design corresponds to "rapid prototyping" which has commonly been used for the development of knowledge based systems, and is sometimes used to aid requirements specification in large software projects. Rapid prototyping involves preparing and implementing a software design quickly before showing it to the client for criticism; the implementation is then altered to take account of any changes which are suggested, and the process is repeated. This iteration normally continues until an acceptable design is reached.

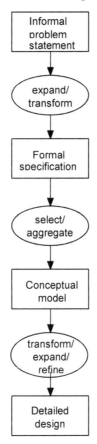

Figure 10.1: The sequential "generic design model" suggested by KADS

The following experiment [112] illustrates the use of iterative design by architectural designers. Postgraduate science students and final year architecture students were given a set of blocks which had some faces coloured blue and some coloured red. The students were told to build a structure which had as few external blue faces as possible. The students were also told that there was another rule which limited their freedom of choice, but they would not be told what that rule was. Instead, they could present possible designs for criticism. They were, however, to present as few intermediate designs as possible.

The experiment revealed that the engineering students tended to focus on determining the unknown rule. Once they had presented enough attempts to deduce the rule, they calculated the optimum configuration of blocks. The design students, however, tended to propose a fairly good solution as a first step; if it was declared to be incorrect, they altered the design slightly, and continued to make slight alterations until they had produced the best design possible which was not declared to be incorrect. Analysis of the results showed that the design students performed as well as the engineering students in reaching an optimum design, and produced a significantly lower number of intermediate designs in the process.

There is documented support for the use of iterative design by architectural designers [111], bridge designers [138] and user interface designers [73] [72], as well as support from the AI community, with its inherent interest in identifying and modelling human cognitive processes [10] [158] [28]. Indeed, Chandrasekaran [28] discusses iterative design which he calls **propose-critique-modify** design, in detail. While Chandrasekaran's preferred name is an accurate description of the processes involved in iterative design, this paper uses the more widely used term "propose-and-revise" to describe this approach to design.

The thesis of this paper is that propose-and-revise design is a commonly used approach to design, and is worthy of being included in the KADS library of generic inference structures, because it is sufficiently different from the approaches already specified in the library. The structure of the paper is as follows:

- The next two sections discuss two key aspects of propose-and-revise design: the role of constraints in design, and the use of previous models as a basis for a design;
- The following two sections bring the conclusions together into a suggested inference structure, and show how that inference structure was applied to a particular project;
- The final section looks at how knowledge acquisition might be performed for a task which uses propose-and-revise design.

10.3 The role of constraints in propose-and-revise design

In any design task, the key elements of the design problem are the constraints placed on the designer. Designers must identify these constraints, and then work within them to produce an acceptable design. If a design cannot be produced which fully satisfies all constraints, then one or more constraints must be relaxed, or abandoned entirely, in order to produce a feasible design.

In propose-and-revise design, a client's criticisms of a possible design effectively place more constraints on the design. However, since criticism requires communication, the designer may take the opportunity to negotiate with the client on which constraints can be relaxed, and how far. It is therefore crucial for the designer to understand each constraint, and the consequences of relaxing it, thoroughly. This is particularly important if there are time restrictions on the design process which reduce the number of explorative iterations which can be performed.

10.3.1   Understanding constraints

In order to understand constraints fully, Lawson [111] suggests that constraints should be analysed on three dimensions:

- Is the constraint imposed *internally* or *externally*? An internal constraint is one imposed by a decision of an interested party; for example, an architectural design may be required to include ramps throughout for use by disabled people, or a graphic design may be required to make use of the colours associated with the client company's corporate image. An external constraint is one which cannot be altered by any decision of the project team; the points of the compass (and hence the position of the sun) is an important external constraint on the design of housing.
- Who imposes the constraint? Is it the designer, the client, the user (if different from the client), or legislators? A graphic designer might decide that a better effect would be achieved if he limits his design to soft pastel colours only which is an example of a designer-imposed constraint. The width of corridors and the number of doors in a building is affected by fire regulations which is an example of a legislative constraint. (As an aside, Lawson notes that legislative constraints tend to be biased towards factors that can easily be measured. This has often led to designer dissatisfaction with legislation which is seen as overly restrictive, or failing to take account of special features of the particular design problem).
- What function does the constraint fulfil? Is it a *radical* constraint, affecting the fundamental purpose of the design, a

practical constraint imposed by the limitations of technology or nature, a constraint on *form*, affecting the style and visual impact of the design or a *symbolic* constraint, affecting the visual symbolism of the design? A radical constraint might be that a school building requires rooms suitable for teaching classes; a practical constraint might be that the site for a building has a certain load-bearing capacity; a constraint on form might be that a graphic designer is required to make an advertisement striking, unusual and memorable; and an example of a symbolic constraint is that the roof of the Sydney Opera House was designed to be parabolic in shape because it is intended to symbolise the surrounding marine environment. Practical constraints can usefully be subdivided into constraints on the parameters of the design and its environment, and constraints on the process of making, testing or assembling the artefact [21].

Gaining an understanding of constraints also requires designers to recognise that they themselves sometimes place implicit constraints on the design process which are nonessential. Lawson [111] reports an exercise in which novice designers (architectural students) were asked to design the floorplan for a block of flats (see Figure 10.2). The students were unable to produce a design which allowed sufficient light into the living room of each flat until they relaxed the constraint *which they had unconsciously imposed upon themselves* that no part of one flat should overlap with a neighbouring flat. The floorplan shown in the lower half of Figure 2 allows plenty of light into both living room and kitchen, makes each flat slightly narrower, and also provides a recessed "entrance area" for each flat. The lesson to draw from this example is that the students did not recognise the constraint on overlapping, and therefore did not realise that this constraint could be relaxed.

10.3.2 Prioritising constraints

A second key factor in propose-and-revise design is that designers who are presented with a large number of constraints to fulfil tend to focus on fulfilling a small number of constraints which are perceived to be important. In another experiment on students of architectural design [111], three groups of students were asked to design an office building for a design competition. They were told that the building would be sited between two major roads, across the line of an existing public footpath, and that it should not present a remote or

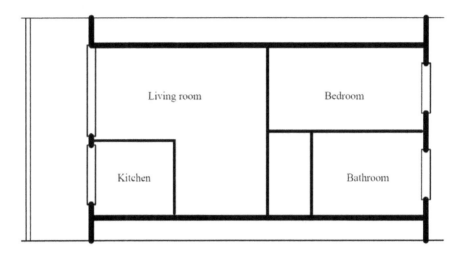

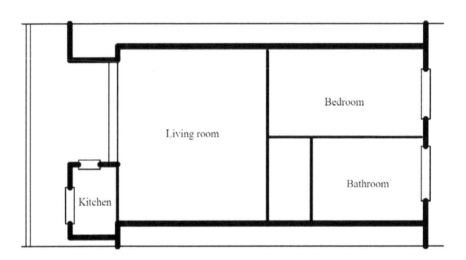

Figure 10.2: Proposed designs for single-bedroom deck-access flats (a)
with a rectangular floorplan (b) with one flat overlapping the next

forbidding image to local ratepayers. The students all appeared to focus
on one aspect of the problem, and to design their whole solution around
that one aspect. One group focussed on the office environment, and
designed an office layout with careful attention to the provision of
service ducts and flexibility of partitioning. Another group focussed on

making the building visitor-friendly, and so designed a building with different departments in different blocks leading off a central court. The third group, however, focussed on the image presented to ratepayers, and particularly on the public footpath. They proceeded to design an arch-shaped building with a covered mall in the centre doubling as the footpath!

It is important that this prioritisation of constraints is made explicit, so that a reasoned decision can be made on the relative advantages of one constraint against another.

10.4   The use of previous designs as a basis for current designs

An obvious possibility for reducing the time required to perform propose-and-revise design is to start with a design used in a previous similar situation which therefore ought to satisfy most of the constraints. The issue of whether it is wise to use a previous design as a basis for a current design has been a subject of considerable debate within the design community. On the positive side, the main advantage of using an existing design is that this design (presumably) satisfies all the constraints which were imposed on it, and so is likely to satisfy many of the constraints which will be imposed in a similar situation. Some would also claim that it is well-nigh impossible for a designer to ignore his previous experience of similar designs when producing a new design, and so the process might as well be explicit. On the negative side, it is claimed that re-use of existing designs stifles creativity in design; the experiment cited in section 10.3.1 showed how the unconscious effects of previous experience hindered the students from arriving at an acceptable solution to their design problem. It is accepted that innovative design is largely dependent on improvement of a feature of an existing design, but it is argued that truly creative design is crucially dependent on freedom from such restrictions. This argument is at the heart of much criticism of designs (from both sides), and it is unlikely that designers will ever agree completely on this matter.

In the AI community, the recent successes of case-based reasoning technology for design tasks [183] have swung the pendulum towards favouring re-use of existing designs. Case-based reasoning attempts to match the key features of the current design task against the key features of previous design tasks. If it finds a previous task which closely matched the current task, it retrieves the solution to that previous task, and then presents that solution to the user for minor modifications, or possibly attempts to make modifications itself.

Given the potential of case-based reasoning, and a degree of suspicion about whether AI is appropriate for "creative" design, it seems pragmatic to assume that any AI-based approach to propose-and-revise design is likely to make use of an existing design as a basis for the current design.

10.5 The inference structure

Based on the above analyses of the process of propose-and-revise design, a generic inference structure should include:
- acquisition of constraints
- ordering of constraints
- creation of a possible solution
- verification of that solution
- feedback from verification to an earlier stage in the process, thus creating an iterative loop
- potential input from previous design models

In some cases, it is possible that attempts at producing a design may prove to be dead-ends, because constraints cannot be relaxed sufficiently to produce an acceptable design. In these cases, the designer has to choose another initial model, and re-start the reasoning process. The inference structure should therefore also represent the possibility of selecting a new initial model from the model library.

The suggested inference structure is shown in Figure 10.3. As described in section 10.2.1, KADS allows inference structure diagrams to be hierarchically decomposed. In this case, it is convenient to decompose the *transform-2* inference function in the top level model. This inference function which represents the process of assigning importance to constraints, is shown in Figure 10.4.

The inference structure shown above is not intended to make every aspect of the design process explicit; it only shows the typical processes in propose-and-revise design. Certain information which is specific to the problem domain must be added for the model to be complete. For example, the model does not indicate which constraints should be relaxed or abandoned if it proves impossible to produce a

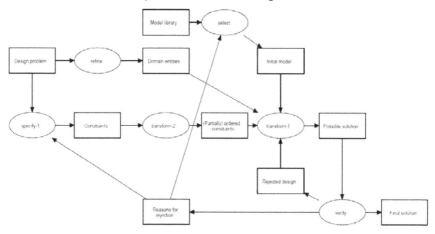

Figure 10.3: Top level inference structure for propose-and-revise design

design which fully satisfies all constraints; nor does it provide any information about how an appropriate initial model is selected from the model library. Both of these factors form a significant component of design expertise, and should be specified as part of the process of instantiating the generic inference structure to a particular task.

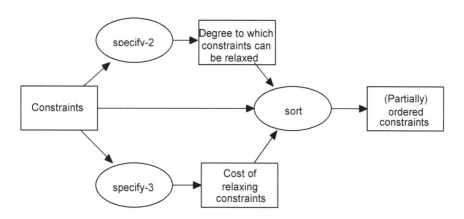

Figure 10.4: Expansion of *transform-2*

Task structure for the top level inference structure

    task design

    goal to synthesise a solution to a design problem

    task structure

    refine(design problem → domain entities)

    specify(design problem → constraints)

    select(model library → initial model)

    for all constraint ∈ constraints do

        specify(constraint → degree to which constraint can be relaxed)

        specify(constraint → cost of relaxing constraint)

        sort(constraints & cost of relaxing constraints & degree to which constraints can be relaxed → (partially) ordered constraints)

        transform(domain entities & initial model & (partially) ordered constraints → possible solution)

    loop

    verify(possible solution → rejected design & reasons for rejection OR final solution)

    specify(reasons for rejection → further constraints OR select new model from model library)

    transform(rejected design & constraints → possible solution)

10.6   Validation of the inference structure

The suggested inference structure has been validated by applying it to a real-life knowledge-based design problem. The problem chosen was that of a consultant or subcontractor negotiating an acceptable workplan for a commercial contract. The tasks to be done, the skills required for each task, and the overall cost of the task must all be defined by the consultant and agreed by the client. Previous workplans may be used as a basis for a current workplan, especially in companies which have well-defined "packages" of work which are sold as a whole.

The application of an inference structure requires the knowledge roles to be instantiated to entities from the domain. If necessary, inference functions and knowledge roles may be added or deleted. In this case, no alterations were required; the mapping is shown in Figure 10.5.

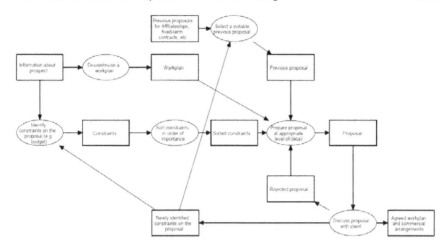

Figure 10.5: The processes involved in discussing a proposal
with a client

This study indicates that the proposed generic inference structure for propose-and-revise design can indeed be instantiated to a real-world design problem.

10.7 Knowledge Acquisition for propose-and-revise design

The process of instantiating a generic inference structure requires that knowledge acquisition is carried out which identifies the information required for each knowledge role. The information which must be acquired includes the domain entities and initial constraint which form the design problem, the contents of the model library, and the format of knowledge generated from these initial inputs.

The most obvious technique for acquiring knowledge for propose-and-revise design is to perform propose-and-revise design; this quickly provides a lot of useful knowledge, particularly about constraints. This technique has been used successfully in a number of knowledge based projects, by using "rapid prototyping" as a basis for knowledge acquisition. However, some information has to be gathered before an initial design can be produced; there may also be some benefit in reducing the number of times that solutions are presented to the client/expert, to avoid causing irritation, or to reduce the total time required for design. It therefore seems wise to devise techniques which can acquire as much knowledge as possible before presenting a solution to a client, and on each iterative loop thereafter.

The most obvious technique for acquiring knowledge for propose-and-revise design is to perform propose-and-revise design; this quickly provides a lot of useful knowledge, particularly about constraints. This technique has been used successfully in a number of knowledge based projects, by using "rapid prototyping" as a basis for knowledge acquisition. However, some information has to be gathered before an initial design can be produced; there may also be some benefit in reducing the number of times that solutions are presented to the client/expert, to avoid causing irritation, or to reduce the total time required for design. It therefore seems wise to devise techniques which can acquire as much knowledge as possible before presenting a solution to a client, and on each iterative loop thereafter.

This section presents some suggested techniques for knowledge acquisition, looking particularly at acquisition of constraints.

10.7.1 Knowledge Acquisition for constraints

According to the inference structure, a design problem can be described in terms of the constraints which are placed on the design, and the domain entities. It is rarely difficult to determine what the domain entities are (although the relationships between them may require a little more thought); many of the difficulties in design revolve around undetermined or underspecified constraints. Knowledge acquisition for a design problem is therefore primarily concerned with the acquisition of constraints.

Interviews

So how can constraints be acquired? An obvious method for acquiring knowledge of any sort is to perform interviews with experts in the field. While interviews have advantages, particularly at early stages of a knowledge engineering project, they also have considerable disadvantages, particularly in the elicitation of tacit knowledge. Many designers find it easier to work on refining an actual design rather than attempting to analyse every constraint, and many design faults are due to unidentified constraints; it follows that many constraints on design problems are either within the designer's mind but unexpressed, or within the problem but unnoticed. These constraints can therefore be classified as tacit knowledge. While it is possible that structured interviews may have value at later stages of the knowledge acquisition process (for example, a designer may be asked to critique a written list of constraints), it seems that knowledge engineers will need to rely on techniques other than interviews in order to acquire constraints successfully.

The Problem Identification Game

For the early stages of constraint acquisition, Lawson [111] suggests the "Problem Identification Game" which was devised at the Open University as an aid to identifying constraints. The 'game' requires designers to start by making a short and simple statement of the design problem as a contrasting pair; an example might be "slum clearance – aged slum dwellers". Next, designers are asked to amplify this statement by considering the following principles:

- Conflict - convert the statement into interested parties who might be viewed as in conflict. For example, "Town planners see a need for change and renewal which is not necessarily appreciated by the aged who have lived in the area all their lives";
- Contradiction - trying to contradict an earlier statement by taking an opposing viewpoint (e.g. "slum clearance – old people need safety & hygiene");
- Complication - identify any factors which should really have been considered when making a previous statement e.g. "Old folk need modern housing because they need safety & hygiene" is subject to the complication "But modernisation usually means increased rent charges";
- Similarity - try to think of, and then think through, an analogous situation (e.g. slum clearance is to housing as a plough is to a field; the process of slum clearance destroys previous street patterns, but opens up the area for new growth);
- Chance - pick a word from a dictionary and see if it sparks any new ideas. For example, the word "softly" might suggest soft music which in turn leads to a consideration of the difficulties of moving grand pianos and other accumulated furniture into modern housing.

It is usually a simple task to extract constraints from these statements, although further analysis may have be done on the degree to which the constraints can be relaxed and the cost of relaxing them. For example, two constraints which can be extracted from the example given above are "Old folk prefer large housing to accommodate their possessions" and "Old folk prefer low-rent housing". However, these two constraints are (usually) in opposition, and further analysis is needed to determine how resistant old people would be to giving up possessions in order to live in smaller housing, or how heavy the financial burden of large housing would be.

Multi-dimensional techniques

Once some constraints have been identified, it is also possible to elicit constraints using multi-dimensional knowledge elicitation techniques such as the *card sort* [152] and the *repertory grid* [93]. To use the card sort technique for acquiring constraints, the name of each constraint is written on an individual index card, and the designer is asked to sort the cards into piles, in any way which seems sensible. This technique is repeated several times, until the constraints have been classified in several different ways. The key step in eliciting constraints is to ask the designer, after each sort has been completed, if there are any other constraints which belong in the categories he has created, but which are not represented on cards. Despite its simplicity, card sorting has proved to be an effective technique in commercial projects.

The repertory grid is used in a similar fashion. The repertory grid technique identifies problem *elements* which have *constructs* (attributes).For constraint elicitation, constraints form the elements of the grid, and the designer is then presented with three constraints (chosen at random) and asked to state how two of them differ from the third. The designer's answer (e.g. "Two of these have a low impact on cost of the design, while one has a high impact") is taken to be an attribute of all constraints, and is defined as a construct. Each constraint is then assigned a value for this construct on a continuous scale. If the scale used for constructs is the same throughout the grid, and is numerical, then repertory grids can be subjected to statistical analysis which produces an implicit clustering of elements. This clustering can be discussed with the expert designer, with emphasis on unexpected assignment to clusters and the nature of the clusters themselves. As with the card sort, it is possible to enquire if any constraints which are not yet represented belong in the clusters.

Eliciting constraints by identifying incompatibilities in possible solutions

It is possible to use a variation of the repertory grid knowledge acquisition technique to analyse constraints, if possible solutions to the design problem (or parts of the design problem) can be defined.

Bradshaw [16] shows how "possibility grids" can be defined, in which possible solutions are assigned "goodness" values on a range of constraints. The grid is then analysed in terms of the "goodness values"; incompatible combinations of values are ruled out, and all other possible combinations are generated. If there is a combination of constraint values which does not match an existing design solution, then either a new possible solution has been found (if this combination is permissible), or a new constraint is elicited (if this combination is deemed unacceptable).

10.7.2 Knowledge Acquisition of model library

At first sight, it might appear that obtaining examples of previous designs would not be difficult. In practice, the situation is more complex. The problem lies in deciding how to represent designs within a library. Either the library will contain a large number of previous designs which must be indexed by some key design features in order to allow for efficient search through the library, or it will contain an abstracted set of "typical" designs, in which certain specific features of real-life designs are not represented.

In either case, it is crucial that the key factors which differentiate designs are defined carefully. The existence of differentiating factors implies an underlying classification scheme; however, there is no agreed classification for design tasks in general. As a result, key differentiating factors must be defined for each domain. This is a significant task in knowledge acquisition. It is possible that machine learning techniques, such as rule induction or neural networks, may be of assistance here, but little empirical work has been done to verify this.

10.7.3 Knowledge Acquisition of inference functions

The best way of acquiring knowledge about the various inference processes in a design task is likely to be highly domain-dependent. If there are a considerable number of procedural steps to be followed, however, then certain knowledge acquisition techniques such as protocol analysis, the laddered grid [152] or the "20 Questions" technique [24] may be useful. For an example of the use of these techniques, see [94].

10.8 Conclusion

This paper has demonstrated that an iterative approach to design which is termed "propose-and-revise design", is used by real-life designers. It is not used by all designers – sequential approaches to design are often used where they are feasible. The existing KADS library of generic inference structures provides a useful classification of techniques for sequential design. However, some designers clearly do use propose-and-revise design, and the library lacks an inference structure for propose-and-revise design. A suitable inference structure is therefore proposed, and tested in the field. Techniques for acquiring the knowledge required for propose-and-revise design are also suggested.

In order to introduce the subject of propose-and-revise design, this paper has given considerable space to discussion of the nature of design tasks. A key conclusion of this discussion is that design tasks can be classified at two levels of abstraction. At the higher level, design tasks can be classified as either sequential or iterative. At a lower level, sequential design tasks can be classified as hierarchical design, transformational design or incremental design. Iterative design tasks currently include propose-and-revise design only; it is possible that further research may produce more categories of iterative design which would help to expand the KADS library of inference structures even further.

The next chapter looks at knowledge acquisition techniques, and how (or whether) they can be used to acquire specific kinds of knowledge as recognised by CommonKADS.

11 Knowledge Acquisition techniques for the Expertise Model

11.1 Introduction

The major difference between knowledge engineering – the science of constructing knowledge-based software systems – and 'conventional' software engineering is the requirement for knowledge engineers to capture, represent, analyse and exploit knowledge in order to produce a successful system. Experience has shown that none of these tasks are simple; taking knowledge capture as an example, knowledge is typically only available within the head of an expert, or implicitly within written procedures or case records, and cannot be extracted from these sources without considerable effort. These difficulties have provided an incentive for the development of a variety of techniques to overcome the problems; techniques for knowledge capture, for example, are known as *knowledge acquisition* techniques. There is considerable literature proposing, analysing and advising on the use of knowledge acquisition techniques (e.g. [125]; [93]).

The task of *representing* the acquired knowledge in a format suitable for analysis is equally important for successful knowledge engineering; yet it has had a comparatively low profile. A number of different approaches have been suggested and used, including encoding the knowledge in a prototype knowledge based system (KBS); identifying and extracting rules within acquired knowledge (both "production rules" [65] and rules for qualitative simulation [110]); using "systemic grammar networks" [89]; and using semantic networks. Sometimes, more than one representation is used which suggests that no one representation is entirely adequate to represent acquired knowledge. It seems that there are different types of knowledge which are better suited to different representations.

The KADS methodology for developing knowledge-based systems has attempted to resolve the problem of adequate representation of acquired knowledge by suggesting that knowledge should be represented and analysed on several different levels simultaneously. KADS encourages the development of *models* of knowledge viewed from different perspectives; these models include hierarchies of domain concepts, "inference structures" which show the inferences required to perform a particular task, and "task structures" which impose procedural information on inference structures. CommonKADS, the recent successor to KADS, has extended and refined the recommended representations for each level, so that CommonKADS now provides a comprehensive suite of representations for the analysis of knowledge. In particular, CommonKADS has introduced a set of ontological primitives for domain knowledge which allows distinctions to be drawn between concepts, properties, relations, and other ontological types at the domain level. These recommendations, coupled with a library of generic templates for inference and task structures, have provided a workable and useful solution to the problem of representing acquired knowledge, with the result that CommonKADS is probably the most widely used methodology for KBS development in Europe.

However, there are no knowledge acquisition techniques which generate output in a form suitable for direct input into CommonKADS models. Instead, knowledge acquisition techniques typically produce textual transcripts, or classifications of domain terms on many different dimensions. This means that the knowledge engineer is required to identify relevant terms within the acquired knowledge, and to classify these manually into CommonKADS' ontology. This is an onerous task, even with the assistance of hypertext-based software support, such as the transcript editors available within ILOG's KADS Tool and Bull's Open KADS. The main difficulty lies in the fact that CommonKADS provides little guidance on how to identify relevant knowledge in a transcript, or to classify acquired knowledge into its ontology; such decisions are dependent on the expertise of the knowledge engineer.

It has been observed, however that the output generated by most knowledge acquisition techniques is not an unsorted jumble of items of knowledge; instead, the acquired knowledge is usually structured in one way or another. All knowledge acquisition techniques produce output which is structured to some degree; even the transcript of an interview is structured according to the rules of natural language. Knowledge acquisition which used to be viewed as the "mining" of chunks of knowledge, is now considered to be more like crystallography; the knowledge must be viewed from various viewpoints in order to determine how individual items of knowledge relate to each other. The implication here is that expert knowledge exists within a structure, and that the output of a knowledge acquisition technique may not reflect the whole structure, but it will reflect some of it. Experience suggests that it is important to discern the structure in order to understand fully the knowledge contained within it; indeed, it has been suggested that knowledge acquisition and subsequent modelling actually helps experts in a domain to develop and improve their own structuring that domain [63] which suggests that even the experts themselves find it useful to discern the structure of their knowledge.

The thesis of this paper is that it is possible to automate much of the identification and classification of domain knowledge by identifying and exploiting the structure of acquired knowledge. Some previous work has been done in this area, including the generation of production rules from a repertory grid (e.g [153]), and the production of a logical framework into which the results of card sorting, laddered grids and repertory grids can be written (cf. [139]). However, no one has yet attempted to make use of the structure of acquired knowledge to perform the classifications required for the CommonKADS ontology.

The purpose of this paper is to describe how such links were devised and implemented in a knowledge engineering toolkit, known as TOPKAT (The Open Practical Knowledge Acquisition Toolkit). The format of the paper is:
- A description of the implementation of TOPKAT;
- A description of the knowledge acquisition techniques which are implemented in TOPKAT;
- A description of the CommonKADS methodology (with particular emphasis on the domain knowledge in the expertise model);
- A description of the links between each knowledge acquisition technique and the CommonKADS classification system.

Figures 11.1 to 11.5 in this paper are drawn from applications modelled using TOPKAT.

11.2 Implementation of TOPKAT

TOPKAT is a hypertext and diagram-based toolkit which supports the acquisition of knowledge using various knowledge acquisition techniques, as well as supporting much of the CommonKADS modelling framework. TOPKAT has been implemented in CLIPS and in HARDY. HARDY [156] is a tool which uses node and link diagrams, hypertext and hyperlinks to allow the creation of graphical models representing many different processes and relationships. The key to HARDY's usefulness in this situation is the ability to define a *diagram type* which allows a system developer to define permitted nodes and arcs for a particular diagramming style; this means that HARDY can be used to produce modelling tools for a wide range of graphical formalisms with little effort. HARDY also provides an interface to CLIPS, allowing CLIPS functions to automate much of the functionality for diagram manipulation which is available interactively. HARDY is available on machines which support X Windows, Open Windows or Microsoft Windows.

TOPKAT consists of a hierarchy of hypercards which act as an index for the different facilities available. The "leaf cards" of the hierarchy each support a diagramming type suitable for a particular knowledge acquisition technique or CommonKADS model; the diagrams are drawn on newly created hypercards which are "instances" of the predefined card, and therefore share the same diagramming type. TOPKAT currently supports the following knowledge acquisition techniques:

- transcript analysis;
- laddered grid;
- card sort;
- repertory grid.

The support for transcript analysis is based on a hypertext card, rather than a diagram card with an appropriate diagram style. HARDY permits the development of a *hypertext type* in a similar fashion to a diagram type; this allows blocks of text, highlighted in appropriate fonts and colours, to be linked to diagram nodes or other hypertext blocks. This linking can be accomplished manually or (as in TOPKAT) it can be automated using CLIPS, so that complex linking operations can be executed with a few mouse clicks.

TOPKAT also provides support for representing the following elements of the CommonKADS Expertise Model:

- Domain Knowledge
    - Domain ontology
    - Domain models
    - Model ontology
    - Model schema
- Inference Knowledge
    - Inference structures
    - Library of inference structures
- Task Knowledge
    - Task structures

In addition, facilities exist within TOPKAT for representing parts of the CommonKADS Task Model, Communication Model and Design Model.

TOPKAT is currently being re-implemented in version 6.0 of CLIPS which permits full integration of object hierarchies with CLIPS' other facilities. This feature is being used to allow CLIPS objects to serve as a knowledge repository, with HARDY being used as a tool for visualising and manipulating that knowledge; this is achieved using a small set of event handlers (daemons) which create TOPKAT nodes or arcs to correspond to CLIPS instances or slot/value pairs, and another set of handlers which generate CLIPS whenever nodes or arcs are created in TOPKAT. This allows the functions within TOPKAT which perform verification, analysis and automated linking to be implemented entirely in CLIPS, thus increasing the portability of TOPKAT.

11.3 Techniques for knowledge acquisition

The most widely used method for knowledge acquisition has been the *interview* which, as the name implies, requires a knowledge engineer to interview an expert, and to record the entire conversation. This approach requires the knowledge engineer to transcribe the interview and analyse the transcript in order to identify and extract relevant items of knowledge. Transcript analysis does provide useful knowledge, and the transcript forms a good record of the source of that knowledge; however, transcript analysis is time-consuming, prone to generate much irrelevant information, and provides no guarantees about the completeness of the knowledge acquired [188]. Alternative methods for obtaining a transcript, such as performing carefully structured interviews, or asking the expert to talk through a case history (*protocol analysis*), have been developed to provide more structured transcripts; such transcripts alleviate the problems associated with transcript analysis, but do not remove them.

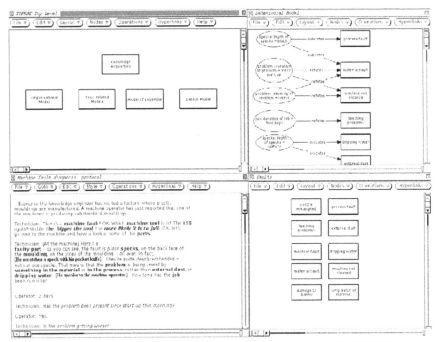

Figure 11.1: Screendump showing some of TOPKAT's hypercards

In order to overcome some of these problems, knowledge engineers have drawn on the field of psychology, and particularly on psychometric testing, to produce techniques such as the *card sort*, the *repertory grid* and the *laddered grid*. The benefits of these techniques are that they provide output in the form of categorisations and relationships; they ensure complete coverage of knowledge, by continual prompting or by requiring all items to be categorised; and they are relatively simple to administer. The repertory grid has been particularly well used, with over 150 applications to date having used this technique successfully [13].

11.3.1 Card Sort

The card sort is a simple but surprisingly effective technique in which an expert categorises cards which represent terms from the knowledge domain [152]. The names of various terms from the domain are written on individual index cards, and the expert is presented with the pile of cards and asked to sort them into piles in any way which seems sensible. When this has been accomplished, the classification of each card is noted, the cards are shuffled, and the expert is asked to repeat the procedure using a different criterion for sorting. This process is repeated until the expert cannot think of any more criteria on which to differentiate the cards.

Refinements to the procedure include sorting large piles into several smaller piles; and asking the expert to name any domain terms which could be in a pile but are not represented on a card. The output of the card sort is a set of classifications of domain terms into one or more categories on many different dimensions.

Figure 11.2 shows the result of a single categorisation of a set of 'cards' representing vehicles. In TOPKAT, the 'cards' are sorted into columns rather than piles; the columns are created by creating an (invisible) arc between the 'card' and its category which updates the list of 'cards' in the category, as well as moving the 'card' into the appropriate column.

11.3.2 Repertory Grid

The repertory grid is a technique derived from psychotherapy in which an expert makes distinctions between terms in the domain on chosen criteria [15]. The criteria are similar to the categories generated by card sorting, except that they are all assumed to be continuous variables; for example, "price" would be a suitable distinction for a repertory grid, because all prices lie on a continuous numeric scale between zero and infinity, whereas "nationality" would not be suitable. Criteria are usually generated by the 'triadic' technique – selecting three domain terms at random and asking the expert to name one way in which two of them differ from the third. All domain terms in the grid are then classified on each criterion (normally using a 1-5 or 1-7 scale), resulting in a grid in which every term is categorised on every variable (see Figure 11.3).

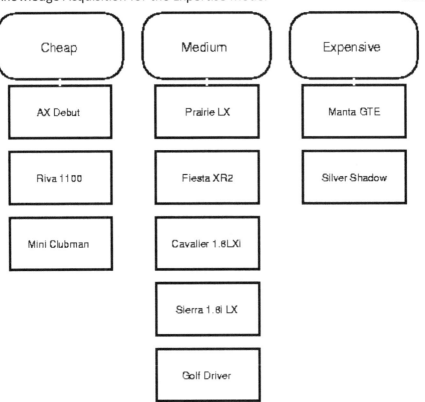

Figure 11.2: A set of cards representing vehicles, sorted by price

One of the features of the repertory grid which sets it apart from other knowledge acquisition techniques is that the classifications in the grid can be analysed statistically, using cluster analysis, to see if the expert has implicitly categorised the terms in any way. The clustering of concepts produced by statistical analysis of the repertory grid is normally represented by a *dendogram* (literally, a tree diagram), in which every domain term is a leaf node, and closeness in the 'tree' represents statistical similarity. However, dendograms often require some interpretation and rationalisation by an expert in order to be meaningful; also, a dendogram bears a considerable resemblance to a taxonomic hierarchy. TOPKAT makes use of these two observations to represent the statistical clustering as a laddered grid, in which the domain terms form the leaf nodes, and the "classes" indicate the level of similarity between domain terms using a percentage value (100%

indicates the two objects are identical on all the dimensions, 0% indicates that they are at opposite ends of the spectrum on every

	Crimes	Pilfering	Theft	Drug taking	Murder	Assault	Rape	Fraud	Speeding
1 = only men / 5 = only women	sex-specificity	4	3	3	3	3	5	3	2
1 = Too long / 5 = Too short	Severity of punishment	3	1	1	2	3	5	3	4
1 = Sensational / 5 = Common	Frequency	3	5	1	1	4	5	4	5
1 = Premeditated / 5 = Casual	Forethought	5	3	1	2	5	4	1	5
1 = Pleasureable / 5 = Nasty	Pleasure for victim	2	2	1	5	5	5	2	4
1 = Nonpersonal / 5 = Personal	Personal nature	2	2	1	5	4	5	2	1
1 = Petty / 5 = Major	Seriousness	1	3	1	5	4	5	4	1
1 = Nonviolent / 5 = Violent	Violence	1	1	2	5	4	5	1	1
1 = Full / 5 = None	Possibility of restitution	1	1	2	5	4	5	1	5
1 = Very small / 5 = Very large	Benefit to perpetrator	2	3	2	3	2	1	5	1

Figure 11.3: A repertory grid classifying crimes

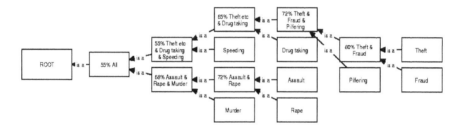

Figure 11.4: A statistical analysis showing an implicit categorisation of crimes

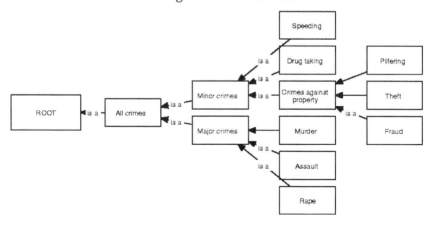

Figure 11.5: The hierarchy of crimes shown in Figure 11.4,
after being rationalised

dimension). The expert and/or the knowledge engineer is then allowed
to rationalise this laddered grid by assigning meaningful names to some
classes and deleting others. For example, Figure 11.4 shows statistical
similarity of crimes (derived from the repertory grid shown in Figure
11.3), and Figure 11.5 shows a rationalised version of this hierarchy.

11.3.3 Laddered Grid
The laddered grid uses pre-defined questions to persuade an
expert to expand a taxonomic hierarchy to its fullest extent [24].
Starting with a single domain term, the questions can elicit
superclasses, subclasses or members of classes which are linked to the
existing object in a hierarchical "grid". Typical questions include "What
is *term* and example of?", or "What other examples of *term 1* are there
apart from *term 2*?". By repeatedly applying the same procedure to
newly elicited objects, an extensive taxonomy can be built up.

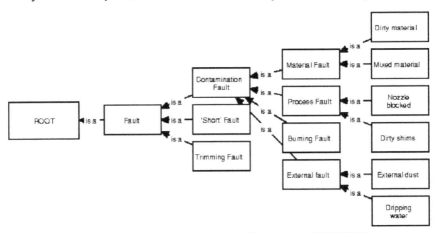

Figure 11.6: Taxonomy diagram in TOPKAT

11.4 Mapping acquired knowledge to the domain level

It can be seen from the previous two sections that the four
knowledge acquisition techniques which are supported by TOPKAT
produce output in differing formats, some of which are similar to

certain aspects of CommonKADS modelling, and some of which are not. The task of the knowledge engineer is to transfer knowledge from the format produced by the knowledge acquisition technique to the formats required for CommonKADS. TOPKAT provides functions for each knowledge acquisition technique to support this transfer process: the functionality is based on the structure provided by the knowledge acquisition technique, and on experience of developing CommonKADS models. The functionality provided is described below.

11.4.1 Transcript analysis according to word class

Textual transcripts differ from the output of the other knowledge acquisition techniques supported by TOPKAT in that they rarely produce knowledge which is obviously structured in a taxonomic or relational manner. Despite this, transcripts are by far the most widely available form of acquired knowledge; they may be produced from interviews, protocol analysis, or scanning of existing documentation. Of course, language has a structure of its own; words are classified as different *word classes* (parts of speech) which may only appear in particular combinations permitted by the rules of grammar. Is it possible to make use of the grammatical structure of language to perform ontological classification?

The starting point for this discussion is Woods' linguistic test [195]. In the course of a discussion on the nature of links in semantic networks, Woods asserts that, given an object O, it is possible to use a linguistic test to determine if A is an attribute of O. The test is that it must be possible to state that "V is the/an A of (some) O". If this test is passed, then in CommonKADS terminology, O is a concept, A is a property of that concept, and V is a value of that property. From a grammatical viewpoint, however, it can be seen that O must be a noun, A must be a singular noun, and V must be an adjective which modifies O. From this analysis, it seems that there is some connection between the CommonKADS ontology and word classes.

A second link between the CommonKADS domain ontology (concepts, properties, relations and expressions, as described in section 8.3) and word classes can be found in the definitions of the different ontological types within CommonKADS:

  • Concepts are classes which represent objects or states. The Shorter Oxford Dictionary defines nouns as "names of persons or things"; if it is assumed that all objects or states are "persons or things" in the "real or mental world of the domain" (cf. [191]), then it can be seen that all concepts can be named using nouns.

• Properties are attributes of concepts. It is difficult to assign attributes to particular word classes, because, while attributes can be represented as singular nouns (according to Woods' linguistic test), they may also be identified using plural nouns (e.g *instances*) or verbs (e.g. *has component*). Nor is the preposition "of" a universal indicator of a property: other prepositions may sometimes be used instead (e.g. O1 is *connected to* O2), and the word "of" may appear in idioms such as "a matter of course".

• Expressions are derived from a concept, a property, and a value. CommonKADS anticipates that values could be strings, numbers, Booleans, or of a domain-specific type; it is difficult to generalise about word classes which are associated with all these types, although it can be seen that certain specific categories of words (such as nouns or adjectives describing numbers) are likely to be associated with values.

• Relations form links between concepts in which one concept affects another. This is normally accomplished linguistically by a verb, and so it seems that a verb which links two objects or states probably indicates a relation. The identification of verbs with relations is further supported by the correspondence between adverbs and CommonKADS' facility which allows relations to have properties of their own; if relations correspond to verbs, then adverbs represent (values of) properties of relations. For example, in the sentence "Peter married Jane yesterday", the adverb (*yesterday*) is a property of the *marry* relation.

From these analyses, it seems that identification of nouns, adjectives, verbs, and the words which they modify (if any) can provide a great deal of information for ontological classification in CommonKADS. There is therefore considerable potential for automated classification if a textual transcript can be parsed (providing grammatical information), or at least lexically tagged, so that the word class of each word is known. TOPKAT uses the analyses above to support semi-automatic classification, in the following manner:

• A textual transcript is written to a file;

• The file is lexically tagged, using a free tagging package;

• TOPKAT re-reads the resulting file to determine the word classes of each word in the transcript.

Once this has been performed, TOPKAT offers the user the options of identifying concepts and properties in the transcript, by:

- Collecting all nouns in the transcript into a list (classifying any instances of two adjacent nouns as a single compound noun);
- Sorting the nouns according to their frequency of occurrence in the transcript, compared with their expected frequency in everyday English. Nouns which appear much more frequently than expected are placed at the head of the list, on the basis that these nouns are more likely to represent domain-specific concepts. Three measures of expected frequency are used (two based on written frequency and one on spoken frequency); an average likelihood from all three measures is used.
- Presenting the list of nouns to the knowledge engineer, and asking which nouns represent concepts that are relevant to problem solving.
- Identifying any adjectives which immediately precede concepts in the transcript, and using a question based on Woods' linguistic test to name the property associated with that adjective.

This approach has been used successfully to produce the classification shown in Figure 11.8. Two features of this approach to classification are immediately obvious: firstly that it is highly interactive; and secondly that it is based on a pragmatic but simple approach to natural language understanding which means that it is vulnerable to errors in lexical tagging and in adjective/noun pairing.

Technician: Here's a *faulty* part – as you can see, the <u>fault</u> is *black* <u>specks</u>, on the *back* <u>face</u> of the <u>moulding</u>, on the sides of the moulding – all over, in fact. [He scratches a speck with his <u>pocket knife</u>]. They're quite deeply embedded – not surface <u>specks</u>. That means that the problem is being caused by something in the <u>material</u> or in the <u>process</u>, rather than *external* <u>dust</u>, or *dripping* <u>water</u>. [He speaks to the machine operator]. How long has the <u>job</u> been running?

Key: **Concepts** are <u>underlined</u>; **Properties** are in *italics*.

Figure 11.7: Transcript classified using semi-automatic natural language analysis

The key to the success of TOPKAT's approach is that these two features balance each other out. Much of the work which has been carried out on understanding natural language has attempted to analyse language with maximum accuracy and minimum human intervention; despite the high level of sophistication of some systems, it has proved very difficult to comprehend language unambiguously without considerable use of general knowledge which is difficult to encode. TOPKAT's natural language capabilities, however, are complemented by the domain knowledge and general knowledge of the knowledge engineer using the system which enables an accurate and largely complete classification to be produced; while for the knowledge engineer, providing guidance to TOPKAT is much less effort than performing transcript analysis without assistance.

TOPKAT thus makes use of the structure of language to identify appropriate mappings between acquired knowledge and CommonKADS domain modelling. While the state of natural language technology does not permit exhaustive identification of ontological types in a transcript using automated analysis, the guidance which is provided is much more useful than simply being presented with a transcript and asked to identify and classify fragments of text. The usefulness of this technique was verified during a training course in which students were asked to identify concepts, properties and relations in a transcript similar to the one shown in Figure 11.5.1. Despite the availability of software support for hyperlinking text fragments to items of domain knowledge, the students spent well over an hour on the task without finishing it. When the semi-automatic classification of TOPKAT was demonstrated during the course, the classification process was completed in 6-7 minutes.

11.4,2 Laddered grid: from one taxonomy to another

The output of the laddered grid technique is a taxonomic hierarchy of domain objects. It is taxonomic because the prompt questions which are used should only generate examples or subclasses of other domain terms[40]; the domain terms are assumed to be objects which are capable of possessing subclasses or examples.

---

[40] The laddered grid technique can also be used with different sets of prompt questions, in which case the taxonomic assumption will not apply. TOPKAT currently only supports prompt questions which will generate a taxonomic laddered grid.

On the basis of this structure, each term in the laddered grid is classified as a *concept* in the CommonKADS domain ontology, and the entire laddered grid is mapped to a taxonomic *domain model* at the CommonKADS domain level.

11.4.3 Card sort: when is a property not a property?

The card sort produces a number of domain *terms* which are classified into different *categories* on a number of *dimensions*. It can be seen that the categories supplied for each dimension form a range of possible values for that dimension; this correlates closely with the relationship between properties and values, and so it seems likely that dimensions will map to properties in the CommonKADS domain ontology, and categories will map to values of those properties. Furthermore, it can be seen that the dimensions must be properties of the domain terms which implies that, as in the laddered grid, the domain terms should be mapped to concepts.

TOPKAT uses the information listed above to map all domain terms into concepts in the CommonKADS domain ontology. However, it turns out that dimensions cannot be uniformly classified as properties. The reason for this is that the flexibility of the card sorting technique; the expert is simply asked to "sort the cards in any way which seems sensible". The resulting dimensions might differentiate the cards in several ways.

For example, if knowledge acquisition was being performed to learn about the task of maintaining a zoo, then a card sort might be performed with the name of a zoo animal on each card. The resulting card sorts might include:

- A sort according to the animals' lifespan, with categories such as "short", "average" and "long". In this case, *lifespan* can safely be assumed to be a property of each animal;
- A sort according to the genus of the animals (reptiles, mammals, etc). This is clearly a *taxonomic* classification of animals;
- A sort according to the zoo collection to which animals belong which may include categories such as "monkey house" or "children's corner". In this case, the animals are considered as *part* of a particular collection which in turn is part of the zoo's overall population. This constitutes a hierarchical (though non-taxonomic) classification of animals.

It can be seen from the above example that dimensions cannot simply be mapped to properties in the CommonKADS domain ontology without further investigation. The approach taken in TOPKAT to classification of dimensions is to ask the knowledge engineer some questions about each sort which help to determine the appropriate classification for that sort. These questions enable the knowledge engineer to make key distinctions between different subtypes of property, including the identification of taxonomic relationships and *part* relationships within card sorts.

TOPKAT's guidance starts by obtaining a name for the property. The name is obtained by asking a question based on Woods' linguistic test (see section 11.5.1). Using the card sort shown in Figure 11.2 as an example, the question derived from Woods' linguistic test would be:

`Cheap is the/a WHAT of Mini?`

which is generated by selecting one card (**Mini**) from the first category (**Cheap**) and instantiating a template question with these two values. Wood's linguistic test is useful in enforcing discipline on the naming of properties, by preventing names with prepositions (*connected-to*), verbs (*is-needed*) or plurals *instances*); instead, these names must be transformed into equivalent singular nouns (such as *connection*, *acquisition procedure* and *instance*). This naming discipline helps to standardise the properties which are created, and the effort of finding a suitable name may also lead to new insights about the conceptual structure of the domain [76].

Once the prospective property has been named, it is necessary to determine whether it really is a property. This is achieved in TOPKAT by asking further questions of the knowledge engineer. The questions are derived from a semi-formal approach to classification emerging from the Italian National Project on Hybrid Systems [76]; they not only determine whether the prospective property is genuinely a property, but they also introduce a sub-classification of properties. [41] This classification is illustrated in Figure 11.8.

It can be seen from Figure 11.9 that classification depends on determining:

---

[41] All the types of "property" described in this section (roles, qualities, and parts) can also be considered as concepts in their own right; Guarino's discussion is phrased in terms of concepts and attributes. This is de-emphasised in this paper, however, to avoid confusion with the CommonKADS domain ontology.

• Whether the prospective property is *founded* or *essentially independent*. A property is considered to be founded if it can only exist if its accompanying concept also exists; for example, the *price* of a car is founded, but the *wheel* of a car is essentially independent, because the wheel can exist even if the car does not exist. The foundedness of a prospective property is determined by asking " Can the/an *property* of *concept* exist if (the/an) *concept* does not exist?"; for example, `Can the/an Nationality of Mini exist even if (the/a) Mini does not exist?`

• Whether the property is *semantically rigid* or not. A property is semantically rigid if it is a necessary condition for the identity of its value; for example, *colour* is semantically rigid, because **red** must be a colour in order to exist, but *driver* is not semantically rigid, since **Fred** does not necessarily have to be a driver of a car in order to exist.

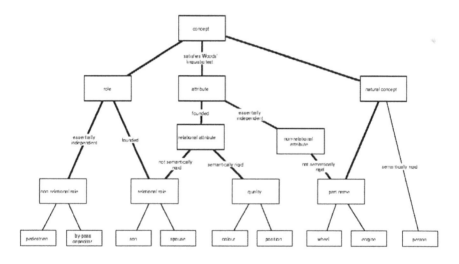

Figure 11.8: Ontology of attributes (from [76])

Developing a suitable question to determine semantic rigidity is not as simple as it first appears. For example, the template "Is *value* necessarily a *property*?" should elicit the correct answer (`No`) when instantiated with **Wheel** and **Part**; it should also elicit the correct answer when instantiated with **Fred** and **Person**. It is therefore suitable for distinguishing between part names and natural concepts (which may, despite Woods' linguistic test, occasionally occur as property names). However, it is likely to obtain the wrong answer (No) when instantiated with **Short** and **Lifespan**, because **Short** is a possible value of many properties. It is possible to circumvent this problem by making use of another of Guarino's observations: that the values of qualities (which are semantically rigid) can be considered as predicates, whereas the values of roles (which are not semantically rigid) can be described as instances of the property. On the basis of this, the question which was devised for distinguishing between relational roles and qualities was "Is *value* an instance of *property*, or a predicate describing the value of *property*?". For example,

```
Is   Fred   an   instance   of   Driver,   or   a
predicate describing the value of Driver?
```

TOPKAT therefore asks if a dimension is founded, and then asks the appropriate question to determine semantic rigidity. On the basis of the answers to these two questions, a property can be classified into Guarino's suggested ontology of attributes. If a property is defined as a relational role or a quality, then it is simply added to CommonKADS' domain ontology as a property; if it is a part name, a **part** relation is created in an appropriate domain model; and if it is a natural concept, then a taxonomic hierarchy is created, in which each category is linked to the dimension by a subclass link. For example, cars could be classified according to their manufacturer; the manufacturer of a car can exist even if the car does not exist (assuming that car is not their only product), and Vauxhall (for example) is necessarily a manufacturer. **Manufacturer** is therefore a natural concept; TOPKAT's response to this situation is to define **Manufacturer** as a concept, and then define each category (i.e. each manufacturer) to be a subclass of *Manufacturer*.

Non-relational roles (such as *pedestrian* or *by-pass capacitor*) should be filtered out by Wood's linguistic test.

11.4.4 Repertory grid: assigning meaning to numbers

The repertory grid technique produces two outputs. The first is the repertory grid itself which is a two-dimensional table in which domain terms (elements) are assigned numeric values on several dimensions (constructs). The second is the statistical clustering produced by comparing these numbers. It has already been seen (in section 11.3.2) that the statistical clustering bears some resemblance to a laddered grid; in order to produce a meaningful hierarchy, the "classes" which represent statistical closeness must be interpreted as representing semantic closeness, or as irrelevant, and the hierarchy must be updated accordingly. TOPKAT currently handles this task by asking the knowledge engineer and/or the expert to perform it.

Once the hierarchy has been rationalised, TOPKAT treats it as if it were a laddered grid. The domain terms (which appear in the repertory grid and in the statistical clustering) are therefore mapped to concepts in the CommonKADS domain ontology, and the (rationalised) statistical clustering is converted into a taxonomic domain model.

Having decided that the domain terms which appear in the repertory grid should be mapped to concepts, it is necessary to decide how the dimensions and the accompanying numeric values should be treated. Dimensions in the repertory grid are restricted to be continuous variables which makes it likely that the majority of them will be *qualities* in Guarino's classification. However, it is possible that binary dimensions will be introduced (e.g. whether a crime is or is not a felony); such dimensions may well represent relational roles, taxonomic hierarchies or part hierarchies, and so the two questions used to determine the correct classification of card sorts must be used again to classify dimensions accurately.

Before the property classification questions can be asked, however, the numeric values in the repertory grid must be translated into textual values. While numeric values are acceptable as values of properties, they are not very informative outside the context of the repertory grid, and numbers make little sense when instantiated into the property classification questions. TOPKAT makes use of the observation that most dimensions in the repertory grid are continuous to generate text which corresponds to each value; this text is based on the name of the dimension, and the names of the poles (low and high values) assigned by the knowledge engineer. The knowledge engineer is then prompted to edit that text until satisfied with it. Using the repertory grid shown in Figure 11.3 as an example, TOPKAT will generate the following text for the *Frequency* dimension:

1.Sensational
2.Fairly Sensational
3.Average Frequency
4.Fairly Common

5.Common

This text will then be used in the property classification questions; so the knowledge engineer will be asked:

```
Can the/an Frequency of Theft exist even if
Theft does not exist?
```

and

```
Is Sensational an instance of Frequency, or a
predicate describing the value of Frequency?
```

The answers to these questions should be "No" and "Predicate" respectively which classifies Frequency as a quality.

The repertory grid can also be used to generate a large number of *expressions* in the CommonKADS domain ontology – one expression for each numeric value in the grid. These expressions could be used as individual conditions of production rules which is the principle used by tools such as KITTEN and NEXTRA to derive rules from repertory grids [153].

11.5 Summary

It can be seen that all the knowledge elicitation techniques supported by TOPKAT produce output which consists not only of knowledge, but of a structure within which knowledge is stored. The output of these knowledge elicitation techniques can be used to generate concepts, properties, expressions, relations, and even domain models directly, with only occasional assistance from the knowledge engineer.

There are many opportunities for future work on improving the linking of knowledge elicitation techniques to CommonKADS knowledge analysis

• For the card sort, the classification of properties into relational roles, qualities, *part* relations and natural concepts could be extended by using the *mereology* (classification scheme for *part* relations) suggested in [70].

• For the card sort and the repertory grid, Woods' linguistic test could be used when dimensions are created. While this might restrict the breadth of the acquired knowledge, it should produce a more coherent set of dimensions which is particularly important in the repertory grid where dimensions are compared against one another. The effort of finding a correct name would also be transferred from the knowledge engineer to the expert by this technique which may lead to further knowledge acquisition as the expert reconsiders the conceptual structure of his knowledge.

- For transcript analysis, there are many possible improvements:
    - Use a chart parser to obtain linguistic information, permitting extensive automatic identification of properties, and perhaps of relations;
    - Feed back linguistic information obtained from a knowledge engineer to the parser or lexical tagger, to improve accuracy;
    - Define and apply a "coding schema" [189] – a set of phrases which are known to indicate the presence of certain ontological types;
    - Use questionnaires or structured interviews to obtain highly structured transcripts which are written in simple declarative sentences. It should be possible to parse these transcripts and classify the knowledge contained therein without human intervention (see [86]).

- For knowledge in the inference and task levels of CommonKADS, define a mapping between knowledge acquisition techniques which acquire procedural knowledge (such as protocol analysis, or the "20 Questions" technique [152]) and CommonKADS inference steps and primitive tasks. TOPKAT already supports a simple decision tree editor.

There is one final CommonKADS model to be considered: the Design model. This is discussed in the next chapter.

12 CommonKADS: Design Modelling

12.1 Introduction

The problem of designing a knowledge based system well is one of the most complex problems that knowledge engineers face. When knowledge based systems are developed by rapid prototyping, good design relies on the knowledge engineer's programming skills, and on his ability to devise, remember, and dynamically update a design specification. This is a difficult task for all but the smallest knowledge based systems, especially if the system intermixes expert knowledge with system control operations.[42] It is possible for the system to get out of control so that even its author cannot understand why apparently small changes have large effects on the overall system.

These problems can be alleviated by producing representations of the expert's knowledge and of the design specification in the form of text or diagrams, thus documenting the expert's knowledge and the important design decisions independently of the system. CommonKADS recommends such an approach, derived from its Expertise Model which models expert problem solving in three components: domain (declarative) knowledge, inference (procedural) knowledge and task (control) knowledge.

The responsibility for representing design decisions is passed to the CommonKADS Design Model. The Expertise Model is intended to represent knowledge at a level of abstraction which is independent of implementation; it neither allows representation of, nor gives guidance on, decisions about which programming techniques to use in order to represent the acquired knowledge.

---

[42] (MYCIN did this; and this was a primary reason for the failure of the GUIDON system which attempted to "teach back" MYCIN's knowledge to users [81].

The Design Model was specified towards the end of the CommonKADS project [180]; apart from a worked example produced by the project team [150], little or nothing has been published describing its use in realistic applications. The purpose of this chapter is to describe the CommonKADS Design Model, including sources of guidance for making design decisions. The chapter illustrates the use of the Design Model by reverse engineering two existing KBS systems to show how the CommonKADS Design Model would have applied to them. The example systems are the same ones which were described in chapter 8.

12.2 The CommonKADS Design Model

The CommonKADS Design Model is intended to support knowledge engineers in choosing knowledge representations and programming techniques in order to produce a good design of a KBS system. It aims to do this in a way which is both generic (i.e. platform-independent for as long as possible), and economical (it encourages preservation of the structures within the expertise model). It also makes use of the CommonKADS Communication Model (see chapter 6) as a source for user interface requirements.

The Design Model supports selection of representations and techniques by encouraging the designer to start with the knowledge contained in an expertise model, and to perform a three-stage transformation process in order to produce design recommendations.

These three stages are:
- *Application design*: choosing an overall approach to design decomposition;
- *Architectural design*: choosing ideal knowledge representation and programming techniques;
- *Platform design*: deciding how to implement the recommended techniques in the chosen software.

12.2.1 Application Design

The application design is the first of these three stages. The purpose of application design is to decompose the knowledge into manageable "chunks". The size and content of each chunk depends on

the approach to decomposition which is used. Broadly speaking, three approaches to decomposition are available:
- Functional decomposition;
- Object-oriented decomposition;
- Various AI paradigms.

Functional decomposition involves treating each *inference step* from the Expertise Model as being a "chunk" of functionality. Functional decomposition is therefore a *structure-preserving* approach to design, because the form of the inference structure is maintained in the design specification. The benefits of this are that the KBS will replicate the expert's problem solving process (or whatever process was modelled in the inference structure); any inference step that is identified as a canonical inference (see [2]) will have its expected functionality clearly defined; and perhaps most important of all, preserving the inference structure usually preserves the task structure from the Expertise Model as well. The task structure is very important for KBS design because it provides a semi-formal specification of the required flow of control for knowledge based processing, while the Design Model recommends only a high-level textual description. Knowledge engineers therefore need to use both the Design Model and the task structure as a specification for KBS implementation.

Object-oriented decomposition treats each *concept* from the domain model as being a "chunk" of information - i.e. each concept is treated as an object class. Since concepts have properties with values, and relationships with other concepts, it's often helpful to represent concepts as objects in object-oriented design. Object-oriented decomposition preserves the structure of the domain models in the expertise model; indeed,

CommonKADS domain modelling can be seen as a generalisation of object oriented data modelling [88]. Preserving the inference and task structures is harder in object-oriented design, though some benefits can be obtained by considering the inference structure to be broadly equivalent to the Object Management Technique's Functional model, while the task model is compared with OMT's Dynamic model. Individual rules can, if necessary, be represented in the domain models using *expressions*; see section 8.3 for a description of these.

Another option for knowledge engineer is to decide that an "AI paradigm" – a well-known approach to AI problem solving – is appropriate. Possible AI paradigms might include blackboard systems; constraint-based programming; qualitative simulation; or model-based reasoning. In this case, the "chunks" of knowledge may be constraints, knowledge sources, cause-and-effect rules or whatever is appropriate for the chosen approach. If an AI paradigm is chosen, it may be that little of the structure of the Expertise model will be maintained. In practice, this means that the knowledge engineer will either have identified the likelihood of an AI paradigm being appropriate earlier in the development process, and will have customised the Expertise model accordingly, or AI paradigms will be considered unfavourably because of the extra effort required to re-analyse the knowledge. Exceptions to this heuristic would be the use of a blackboard architecture (where only the task structure of the Expertise Model needs to be revised) or the use of an AI paradigm for a system subcomponent e.g. model-based simulation to perform diagnostic tests on a system, under the overall control of a diagnostic inference structure.

Once decomposition has been performed, it's necessary to characterise the contents of each "chunk" in a way that specifies further design requirements. For example, if functional decomposition has been performed, it's helpful to designate the operation being performed by each inference step in the form of an *architectural command* – a "function name" which describes the action which the function performs. Typical operations might be *subset*, *get-property-value*, or *calculate*. As mentioned above, the definitions of canonical inference steps in the CommonKADS expertise model may be helpful in defining appropriate architectural commands; for example, an inference step of type *select-subset* is very likely to be implemented by a *subset* operation. This process also helps validate the Expertise Model; if the architectural command differs significantly from the inference step definition, then a possible error in labelling or understanding the inference structure has been highlighted. A full set of possible architectural commands has not been published, but a suggested BNF for these commands is given in [150], and knowledge engineers are encouraged to use this to help them develop their own set of commands.

12.2.2 Architectural Design

The task of architectural design is to define a computational infrastructure capable of implementing all the architecture commands defined in the application design. It is at this stage that the preferred knowledge representation and programming techniques are selected.

Knowledge representations available to knowledge engineers typically include objects, facts, and production rules, as well as more "conventional" representations such as tables or arrays. Many *programming techniques* are available including data- and goal-driven reasoning, truth maintenance, meta-rules, and various search strategies. The architectural commands specified during the previous phase provide guidance to the knowledge engineer on which representations and techniques are appropriate; for example, a *get-property-value* operation specifies a preference for objects as a knowledge representation technique, because properties are an essential feature of objects. The emphasis in this phase is on choosing *ideal* techniques; the appropriateness of these for the available software tool should be considered in the next phase. In practice, most knowledge engineers know which tool they will be using when this phase is performed, and so will not select representations or techniques which will be impossible to implement; this phase is still useful, however, in assessing the appropriateness of the chosen tool or the chosen AI paradigm.

It is at this stage of design that the experience of a knowledge engineer can be brought to bear in making good design decisions. If the knowledge engineer knows that a particular technique or representation has proved suitable (or otherwise) for a similar problem in the past, then a knowledge engineer can use this information to guide his choices. There have been some attempts to capture and encode this knowledge for the use of less experienced knowledge engineers; it turns out that there are a large number of features of knowledge based problems which affect the choice of representations and techniques, so many that an entire book has been filled with *probing questions*. Probing questions ask if certain features are present in a knowledge-based problem, and suggest suitable functionality based on that feature. An example of a probing question is given below:

```
On average, do we know five or more new
facts about a domain object simply by being told
that it is of type X?
    OR
```

```
          Are    these    new    facts    not    known    with
certainty, but assumed unless there is evidence
to the contrary?
          Yes →Place the object in a data structure
(e.g. frames, semantic nets or objects) whose
inheritance mechanism will provide the facts
when needed, and whose default values will be
assumed unless an exception is specifically
asserted.
          No →Assert the new facts explicitly which
is a 'cheap' solution.
```

Kline & Dolins' book [104] contains probing questions based on successful AI systems up to the time of publication. AIAI has done some further knowledge acquisition and system development in this area (see appendix D), but there is a need for more research and development of probing questions to keep pace with new technologies and techniques.

12.2.3 Platform Design

The final phase of the CommonKADS Design Model considers how (or whether) the ideal knowledge representations and inference techniques should be implemented in the chosen software. Most modern KBS tools support both objects and rules, so knowledge representation is rarely a problem. However, some programming techniques can be awkward to implement; for example, implementing data-driven reasoning in a tool which primarily supports backward chaining. The restrictions of the tool may mean that a different programming technique needs to be used.

12.3 Worked Example 1: IMPRESS

The use of the CommonKADS Design Model will be demonstrated with two worked examples – IMPRESS which diagnoses faults in plastic moulding machinery, and X-MATE which assesses the risk of mortgage applicants failing to make repayments. These two projects have been chosen because their expertise models have been described in some detail in chapter 8.[43]

IMPRESS (the Injection Moulding Process Expert System) diagnoses the causes of faults in plastic injection mouldings. Given data about the type of fault (e.g. "black specks in the moulding"), IMPRESS considers all possible causes of the fault, suggests tests for the system user (a technician or machine operator) to perform on the system, and iterates through a cycle of test-discard hypotheses-suggest tests until there is only one hypothesis left.

12.3.1 IMPRESS: Application Design

No AI paradigms appeared to have overriding advantages for IMPRESS, so the choice of application design became a choice between functional and object-oriented decomposition. A few relations had been identified at the domain level, and a detailed inference structure with a little extra procedural ordering information had also been developed, so there was more detail in the inference structure than in the domain models.

It was decided to break down the expertise model using functional decomposition i.e. to preserve the inference structure which is shown in Figure 12.1. The chosen functions are described in Table 12.3.1. It can be seen from the architectural commands that IMPRESS requires a *subset* operation, where a set (of possible fault states) is reduced to a smaller set which are compatible with all observed symptoms and measurements; several *get-property-value* operations which obtain values such as the expected value of an observable if a particular hypothesis is true; a *sort* of tests according to the time required to undertake them; a *transfer task* which asks a user to perform a test which will observe or measure some relevant parameter of the machine, and to report the measured value to IMPRESS; and a *match-2* operation (a match between 2 values) to compare an observed measurement against the expected value of that observable in each fault state.

---

[43] The initial development of these systems pre-date CommonKADS, and so the design models used in these projects have been reverse engineered, to show how the decisions which were actually taken during system design would have been represented if a CommonKADS design model had been developed.

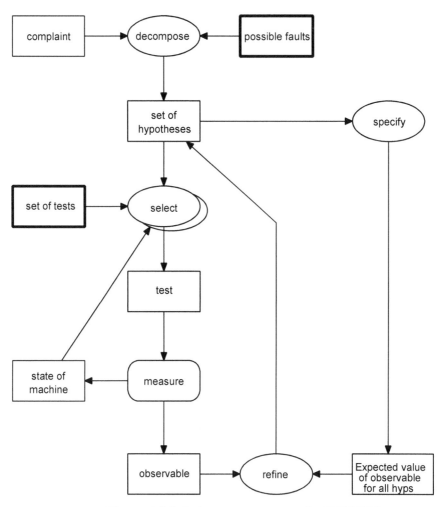

Figure 12.1: Inference structure for IMPRESS

An observation on this mapping is that the *decompose* inference step in IMPRESS is mapped to a *subset* operation, whereas CommonKADS' definitions of canonical inference actions suggests that *decompose* requires replacing a single concept with a set of its component concepts. The reason for this difference is discussed in chapter 18.

Inference step	Function	Arguments
decompose	subset	:set all-faults :set hypotheses :key symptom
specify	get-property	:concept hypothesis :property expected-value :key observable
select	get-property	:concept hypothesised-fault :property distinguishing-observables
	subset	:set all-tests :set discriminating-tests :key distinguishing-observables
	get-property	:concept test :property time-required
	sort	:set discriminating-tests :key time-required
measure	Transfer Task	
refine	get-property	:concept hypothesised-fault :property expected-value :key test
	match	:element observed-value :element expected-value
	subset	:set hypotheses :set remaining-hypotheses :key difference

Table 12.1: Application Design for IMPRESS

12.3.2 Architectural Design

It should be noted here that a functionally decomposed Design model actually consists of three diagrams; one for the inference steps, one for the knowledge roles, and one for the communication transactions. Each of these reflects the three steps of application design, architectural design and platform design. The relevant diagrams for IMPRESS can be seen in Figures 12.2, 12.3 and 12.4.

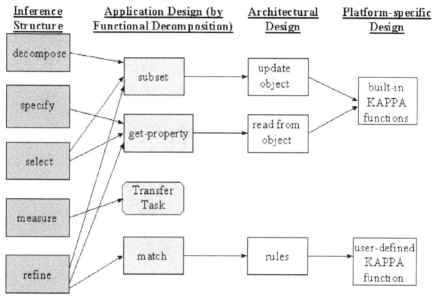

Figure 12.2: IMPRESS Design Model: Inference steps

The design for the inference steps identified a preference for production rules to carry out the *match* step. The other steps were identified as capable of being implemented with simple object-based operations: the *subset* operation involved a *member-of* operation on the symptoms, plus changing values of the "set membership" slot from Yes to No, while the *get-property* operation requires reading the value of a slot in an object. The measurement task was considered to be a transfer task, so the only design requirements were for the user interface to instruct the user on the task, and obtain the result correctly.

The architectural design for IMPRESS' domain knowledge was not too complex; fault states, tests and other concepts were implemented using objects, and domain relations were to be represented using slots. Set membership was also indicated using a slot which carried the name of the set, and possible values of *Yes* and *No*.

The user interface design was also fairly simple, since the most complex user interface feature required was a multiple-choice menu.

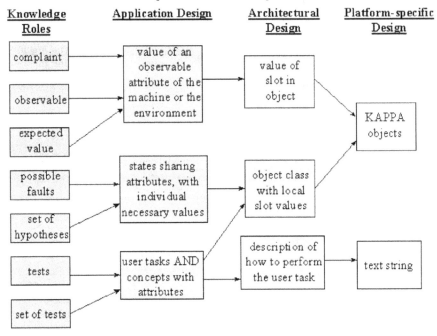

Figure 12.3: IMPRESS Design Model: Domain Knowledge

12.3.3 Platform Design

IMPRESS was implemented in KAPPA-PC on a Compaq 386 PC. KAPPA-PC provided good support for object representations and object accessing functions, so the relevant architectural design recommendations were followed exactly. However, the rule system in that version of KAPPA-PC effectively operated as an add-on module to the rest of the system; it needed to be carefully set up and explicitly invoked. Since the matching algorithm only needed to match 2 parameters (test results against faults), and there were approximately 40 faults and 40 tests in the knowledge base, then the maximum number of possible matches was 1600, and a quick survey of the knowledge base established that the mean number of matches was much lower – less than 100. It was therefore feasible to perform the matching with a doubly-iterative function, thus avoiding the need to introduce the rule system into the program at all.

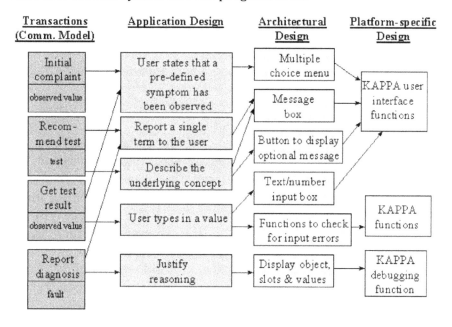

Figure 12.4: IMPRESS Design Model: User Interfaces

12.3.4 Flow of Control

Design decisions on flow of control are made on the basis of the task structure from the Expertise Model. The knowledge representations and programming techniques recommended by the Design Model must be chained together in order to replicate the *task body* specified. For IMPRESS, the task body (see section 8.4.1) specifies a generate-and-test approach: an initial set of candidate faults is identified, and then the system enters a REPEAT-UNTIL loop in which tests are selected, performed, and the set of possible faults is narrowed down, until the set of possible faults has 1 or less members in it. This was easy to implement in KAPPA-PC.

12.4 Worked Example 2: X-MATE

X-MATE (eXpert Mortgage Arrears Threat Advisor) [95] was developed for a large UK building society by Hewlett Packard's Knowledge Systems Centre with assistance from AIAI. Its task was to assess the likelihood of mortgage applicants meeting their loan repayments.

The building society's problem was that the percentage of defaulters was too high, and it was difficult to enforce quality control on acceptance of applications because, within certain guidelines, the acceptance or rejection of applications was almost entirely at the discretion of the local branch manager. The system was intended to support a branch manager or branch clerk by highlighting applications which were worthy of further investigation, and assisting the user in performing some further checks on the application. It did this by identifying the key features of "typical high risk customers", determining what data on the application form would indicate these features, and then scanning application forms (and, if necessary, data supplied from other sources) for the presence of these high risk indicators.

12.4.1 X-MATE: Application Design

X-MATE was also decomposed using functional decomposition. The inference structure for X-MATE is shown in Figure 12.5. The application design for X-MATE can be seen in Table 12.4.1.

The most obvious factor about this design is that several inference steps are labelled "pre-compiled", and no architectural commands are defined for these steps. What has happened is that several of the problem-solving steps required to perform mortgage application assessment have been carried out once and for all by the experts who supplied the knowledge for the system; the system only contains the results of that process. This "distilled wisdom" is considered to be "shallow" knowledge (i.e. direct associations between key inputs and important outputs.) in AI terminology, replacing the "deep knowledge" of the full problem-solving process. This can be reflected in a revised version of the inference structure; see section 8.2.2.

The application design also contains an extra problem solving step (the selection of a particular data source) which did not appear in the inference structure. This extra step reflects a design decision to run the system up to four times, using different sets of data; the reason for this was to speed up processing by making all automatic checks first,

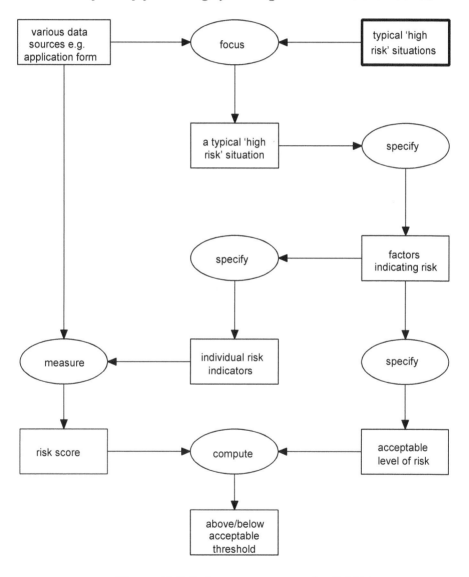

Figure 12.5: Inference structure for X-MATE

and only proceeding to ask the user to input data if the application is deemed to be medium or high risk. While this is a control issue, and therefore is largely the concern of the task structure, it was necessary to select the appropriate data source for each run, and this had to appear in the Design model.

Inference step	Function	Arguments
focus	subset	:set all-risk-indicators :set some-risk-indicators :key situation
select	select-simple	:set available-data-sources :key phase-of-problem-solving
specify	pre-compiled	
specify	pre-compiled	
specify	pre-compiled	
measure	match-N	:elements application-form-data :elements risk-indicators
compute	calculate	:number risk-score :number risk-threshold

Table 12.2: Application Design for X-MATE

The *select-simple* function is given a list of four data sources; its functionality is to select the next data source from the list. *match-N* performs pattern matching between 2 or more items, while *calculate* performs arithmetic calculations.

12.4.2 Architectural Design

The architectural design for X-MATE's processes is as follows:

• Select data sources: the key to this selection is the phase of processing. It can be implemented as a *case* statement i.e. "if phase 1, select source X; if phase 2, select source Y; etc."

- Matching should be implemented using production rules. X-MATE correlates multiple features in order to determine risk, whereas IMPRESS only matched pairs of properties; so the theoretical set of possible matches is much larger in X-MATE.
- Focus on a set of risk indicators: choose an appropriate rule set.
- Computation should be implemented using arithmetic functions.

As for the domain knowledge design, the application form was represented using 2 or more objects: one object for each applicant (instances of an *Applicants* class) and one to represent the "case" (details of the property, and other non-applicant-specific information).

12.4.3 Platform Design

X-MATE was also implemented in KAPPA-PC 1.1 on a HP Vectra 386 PC. The platform design mirrored the architectural design; no changes were deemed necessary.

The full design model for X-MATE's inference steps can be seen in Figure 12.6.

12.4.4 Flow of Control

The flow of control specified for X-MATE (see section 8.4.2 is to `repeat` running through the *whole* inference structure `until` the computed risk score doesn't meet a particular threshold, or until there are no more rule sets to be processed (each rule set corresponded to a different data source). When an application comes in, the first rule set is selected and is run on the objects representing the applicants and the case. If the resulting risk score does not reach a certain threshold, the application is deemed OK; if it does reach the threshold, another rule set is loaded and run on the same objects *after* extra data have been added by an automatic request to a credit search bureau. If a second threshold is breached, a third rule set is loaded which asks the user questions about the text in the application and accompanying references; if another threshold is breached, then the system loads its final ruleset which requires the applicants themselves to attend an interview to answer further questions.

The final accumulated risk score is then recorded and can be displayed later, or sorted to produce a list of the riskiest applications for forwarding to Head Office. The system has been designed not to reject any applications without further consultation.

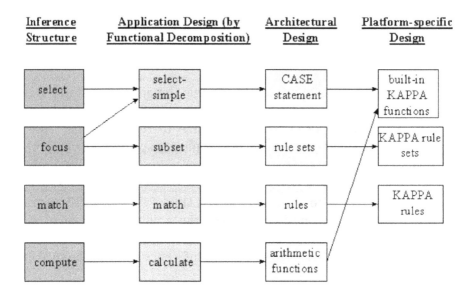

Figure 12.6: X-MATE Design Model: Inference steps

12.5 Conclusion

It can be seen that the CommonKADS Design Model is a useful way of recording design decisions, and of viewing how one design decision flows from another; it therefore provides useful documentation of the process of system design. The separation of flow-of-control design from selection of representations & techniques is a consequence of a similar separation in the Expertise Model; this encourages greater modularity and reusability of designs. The three-stage design process helps to validate the Expertise Model and to separate decisions on good design techniques from decisions on what can be implemented.

Weaknesses in the Design Model include a lack of guidance on selection of techniques; probing questions provide some remedy for this. The lack of a defined set of architectural commands is also a weakness.

In summary, the CommonKADS Design Model is a useful aid to knowledge engineers in representing and recording design decisions, especially if an Expertise Model and a Communication Model have been developed previously. The usefulness of the Design Model will be improved by further recommendations on content (particularly architectural commands) and guidance on making selections (i.e. development of further "probing questions").

The final chapter of this book (excluding the "critical review" chapters) suggests which aspects of CommonKADS are really necessary, in the context of a very short KBS development project.

13 Pragmatic KADS: Using KADS for a small project

13.1 Introduction

It might be thought that KADS, with its specific guidance for the system developer and flow of information for the project manager, would quickly become the standard approach to KBS development.

There is, however, a vociferous faction amongst KBS developers which believes that methodological approaches to KBS development add so much overhead to some projects that they are not worth using. For example, the KADS methodology has been criticised both for the time required to construct all the detailed models, and for the large number of reports which are required to document progress made and decisions taken. KADS' approach may be essential for large-scale commercial projects, but it is argued that this approach is not appropriate for many KBS developments.

This overhead causes particularly severe problems for small and medium-sized KBS projects. There is also less perceived need for methodology on these projects, since they are typically least at risk from informal KBS development procedures. In order to solve this problem, some KBS developers have rejected methodological approaches altogether; others have developed their own streamlined methodology; and others still have used parts of a recognised methodology, attempting to extract the benefits of formalisation and guidance for developers while minimising document preparation and other overheads.

COURSE SELECTOR is a small KBS, developed by the Artificial Intelligence Applications Institute of the University of Edinburgh in 6 man weeks. The use of a full-scale method for such a short project would have been prohibitively time-consuming, and so a pragmatic version of the KADS methodology was used. This paper describes the use of "pragmatic KADS" in the development of the course selector system, highlighting those parts of KADS which were found to be particularly useful. For comparison purposes, it also shows CommonKADS models that represent the same knowledge.

13.2   COURSE SELECTOR: **The problem**

The COURSE SELECTOR system was implemented for the Department of Business Studies in the University of Edinburgh. The Department's problem was that, in the first two weeks of the Autumn term, every student is required to choose courses for the coming year. Each student has a Director of Studies who is responsible for ensuring that a legitimate combination of courses has been chosen, and every Director of Studies finds that the whole of the first week of term, plus a significant proportion of time thereafter, is taken up with advising students on this complex problem. The task of choosing an acceptable combination of courses is complex, for the following reasons:

• The University of Edinburgh permits students to choose from a very wide range of courses. While most Business Studies students choose their courses from the 20 subjects offered within the Faculty of Social Science, it is not unknown for students to take courses such as Chinese Civilisation, or Forensic Medicine. As a result, there are a large number of potential timetable clashes.

• The Department of Business Studies requires students to take certain combinations of courses in their second and third years. All Honours students are required to take Business Studies 1, Business Studies 2 and Business Studies 3 in their first three years; in addition, most students must take six other courses, in one of the following combinations:

– Levels 1, 2, and 3 in a single subject, and three other level 1 courses

– Levels 1 and 2 in two subjects, and two other level 1 courses

– Levels 1 and 2 in a single subject, three level 1 courses, and two extra half-courses in Business Studies

These regulations can be difficult to coordinate with timetable clashes and students' preferences.

• The Department of Business Studies offers ten different Bachelor degrees which include a Business Studies component. Each of these has different compulsory courses, and some require 2nd and 3rd year students to take more than six courses (in addition to Business Studies 1, 2 and 3).

- Students are permitted to transfer to Business Studies from other degrees, possibly from other Faculties, and students with appropriate qualifications are permitted to start in 2nd year.
- All the above requirements may be overridden at the discretion of the Head of the Department(s) concerned.

The current procedure (in theory) is for the students to examine the University Calendar, an 800-page volume describing the regulations and timetables of every available course, and to make their course choices which are then verified by their Director of Studies. In practice, many students rely on their Director of Studies to be a source of wisdom, making little or no effort to look at the University Calendar themselves. The result is that the Director has to conduct one or more lengthy interviews with each student. Since each Director is currently responsible for 60 students, the workload is large. There is also considerable scope for error; the number of possible interactions between courses is so great that, during the development of the course selector system, the University Calendar itself was found to have omitted to mention a timetable clash between two courses which were recommended for a particular degree.

The COURSE SELECTOR system was designed to encode the knowledge stored in the University Calendar, with some additional input from two experienced Directors of Studies. It was initially used by 2nd and 3rd year undergraduates and later by 1st years as well.

13.3 Analysis: Modelling expertise

Despite the short time available for the construction of the course selector system, it was decided that the guidance for KBS development provided by an Expertise model was worth the effort required to develop the model. A communication model was also developed, as a necessary input to the design phase.

As described in chapters 7 and 8, the Expertise model consists of one or more models of:

- Domain knowledge: knowledge about concepts, objects, properties, and values that are important in this domain.
- Inference knowledge: knowledge about the deductions that must be carried out to solve a problem.
- Task knowledge: knowledge about the order in which inferences are carried out.

The development of the expertise model for the course selector system proceeded as follows:

13.3.1 The model of expertise: Domain knowledge

The vast majority of the domain information was laid out clearly and succinctly in the University Calendar. Only one knowledge acquisition session (plus a few telephone calls) was necessary, in order to elicit some Department-specific regulations which were not represented in the University Calendar; some knowledge about optional courses which fitted well with certain degrees; and some examples of typical course combinations. As a result, the creation and structuring of the domain knowledge model required comparatively little effort.

13.3.2 The model of expertise: Inference knowledge

The creation of an inference structure involves:
- deciding what type of task the KBS is tackling;
- finding the interpretation model for that task type;
- adapting and instantiating that interpretation model for the particular domain.

It was decided that the task of generating a schedule of courses which fitted in with a range of different restrictions was a *configuration* task. An example of a configuration task is the task tackled by the XCON knowledge based system, where a number of components had to be chosen and then correctly placed into boxes to create a VAX computer [124]. In the course selector system, a course schedule must be built up from a number of individual courses, some of which are incompatible with each other; the task is therefore analogous to the task performed by XCON, with a course schedule replacing a VAX computer, and individual courses replacing computer components.

Having decided that the course selector system was performing a configuration task, the next step was to find the appropriate generic inference structure for modelling configuration tasks. The library of generic inference structures available when course selector was developed [20] did not include an inference structure for configuration tasks; instead, a 'generic' inference structure was adapted from the inference structure used in a previous case study [190] that used KADS to support the development of a KBS for configuring industrial mixers. This inference structure is shown in Figure 13.1.

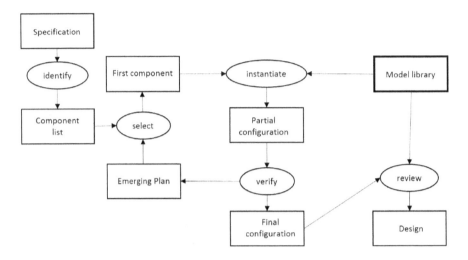

Figure 13.1: 'Generic' inference structure for configuration tasks

According to Figure 13.1, a configuration is generated by:

1. Producing a list of all components that need to be added to the configuration(the **component list**);

2. Adding one component to a partial configuration (represented by the **instantiate** inference action)

3. Calculating all the ramifications of that addition (represented by the **verify** inference action)

4. If the configuration is not yet complete, and is still within its constraints, return to step (2)

5. If the configuration is complete, perform some final actions and produce some output

This generic inference structure was adapted for the course selector system to produce a problem-specific inference structure which is shown in Figures 13.2 and 13.3. While this inference structure appears to differ considerably from the generic inference structure, it follows the same principles:

- All students are required to take certain courses, and these are added to the course schedule first (one at a time) - this is represented by the **identify-1** and **assemble** inference steps.

Students are then allowed to select further courses, a process which is represented by the inference step **select**. These courses (both required and optional courses) correspond to the component list in the generic inference structure.

• Each course is then added to the course schedule (one at a time). This is represented by the **assemble** inference step which corresponds to the **instantiate** inference step in the generic inference structure.

• The *current course schedule* knowledge role corresponds to the *partial configuration* in the generic inference structure.

• The selection of a course may make some other courses ineligible, because of timetable clashes or University regulations on the allowed combinations of courses. This is represented by the inference step **refine-1**. This has no corresponding inference step in the generic inference structure; the fact that adding items to the configuration constrains the list of eligible components is not represented in the generic inference structure.

• The student continues selecting courses until his schedule is full. The check on whether a student's course schedule is full is represented by **compare** on the left hand side of the diagram, which corresponds to **verify** in the generic inference structure..

Sometimes, certain inference steps are sufficiently complex that they must be decomposed into a number of inference steps and knowledge roles. This is the case with the **refine-1** inference step. The breakdown of this inference step is shown in Figure 13.3.

These two diagrams describe the instantiated inference structure (or, in the language of the Zachman framework, the system level process model) for the COURSE SELECTOR system.

13.3.3 Strategy level
Strategy level comments for this system include:

• When generating or updating the initial list of Eligible optional courses, course combination regulations will rule out some courses. It is probably more efficient to generate the list once and to remove non-permitted courses from the Eligible optional courses than to repeatedly construct a new list of those which are still permitted. This is because it is likely that only a few courses will be forbidden whenever a new course is added to the course schedule.

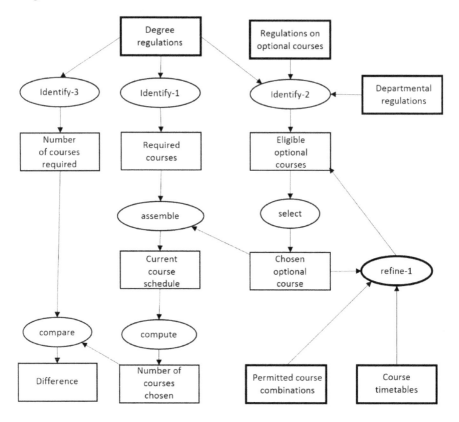

Figure 13.2: Instantiated inference structure for COURSE SELECTOR: top level

- A caveat to the statement above is that the user may sometimes want to 'undo' selections which could require adding deleted courses back into the list. Consequently, a form of *truth maintenance* should be used; the preferred option is a "negative truth maintenance" approach where the system maintains a set of all courses that the user might be permitted to choose; when a choice is made, courses that clash with the chosen course due to timetabling or regulations are marked as unavailable *due to that course.* An advantage of this approach is that a course which is unavailable due to clashes with two selected courses will not become available again if one of the two clashing courses is de-selected.

- The inference structure suggests that the generation of eligible courses, and the initial filtering based on last year's grades, can be done in parallel to the identification of required courses. In practice, it is proposed that the list of eligible courses is generated **before** the required courses are dealt with; furthermore, it is proposed that the list of eligible courses should initially include the required courses. This is because the initial filtering based on low grades may apply equally to required courses as to optional courses.

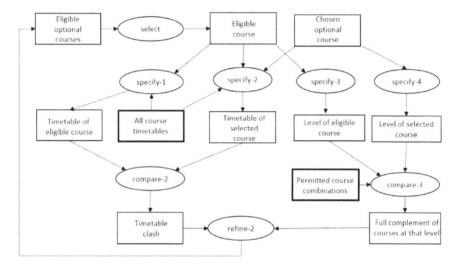

Figure 13.3: Instantiated inference structure for COURSE SELECTOR: expansion of *refine-1*

13.3.4 The model of expertise: Task knowledge

Once an instantiated inference structure has been developed, and the strategy level issues have been identified, a *task structure* must be developed to determine the order in which these tasks are carried out. This task structure describes the task (control) knowledge within the model of expertise. The chosen order is shown below; it can be seen that, although this may have been a short project, it required a lot of inference and control knowledge.

task *configure-course-schedule*
goal allow a student to select a legitimate combination of courses
control-terms
Eligible courses → the set of all courses which students can choose
Required courses → those courses which this student must take
task structure

configure-course-schedule (Initial Specification + Regulations → Course Schedule)

obtain(Initial Specification) *i.e. the student's name, degree course, and year of study*

identify-1(Initial Specification + Degree regulations → Required Courses)

identify-2(Initial Specification + Regulations on allowed optional courses + Department's own regulations → Eligible Courses)

identify-3(Initial Specification + Degree regulations → Number of Courses to be taken)

for all (course in Required Courses)

assemble(Course Schedule + course → Course Schedule)

inform(user)

end

begin loop

compute(Course Schedule → Number or courses chosen so far)

compare(Number of Courses chosen so far *vs* Number of Courses to be taken)

if comparison = equal then exit loop

ask(user)

select(Eligible Courses → Chosen Course)

assemble(Course Schedule + course → Course Schedule)

inform(user)

refine-1(Eligible Courses → Eligible Courses):

> **remove**(Chosen Course + Eligible Courses→
> Eligible Courses)
>> for all (course in Courses with timetable
> clashes with Chosen Course)
>>> **refine-2**(course + Eligible Courses →
>> Eligible Courses)
>> end
>> for all (course in Courses no longer permitted by
>> course combination regulations)
>>> **refine-2**(course + Eligible Courses →
>> Eligible Courses)
>> end
>> *ask*(user)
>> select(Course Schedule → Deselected Course)
>> assemble(Course Schedule + Deselected Course →
>> Course Schedule)
>> *inform*(user)
>> **refine-1**(Eligible Courses → Eligible Courses):
>>> **add**(Eligible Courses→ Eligible Courses +
>> Deselected Course)
>>> for all (course in Courses with timetable
>> clashes with Deselected Course)
>>>> **add**(Eligible Courses → Eligible Courses +
>> course)
>>> end
>>> for all (course in Courses not permitted by
>> course combination regulations)
>>>> if level of course = level of
>> Deselected course
>>>> then **add**(Eligible Courses →
>> Eligible Courses + course)
>>>> end
> end loop

The primary purpose of the task structure is to specify a procedural ordering of tasks. For example, the step of comparing the number of courses chosen against the number required to be taken was placed at the beginning of the loop, because it is possible that the student's course schedule may be filled by the required courses; so the loop may never need to be executed at all.

Some parts of the task structure would benefit from further explanation. It might appear that the task structure given above is self-defeating: within the loop, the user adds a course to their schedule and then removes a course, thus ensuring that the schedule will never be complete. This is not the case; it is envisaged that the user will be offered a menu of options which will include adding a course to their course schedule or removing a course from their course schedule. Neither of these options is compulsory, and since the execution of the loop is dependent on the user's selected option, the loop will not always be executed in its entirety.

13.4 Analysis: Modelling Communication

The communication model was developed by identifying all tasks identified in the task structure, identifying dependencies between tasks to the diagram, and then making a decision about which tasks would be performed by the KBS, and which by the student – in other words, a *model of interaction* was developed. The result which is shown in Figures 13.4 to 13.6, suggests that most of the tasks will be performed by the knowledge based system; this is to be expected, since the KBS is intended for (highly) non-expert users. However, the completed communication model also highlights several occasions in which the KBS is required to communicate with the user or with files elsewhere in the system; this information is worth modelling for completeness, and as an input to the design phase.

The equivalent CommonKADS Communication model can be seen in Figure 13.7.

13.5 Design phase

The design phase is the next major phase of the KADS methodology. In both CommonKADS and Pragmatic KADS, this involves the construction of a Design Model.

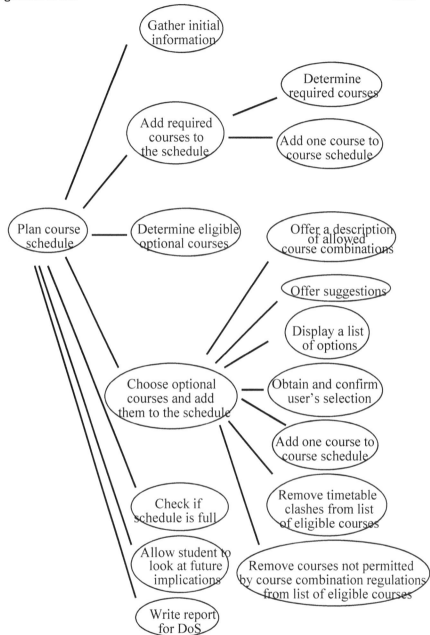

Figure 13.4: Task hierarchy in COURSE SELECTOR

13.5.1 COURSE SELECTOR: **Application design**

Application design was performed using functional decomposition for the course selector project. The functional decomposition can be found in the Application Design columns of Figures 13.5 and 13.6

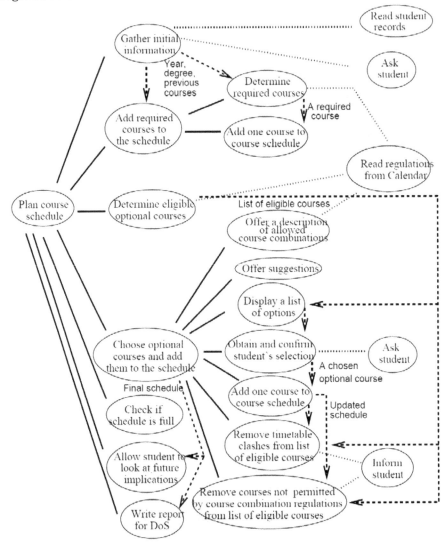

Figure 13.5: Tasks plus dependencies in COURSE SELECTOR

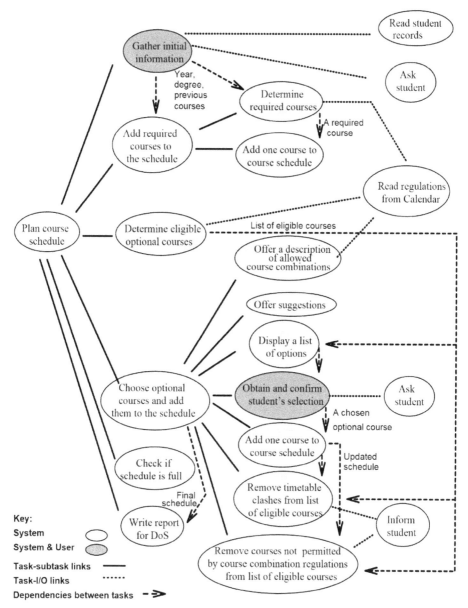

Figure 13.6: Model of interaction for COURSE SELECTOR

A more detailed functional decomposition, showing the links between inference steps, knowledge roles and interface functions, was also prepared. This was recommended by the original KADS methodology, and users of Pragmatic KADS may use this approach in preference to the CommonKADS Design Model if they prefer, since it summarises more information in fewer diagrams than the Design Model achieves. However, this approach is only recommended for systems with less knowledge than the COURSE SELECTOR system; it can be seen from Figure 13.8 that this diagram quickly becomes too detailed to be of any real use.

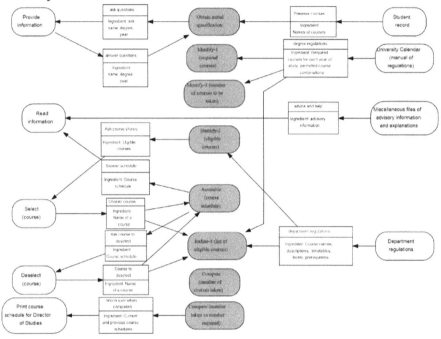

Figure 13.7: Communication model for COURSE SELECTOR

Developing this detailed functional decomposition did prove useful in identifying a few communication paths and minor knowledge roles which had been omitted from, or not fully specified in, the Expertise and Communication models.

13.5.2 Architectural design

KADS and CommonKADS provide almost no guidance on architectural design; while this is consistent with the overall descriptive rather than prescriptive approach, guidance is particularly missed at this stage. What guidance there is can be found in [146], but the suggestions provided are not very detailed, and there is no guidance at all for configuration tasks. As a result, the "probing questions" approach (see chapter 12) was identified (based on the work of Kline & Dolins at Rome Labs [105]) and used.

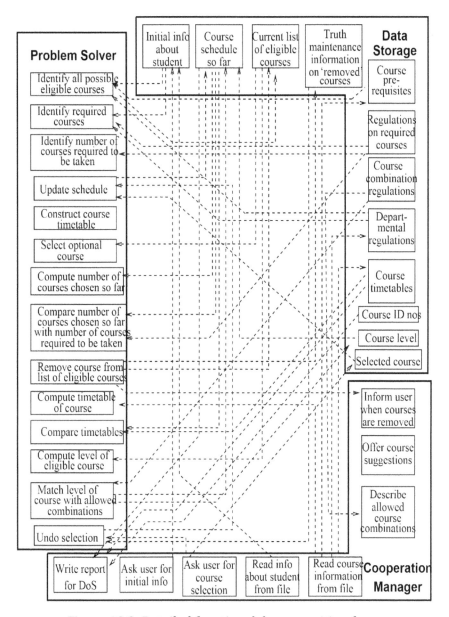

Figure 13.8: Detailed functional decomposition for COURSE SELECTOR

The full set of probing questions asked of the course selector system can be seen at the end of this section. Only two "probing questions" (6 and 15) affected the architectural design. Question 6 asked whether it was sensible to enumerate all possible solutions to the problem, or whether the system should be capable of generating solutions. In a configuration problem, there are a very large number of possible solutions, and so it is better that solutions are generated. *Data-driven reasoning* is therefore suggested. It is also likely that the partial configuration will need to be represented which suggests the use of *objects* and *dynamic object creation*. Question 15 asked whether the system has to re-make elaborate decisions; the answer is yes, if the user should decide to undo a choice. The consequent suggestion is to use either *backtracking* or *truth maintenance*. Since it is very difficult to combine backtracking with data-driven reasoning, truth maintenance seems to be the preferred approach.

As far as KBS programming is concerned, the probing questions analysis recommended the use of data-driven reasoning and truth maintenance. It also suggested that objects, with dynamic object creation, might be useful as well.

Architectural design is recommended not only for problem solving techniques, but also for domain information, and for communication. An analysis of the maintenance requirements for the course selector system had determined that the characteristics of courses are likely to change frequently (every year, at least). Probing question 16 suggests that it would be helpful if the domain information about courses could be read from a file, rather than being hard-coded into the KBS, thus allowing it to be updated without having to re-program the whole KBS. This suggestion was adopted; its main effect on the architectural design is that the chosen representation for courses should be human-readable as well as machine-readable.

The decisions regarding communication design were fairly simple, since there were only three types of communication that needed to take place: users had to type in text, the system had to offer menus that the users selected an item from, and the system had to display explanatory text when the users requested it.

See the "Architectural design" columns of Figures 13.5 and 13.6 for a summary of the architectural design decisions made for COURSE SELECTOR.

Probing questions for course selector

1. How well designed is the project? A weakly designed one may need a broad range of features for prototyping.

Answer: The course selector system has been designed in detail using KADS design techniques.

2. Is the KBS attempting to produce an optimal solution or just a satisfactory one?

Answer: A satisfactory one.

3. How much confidence can one have in the results of the system?

Answer: A lot, since they are based on regulations, rather than possibly inexact measurements

4. Does the system have to "fuse" data from different sources?

Answer: Not to such an extent that this fusion requires management

5. Will the KBS be using 'deep' knowledge?

Answer: No.

6. Is it sensible to enumerate all possible solutions, or should the system be capable of generating solutions?

Answer: In a configuration problem, solutions should be generated. It is likely that the partial configuration will need to be represented which suggests the use of *objects* and *dynamic object creation. Data-driven reasoning* is also suggested.

In practice, the partial configuration is unlikely to be very complex (it is simply a list of the names of courses plus their timetables), and so objects may not be necessary to represent this.

7. How many things will the system have to consider simultaneously?

Answer: One course at a time.

8. Will the KBS have to reason about relationships between things?

Answer: No, with the exception of courses that make other courses ineligible.

This isn't a relationship in the normal AI use of the term.

9. Will the KBS include a hierarchy of classified objects?

Answer: No.

10. Will the KBS have to consider a number of possibilities simultaneously?

Answer: No. Only one course schedule will be considered at a time.

11. Will the system have to determine what step to take next, depending on thepartial solutions?

Answer: No. While the system will perform some reasoning based on partial solutions, it will not alter its order of reasoning.

12. Is the system expected to reason with incomplete data?

Answer: No.

13. How large will the system be?

Answer: Not large enough to consider using an AI language rather than a shell or toolkit.

14. Does the system have requirements for speed?

Answer: No stated requirements.

15. Does the system have to re-make elaborate decisions?

Answer: Yes, if the user decides to undo a choice. The consequent suggestion is to use either *backtracking* or *truth maintenance* which had already been identified as options.

16. Does the information vary over time?

Answer: No, as far as the system is concerned. It changes every year; this will be handled by representing certain information in a spreadsheet file that can be updated by someone who has no KBS programming knowledge.

17. Will the system allow the user to request explanations, refuse to answer a question, or volunteer information?

Answer: No.

18. Does the system have any real time constraints?

Answer: No.

19. Does the system have to produce responses within a certain time?

Answer: The system is supposed to be interactive.

20. Does the system have to handle multiple problems concurrently?

Answer: No.

13.5.3 Platform design

There are two major issues in the platform design of a knowledge base that has been developed using KADS: preserving the structure of the model of expertise (unless an AI paradigm is being used), and deciding how to implement the chosen architectural design. In the course selector project, the knowledge base of the course selector system was designed to be broken down into a number of files, where each major inference step was implemented by code stored in a separate file.

The second issue was deciding on the most appropriate programming tool. In the course selector project, as in many projects, there were a number of other factors apart from the architectural design components affecting the choice of tool: principally that the COURSE SELECTOR system should be able to run on an 8086 PC with 640Kb of RAM[44], and that the tool should cost very little.

The tool chosen was CLIPS version 5.0. CLIPS is a KBS toolkit whose primary form of representation is forward chaining rules which are similar to the rule-based component of Inference ART[85]. It includes a simple truth maintenance system, and dynamic creation of symbolic facts. Version 5.0 of CLIPS also introduced object-oriented programming and functions, but one of the advantages of CLIPS for this project was that it can be compiled with or without its various program components; because of restrictions of speed and memory on the target PCs, the object-oriented and function facilities of CLIPS were compiled out.

The platform design chosen for each of the architectural design components was:

• Data driven reasoning would be implemented using forward chaining rules.

• The required object functionality would be implemented using multiple facts, where the first element in each fact was the name of the "object".

• Truth maintenance would also be implemented using facts, since the built-in truth maintenance facility was not sufficiently expressive to represent the reason(s) that a course was unavailable. Truth maintenance was implemented by the simple but powerful technique of creating a fact to represent a course which was known **not** to be eligible for selection. This contrasts with the normal truth maintenance technique of keeping track of **valid** assumptions; the reason for this choice is that there are

---

[44] The COURSE SELECTOR system was developed in 1991, and the system was to be used in a student computing laboratory filled with low-specification PCs.

likely to be fewer ineligible courses than eligible ones, and so fewer facts will be required. The "truth maintenance" facts note the reason for the creation of the fact which will be the addition of a certain course to the course schedule; if that course is ever removed from the schedule, then any "truth maintenance" facts associated with it are also removed. This technique is powerful because it is able to handle a situation where a course is ineligible for more than one reason; a course is only considered eligible if *all* the "truth maintenance" facts affecting it are removed.

• The external file of course information was developed by using a spreadsheet, and writing out a text file containing the fields of the spreadsheet. This file was then parsed using an ASCII parser.

See the "Platform design" columns of Figures 13.5 and 13.6 for a summary of the platform design decisions made for course selector.

13.6 The KADS methodology: Implementation phase

The implementation phase is the last major phase of KBS development; it involves writing code, interfacing with other software, and verification and validation. Both CommonKADS and Pragmatic KADS have very little to say about it; once the platform design has been completed, implementation is seen as a programming task, where engineering methods can be applied without any adaptation. However, this worked example will include some implementation details to show how the recommendations of the Design model were implemented.

For the course selector system, the code was divided up into various files, with one file for each major inference step in the instantiated inference structure; there were also separate files for the interface functions and the overall control (loading, passing control between phases, etc.). For example, there is a file that implements the comparison of timetables between selected courses and currently eligible courses; this implements the inference step *compare-2*, and, by pattern matching, implements *specify-1* and *specify-2* as well. This file contains seven rules; the first one is shown below.

Inference steps	Application design	Architectural design	Platform design

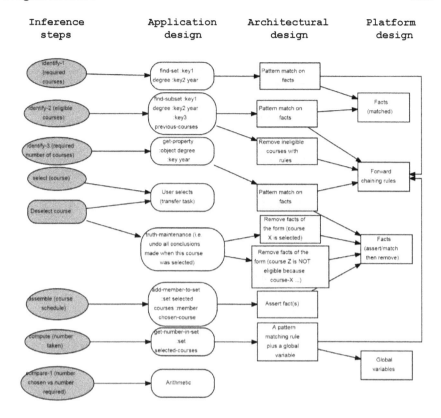

Figure 13.9: Design model: inference steps: top level

13.6.1 Example rule: identify timetable clashes

```
(defrule reject_clashing_whole_courses
    (declare (salience 10000)) ;; must be higher
than the menu rules
    (phase check_for_rejects)
    (check_timetable_clashes ?course)
    (status ?course 1);; it is a whole course
    (lecture  ?course $? ?day ?time&:(integerp
?time) $?) ;; if any lecture (described
    (lecture    ?course2&~?course    $?    ?day
?time&:(integerp ?time) $?)
  =>
    (assert  (timetable_clash  ?course2  ?course
?day ?time))
  )
```

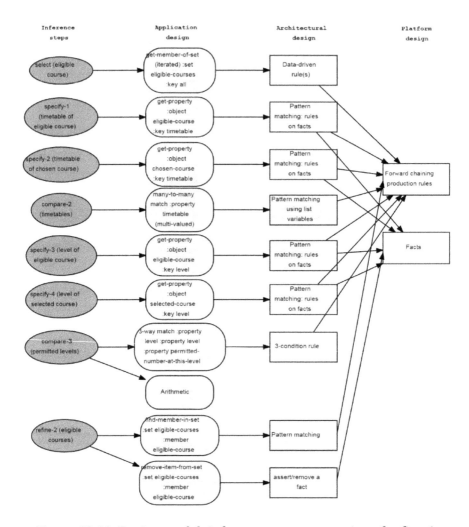

Figure 13.10: Design model: inference steps: expansion of *refine-1*

A typical set of facts that could match this rule would be:

```
(phase check_for_rejects)
(check_timetable_clashes        Accounting1)
(status Accounting1 1)
(lecture Accounting1 M 10 Tu 12 Th 2)
(lecture Geography1 M 12 Tu 9 Th 2)
```

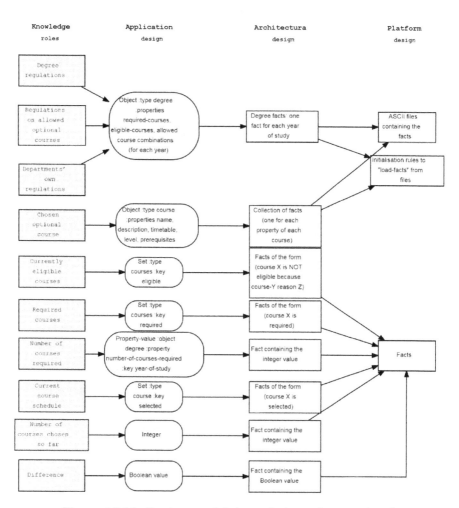

Figure 13.11: Design model: knowledge roles: top level

In CLIPS, almost everything preceding the arrow (=>) represents a pattern that must be matched; every pattern must be matched, and variables instantiated appropriately, if the whole rule is to be matched. The actions of the rule appear after the arrow; if the conditions are matched and the rule is "fired", these actions are carried out.

In this rule, the *salience* is a control feature that awards this rule high priority; i.e. it is more likely to be "fired" if several rules have their conditions matched simultaneously. The second line is also a control feature; it will only match if the fact *(phase check_for_rejects)* exists in the working memory. The creation and deletion of *(phase ...)* facts is used to impose a general sequencing on the system as a whole.

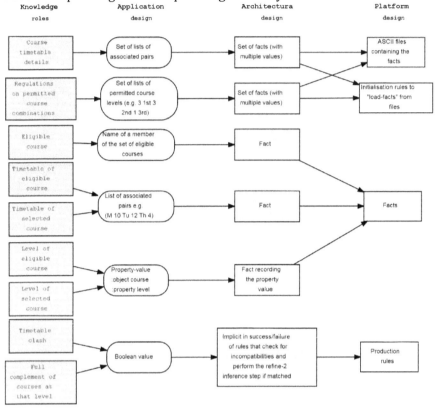

Figure 13.12: Design model: knowledge roles: expansion of *refine-1*

The second pattern is *(check_timetable_clashes ?course)* which serves a dual purpose; it provides even more control by saying "it's now time to check for timetable clashes against this course", and it identifies the selected course (thereby implementing the *select* inference step). This fact will be matched by **any** fact in the working memory that has two terms in it, where the first term is *check_timetable_clashes*; however, if the rest of the system is operating correctly, there should at most one fact in the working memory of that format at any one time.

The third pattern is *(status ?course 1)* which is intended to state that the selected course is a whole course; there are separate rules for checking timetable clashes between half courses and other courses.

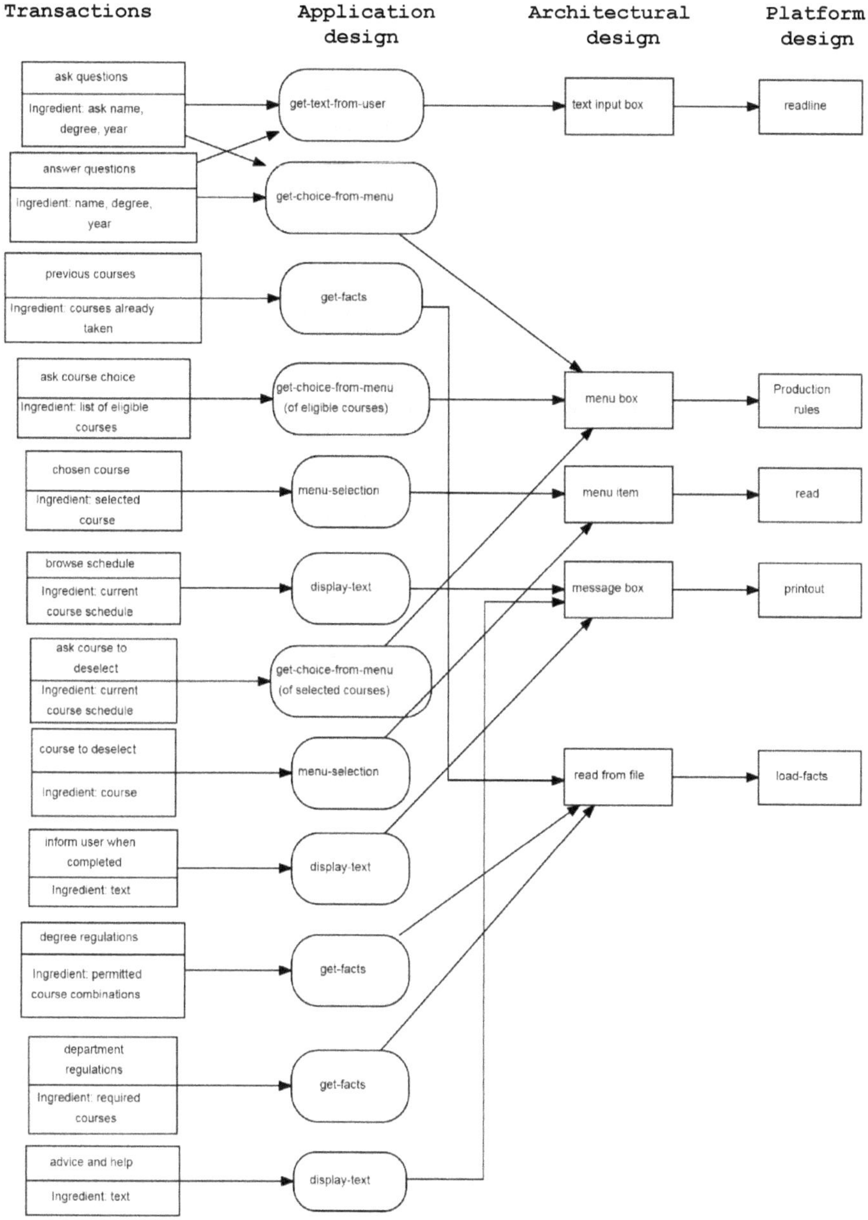

Figure 13.13: Design model: communication

The fourth and fifth patterns do the real work of the rule; in terms of the inference structure, these two conditions implement *specify-1*, *specify-2* and *compare-2*. Expressing these patterns in pseudo-English, they read:

```
IF there is a lecture on the selected course on
day DAY at time TIME AND there is another course
which is not the selected course, with a lecture on
the same DAY at the same TIME
   THEN there is a clash
```

The implementation of "the same" day and time is achieved by using the same variables for the day and the time in the two patterns; they must be instantiated to the same values for the whole rule to be matched. The *integerp* test and the $? symbols are used to make one rule match on all elements of an association list: the $? symbol will match on zero or more items, so no matter how many lectures a course has, every pairing will be tested by the rule. The *integerp* test on the lecture time is a simple way of ensuring that the rule doesn't consider "12 Th" to be an associated lecture pairing, but only "Th 2".

If all these facts are matched (as they would be by the facts given above), then the rule is eligible to be "fired". If it is "fired", the fact *(timetable_clash Geography1 Accounting1 Th 2)* is added to the working memory. This fact is then used by the rules that implement the *refine-2* inference step to make Geography1 ineligible for selection.

13.7 Discussion

What can we learn from our example of Pragmatic KADS?
• Major benefits can be obtained from developing an inference structure. Generic inference structures were found to be very useful as a basis for structuring the knowledge, and also for providing a structure for the final implemented system.
• The "abbreviated" models suggested by Pragmatic KADS – the model of interaction and the 'all-in-one' functional decomposition – are more compact than those recommended by CommonKADS. This is both a strength and a weakness; it is a strength because they represent more perspectives on knowledge in a single diagram and can therefore represent more interactions, but it is a weakness because these models quickly become too cluttered and complex for use. Given that most of the well-known modelling techniques covered in chapter 2 seem to represent only one or two perspectives on knowledge, it seems that Pragmatic KADS'

"abbreviated" models are likely to be of use only for small KBS projects.

• The "hints and tips" of the Strategy level were a useful addendum to the model of Expertise, and could usefully be included in the full CommonKADS methodology.

• The use of probing questions often offers fewer recommendations than might be expected; however, it's useful to rule our some considerations explicitly since this reduces the risk that the project might encounter an unexpected technical issue.

• As for implementation, it can be seen that the CommonKADS Design Model is a guide but not a template for implementation; good software engineering practice (modularity, commenting, etc.) needs to be followed as well. In rule based systems, the biggest consideration is usually flow of control in the system; making sure that each piece of code not only works in turn, but is not accidentally triggered out of turn. The use of "phase" facts is a common way of reducing this problem to manageable levels.

Pragmatic KADS has been applied and used successfully on a number of student projects within the University of Edinburgh. See e.g. [48] and [136].

Part IV: Issues for Further Research

14 Critical Review

The purpose of this review is to consider issues raised by each chapter of the book, with the overall remit of testing the two propositions laid out in the introduction to this book: whether CommonKADS' models are adequate to represent real-world knowledge; and whether multi-perspective modelling is indeed a necessary and sufficient foundation for knowledge engineering and knowledge management. The issues to be discussed are identified below, according to the order of the chapters.

14.1 Issues raised by chapter 2

Chapter 2 looks at the principles of multi-perspective modelling – at the benefits of representing a single artefact from different perspectives, at the content of these perspectives at different levels of detail, and at the techniques that can be derived from meta-modelling of the Zachman framework for multi-perspective modelling. Its conclusion is that a full set of multi-perspective models (i.e. modelling every perspective at every level of detail) should represent all the knowledge that might be needed for both knowledge management and knowledge engineering, and should alleviate some of the problems that arise from the elimination of (apparently) irrelevant knowledge that is inherent in the act of modelling. The biggest disadvantage is the effort required in preparing so many models.

In the course of its discussion, this chapter raises a number of issues that are worthy of further discussion, and are considered in the remaining chapters of this book. The issues that will be considered in this review are:

- Given that the Zachman framework was originally intended for supporting *information* systems, what are the differences between data, information and knowledge? (See chapter 15).

• Can the Zachman framework really capture and represent all the knowledge needed for knowledge management? (See chapter 16).

• Are there parts of the Zachman framework that don't really need to be filled in order to 'accomplish' knowledge management? Conversely, is there anything required by knowledge management that can't be represented by the Zachman framework? (See chapter 16).

• What is different about the WHY perspective that allows it a dual interpretation? Does this apply to any higher levels? (See chapter 15).

14.2 Issues raised by chapter 3

This chapter reviews a number of common problems that arise with ontologies, and shows how the development of multi-perspective ontologies can resolve some of them. There are therefore clearly advantages to developing multi-perspective ontologies. However, the chapter specifically highlights two issues that are not obviously solved by multi-perspective ontologies: defining agreed "levels of detail" for ontologies, and determining the most appropriate set of definitional properties for ontological concepts.

These will be discussed further in chapter 17.

14.3 Issues raised by chapter 4

This chapter discusses the ACM classification scheme, and its extension for Artificial Intelligence topics. It then considers whether multi-perspective modelling is necessary for a full and accurate indexing scheme – and also, where knowledge management, knowledge engineering, and knowledge acquisition fit into the scheme. The paper is mostly discursive rather than empirical, and so there aren't too many issues for discussion that aren't covered in the paper. However, one question that does arise concerns the primacy of the WHAT and HOW perspectives over the other four perspectives; is this a common feature, and if so, why? (See chapter 16 for a discussion of this issue).

14.4 Issues raised by chapter 5

Chapter 5 outlines how CommonKADS instantiates the multi-perspective modelling approach recommended in earlier chapters, and describes two of CommonKADS' six models. It raises the following issues:

• Does CommonKADS propose models that fill all the cells in the Zachman framework?

• If not which perspectives does it address at which levels of abstraction?

• Are there other knowledge modelling methods which are "better" than CommonKADS for one or more perspectives or levels of abstraction?

See chapter 16 for a discussion of these issues.

14.5 Issues raised by chapter 6

As with chapter 5, this chapter is largely descriptive and therefore does not raise too many issues. However, the concluding discussion prompts the following questions:

• How useful is it to apply CommonKADS models – or other knowledge models, for that matter – prescriptively rather than descriptively?

• What features in a system level Communication model suggest that certain subtasks should or should not be carried out by a user?

These issues are considered in chapter 18.

14.6 Issues raised by chapter 7

This chapter describes one of my earliest attempts to apply KADS (the forerunner of CommonKADS) to development of a real-world knowledge based system. The task was to diagnose faults causing contamination (unwanted marks) on commercial plastic mouldings, such as computer casings, or panels for video recorders. The aim of the project was to develop a system that could be used by non-expert machine operators to diagnose faults; and since the company were looking for a solution to a specific business problem, most of the effort of the project was expended on developing an Expertise model, and implementing the system, rather than on the preliminary stages of organisational modelling or agent modelling. The objective of the project was therefore to acquire knowledge and build an Expertise model that was sufficiently accurate and detailed to be used as a basis for a usable and useful knowledge based system. Since it was one of my earliest applications of KADS, there was also a secondary research objective: to test the adequacy and benefits of using KADS to build an Expertise model, and of using that model as a basis for design and implementation of a knowledge based system.

Since the project was completed successfully, it can be assumed that the Expertise model that was developed was sufficient to support development of a commercial KBS. However, during the process of developing the models, a couple of issues were discovered that affected the model development process, and that were not obviously solved by the CommonKADS models or documentation. These issues were:

- Is knowledge engineering using CommonKADS a purely sequential process, or are there feedback loops to earlier models?
- Is there any guidance on "correct" instantiation of generic inference structures?
- What does a 'bad' Expertise model look like?

See chapter 18 for consideration of these issues.

14.7 Issues raised by chapter 8

The chapter describes and examines the CommonKADS Expertise Model (as opposed to the KADS Expertise model) by re-modelling two existing knowledge based systems, both of which were originally modelled using KADS. The purpose of this re-modelling exercise was to provide a realistic test of the adequacy and applicability of the CommonKADS Expertise Model, by determining how well it represented two collections of real-life knowledge. Particular attention was paid to the utility of features in CommonKADS that were not defined or proposed by the KADS Expertise model; could CommonKADS provide a clear representation of fine distinctions, viewpoints, or knowledge items that were represented obliquely or not at all in the KADS Expertise Model?

To summarise the answers to the above questions: CommonKADS did indeed prove able to represent knowledge, to represent modelling decisions, and to support modelling in ways that were not obvious or possible in KADS. However, there is still a need for further guidance on *how* to develop models. Issues identified include:

- how to select the "right" inference step;
- how to decide if a domain item is a concept or a property;
- deciding whether to develop knowledge models bottom-up (i.e. finding all relationships in acquired knowledge) or top-down (finding all acquired knowledge that can be instantiated to the generic inference structure).

These are discussed in chapter 18.

14.8 Issues raised by chapters 9 and 10

These papers are included in the book because the library of expertise models is often considered the single most useful contribution of the CommonKADS methodology to knowledge engineering, and any extensions to it – particularly extensions that have been developed in accordance with the original principles of the library, and have been shown to work in real-world applications – are likely to be seen as valuable by the knowledge engineering community. Both inference structures promise real-world validity because they are based on real-world systems or studies; the inference structure for planning described in chapter 9 was derived from the O-Plan system [170], while the inference structure for design proposed in chapter 10 was based on studies of designers' behaviour.

Developing these models was essentially an empirical exercise, so there aren't many technical and technological issues to discuss. It might be argued that drawing out a generic inference model based on a few example systems (or one system, in the case of O-Plan) is not a wise approach, but this argument really comes down to the distinction between domain and inference knowledge; if it is possible to strip domain knowledge out of a system and leave only the inference knowledge, and this inference knowledge is re-usable across domains (as CommonKADS claims), then an inference model derived from any well-designed AI system should be usable in several other systems.

14.9   Issues raised by chapter 11

This chapter demonstrates how the output of various tried and tested knowledge acquisition techniques can be mapped into the CommonKADS domain ontology. Such guidance is almost wholly lacking in the knowledge engineering community; this is probably due to a combination of factors, including the limited range of knowledge acquisition techniques available; the lack of agreement on a standardised modelling method (or, to be more accurate, a standardised ontology or ontology framework) among knowledge acquisition researchers; and the focusing of research on domain-specific or task-specific knowledge elicitation tools with the aim of allowing direct knowledge inputting by experts, thus (apparently) bypassing knowledge engineering decisions. The subject of this section of the review will be research or discussion that seeks to address each these three factors.

The specific questions that will be addressed are:
• Where have domain-specific and task-specific knowledge acquisition tools been successful? Why? (See chapter 17).
• Are there knowledge acquisition techniques to cover all six perspectives proposed by the Zachman framework? If not, why not, and could techniques be devised? Is there a need for different techniques at different levels of abstraction? (See chapter 16).
• Why are different knowledge acquisition techniques appropriate for certain types of task? (See chapter 15).
• Could ontologies and knowledge acquisition techniques support each other? (See chapter 17).

14.10 Issues raised by chapter 12

Chapter 12 puts the Design model into practice by discusses the three stages of building the Design Model – Application Design, Architectural Design and Platform Design – and then providing examples. The issues raised by this chapter are:

Stage 1: Application Design At this stage, it is necessary to decide whether the design will be primarily based on functional decomposition, object-oriented decomposition, or a known AI paradigm. The issue is in determining which approach is best for a particular problem.

Stage 2: Architecture Design There are two issues here: firstly, assessing the pros and cons of a "probing questions" approach to making architectural decisions; and secondly, considering the adequacy of the languages proposed by CommonKADS for representing detailed application design and detailed architectural design.

Stage 3: Platform Design The issue here is determining how to match correctly the capabilities and strengths of a programming tool to the design, and adapting the design to the strengths of the tool.

See chapter 19 for a discussion of these issues.

14.11 Comments on chapter 13

Chapter 13 is presented as a possible solution/workaround to some of the issues raised by the earlier chapters, and so it is considered that a review of issues raised by this chapter is not appropriate. Instead, a "manual for pragmatic KADS" is included as an appendix to this book.

15 Epistemological   issues: The Nature of Knowledge

A number of the issues highlighted by the earlier chapters in this book are concerned, directly or indirectly, with the nature of knowledge. These include the over-arching question of whether knowledge can indeed be represented using models; the need to distinguish data, information and knowledge; the need to determine why certain knowledge acquisition techniques are better for certain types of task; and the question of why the WHY perspective appears to be different to the other perspectives in the Zachman framework.

15.1   Epistemology

The nature of knowledge is such a vast subject that an entire sub-branch of philosophy, known as epistemology, is devoted to it. A number of theories have arisen that relate to the mutability of knowledge, ranging from those that stress the "absolute, permanent" character of knowledge to those that put the emphasis on its relativity or situation-dependence. Two of these theories are of particular interest to us: the *pragmatic* or *cognitive* theory and the *constructivist* theory. The pragmatic/cognitive theory is described in the following quotation:

> "[...] The next stage of development of epistemology may be called **pragmatic**. Parts of it can be found in early twentieth century approaches, such as logical positivism, conventionalism, and the "Copenhagen interpretation" of quantum mechanics. This philosophy still dominates most present work in cognitive science and artificial intelligence. According to pragmatic epistemology, knowledge consists of models that attempt to represent the environment in such a way as to maximally simplify problem-solving. It is assumed that no model can ever hope to capture all relevant information, and even if such a complete model would exist, it would be too complicated to use in any practical way. Therefore we must accept the parallel existence of different

models, even though they may seem contradictory. The model which is to be chosen depends on the problems that are to be solved. The basic criterion is that the model should produce correct (or approximate) predictions (which may be tested) or problem-solutions, and be as simple as possible. Further questions about the "Ding an Sich" or ultimate reality behind the model are meaningless.

The pragmatic epistemology does not give a clear answer to the question where knowledge or models come from. There is an implicit assumption that models are built from parts of other models and empirical data on the basis of trial-and-error complemented with some heuristics or intuition. A more radical point of departure is offered by constructivism. It assumes that all knowledge is built up from scratch by the subject of knowledge. There are no 'givens', neither objective empirical data or facts, nor inborn categories or cognitive structures. The idea of a correspondence or reflection of external reality is rejected. Because of this lacking connection between models and the things they represent, the danger with constructivism is that it may lead to relativism, to the idea that any model constructed by a subject is as good as any other and that there is no way to distinguish adequate or 'true' knowledge from inadequate or 'false' knowledge.

We can distinguish two approaches trying to avoid such an 'absolute relativism'. The first may be called *individual constructivism*. It assumes that an individual attempts to reach coherence among the different pieces of knowledge. Constructions that are inconsistent with the bulk of other knowledge that the individual has will tend to be rejected. Constructions that succeed in integrating previously incoherent pieces of knowledge will be maintained. The second, to be called **social constructivism**, sees consensus between different subjects as the ultimate criterion to judge knowledge. 'Truth' or 'reality' will be accorded only to those constructions on which most people of a social group agree.[58]

This analysis cuts to the heart of many of the debates over the definition of knowledge management. To a pragmatic epistemologist, modelling knowledge (whether in diagrams or in an automated system) is the obvious approach to making knowledge more widely available; to a constructivist, anything that claims to be or to contain 'knowledge', but is apparently independent of an individual's body of coherent knowledge or a group's consensus, is highly suspect. Furthermore, the famous "knowledge creating cycle" of Nonaka & Takeuchi [132] is revealed to be heavily based on a constructivist viewpoint; in its essence, the cycle combines individual constructivism and social constructivism into a continuous process of knowledge creation & refinement.

The above analysis also reveals some of the strengths and weaknesses of each approach to knowledge management which should map well to the goals of an organisation's knowledge management activities. Is it important to simplify knowledge in order to make it more widely available, or is it more important to have decision-makers understand all the implications and ramifications of their decisions? Is it important that the knowledge should have a "trace log" by which it can be justified? Does it matter whether the knowledge can be written down in some form so that it can be externally verified? One of the biggest determining factors can be identified from Binney's KM spectrum (discussed in chapter 2); is the knowledge old and stable and merely needs to be analysed, or new and uncertain and needs to be synthesised? For current purposes, it will be assumed that knowledge management is, in fact, a collection of different approaches from which a good knowledge manager will select the one(s) that fit his organisation's goals, and that Binney's KM spectrum provides a full list of options to choose from.

15.2   Applying Zachman perspectives to the nature of knowledge

The analysis above has shed some light on one of the issues identified at the start of this chapter: determining the best approach to knowledge management. However, taking a 'meta' view, the above debate can be considered to be the WHY perspective on the nature of knowledge (i.e both the cognitive and constructivist viewpoints provide an explanation of why knowledge is what it is). Are there other Zachman perspectives on the nature of knowledge that may help answer some of the other identified issues? The remainder of this chapter will consider other perspectives on the nature of knowledge, starting with the perspective of *ontology*.

15.3   Ontology: the WHAT perspective on knowledge

When discussing the nature of knowledge, it is perhaps easiest to think of ontology as the WHAT perspective on the nature of knowledge – that is, it describes (or at least labels) the nature of each "chunk" of knowledge, and of the relationships between "chunks". Ontology-related issues are discussed in more detail in chapter 17.

15.4   Data, information and knowledge: the HOW perspective

The next perspective to consider is the HOW perspective: what can we say about the manner in which knowledge is generated? Some insights can be drawn from a discussion of the relationship between data, information and knowledge.

A simple definition of the difference between data, information and knowledge is that information is "data that makes a difference"; knowledge is "information that makes a difference". This definition of data, information and knowledge is based on that given by Davenport and Prusak [41]. They see data as

> "a set of discrete, objective facts about events – for example, when a customer goes to a gas station and fills the tank of his car, the transaction can be partly described by data: when he made the purchase; how many gallons he bought; how much he paid. But in and of themselves, such facts say nothing about whether the service station is well or badly run, whether it is failing or thriving. Peter Drucker once said that information is "data endowed with relevance or purpose" which of course suggests that data itself has little relevance or purpose. But it is essential raw material for the creation of information."

Davenport & Prusak's definition of information is that it is a *message*, usually in the form of a document or an audible or visible communication, intended to 'shape' the outlook or insight of the person who gets it. But they consider that not only does it potentially shape the receiver, it *has* a shape; it is organized to some purpose. Organisation may occur by placing the data in context; by categorisation; by calculation; by correction; or by condensing the data into a summarised form. But, in essence, information is data with a structure and a purpose.

Davenport & Prusak consider that knowledge derives from information as information derives from data, but that "humans must do virtually all the work" in giving knowledge its structure and purpose. They argue that knowledge "originates and is applied in the minds of knowers. In organizations, it often becomes embedded not only in documents or repositories, but also in organizational routines, processes, practices, and norms." The processes that assign this structure and purpose to knowledge include comparison between information; consequences (i.e. considering cause and effect); connections between information; and conversation with others.

It's worth noting that the processes that Davenport & Prusak assign to the data-information transformation are largely analytic processes, while the processes for information-knowledge transformation are generally synthetic. If Davenport & Prusak's definition is wholly correct, therefore, perhaps CommonKADS' analytic tasks do little more than generate information from data, while "knowledge" is limited to the synthetic tasks. Alternatively, Davenport & Prusak may in fact be distinguishing new, uncertain, constructed knowledge from old, stable, structured knowledge. Whichever is true, it seems that we can summarise the HOW perspective on knowledge by saying that knowledge must be generated from information by one or more (knowledge-based) processes, just as information is generated from data by other knowledge-based processes; whether these processes reside only in humans, or are only capable of residing in humans, is yet another aspect of the cognitive/constructivist debate.

15.4.1 The WHEN of knowledge: Boisot's I-Space

The most important feature of knowledge in terms of time is whether it is new or old ... or more specifically, whether it is narrowly known (new) or widely known (old). This concept is discussed by Boisot [12], where he describes a progression of knowledge from being 'emergent' through 'key' to being 'widespread'. He judges this by placing the knowledge on three dimensions; whether it is codified or uncodified, abstract or concrete, and diffuse or scarce. Emergent knowledge is typically abstract, uncodified, and scarce; key knowledge is concrete, codified, and scarce; and widespread knowledge is concrete, codified and diffused. Boisot illustrates how this applies to various theories of economic markets as well as to knowledge.

Boisot's observation is that key knowledge (which has the highest value to an organisation) differs only from widespread knowledge in its degree of diffusion. Yet, for an organisation to make use of its key knowledge, it must make it available to its members in some form ... which will eventually lead to it being widely diffused, as people leave the organisation and take their knowledge with them, or if an external agency obtains and publishes some of the organisation's knowledge.

This observation has important implications for an organisation's choice of knowledge management approach ... or, indeed, whether a knowledge management approach is to be used at all. If the knowledge concerned is 'emergent' knowledge that stands a good chance of becoming 'key' knowledge, then a codification process is required (for which knowledge acquisition and knowledge modelling may be valuable), but it may be desirable to limit access to the knowledge to a very few people in the organisation. In this case, a 'personal development' (i.e. staff training) knowledge management approach may be approp13riate. If the knowledge is 'key', however, and it is desirable to spread it widely within the organisation, then a technology-based approach might be more appropriate.

15.4.2 The WHO and WHERE of knowledge

It's easy to confuse the WHO and WHERE perspectives on knowledge. The WHERE perspective tells us where knowledge resides, or is generated, or is communicated (so saying "John has the knowledge" is part of the WHERE perspective); the WHO perspective tells us who is responsible for creation, maintenance, updating, and general management of knowledge.

The answer to the question, "Where does knowledge reside?" will be different depending on the respondent's opinion on cognitive vs. constructivist views of knowledge. Both groups agree that knowledge often resides within an individual's head. But a number of other questions – whether knowledge also resides in the shared consensus of a group, or in knowledge 'models', or in a knowledge based system – remain unresolved.

There has also been remarkably little work within the knowledge management community on the communication of knowledge to or from individuals and groups (apart from Nonaka & Takeuchi's "knowledge creating cycle", and even this only describes the process in general terms), and on effective communication methods in general. Some general arguments are made for the pros and cons of apprenticeships, simulations, and lecture-based training courses, but translating these ideas into effective knowledge communication techniques seems to be a fruitful area for future research.

The question of who is responsible for knowledge is highly dependent on the answer to the question of where the knowledge resides. It's also, perhaps, the area of knowledge management that an organisation has the least direct control over; the organisation can encourage individuals to keep their knowledge up to date, and can even pay them to do research and development, but it cannot force them to do so, nor can it guarantee that their work will result in 'key' knowledge for the organisation. Perhaps the subject of effective research incentives is another area of research that the knowledge management community would benefit from becoming involved in.

In summary, looking at the nature of knowledge using the Zachman perspectives has provided some useful insights, and raised possibilities for future work. It has also illustrated once again the value of the Zachman framework as a structure for analysis of knowledge of almost any kind.

This chapter has also shown how the cognitive/constructivist debate permeates many discussions within knowledge management, and it is essential to tease out these two perspectives (and any others that may exist!) before any debate can be meaningful.

16 Issues with Multi-Perspective Modelling

The issues raised by this book that are concerned with the multi-perspective modelling are:

• Can the Zachman framework really capture and represent all the knowledge needed for knowledge management and knowledge engineering? Are there parts of the Zachman framework that don't need to be filled in order to accomplish knowledge management? Conversely, is there anything required by knowledge management that can't be represented by the Zachman framework?

• Does CommonKADS propose models that fill all the cells in the Zachman framework? If not which perspectives does it address at which levels of abstraction?

• Are there knowledge acquisition techniques to cover all six perspectives proposed by the Zachman framework? If not, why not, and could techniques be devised? Is there a need for different techniques at different levels of abstraction?

• Is it common for the WHAT and HOW perspectives to dominate the other perspectives? If so, why?

16.1 The Zachman framework and Knowledge Management

Determining whether the Zachman framework is adequate to support knowledge management requires revisiting the question of what knowledge management actually is. For the purposes of this discussion, the seven approaches to knowledge management identified in [78] will be considered in three categories:

1. Approaches that result in a computerised decision support system of some kind('transactional', 'analytical' and 'asset improvement');

2. Approaches that result in some kind of (indexed) library of knowledge ('asset management' and 'process management');

3. Approaches that result in more knowledgeable people ('developmental' and 'innovation').

16.1.1 'Decision support system' knowledge management

The Zachman framework is most obviously representative of this type of knowledge management, not least because the discussion in section 2.6 shows how the rows of the Zachman framework correspond to the various steps in a typical software engineering project at multiple levels of abstraction: at an abstract level it corresponds to a spiral project management lifecycle, at a 'normal' level it corresponds to a waterfall (i.e. sequential) model of software development, and at a more detailed level it illustrates that sub-tasks of software development have their own sequential series of activities.

The question of whether all the cells in the Zachman framework are needed for this type of knowledge management is difficult to answer outside the context of a specific project. If an organisation commissions a system to address a specific problem, for example, as described in chapter 7, then there is little need to develop nmodels to represent the Scoping and Enterprise levels of the framework. However, if the purpose of the exercise is to carry out an organisational SWOT (strengths, weaknesses, opportunities and threats) analysis, issues may arise anywhere in the Zachman framework ... for example, the weakness "our system designs are based on old assumptions" belongs to the Technology row and the Why column); "our corporate structure has too many levels" belongs to Scoping and What); and "we have world class experts in our research department" can be assigned to the System level and the Who perspective.

It seems, however that the parts of the Zachman framework that are most relevant to knowledge management are the top two rows – the scoping and enterprise levels. This is because the goals of knowledge management – "the identification and analysis of available and required knowledge assets and knowledge asset related processes, and the subsequent planning and control of actions to develop both the assets and the processes so as to fulfil organisational objectives." [118] – are focused more on knowing what knowledge exists in the organisation, and deciding what to do with it, rather than on knowing the knowledge itself. Knowledge management should therefore be more of a strategic task in organisations that an operational one, and hence the "scoping" and "enterprise" levels which focus on business processes at a high level, are most appropriate to it.

The answer to the opposite question – whether there are any aspects of 'decision support system' knowledge management that aren't covered by the perspectives and rows in the Zachman framework – seems to be 'no'. To say otherwise would be to contradict the main point of chapter 2. This may not be equally true for the other categories of knowledge management.

16.1.2 'Indexed library' knowledge management

For the asset management and process management approaches to knowledge management, the Zachman framework's primary support lies in its columns – the perspectives – rather than its rows. The perspectives inherent in the Zachman framework provide a wide-ranging indexing approach that makes it easier for users to find the information that they are looking for, as described in chapter 3. The actual guidance on what these multi-perspective indices should contain is limited to a few suggestions such as "networks" or "events" (see table 2.1), but as the discussion of chapter 3 argues, the mere inclusion of a multi-perspective index should be an advance over current ontology indexing techniques.

16.1.3 'Knowledgeable   people'   knowledge management

Many researchers who favour the 'knowledgeable people' approach favour a constructivist view of knowledge which rejects "the idea of a correspondence or reflection of external reality [with knowledge]." Instead, constructivism assumes that an individual attempts to reach coherence among the different pieces of knowledge, maintaining only 'constructions' that succeed in integrating previously incoherent pieces of knowledge. The emphasis is therefore on knowledge relationships and structures rather than individual 'items' of knowledge. Furthermore, constructivism rejects the idea of 'givens': "neither objective empirical data or facts, nor inborn categories or cognitive structures". To these researchers, the Zachman framework seems to be an encouragement to engage in unhelpful separation and classification of knowledge items.

Yet even to a constructivist, the concept of multi-perspective modelling has value. If there is a complex knowledge structure in someone's head, and it is desirable to bring it into the open ('acquire' it in knowledge engineering jargon; 'externalise' it in the words of Nonaka & Takeuchi), then looking at it from multiple perspectives can help determine the structure itself as well as the components of the structure, just as crystallography examines a crystal from different angles to obtain an understanding of the structure of the crystal.

Let's take an example of 'constructed' knowledge – a situation in which a machine has an unknown fault, and a visiting technician, after failing to fix the machine, sits down for a drink with the local maintenance operator. As each shares with the other their experience of the machine, they begin to develop a joint 'story', consistent with the past experiences of both of them, about how the machine might be operating. This 'constructed' view of the machine's (faulty) operation then allows them to diagnose the fault.

The thesis being presented here is that there would be some benefit to this conversation if it were structured around Zachman's six perspectives. Would it help the technician if the operator stuck to describing WHAT had happened, rather than speculating on HOW? If the fault is intermittent, is that enough information or would it help to construct an approximate schedule of WHEN the fault had occurred? Does it make any difference WHO the operator was when the fault occurred? (In one anecdote from computer technical support, a computer made repeated beeping noises only when used by a particular secretary. The problem turned out to be a low chair, so that her large breasts were resting on the keyboard!). No research is known in this area, but it seems a good opening for future work.

The constructivist view does highlight what is possibly the biggest weakness of the Zachman framework, though, and indeed of knowledge modelling in general ... the very act of separating knowledge risks losing some of the information about the links between items of knowledge. However, as chapter 3 makes clear, the complementarity of models recommended by multi-perspective modelling helps to reduce this problem. Still, it can be argued that representing complex knowledge structure is indeed an area where the Zachman framework may be insufficient to support knowledge management.

The development of knowledge based systems has grown from the development of research prototypes into a industry that is able to produce robust, reliable, commercial software. The concept of 'knowledge engineering' – a term coined by Ed Feigenbaum, defined as "the systematic application of engineering techniques and methods to the development of expert systems" – arose from a desire by the customers for these systems to have such reliability and robustness, and the response by researchers to seek for an equivalent approach to the software engineering approaches used for more conventional software systems. The process of developing a suitable "knowledge engineering" approach produced several false starts and (arguably) one new software engineering method – the whole area of object oriented analysis and design has its roots in the knowledge representation technique of 'frames', first publicised by Marvin Minsky – but once the KADS methodology appeared, it became clear that nearly all other knowledge engineering methods that were subsequently proposed (or revised) were drawing on KADS' library of interpretation models (used as templated for part of the Expertise model). KADS, and later CommonKADS, therefore became a *de facto* standard for knowledge engineering.

It's the System level of the Zachman framework that maps best to CommonKADS' Expertise model. Since the lowest level of the Zachman framework is an implemented system which is also the end result of a knowledge engineering process, it can be assumed that four lower rows of the Zachman framework are all relevant to knowledge engineering; but since CommonKADS' Expertise model is by far the most detailed of its models, the discussion below will concentrate on the System level.

16.3 Multi-perspective modelling and the Expertise model: perspectives

What perspectives on knowledge are represented at the System level? It's possible to provide a short answer to this question: the Expertise model covers the *what*, *how* and (arguably) *when* perspectives through its domain models, inference structures and task structures respectively. The discussion below therefore centres on the remaining three perspectives.

16.3.1 Representing who, where and why at the System level

The main argument of chapter 6 is that the CommonKADS Agent and Communication Models which CommonKADS considers to belong to the Enterprise level and the System level respectively, can both be usefully applied at both levels of abstraction. If these 'system level' Agent and Communication models are developed, this will provide both "who" and "where" perspectives at the System level.

As for "why" knowledge, chapter 2 has noted that "why" knowledge is often considered to be supplied by the context of knowledge (i.e. the role it plays in a higher level of abstraction). If this is true then no separate modelling of "why" knowledge is needed at the System level. However, section 2.3.6 has demonstrated that there are some domains or tasks for which "why" knowledge ought to be modelled, because justifications and rationales need to be explicitly identified. Knowledge engineers who need to model "why" knowledge are encouraged to use the variant QOC technique presented in section 2.3.6, the simplified 'Strategy' knowledge suggested in section D.5.2, or some adaptation of these that suits their needs.

It's also arguable that "when" knowledge experiences – or suffers from – the same dual representation as "why" knowledge. "When" knowledge can be considered to be either knowledge about time, or knowledge associated with ordering and sequencing – i.e. control over the "how" perspective. From this viewpoint, it might be considered that "when" knowledge is also under-represented in CommonKADS models.... control knowledge is expressed in more than one model, but temporal knowledge only addressed explicitly within the Organisation model.

16.4   Knowledge acquisition

16.4.1 What types of knowledge need to be acquired for different task types?

KADS and CommonKADS both provide a library of task types (actually "problem solving methods"), with associated interpretation models or inference structures. The library is categorised at the top level into *analytic* tasks, *synthetic* tasks and *modification* tasks. Analytic tasks (classification, diagnosis, assessment, monitoring, prediction) are those that analyse an existing situation or artefact; synthetic tasks (design, configuration, planning, scheduling) are those that create some new artefact or situation; and modification tasks (control, repair) are those that alter an existing artefact or situation which normally requires elements of both analysis and synthesis.

This classification has major implications for the design of knowledge based systems to support these tasks (see chapter 12), and it also affects the types of knowledge required for tasks: synthetic tasks all require knowledge of constraints on the parameters of the created artefact, while analytic tasks rarely require this type of knowledge.

Below this level of detail, however, the major influence on the type of knowledge needed by various tasks seems to be not the source of the knowledge, nor the way in which its component information is combined, nor the form of the knowledge; instead, it is the perspective that they address (i.e. WHO, WHAT, HOW, WHEN, WHERE or

WHY). Classification and assessment tasks address WHAT knowledge (i.e. categorisation according to features) whereas diagnosis and monitoring are more concerned with HOW a system works (or should work). Planning and scheduling focus on WHEN tasks are carried out while configuration and design look at WHERE items should be placed, with design also considering WHICH items will play a particular role – which is analogous to the WHO perspective. The correlation of the WHEN and WHERE perspectives with synthetic tasks, and the absence of tasks that use WHY knowledge (and minimal consideration of the WHO perspective), are indicators worthy of further attention.

Before speculating on these correlations, however, a word must be said about the 'primitiveness' of problem solving tasks. The list of task types used by KADS and CommonKADS was originally proposed by Joost Breuker in the very first KADS report [20]. But Breuker himself has proposed more recently that CommonKADS' tasks are actually composed from a smaller set of more primitive tasks [18]. He suggests that the minimal set consists of just six tasks from which all other task types can be composed: modelling, design, assignment, prediction, monitoring and diagnosis. Breuker defines these as follows:

- Modelling is concerned with the identification of what is a system and what is its environment, or more precise: what is its behavioural interface with the environment.
- Design has as its conclusion a structure of components and their connections. The components may be objects or processes, physical or symbolic.
- Assignment distributes (additional) elements (components, actions) over a structure. If the structure is a plan, the assignment problem is generally called scheduling. If the structure is a design the problem is often called configuration.
- Prediction delivers the resulting states of a system over time, starting with an initial state. When one derives an initial state from some output states one may speak of postdiction.
- Monitoring yields a discrepancy between a predicted state and an observed state.
- Diagnosis finds components or structures which conflict with their behavioural model or design.

Furthermore, Breuker sees these six tasks as being sequential: so modelling is a prerequisite for all the others, a design can be transformed into an assignment, and so on.

There is a good correlation between Breuker's six basic task types and the six perspectives recommended by the Zachman framework:

- Modelling is concerned with the WHAT the current system is;
- Design is concerned with WHICH components will play particular roles in the new system which is analogous to WHO knowledge;
- Assignment is concerned with WHERE the components will fit;
- Prediction is concerned with state of the system at a particular time (WHEN);
- Monitoring is concerned with comparisons (information to knowledge conversion, according to Davenport & Prusak);
- Diagnosis tells us WHY any discrepancies observed by monitoring exist, based on knowledge of HOW the system functions.

So each task will require different types of knowledge, and will thus require different knowledge elicitation techniques. Modelling will be concerned with categories, properties, taxonomies and ontologies; design with capabilities and roles; assignment with connections and constraints; prediction with time and states; and diagnosis with procedures, processes, rationales and justifications. Monitoring may require detailed knowledge of monitoring procedures or of methods of interpreting monitoring data, but it does seem to be more of an information-processing task than a knowledge-based task in many cases.

In short, it seems that the Zachman framework's perspectives should cover all the types of knowledge that need to be acquired in order to support any knowledge based task (or at least, any knowledge-based task that has an associated 'interpretation model' in CommonKADS).

16.4.2 Knowledge acquisition techniques

We have determined that the perspectives in the Zachman model are sufficient to represent all the knowledge that might be needed for any task for which a CommonKADS interpretation model exists. But are there knowledge acquisition techniques capable of capturing all these types of knowledge?

Chapter 11 argues that there are existing knowledge acquisition techniques for acquiring declarative and procedural (WHAT and HOW knowledge). A mapping of the knowledge acquisition techniques presented in that chapter to perspectives might look like Table 16.1.

In addition, the repertory grid can be applied to acquiring features of tasks by prepopulating the grid with task-related attributes, or to acquire "goodness" values for constraints, using the "possibility grid" approach [16] referred to in Chapter 10.

From this, it can be seen that acquisition of "what" and "how" knowledge is well provided for by current knowledge acquisition techniques, but very few techniques are specifically intended for acquiring other types of knowledge. Constraints (primarily WHEN knowledge), roles and responsibilities (WHO knowledge), networks and structures (WHERE) and rationales and justifications (WHY) are all poorly catered for by existing knowledge acquisition techniques. The lack of a good technique for acquiring networks and structures (unless they are taxonomies) is perhaps the biggest need.

There may be deeper reasons why it is difficult to design knowledge acquisition techniques for perspectives that are associated with synthetic tasks - WHEN, WHERE and WHY knowledge. The next two sections look at knowledge associated with these perspectives in more detail, and will also look at the question of why WHAT and HOW knowledge seem to dominate the other perspectives

Technique	Knowledge acquired
Laddering	Concepts, **is-a** relations, taxonomy
Card sorting	Properties, values, concepts, possibly **is-a** or **part-of** relations
Repertory grid	Properties, values, conceptual clustering (might be taxonomic)
Laddering with alternate questions	Tasks/actions/activities, processes, states, sequencing
Protocol analysis	Tasks/activities/actions, sequencing, durations, (some) communication links, communication content
20 questions	Tasks/activities/actions, sequencing
Rapid prototyping	All types
Conflict	Agents, constraints
Contradiction & complication	Constraints, concepts, properties
Similarity	Constraints, concepts[1]
Chance	Concepts

Table 16.1 Mapping propose-and-revise knowledge acquisition techniques to perspectives

16.4.3   WHEN and WHERE and determinable concepts

The answer to the question regarding the association of WHEN and WHERE with synthetic tasks is probably tied to the difference between determinate and determinable concepts highlighted in chapter 3. Both time and spatial location are determinable concepts – while one or two commonly used time intervals have real world correlates ('day', 'year', and 'lunar month'), most time intervals are arbitarily determined (why should a day be divided into twenty four hours, for example?); and spatial location is perhaps the ultimate determinable concept, requiring at least three and maybe as many as six points on arbitrarily determined scales (distance measurements – one or two points on each of three dimensions) to identify it accurately. So we see that where a task requires dealing with determinable concepts, a solution typically has to be synthesised rather than analysing an existing situation.

This link probably arises because determinable concepts can overlap much more easily than determinate ones, and this increases the complexity of constraints and the size of the search space. It's much easier to envisage time intervals or spatial locations that overlap with each other than people or objects that overlap; even processes rarely have sub-activities that help to fulfil more than one higher level activity. In other words, it is the size of the search space induced by determinable concepts such as time or spatial location that require a synthetic task; if the search space is small, synthetic tasks can usually be boiled down to analytic tasks, such as selection from a set of pre-defined options, or assignment of components to vacant slots.

What can we derive from this analysis? We can postulate that knowledge engineering tasks that are heavily based on determinable concepts are likely to produce a large search space, and therefore to require synthetic approaches. Perhaps this is the reason for the popularity of neural networks and data mining in stock market trading and other financial applications – not only is there a vast amount of data that needs to be categorised, but financial value is a determinable concept (it's a function of two other determinable dimensions, supply and demand), and there are therefore no "natural" value categories to use as a framework for analysis. The combination of large amounts of data and the need for a synthetic approach leads naturally towards "machine learning" approaches such as neural nets or data mining.

Other determinable concepts include colour (based on three determinable dimensions: level of red, green and blue light); temperature (with the exception of absolute zero); physical parameters such as age, weight or velocity; and status. In fact, all measurements based on the three spatial dimensions or on the fourth dimension of time are ultimately determinable rather than determinate; so are all measures based on energy levels – luminance, radiation, mass, and so on. Colour is fundamentally an energy-based concept. It is perhaps worth distinguishing these "physically determinable" concepts from "societally determinable" concepts such as value, status, and perhaps even codes of laws. I do not intend to continue this line of argument to the conclusion that the social constructivist epistemologists have reached – that because so much of the 'world' is fundamentally determinable rather than determinate, 'truth' or 'reality' will be accorded only to those constructions on which most people of a social group agree – for the task of knowledge engineers is normally to work within societal codes (and in addition, within the knowledge-owning company's codes of practice) and to achieve better knowledge management within an existing agreed framework; but it is worth considering that the problem faced by ontologists of boiling everything down to "primitive" levels of detail (see chapter 3) may be insoluble in practice, because so many apparently "primitive" concepts are determinable rather that determinate. For practical purposes, knowledge engineers should be aware that they are likely to run into difficulties and disagreements if they try to produce a classification of obviously determinable concepts, and they may find benefit in choosing a synthetic approach instead.

It is perhaps this determinable/deterministic distinction that explains the popularity of the WHAT and HOW perspectives, certainly for classification tasks such as the one described in chapter 4. The answer is simply that WHAT and HOW concepts are deterministic, and therefore more widely accepted, than concepts from other perspectives (roles from the WHO perspective are largely determinable, being defined by the list of responsibilities associated with them). However, there are further questions that could be solved by future research, though ... is all knowledge associated with these two perspectives deterministic? How should non-taxonomic knowledge, and HOW knowledge in particular, be best used for indexing? Is there a deterministic link between deterministic WHAT knowledge and deterministic HOW knowledge?

16.4.4 Where is the WHY perspective?

The observation above also helps us understand the frequent absence of a WHY perspective that has been observed at all levels of knowledge modelling. Chapter 2 observed that the answer to the question "why are you doing this?" or "why is this so?" can be on two levels; it can be goal-based e.g. "I am doing it to achieve this higher level goal" or it can be based on rationale and justification (e.g. "I am doing this because it is industry best practice"). In that discussion, it was assumed that the reason the WHY perspective was frequently not mentioned in knowledge modelling was that most answers were goal-based, and since the goals had already been described at a higher level of knowledge modelling, there was no need to repeat this.

But now we see that the rationale-based answer to "why" also has difficulties, because knowledge engineers work within (often unstated) societal codes or organisational practices. So a rationale that states "I am doing this because it is industry best practice" or "I am doing this because it fits the ethos of this organisation" inevitably leads on to further questions: "Why is this believed to be industry best practice?" or "why does the organisation have this ethos?". In essence, the questions are asking "What are the primitive absolutes on which this justification is based?", and there often are no primitive absolutes; instead, the justification is based on agreed societally determinable concepts such as ethics or laws (normally indicated by the answer "that's just the way things are").

In a few cases, there is empirical evidence that a particular approach is the best one (see for example [122] who argue strongly for taking an evidence-based approach to clinical practice in medicine); but equally often, the rationale for a procedure is not even a societally agreed concept, but simply based on the opinion of one or two senior individuals in the organisation, or on one or to past experiences of "experts" in the organisation. Furthermore, it's a well-known psychological feature of human decision making that generalisations are often based on only two or three examples (see [60]. The "why" perspective is therefore often not developed for two reasons: because it is unprofitable to record "that's the way it is" justifications, and because it's sometimes to the organisation's or individual's advantage to cover up the lack of an empirical or otherwise well-justified basis for their actions.

There are some circumstances where the WHY perspective is explicitly recorded, and is very beneficial. The consideration of empirical studies which make conflicting recommendations is one such area, as illustrated in chapter 2. Another area where the WHY perspective is very useful is in representing the knowledge required to agree on societal norms; see for example the PLINTH system [26], used to represent supporting arguments and related statutes when developing building regulations. And then there is the task of diagnosis, whose goal is to answer the question "Why is this system not working?". Diagnostic reasoning must be ultimately based on a cause-and-effect model of how the system works, and it may be that the principles of cause-and-effect are closer to being primitive absolute concepts than any other concepts that knowledge engineers work with.

17 Ontological issues

The issues that will be discussed in this chapter are as follows:
• How is it possible to determine if a domain item is a concept or a property?
• Is it possible to build a library of reusable domain models, akin to the library of generic inference structures?
• Could ontologies and knowledge acquisition techniques support each other?
• Would a domain-specific ontology provide more support to knowledge acquisition than the CommonKADS domain ontology? Conversely, would a domain-specific ontology overly restrict knowledge acquisition?
• Where have domain-specific and task-specific knowledge acquisition tools been successful? Why?

The definition of 'ontology' being used in this book is that it is an explicit specification of a conceptualisation; in knowledge engineering practice, it defines what can be represented in a computer system. From the pragmatic viewpoint of a knowledge engineer, ontologies are a way of *organising* and *standardising* the terminology used to describe the knowledge that is captured and presented in knowledge models. The CommonKADS domain knowledge classification scheme (concepts/properties/relations/expressions) can be considered to be a simple, domain-neutral ontology.

17.1 Ontological classification of domain knowledge

The first issue that appears above is how to decide whether domain items should be classified as concepts or properties. It may seem obvious that "objects" should be classified as concepts while "attributes" of those objects should be classified as properties. In Chapter 11, a simple "linguistic test" was suggested for distinguishing concepts and properties, based on the part of speech (nouns and adjectives).

But it turns out that this "linguistic test" only works in the context of a particular application. The truth is that "one man's concept is another man's property" – in other words, ontological classification is task-specific. Data, information or knowledge that functions as a concept in one task might be a property in another. To give an example, "colour" is likely to be a concept when the task is digitally editing a photograph (with properties such as "density" and "hue"), but a property when the task is choosing a car. Even a car – which is clearly an object – may not always be considered to be a concept; if the task is to solve the "travelling salesman" problem, then the car itself may be considered to be a property (of the salesman) rather than a concept.

This variety of function seems to strike at the heart of the assumption that a single "ontology" of the entire world can be developed, in which every item is uniquely defined, and has a unique ontological type (i.e. concept/property/whatever). If this assumption is false, projects such as the development of Cyc [114] seem unlikely to succeed. But is it possible to develop a single ontology of the world where items have unique definitions but do not have unique ontological types? If so, then there is hope once again for grand ontology projects.

Let's consider this question by examining the ontological classification of "colour" in more detail. First, let us try to define 'colour' according to "first principles". 'Colour' is defined in the *Shorter Oxford English Dictionary* as

1.The quality in virtue of which objects present different appearances to the eye, in respect of the kind of light reflected from their surfaces.
2.A particular hue or tint; often specifying one distinct from the prevailing tone.
3.Complexion, hue; freshness of hue
4.Colouring (especially in Art)

In the *Cambridge Encyclopedia*, "colour vision" is defined as

"The ability to detect differences between light of various wavelengths by converting them into colours. It is dependent on the presence of light-sensitive pigments in the cones, each being sensitive to light of a particular wavelength. The cones send coded information to the brain

(via certain retinal neurones and the optic nerve) for processing and colour appreciation. In humans, the cones contain pigments most sensitive to red, green or blue light."
From these definitions, it is clear that:
- Any coloured object has a colour hue, and (by extension) other properties such as colour density;
- The "thing" that causes colour is light of a particular wavelength;
- The appearance of colours is dependent on the ambient light, and different people may perceive colours differently.

So there is (in theory) a fundamental "ontology" of colour that can be universally accepted. But very few ontologies define colour in terms of wavelengths of light because such detail isn't necessary for the task being tackled. It seems that ontologies define concepts at different levels of abstraction from the fundamental definitions, where the chosen level of abstraction is task-dependent. For example, digital manipulation of photographs requires matching of colour hues and colour densities; if these are properties that need to be considered, then colour must be a concept. So while it may be possible to identify 'primitive' properties from the dictionary or "first principles" definitions, an ontology that was based on such "primitive" properties would rarely be directly usable for problem solving, because it would not match the properties that were important to the tasks.

Is it possible to characterise the various levels of abstraction that can be used? If it is, it may be possible to specify how any given ontological definition is derived from first principles, and therefore to provide a link between any given ontology and a universal ("first principles", and therefore task-neutral) ontology of that domain. This is still a topic for research, but the field has been opened up for debate by Nicola Guarino, in his paper, "Some Ontological Principles for Designing Upper Level Lexical Resources" [128]. Guarino proposes that there are no less than nine levels of detail that might be considered relevant, ranging from the "atomic level" through the "topological level" and the "biological level" up to the "social level". It can be seen how each level can be derived from the next higher level of detail.

If Guarino's "nine levels" argument is correct, then it should be possible to develop a 'grand ontology' with unique definitions for each concept, at the "first principles" level, and to link conceptual definitions in other ontologies to these universal definitions by identifying the level of abstraction being used. So even if a suitable level of detail cannot be agreed, different levels of detail can be identified. Guarino's definitions of the different levels also go some way towards establishing definitional properties for ontologies.

17.2 Ontologies and re-usable domain models

A re-usable domain model consists of a set of concepts that describe a domain and can be incorporated into any knowledge based system that deals with that domain, whatever the task is. In theory, an ontology of the domain should provide all the functionality that is expected from a re-usable domain model. In practice, however, ontologies do not necessarily generalise well if the task they are being used for is not similar to the task they were designed for. For example, an ontology of diseases designed to support diagnosis might be re-usable for deciding on treatments for the patient, but less useful for public health officials trying to prevent disease transmission.

There seem to be two reasons for this lack of re-usability. One reason is the concept-vs-property issue discussed above; the level of abstraction selected for concepts in an ontology varies according the type of task being tackled (e.g. digital manipulation of a photograph vs. identifying a car by its colour). The second reason is that the required *viewpoint* on information – that is, the properties of concepts that are considered relevant – also changes according to the task.

Here's an example of viewpoints from the ESPRIT-funded KACTUS project [134]:

"If one wants to re-use a notion like "heat exchanger", it quickly becomes clear that this term can have different meanings in different contexts. For example, from an oil-platform design perspective the physical properties will be the main emphasis: physical dimensions, types of connections, etc. In a diagnostic setting functional properties such as the difference in temperature between the different inputs and outputs are likely to be the prime focus of attention. For dynamic simulation applications, behavioural properties such as mathematical properties of the heat exchange process would need to be modelled in association with 'heat exchanger'."

In other words, the requirements placed on an ontology vary according to the level of detail required, and on whether the emphasis is on WHAT, HOW, WHY or some other perspective on knowledge.

So is this argument leading to the conclusion that a separate ontology is required for each of the thirty-six cells in the Zachman framework? Perhaps this is what might be required in theory, but in practice this is unworkable. It is better to make some compromises on the reusability of a single ontology than to try to develop thirty-six ontologies for every domain.

So how many ontologies are needed? On the subject of levels of detail, the KACTUS project proposed developing ontologies at four different levels:

Application ontology : An application ontology is simply an ontology used by an application. It contains the information structures we use for building a software system. It can be very specific for this application, or also have general features. In KACTUS we are interested in the question how one can flesh out the meaning of parts of an application ontology for future reuse, and how we can construct (part of) an application ontology from existing ontologies.

Domain ontology : Domain ontologies are ontologies that are specific for a particular type of artefact. Example domain ontologies could be ontologies for ships, oil platforms, and electrical networks. A domain ontology generalises over particular application tasks in that domain. Thus, a domain ontology for ship design would need to be independent of both a design assessment application, and of a design construction application.

Basic technical ontology : Basic technical ontologies generalise over particular artefacts, and describe general features of artefacts. Basic technical ontologies usually define a viewpoint related to some physical process type: flow, heat, energy, power, electricity. Such processes re-appear in many different technical domains. For example, flow processes occur in both oil platforms and in electrical networks.

Generic ontology : A generic ontology describes a "top-level category". One can see a generic ontology as a basic mechanism for "carving up the world". It is related to the Aristotelian notion of categories. The main difference is that in KACTUS we are not aiming at a complete set of generic ontologies, but are only interested in those categories that frequently occur. Example top-level categories that were identified are notions like physical, functional, and behavioural entities, connectedness, part-whole, and topology.

No work is known on the number of perspectives that are needed as a pragmatic minimum, although given that 80% of all successful KBS applications perform either diagnosis or assessment tasks, it seems that the WHAT and HOW perspectives are probably the most widely used.

The KACTUS project, whose purpose is to "develop methods and tools to enable reuse and sharing of technical knowledge", also considers issues relating to the primitives of ontology specification languages, and the relationship of ontology definitions to software engineering approaches, such as the ANSI/SPARC definition of databases. All of these are described briefly in [134].

In summary, ontologies are theoretically re-usable for multiple tasks, but only if the tasks tackle the same domain *and* the desired viewpoints/perspectives are the same *and* the required level of abstraction is the same. This is rarely true unless the task being tackled is very similar to the task that the original ontology was designed for.

17.3   Ontologies   &   domain/task-specific knowledge acquisition

The idea of using ontologies to support knowledge acquisition is an obvious one; for if an immensely detailed (and relevant) ontology was used, acquisition of domain knowledge would be reduced to determining which items from the ontology were present and which were absent in the relevant expert knowledge. Yet this approach is unrealistic, not only because of the sheer size of the ontology that would be needed to represent all possible knowledge in even a narrow domain, but also because it does not take account of the practicalities of knowledge acquisition. Knowledge acquisition is not only about identifying items of knowledge but also choosing the appropriate level of abstraction for each item of knowledge; it's not only about determining what domain knowledge is *present* in the expert's knowledge but also about what is *relevant*; and it's not only about defining knowledge ontologically, it's also about considering how that knowledge will be applied.

There are, broadly speaking, three approaches that aim to make use of ontologies to support knowledge acquisition:

• The first approach is to supply a tool that makes it easy for an domain expert to define an ontology; this ontology can then be used to support knowledge acquisition. A well-known tool in this category is Protege [126]. Protege is intended to be a tool which allows the user to construct a domain ontology, customize knowledge-acquisition forms or enter domain knowledge; it is also a platform which can be extended with graphical widgets for tables, diagrams, animation components to access other knowledge-based systems embedded applications, and a library which other applications can use to access and display knowledge bases. Tools such as Protege may speed the process of ontology editing, but their support for the conceptual task of defining an appropriate ontology is limited to general techniques such as encouraging hierarchical classification of concepts.

• The second approach is to provide pre-defined ontologies at an abstracted level, so that each node in an abstract ontology represents a class, instances or possibly a whole taxonomy in the domain knowledge. In other words, provide an ontology at the level of the "basic technical ontology" suggested by the KACTUS project, and use it as a guide to the creation or instantiation of a domain ontology. The system that has tried this approach most thoroughly is CUE [182]. This approach seems promising because of its similarity to the CommonKADS generic inference models, but no empirical work on its usefulness (or potential restrictiveness) is known.

A variation on this approach has been to provide pre-defined ontologies for tasks rather than domains. The most common task tackled in this way has been diagnosis (OPAL [117]; Emerald Intelligence's Mahogany Help Desk; MOLE [57]; MORE [91]; and Carnegie Group's Testbench) although other tasks addressed include propose-and-revise design/configuration (SALT [123]) and design evaluation (KNACK [106]).

It might even be argued that the task of classification is supported by tools such as Protege, or by tools that support particular knowledge acquisition techniques such as the repertory grid (e.g. NEXTRA, a front end to the Nexpert Object expert system shell, or AQUINAS [14], a knowledge acquisition workbench), although this argument does require stretching the definition of a "classified ontology" to include "those distinctions that a repertory grid is able to make".

• The third approach is a combination of the previous two approaches: a predefined ontology is provided, but with appropriate training, experts are able to edit the ontology. A well-known tool that supports this approach is EXPECT [165] which is a task-specific knowledge acquisition tool focused on propose-and-revise design/configuration tasks.

A major experiment on this approach was carried out within the DARPA-sponsored Rapid Knowledge Formation (RKF) project, in the domain of molecular biology [173], using two different generic ontologies but the same domain. The results (in terms of fast, accurate ontology development) were impressive, though the required level of training for the experts in ontological concept definition proved to be higher than first thought.

Which of these approaches works the best? For experts with little or no understanding of ontological terms, tools that support pre-defined ontologies would appear to be recommended. But this requires careful tool selection by the knowledge engineer, because the pre-defined ontology must fit the domain or task to be tackled. If the task is non-standard in any way (e.g. a configuration task requires prioritisation of components), then the "ontology editing" tools would seem preferable. Alternatively, the knowledge engineer could use tools such as Protege to develop his own pre-defined ontology-based knowledge acquisition tool.

18 Knowledge Engineering: CommonKADS' Expertise Model

The next two chapters of the review consists of a detailed overview of the process of developing a set of CommonKADS models for domain-specific knowledge. This chapter focuses on the Expertise model, the next on the Communication and Design models. The issues that are covered in this chapter are:

- How useful is it to apply CommonKADS models – or other knowledge models, for that matter – prescriptively rather than descriptively? In other words, is it better to start with a generic knowledge model and use it as a guide to what knowledge should be needed to solve the task (a top-down approach) or to start by analysing knowledge acquired through interviews or other methods and to determine which knowledge model(s) it fits into? (a bottom-up approach)?
- Is knowledge engineering using CommonKADS a purely sequential process, or are there feedback loops to earlier models?
- Is there any guidance on
    - "correct" instantiation of generic inference structures?
    - how to select the "right" inference step?
- What does a 'bad' Expertise model look like?

18.1 Top-down or bottom-up knowledge modelling?

As with many issues that have been widely debated in computer science, both top-down and bottom-up knowledge modelling have some advantages. Top-down modelling maximises re-use of previous knowledge and avoids the need to analyse acquired knowledge that has little relevance to the actual problem solving task. On the other hand, it risks missing out on knowledge that is relevant just because it is not expected; the issues are similar to those debated in earlier chapters regarding the value of modelling as a knowledge management technique. If a poor choice of generic model is made, top-down modelling also risks forcing acquired knowledge into a 'box' that is not suitable for it.

Bottom-up modelling, by contrast, risks spending much time on acquisition and analysis of knowledge that is not ultimately useful, and may also become unfocused or undirected, with knowledge acquisition sessions following the expert's whims.

The supporters of both the top-down approach and the bottom-up approach have recognised the strengths and weaknesses of their own approaches, and have suggested modifications. Much of the discussion in this section is focused on using CommonKADS top-down, and on guidance that is available on selecting the best generic inference structure and on configuring inference structures that do not quite match the task being addressed (or are not specific enough). A short section on "Assembling an inference structure from components" considers the opposite viewpoint, showing how bottom-up modellers may identify small components of inference structures that may then be assembled into bigger structures.

The recognition of these weaknesses in each approach largely answers the question of whether CommonKADS' models should be developed sequentially or with loopback. If the chosen approach fits perfectly first time – the top-down approach completely instantiates a model with the expert declaring that all relevant knowledge has now been acquired, or the bottom-up approach acquires all available knowledge and then builds a suitable knowledge model from it – then no loopback should be required. However, it will be rare for either of these situations to apply. More frequently, the top-down modeller will discover some knowledge that cannot be fitted into the generic model and must return to the generic model and configure it; or the bottom-up modeller will identify a component knowledge model, only to realise that he does not have sufficient knowledge to instantiate that model and must return to the expert. So looping back should be considered the norm.

18.2 Top-down: Selecting and configuring inference structures

This section will discuss the three stages involved in using a generic inference structure to develop an instantiated inference structure within an Expertise model:

- selection of generic inference structures from CommonKADS' library of inference structures;
- configuration of inference structures to match specific knowledge-based tasks;
- instantiation of an inference structure to domain-specific knowledge

18.2.1 Selecting a generic inference structure

CommonKADS (and KADS before it) offers a library of generic inference structures. This library has probably been CommonKADS' single biggest contribution to the overall science of knowledge engineering. The library is indexed by task type; that is, the library can be organised according to a taxonomy of generic task types. See Figure 18.1 for the first proposed version of this taxonomy [20].

Simple selection of a generic inference structure

Simple selection of a generic inference structure requires a knowledge engineer to identify the type of the knowledge based task that needs to be modelled, and then to obtain a model from the library that corresponds to that task type. This requires an understanding of the taxonomy of task types.

At the top level of the taxonomy is a distinction between *System Analysis* tasks that require analysis of an existing state or artefact; *System Synthesis* tasks that require creation of an artefact that did not previously exist; and *System Modification* tasks, a small number of tasks that are considered to combine analysis and synthesis. The first two categories are decomposed further:

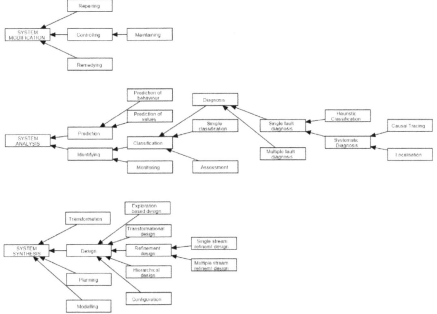

Figure 18.1: Taxonomy of task types

• Analytic tasks are classified as *Identification* tasks or *Prediction* tasks, depending on whether a current or future state or artefact is being analysed. The Identification category contains inference structures for assessment tasks, for simple classification tasks, and for a range of diagnostic tasks ranging from heuristic classification to multiple fault diagnosis; the Prediction category includes a couple of inference structures for different varieties of predictive task.

• The System Synthesis category is broken down into categories of *Planning* and *Design*. Inference structures for design cover several different approaches to design (transformational design, refinement design, etc.) as well as configuration tasks; configuration is a subset of design, since the solution must still be synthesised, but the design parameters are firmly fixed. Similarly, inference structures for planning tasks include various approaches to AI planning and to scheduling.

Indexing according to task type can be very useful. At the higher levels of the taxonomy of inference structures, the distinctions made were very powerful: for example, System Analysis tasks such as classification, diagnosis and assessment can be addressed using backward chaining rules if desired, whereas System Synthesis tasks cannot use backward reasoning as their sole programming paradigm, because to do so would require representing a (possibly infinite) space of solutions. The distinction between planning and design also tells the knowledge engineer immediately about the likely requirements for temporal and spatial reasoning.

One way of helping knowledge engineers select the "correct" inference structure is by treating the taxonomy of inference structures as a decision tree, and devising questions about the problem being tackled that guide the knowledge engineer on which branch of the "decision tree" to follow, eventually arriving at a recommended inference structure. This approach was investigated by [108], and a prototype system was developed. If a knowledge engineer asked the system for more detail, explanations were provided based on the descriptions given in [20].

Refining selection of inference structures by type of result

While simple selection of a generic inference structure is often sufficient, there are occasions where it's difficult to identify precisely the best generic inference structure. Choosing the "wrong" one rarely causes the project to fail, but it does mean that a lot of extra work is done in configuring the inference structure to the problem. Experience has shown that researchers usually agree on the task type of a knowledge based task, but have difficulty in agreeing on the optimal inference structure for any given application; a good example of this can be seen in the Sisyphus elevator design project [68]. Four research groups tried to model the same set of elevator design knowledge using CommonKADS, and managed to produce four inference structures that appeared very different from each other.

One of the difficulties lies in the fact that a small change to an inference structure may imply a large change to the problem solving approach. An example can be found in chapter 7 (section 7.4.1), where changing the name of a single inference step (from *decompose* to *select*) implies a change from a model-based approach (i.e. an approach based on cause and effect reasoning) to a simpler approach based on pre-defining expected results of tests. The reason for this was pointed out in 1997 by Joost Breuker [18], the author of the original taxonomy of task types: once a task has been identified as a diagnostic task, a further refinement is needed based in the type of result required. An inference structure that "decomposes" a system model expects to locate a faulty component as its result, and so the machine is progressively "decomposed" into subassemblies until a single faulty component is located – the tests that are run must simulate the inputs and outputs to each sub-assembly, and so the overall approach is model-based. In contrast, an inference structure that "selects" a system model is using the Sherlock Holmes approach of starting with a set of hypothesised faults, and progressively narrowing down that set; the faults may or may not be linked to individual components.

Breuker proposes that there are three possible result types that may be desired. These are:

1. Case – the state which the system is in;
2. Solution – the solution to the problem;
3. Argument – how the solution was derived from the case.

In a diagnostic task, faults correspond to cases, while components to be replaced (or other repair actions) constitute solutions. It is sensible for IMPRESS to use the fault-based Sherlock Holmes approach because there are several possible faults that are not caused by components in the system (e.g. a dusty environment is considered to be a "fault" if the dust gets into the plastic moulding machines); it would therefore be difficult to represent these using a component-focused diagnostic approach. Ideally, a generic inference structure that used a "select" rather than a "decompose" inference should have been selected initially; in practice, I was not aware of this distinction when I carried out the IMPRESS project, and so I merely changed the "decompose" to a "select" when I configured the generic inference structure to the problem. It seems likely that many other users of KADS and CommonKADS may have made similar "modelling hacks" which could account for the divergence in models seen in the Sisyphus project.

For the record, an "argument" solution for a diagnostic task corresponds to the relationship between the component and the faulty state. Argument solutions are perhaps of most use in devising expedient solutions to problems; consider the following (true) example of a diagnosis and recommended workaround:

> "Your computer crashes when you use the floppy drive. This is due to a fault in the bus. This limits the number of system devices that can be handled simultaneously; using the floppy drive adds another device, so the system crashes. However, replacing the bus is uneconomic. If the machine is rebooted into 16 colour video before using the floppy drive that will reduce the number of devices being used, and so the floppy drive can be used without crashing the computer."[45]

Here, the first sentence expresses the faulty state, the second sentence identifies the component and the third expresses the argument. The fourth sentence expresses the need for an expedient solution, and the last sentence uses the argument to devise a workaround solution rather than a fix for the fault.

Breuker's typology of results – case, argument and solution – is probably applicable to other tasks apart from diagnosis; it is almost certainly applicable to all analytic tasks, and may be applicable to synthetic tasks as well. It is therefore recommended that, where simple selection is not sufficient for identifying the optimal generic inference structure, the type of result desired should also be considered.

18.2.2 Configuring a generic inference structure

If an inference structure, once selected, could be used merely by instantiating its knowledge roles to problem-specific domain knowledge, then the issue of configuration would not arise. But in practice, few real-world tasks conform exactly to the inference structures contained in the CommonKADS library of inference structures; as suggested in chapter 8, selection of an inference structure from the library is usually followed by configuration of that inference structure (adding or removing a few inference steps or knowledge roles) before finally instantiating it to the domain. If configuration only involves removing components from a generic inference structure, then it may be that some of the inference steps have been "pre-compiled"

---

[45] My thanks to Richard Wheeler, formerly of AIAI and Starlab, for spending the hours necessary to arrive at this diagnosis, and to allow me to read floppy disks again.

into *static knowledge roles* i.e. all possible inputs to an inference step are processed through an inference step, the set of all possible results is stored, and then the inference step no longer needs to be performed during problem solving; a simple look-up of the set of all possible results (the "static knowledge role") is sufficient. This is actually quite a common feature of knowledge based programming, and it can be seen in the description of the configuration of the X-MATE inference structure in chapter 8. But if configuration requires adding any inference steps or knowledge roles, as in the generic inference structure for IMPRESS in chapter 8 where the "state of the machine" is added as a knowledge role, then it becomes clear that the generic inference structure has failed to characterise the problem completely.

A top-down approach to this problem is the "configurable inference structures" approach discussed in chapter 8. This approach uses principled (and recordable) transformations, and seems promising for further development and refinement of the CommonKADS library of generic inference structures. It is also supported by the very good definitions of inference steps given by Manfred Aben in his Ph.D. thesis [2]; he gives a very good description of the expected inputs, outputs and function of each type of inference step.

However, this approach has currently only been developed for assessment tasks [177] (although a tree-based analysis of assumptions in diagnosis tasks [59] might also support this approach), and it may not be able to cover all configurations that are needed by a particular domain.

18.3 Bottom   up: Assembling   from components

Some researchers have tackled the problem of customisation by reducing the "grain size" of generic inference structures; in other words, they propose that the library of inference structures should be made up of inference components, each containing a few inference steps, and the knowledge engineer should assemble a problem-specific inference structure from these components. This approach is seen most clearly in the "Components of Expertise" work of Luc Steels [161], but it is also a major theme in the VITAL approach to knowledge modelling that originated from the ESPRIT ACKnowledge project [51], and it is a feature of the "Generic Tasks" approach of Chandrasekaran [27]. This idea even arises in post-project work on CommonKADS; Joost Breuker [18] has proposed that the twenty or so task types that characterise the CommonKADS library of generic inference structures should be cut down to six task types from which other tasks can be assembled. For example, inference structures for Repair tasks can be assembled from an inference structure for Diagnosis (which is itself a specialisation of Assignment, in Breuker's scheme of things) followed by an inference structure for Planning (a specialisation of Design, according to Breuker).

It can be argued that this "assembly approach" to building inference structures tends to support a bottom-up approach – acquiring some knowledge, determining which "components of expertise" are present, and then assembling these into a larger inference structure. So which method is better; top-down or bottom-up modelling? Unfortunately, it is difficult to give an answer that applies to every case. Top-down modelling does appear to have the advantage of providing some guidance from re-use of previous knowledge engineering approaches. However, it is advisable to do some initial knowledge acquisition before making the decision whether to proceed top-down or bottom-up. As a rule of thumb, if there is a lot of knowledge available about the task (e.g. a textbook), then a top-down approach may be advisable to restrict the knowledge acquisition to just the relevant factors; if the task type is unclear from the initial knowledge acquisition, or appears to be a combination of task types, bottom-up modelling may be advisable.

18.4 Instantiation of generic inference structures

Instantiating an inference structure requires the replacement of the generic names of knowledge roles with domain-specific labels. For example, "universum of observables" might be replaced with "set of automatic tests" in an application involving computer diagnosis from a remote site. If the generic inference structure has been configured correctly, then it should resemble the domain model schema (see section 8.3.1) in structure. If this is the case, then t may be possible to transfer the labels in the domain model schema almost verbatim to the knowledge roles in the inference structure. But even if this is the case, it's worth double-checking that the knowledge roles match the input and output types expected by inference steps. For example, a "select" inference step must have at least one set as an input, and should produce a single element from that set as an output. Such checking is usually done informally, though more formal checks could be done using the definitions from [2].

18.5 Problem solving methods: the CommonKADS task structure

It's easy to think that, having selected, configured and instantiated a generic inference structure, the HOW component of the Expertise Model has been completed. However, this is not the case, because a single generic inference structure may support more than one problem-solving approach – which helps to explain the observation above that a small change in an inference structure may imply a large change in the problem solving approach. The main purpose of the task structure of the Expertise Model is to describe the problem solving method that has been chosen.

Researchers such as Richard Benjamins [9] have designed, described, and collected problem solving methods (PSMs). A survey can be found in [33] which describes how diagnosis problems can be solved by methods ranging from consistency-based diagnosis through hierarchical diagnosis to abduction. As with generic inference structures, methods can be selected from a library and configured, or constructed bottom-up. At the University of Amsterdam, the construction of problem solving methods has been treated as a knowledge-based task that can be modelled using CommonKADS; they represent the construction of problem solving methods as a parametric design task [174]. Parametric design is actually a simplified form of configuration which is in turn a simplified design task. In configuration, both the set of possible components that must appear in the design and the set of possible connections between components are fixed, thus simplifying the design task by reducing the range of possible solutions;

in parametric design, the actual connections between components are already fixed in a given structure. Since the connections within CommonKADS' problem solving methods are defined by the related inference structure, constructing a problem solving method is indeed a parametric design task.

The generic inference structure for parametric design is therefore selected from the library. The problem-solving method chosen was propose-and-revise. Some may consider that selecting this method from a library, rather than constructing or configuring it, undermines the argument that a system to support construction and configuration of PSMs is needed; but in fact this argument is similar to the argument about top-down vs bottom-up creation of domain-specific inference structures – sometimes bottom-up construction will be needed, sometimes not. A good worked example of the use of this system appears in [174].

The problem of configuring PSMs to a particular domain has been tackled by various researchers by using a method-decomposition tree approach to describing a method which allows configuration of a method by re-constructing a method from different components; using this approach, the configuration problem is therefore a specialisation of the construction problem. See [9] or [163] for examples of this approach.

A scheme for describing problem solving methods

Research on selection of problem solving methods from libraries is still fairly sparse. One piece of research that could potentially support the selection of problem solving methods was carried out as part of the DARPA-sponsored High Performance Knowledge Bases program. A set of attributes for describing the contents of a PSM library in order to aid selection was developed [3]. These attributes were generated after surveying a range of methods: SPAR [171], the CommonKADS library of generic inference structures[147], CommonKADS' competence theory [5], the Components of Expertise approach (Steels [161]), the results of the EuroKnowledge ESPRIT project [61, 129], the Cokace PSM library tool [36], and the "design patterns" approach to object oriented programming [69]. In addition, discussions with other HPKB participants concerning systems such as MAITA [52] and EXPECT [165] produced several useful suggestions relating to executable PSMs. The attributes are divided into those that are useful for selecting methods from the library, those that are useful for configuring methods, and those that are important when executing methods. The attributes are listed below, with brief descriptions of each:

```
PSM Capability Statement
     Competence (to support the selection process)
          Goal
          Problem Type
          Generic Solution
          Solution Component
          Solution Properties
          Context
          Rationale

Configuration (to support configuration & selection)
          Domain Theory Requirements
               Type
               Field
               Ontology
               Representation
          Submethods
          Environmental Requirements

PSM Process Description (i.e. a description of the process
to support system design)
          Input (input to PSM)
          Output (output of PSM)
          Resource                (available          KBS
     shells/toolkits/languages)
          Precondition
          Constraints (user-requirements)
          Agent

PSM Efficiency description (i.e.  a description  of  an
implemented PSM to support system execution)
     Search efficiency
     Solution optimality
     Coverage (how much of the potential/actual domain
knowledge can be handled?)
     Constraints on inputs
     Representational power Tool support
     Method (pseudo code description)
```

Figure 18.2: An indexing scheme for PSMs

Competence:

Goal The goal of a PSM. Specifying the goal requires a standard terminology. Goal is a task feature in CommonKADS.

Problem Type The generic type of problem a method applies to. A set of six problem types has been identified (Breuker [18]) they are: { modelling, design, assignment, prediction, monitoring, diagnosis }. Problem Type is a component of task knowledge in CommonKADS.

Generic Solution Types of solution that can be generated for problems. For example, there are three generic solutions for diagnosis: { set of faulty components, fault classification, causal explanation of fault }. An example of a fault classification in a medical domain is an infection, following Bredeweg [17]. Other problems will add to this set - generic solutions will be problem specific. Generic Solution is a component of task knowledge in CommonKADS.

Solution Component Three solution components have been identified (Breuker [19]) { conclusion, argument structure, case model } The argument structure justifies the conclusion (as in a proof), while the case model explains the data. These components are not problem specific.

Solution Properties Solution properties are properties that hold between knowledge roles in the conceptual model of a PSM (some knowledge roles are also inputs and outputs of the method as a whole). Example properties of diagnosis methods are: consistency between complaints and diagnosis, consistency between complaints, observations and diagnosis, minimality of the explanation, and more generally, optimality of the solution. These Solution Properties were identified by Akkermans [5] for CommonKADS models (but were not used as task features).

Rationale Rationale includes a textual description of why and when the method might be used. The conceptual model of the method (the inference structure in KADS) could be used to explain the problem-solving process. Rationale is a feature of indexing schemes for reusable software components.

Configuration:

Domain Theory - Type The type of the domain theory e.g. a causal theory. Knowledge types are a similar task feature in CommonKADS.

Domain Theory - Field The field of knowledge of a domain theory, e.g. medicine.

Application field is a feature in the Cokace library tool.

Domain Theory - Ontology The ontology of the domain theory. Ontology is a feature in the Cokace library tool.

Domain Theory - Representation The language in which the domain theory is represented.

Submethods A specification of submethods required in the configuration of this method. Submethods can be specified using the same categories that describe the main method – submethod descriptions are embedded in method descriptions.

Environmental Requirements A characterisation of the operating environment of the KBS. Environmental conditions are a task feature in CommonKADS.

PSM Process Descriptions: The following categories can be found in process modelling.

PSM - Input Data input to PSM. Form, content and time pattern of input are task features in CommonKADS.

PSM - Output Data output by PSM. Form, content and time pattern of input are task features in CommonKADS.

PSM - Resource Resources used during execution of PSM. Costs are a similar task feature in CommonKADS.

PSM - Precondition Conditions that have to hold before a PSM can be executed. **PSM - Agent** Agents involved in the execution of the method.

Search efficiency: does this method use informed or uninformed search? In some cases, the problem space is sufficiently small that the difference is not noticeable; in other cases, good search techniques can have a significant effect on the efficiency of the system

Solution optimality: if there is more than one possible solution, does this method find the best solution? If not, how close to the best solution does it typically get? Does it even find more than one solution?

Coverage: how comprehensive is the system's knowledge? For example, in constraint-based search, does it take account of all possible constraints? Does it know which constraints can be relaxed if there are too many constraints to find any solution? Note that this refers to the capability of the method; so if the problem was to choose between alternatives (let's say insurance schemes), and the system only had domain knowledge of a few insurance schemes, this is *not* a problem with the coverage of the PSM. However, if there were three different types of insurance scheme, and the PSM only had enough procedural knowledge to analyse two types correctly, then this *is* a coverage problem.

Constraints among inputs: These will be most important where the system is taking a stream of inputs (e.g. in a process monitoring task). Constraints may include timing conditions, distributions, accuracy, reliability, and interruptibility. For example, a PSM for monitoring and predicting the health of a cardiac patient might have constraints on the maximum time between inputs; inputs from several different physiological sensors, with more frequent inputs from sensors near the heart; a minimum accuracy of 95% from each sensor; an expected reliability of 99% from each sensor; and some inputs might require invasive surgical procedures, implying very low interruptibility.

Representational power: Can the method represent temporal or spatial information, and what ontology does it use to do so? Can it represent events, actions or states? Can meta-level information be represented?

Tool support: Is there a software tool available that eases, or fully automates, instantiation of a PSM with a new set of domain knowledge?

Method A description of the approach taken by the implementation, in pseudo-code, logic, or whatever.

An example of the application of these attributes to one PSM is given in [3] and is reproduced in Figure 18.3.

These attributes appear to provide a classification scheme for problem solving methods that should prove very useful in helping knowledge engineers describe which method to select.

```
------------------------------------------------------------------
Cover and Differentiate for diagnosis
Competence
        Goal                  :diagnosis
        Problem Type          :{diagnosis}
        Generic Solution      :fault-cause
        Solution Component    :{case-model}
        Solution Properties   :consistency(Complaint,
                               Diagnosis)=True
        Rationale             :''This method should be used when a
                                  causal theory of the behaviour of
                                  the system is available. The 'cover'
                                  inference has input knowledge role
                                  'Complaint' and output knowledge role
                                  'Hypothesis.
                                  [Complaint]->cover->[Hypothesis] ...''

Configuration
        Method-Ontology       :causal-theory-of-behaviour
        Domain Theory
            Field             :{motor-vehicles}
            Ontology/Mapping  :{{engineering-Cyc, equality)}
            Representation    :CycL
        Submethods            :{}


PSM Process Description
        Environmental         :software-installed(Cyc)=True
        Resource Constraints  :cpu-cycles-free (99,%)=True
        Actor Constraints     :currently-executing(Cyc)=True
        World Constraints
          Data Input          :(Complaint, <set-of-concepts>)
          Data Output         :(Diagnosis, <concept>)
        Sub-activities        :{}

------------------------------------------------------------------
```

Figure 18.3: An example capability description

18.6 A 'bad' expertise model

What constitutes a 'bad' expertise model? This question can best be answered by giving an example of a 'bad' model. The example comes from one of the publications of the KADS-II project – the original CommonKADS report on applying the Design Model [55]. The application was air crew flight scheduling. Normally, one would expect to see a domain model that identified tasks (in this case, flight segments) and their properties (time, duration, skills needed, etc.), and an expertise model, perhaps based on a generic inference structure for configuration or scheduling that included inference steps that demonstrated how to match the constraints of tasks against an existing schedule and detect any conflicts that arose. However, in this example, one of the domain models in the Expertise Model included a concept of "the best return flight for each outward flight". In other words, much of the reasoning about flight matching was "pre-compiled" into this concept. This is bad modelling practice for the following reasons:

- It would be normal to deduce this concept from constraints such as turn-around time, obligatory crew rest periods, etc. rather than to hard-wire it, in case there are unusual circumstances which affect the best matches;
- Creating this concept means there is no need to represent knowledge about how the matches are made, and so key inference knowledge is not recorded.

In the language of CommonKADS, the concept of "the best return flight for an outward flight" acts as a *static knowledge role* in the inference structure. It's not unusual for some inputs to the task to be pre-compiled into static knowledge roles, but this is not normally done with concepts that form key outputs of the task. By creating a static knowledge role from an output concept, most of the inference structure has been rendered superfluous.

It turned out that there were 'political' reasons for this knowledge structure: the knowledge engineers wanted to avoid disclosing unofficial and sensitive knowledge about the actual allocation process used in a publicly available document [personal communication]. However, it resulted in a good example of bad knowledge modelling practice. The models should be perspicacious, so that the reasoning that is carried out is reflected in the models and can be examined and linked to other models easily.

18.7 Issues affecting inference knowledge: summary

Overall, it appears that the process of using a model from CommonKADS' library of generic inference structures has more intricacies and more pitfalls than might be expected at first sight. Having said that, many knowledge engineers have managed to use these inference structures and associated problem solving methods to model knowledge and build systems successfully; it seems that although these inference structures may be difficult to use perfectly, they can bring benefits even to novice knowledge engineers.

19 CommonKADS,   Design and Implementation

The issues that are covered in this section are:

• What features in a system level Communication model suggest that certain subtasks should or should not be carried out by a user?

• How should good design decisions be made when creating the Design Model?

The chapter also looks briefly at the stages of knowledge engineering that follow design modelling.

19.1   Communication Modelling

The Communication Model is used to model the communication that takes place within a problem solving task, and to assign subtasks to agents. At the System level, the agents may be the user, the system, or the two working together.

CommonKADS does not give a lot of guidance on human factors issues. However, deciding whom to allocate a particular task to depends largely on the "interface function" being performed. It would be very helpful to define a standard set of "interface functions" that would be specified in the final stage of communication modelling and could be directly used in design modelling (see chapter 12). As a guideline, I will suggest that all interface functions should specify at least three aspects of the information being communicated:

• Whether the information is being communicated with a user, a database, or any other type of IT system. If no information is being communicated to or from a user, the task should (obviously) be allocated to the system; conversely, any communication to or from the user requires user involvement.

• What the type of the information is (text, integers, real numbers, Web addresses, or whatever). If the system requires input of unrestricted text, this will probably be considered a task for the user alone. If the system requires input of multiple-choice values or other restricted inputs, this should probably be assigned to the user and the system working together, especially if the system also performs some kind of error checking on the input.

• Whether the communication will be of a single value, a list, an array, or a set of values. This information is of more use in system design than in subtask assignment, but it may have some implications for the latter; for example, if the input consists of a very long list, or a highly structured array, a good designer will search for ways to obtain such information from an online source rather than forcing the user to spend a long time inputting the relevant data.

19.2   Design Modelling: Producing a KBS Design Specification

What constitutes a good design for a knowledge based system? Schrooten & Duursma [151] identify a number of principles drawn from the AI literature:

• Represent all knowledge explicitly;
• Keep elements of the knowledge base as independent and modular as possible;
• Separate the knowledge base from the programs that interpret it;
• Use as uniform a representation as possible;
• An object-oriented paradigm offers the most flexibility;
• Exploit redundancy.

The CommonKADS Design Model allows explicit consideration of design decisions, and representation of decisions made. The Design Model resembles the other models in CommonKADS because it recommends step-by-step transformation of concepts into more concepts. If the knowledge engineer chooses to use the Expertise Model as a basis for the Design Model (which is encouraged because doing so will re-use existing knowledge structure, will typically fulfil the principle of independence and modularity, and may fulfil other principles of good design too) then it will also take different perspectives on the design; there will be separate components of the

Design model for inference steps ("how" knowledge), knowledge roles ("what" knowledge) and communication ("where" knowledge). However, it is important to consider how decisions made in one perspective will affect another perspective.

Chapter 12 puts the Design model into practice by discussing the three stages of building the Design Model – Application Design, Architectural Design and Platform Design – and then providing examples. The issues raised by this chapter are:

> **Stage 1: Application Design** At this stage, it is necessary to decide whether the design will be primarily based on functional decomposition, object-oriented decomposition, or a known AI paradigm. The issue is in determining which approach is best for a particular problem.

> **Stage 2: Architecture Design** There are two issues here: firstly, assessing the pros and cons of a "probing questions" approach to making architectural decisions; and secondly, considering the adequacy of the languages proposed by CommonKADS for representing detailed application design and detailed architectural design.

> **Stage 3: Platform Design** The issue here is determining how to match correctly the capabilities and strengths of a programming tool to the design, and adapting the design to the strengths of the tool.

The first two issues are discussed below; the remaining two issues are covered well by other authors, and a brief review of their work is provided.

19.2.1 Application Design: Functional, Object-Oriented, or AI Paradigm?

The discussion in section 12.2.1 suggests that the main criterion for determining whether to use functional decomposition, object-oriented decomposition, or a recognised AI paradigm is the degree of effort that has been put into the various components of the Expertise model. If the Expertise model contains many domain concepts and relations but only a few inference steps, then object-oriented decomposition is the preferred approach to application design; if the richest knowledge in the Expertise model is in the inference structure, then functional decomposition is recommended; and in some circumstances, the Expertise model is effectively discarded in favour of a recognised AI paradigm.

Assuming this advice is sound, the question of AI paradigms should be discussed further. Why should any knowledge engineer choose to discard a (presumably) good set of knowledge models? To answer this question, I will look at one AI paradigm – model-based reasoning – in the context of three well known expert systems: MYCIN, CASNET and INTERNIST [90].

MYCIN, CASNET and INTERNIST are all knowledge based systems that tackle diagnostic tasks (indeed, all tackle diagnosis in the same domain - medicine), but they are implemented very differently. MYCIN is a backward chaining rule based system that uses certainty factors for diagnosing bacterial infections; CASNET uses a multilayer "findings influence hypotheses" approach to diagnose glaucoma, an eye disease; and INTERNIST uses a large object-based model to represent "the whole of internal medicine". It could be argued that the three systems used different problem solving methods for diagnosis, and should therefore have drawn on different inference and task structures from the CommonKADS library; however, this explanation is not only unproven, but also nowhere near powerful enough to explain the magnitude of the differences between these systems.

What has occurred is that major differences have arisen at the design stage; MYCIN has effectively followed a functional decomposition approach, while both CASNET and INTERNIST claim to use the AI paradigm of model-based reasoning. MYCIN's knowledge is "shallow" knowledge linking combinations of symptoms with diseases; all its knowledge has been represented in (backward chaining) production rules. CASNET chose to encode explicit relationships between findings and hypotheses (i.e. the acquired knowledge also linked symptoms to diseases but in a "deeper" way); when evidence is found for a "finding", a weight is attached to (or occasionally subtracted from) a linked "hypothesis", in much the same way that simple neural networks operate.[46] The end result is a system that drives its reasoning based on relationships from the domain knowledge, either by propagating knowledge about new findings (symptoms) to hypotheses (diseases or disease states), or by determining what symptoms must be

---

[46] CASNET also has some hypothesis-to-hypothesis links.

checked for to confirm or rule out a particular hypothesis; in other words, CASNET's "deep" representation of knowledge supports both forward and backward reasoning which seems to reflect the way that doctors operate. As for INTERNIST, its developers decided that, to represent the processes of internal diseases and medicine accurately, it was necessary to simulate the cause-and-effect processes of diseases and medicines, and then to perform reasoning based on that simulation. In other words, INTERNIST's knowledge is about as "deep" as knowledge can get, because it aims to perform explicit simulation of physiological processes. This knowledge is (strictly speaking) neither domain nor inference knowledge for the diagnosis of diseases; instead, it belongs to a more detailed level of knowledge[47] that doctors typically fall back on when their standard practices prove inadequate. As a result, while INTERNIST can support different types of reasoning, different types of task, and can represent many different diseases (INTERNIST claims to handle about 80% of "internal medicine"), it required an enormous effort to construct it, and powerful computers to run it.

It can be seen that while ease of modelling knowledge is probably the most important factor in determining a suitable application design, it is by no means the only factor. CASNET chose to represent relationships between symptoms and diseases explicitly in order to represent doctors' reasoning better, while INTERNIST chose a simulation-based approach because in a complex system such as the biological processes within a human, it is difficult to predict all the outcomes of a single event without simulating the processes. In other words, model-based reasoning, to a greater of lesser level of detail, should be used when the complexity of the system or the depth of reasoning required is so great that its benefits outweigh the extra efforts required to build the system.

A similar argument could be made for other AI paradigms: for example, it could be argued that constraint-based reasoning should be used where there are so many constraints on a process that it is difficult to represent the effects of all constraints without reasoning about them explicitly, and qualitative reasoning should be used where there is so much uncertainty about quantities that no meaningful conclusion can be drawn without using qualitative reasoning.

---

[47] See section 2.6 for a discussion of levels of detail in knowledge.

19.2.2 Architectural Design: Probing questions

The "probing questions" approach does seem to be a promising one, especially if particular questions can be tied to particular stages of decomposition; in other words, it's necessary to categorise the probing questions in order to determine which ones are most applicable to each stage of development. The probing questions approach has been developed further, and implemented, by Colin Macnee ([120]; see also [98]). Macnee developed his own categorisation of probing questions:

Knowledge Structure – (a) domain objects and relationships
Knowledge Structure – (b) inferences and generic tasks
Validity of conclusions
Solutions
Data
Dialogue & explanation
Computational efficiency
Development, maintenance & expansion

Table 19.1: Macnee's classification of probing questions

It can be seen that parts of his classification correlate with the three main components of the Design model (domain objects and relationships; inferences and generic tasks; dialogue & explanation) but other parts concern topics that the experts he talked to deemed worthy of detailed investigation. It may be that these are the areas that trigger design differences such as those found between MYCIN, CASNET and INTERNIST; for example, the ratio of data to solutions acts as a simple heuristic for deciding whether to consider forward chaining (few data, many solutions), backward chaining (many data, few solutions) or a model-based/constraint-based approach (many data, many solutions).

Macnee's collection of probing questions has both strengths and weaknesses which reflect the strengths and weaknesses of many an AI system. The strengths lie in the ease of use and ease of understanding of the questions; a rule based format can be understood readily, and phrasing the questions in this way ensures that any terms not understood by a knowledge engineer can be identified within the rule-based format and looked up quickly. The weaknesses derive mostly from the "shallowness" of the knowledge; like MYCIN, there is almost no explanation of the recommendations; and if an unexpected set of circumstances arises, rule based systems can offer only a little advice whereas a simulation-based system might be able to work out the answer from first principles. On the whole, though, this set of questions represent a significant advance in available guidance for knowledge engineers.

19.2.3 Adequacy of Design Model representation languages

It is difficult for me to comment authoritatively on the adequacy of the languages recommended for detailed application design and detailed architectural design in CommonKADS, since I have never found a need to represent a design in that level of detail; the graphical models have always proved sufficient for me. Furthermore, the main worked example published during the KADS-II project is based on the flight scheduling knowledge base that was used as an example of a 'bad' expertise model in the previous chapter [150]. However, the language does appear to have the benefit of clearly identifying design decisions that have been made which promises some benefits for development and future maintenance of the system.

19.2.4 Matching design characteristics to tools

Robertson [141] [98] makes use of the results of probing questions to make recommendations about suitable tools for KBS implementation. His aim was to select the simplest (and, usually, cheapest) tool that was capable of handling all the knowledge representations and reasoning techniques required. He found that the choices made at the stage of application design had the biggest effect on tool selection; functional decomposition tended to favour a rule-based implementation, object-oriented decomposition favoured an object-oriented implementation, and AI paradigms favoured tools that are specialised for those paradigms. He also found that certain probing questions had a major effect on selection; for example, the question about the ratio between data and solutions is often a strong indicator of the need for forward or backward reasoning. Some tools are simply not capable of supporting one or other of these reasoning strategies.

The main features by which tools were differentiated were, according to Robertson:

Knowledge representation	rules, objects, both, other
Inference types	data-driven and/or goal-driven reasoning
Inference control	breadth-first search, depth-first search, other
Uncertainty	numerical methods, truth maintenance systems
Interfaces	to the developer, to other systems and the user
Knowledge acquisition support	
Numerical functionality	
Extendability	
Runtime options	
Security	
Physical environment	development hardware, delivery hardware, operating system

Table 19.2: Features on which AI development tools differ

A detailed analysis of each of the above features could require an entire textbook, and so will not be attempted here. Readers who are interested in this topic should note that the current "state of the art" largely focuses on tools written in Java or other Web-based languages, such as the Java Expert System Shell [67].

19.3 Implementation and beyond

CommonKADS' models end with the Design model; the task of implementing a KBS is not directly supported by any recommendations from CommonKADS, apart from the project management lifecycle models. In this section, a brief review will be given of the tasks that remain to be performed between completion of the Design Model and completion of a knowledge based system.

19.3.1 Implementing a knowledge based system

The skills required for good implementation of KBS are much the same as the skills required for good implementation of any software project: planning, milestones, documentation, modularity, etc. Knowledge engineers who have used CommonKADS would be advised to use the models they have developed to assist them in these tasks. My own practice is to divide up the reasoning component of an implementation into a number of files, where each file represents a single inference step from the Expertise Model. This ensures modularity (since each inference step is independent of others), completeness, and ease of verification (because the inputs and expected outputs of each step are defined). It has also been suggested in [103] that some models can act as user interfaces for systems.

19.3.2 Verification and validation of knowledge based systems

After the implementation is completed (and preferably also at stages during the implementation), the question of **verification and validation** arises. Verification of knowledge based systems is checking that the knowledge is correct, ("doing the right thing"); validation ensures that the system's design reflects its design requirements ("doing the thing right"). Verification of knowledge based systems requires checking that the system's performance matches the acquired knowledge which is greatly simplified by the existence of a set of models such as those produced by CommonKADS. It should also require checking the accuracy of acquired knowledge (i.e. the contents of the models), but in practice, informal approaches are often used, such as peer review or having the expert sign off the models as correct. Validation, however, can partly be automated within knowledge based systems; [131] and [62] show how the conditions of rules can be encoded in a matrix which is then analysed to determine if there are any useless rules (their conclusion is not used in any rule conditions), inaccessible rules (their condition is not concluded by any other rules, either directly or via user interaction), or circular rules (where one rule states "if A then B" and another states "if B then A").

19.3.3 Delivery and installation

As with implementation, the techniques required for this are similar to any software project. It's worth noting that KBS are often designed to run locally on desktop machines rather than running on servers and being accessed by many users simultaneously; if a client-server architecture is desired, care must be taken to select a programming tool that supports this. Examples of such tools include Nexpert Object, the Aion Development System, and the Java Expert System Shell [67].

19.3.4 Maintenance and decommissioning

The delivery of the system does **not** end the development of a knowledge based system. The knowledge has to be kept up to date which is effectively a full knowledge engineering process of acquiring new knowledge, analysing it, and implementing the resulting changes. It is here that the use of CommonKADS really shows its benefits, for if maintenance simply involves some small changes to a few existing models, it's easy to see what parts of the implementation should be changed and what should not, and it's easy to create a new set of consistent and accurate documentation. It's wise to allocate 5-10% of a knowledge engineer's time to maintain each system that the company has in use.

Decommissioning is the process of phasing a system out of service. Here again, the principles to follow are the same as for other software engineering projects. The golden rule is, don't turn off the old service until the replacement service is known to be working. This often involves parallel running of the old and new services for a few weeks or months.

19.4 Summary

We have seen that the CommonKADS Design Model is a useful way to record design decisions, but that the decisions that must be made are wider-ranging than the three steps in the model might suggest. Application design – deciding whether to use an AI paradigm or to decompose the Expertise model – is dependent on an assessment of the level of complexity required of the knowledge and of the reasoning which is in turn dependent on user requirements and organisational goals that are more likely to appear in the Communication or Organisation models than in the Expertise model. Architectural design is dependent on so many factors that the "probing questions" practically form a knowledge base in their own right. And platform design is far from being the end of the knowledge engineering process; implementation, verification and validation, installation and maintenance must all be considered.

And yet the Design model has the advantage that, simply by ensuring that design decisions are recorded, it prompts the knowledge engineer to carry out many of these steps; it is also relatively lightweight, for it does not require the production of a large number of complex diagrams. On balance, therefore, the Design model is a worthwhile addition to a knowledge engineer's toolbox.

20 Summary and future work

This book has demonstrated how a framework for representing information knowledge can be applied, and has been applied, to assist in both knowledge management and knowledge engineering. A number of suggestions have been made for future work on developing these methods further. These are summarised below.

20.1 Suggestions for future work: knowledge management

This book has suggested that field of knowledge management is, in fact, a collection of diverse methods grouped under a single heading. The biggest difference is between "cognitive" methods (typically computer-based decision support systems) and "constructivist" methods (typically facilitation of personal development or group knowledge sharing).

Research in this area is sparse, and so a number of suggestions are made for future work. These are:

• How is knowledge communicated within groups, and between groups and individuals? Can this communication be enhanced by any method? This book has suggested using the perspectives of the Zachman framework as a basis for a structured dialogue, but it is not known how effective that would be. Some general arguments are made for the pros and cons of apprenticeships, simulations, and lecture-based training courses, but translating these ideas into effective knowledge communication techniques seems to be a fruitful area for future research.

• What incentives are effective to persuade individuals to update their own knowledge?

• What are the goals of a knowledge management project that would match well with either a cognitive or a constructivist approach?

20.2 Suggestions for future work: knowledge engineering

The suggestions for future work in knowledge engineering focus on the knowledge itself in more detail.

- Can structured interviews for knowledge acquisition be structured using the perspectives from the Zachman framework?
- How can WHY knowledge be used more effectively? Are there good modelling techniques for representing WHY knowledge? Can decision trees be used as a representation for WHY knowledge?
- Is knowledge associated with the WHAT and HOW perspectives always deterministic? Is there a deterministic link between deterministic WHAT knowledge and deterministic HOW knowledge (which might appear in a generic inference structure), or are such links determinable?
- Can non-taxonomic knowledge, and HOW knowledge in particular, be used for indexing? If so, how?

20.3 Suggestions for future work: ontology

It is hard to distinguish questions that affect knowledge engineering from questions that affect ontology, but some suggestions for future work are clearly more related to ontology.

- Could the knowledge acquisition technique of cluster analysis be used to generate a "natural" ontology? (This develops the argument put forward in chapter 17 that repertory grid tools can be used to generate a classified ontology).

20.4 Suggestions for future work: knowledge acquisition

The suggestions below focus on better linking of common knowledge acquisition techniques with CommonKADS' models.

- For the card sort, the classification of properties into relational roles, qualities, *part* relations and natural concepts could be extended by using the *mereology* (classification scheme for *part* relations) suggested in [70].

- For the card sort and the repertory grid, Woods' linguistic test could be used when dimensions are created. While this might restrict the breadth of the acquired knowledge, it should produce a more coherent set of dimensions which is particularly important in the repertory grid where dimensions are compared against one another. The effort of finding a correct name would also be transferred from the knowledge engineer to the expert by this technique which may lead to further knowledge acquisition as the expert reconsiders the conceptual structure of his knowledge.

- For transcript analysis, there are many possible improvements:
    - Use a chart parser to obtain linguistic information, permitting extensive automatic identification of properties, and perhaps of relations;
    - Feed back linguistic information obtained from a knowledge engineer to the parser or lexical tagger, to improve accuracy;
    - Define and apply a "coding schema" [189] – a set of phrases that are known to indicate the presence of certain ontological types;
    - Use questionnaires or structured interviews to obtain highly structured transcripts that are written in simple declarative sentences. It should be possible to parse these transcripts and classify the knowledge contained therein without human intervention (see [86]).

- For knowledge in the inference and task levels of CommonKADS, define a mapping between knowledge acquisition techniques which acquire procedural knowledge (such as protocol analysis, or the "20 Questions" technique [152]) and CommonKADS inference steps and primitive tasks. TOPKAT already supports a simple decision tree editor.

The list of questions above shows how knowledge management, knowledge engineering and ontology engineering are disciplines that touch subject areas far beyond computing. Research in many branches of psychology, cognitive science, business studies and librarianship is all relevant. It seems that wherever there is knowledge, knowledge management may be of benefit; and this book postulates that wherever there is knowledge management, the Zachman framework, with the assistance of perspectives such as Binney's knowledge management spectrum and Boisot's I-Space model, supplies a structure for carrying out the task(s) effectively.

20.5 Partial re-use of ontologies

This book has answered many questions concerning the use of multi-perspective models to support knowledge management and knowledge engineering. However, two big questions remains unanswered. The first is: are these methods necessary in their entirety, or can they be used in part? The discussion surrounding Pragmatic KADS was intended to show that CommonKADS can indeed be used in full or in part, as dictated by the demands of the project. It has also been proposed that ontologies could be subject to the same process; either the ontology could be modularised by the developer, or the ontology could be "winnowed" [6] when it is used in order to restrict its size. The motivation for this is that inclusion of multiple ontologies which may exist at more than one of Guarino's nine levels of ontology (e.g. using an engineering ontology may require inclusion of an ontology of mathematical principles), can create unmanageably large ontologies within an application. Whether such an approach would benefit from identifying ontologies as belonging to one or more of Guarino's nine levels, and choosing only to include those terms that exist at a particular level, is another question for future research.

20.6 Methodology or anarchic development?

The second big question that has not been answered is: are these methods necessary at all? Can knowledge management solutions or knowledge engineering systems be developed by other means – and if so, are there benefits to the other approaches?

An alternative model for developing knowledge systems is the "knowledge services" model. This approach is analogous to the "blackboard systems" that were developed in the early days of artificial intelligence. In blackboard systems, a central data store records a problem to be solved and its current state, and sends out a request to distributed knowledge-based problem solvers to ask if they can contribute anything to change the current state of the problem. If the state can be changed, one problem solver may be selected to change the state; the new state is recorded centrally; and the process repeats until the desired goal state is reached.

The knowledge services approach is similar, but with one key difference; the individual problem-solvers are not written or even chosen by a single developer. Instead they are developed according to perceived need by anyone who wishes to contribute, with or without reward. Marty Tenenbaum in his article *AI Meets Web 2.0: Building the Web of Tomorrow, Today* calls this "anarchic" development resulting in "collective intelligence", and compares it to the development of other Web Services. Examples of such knowledge-based services include installable services such as Book Burro [164] which is triggered by a search for a book on Amazon.com, and searches for prices for the same book at other web sites; shared knowledge sources such as Java libraries; and knowledge bases built by multiple (voluntary) users, such as the Open Mind project [162]. Tenenbaum argues that each of these is simply a knowledge-based extension of an existing common Web activity or service: looking up multiple e-commerce websites (for the same edition of the same book); writing code to develop Web applications; or developing Wikipedia.

If Tenenbaum's arguments about the development of intelligent services on Web 2.0 are sound, does this mean that knowledge based systems developed using methods such as CommonKADS are obsolete? The answer is probably 'No'; but users would be wise to consider which approach might suit them better. For applications requiring specialised or rare knowledge, a methodological approach seems essential, because the knowledge is highly unlikely to arise from anarchic development, and because there may be an understandable reluctance to share such rare knowledge with the whole world.. Conversely, Tenenbaum points out that the insurance industry, one of the early application areas for many 'monolithic' knowledge based systems, no longer uses such systems but is moving towards a knowledge based web services model (see e.g. *webifysolutions.com*, described as a "simple agent-based knowledge system" by Tenenbaum.) Tenenbaum attributes this to the insurance industry being a "complex distributed ecosystem [including] the primary carriers, their agents, underwriters, and claims adjusters, re-insurers, fraud investigators, and many other service providers" where "integration and automation are best approached incrementally, one organization and one task at a time."

In short, the decision on whether to use a methodological approach or to encourage an anarchic approach to knowledge based system development should be a knowledge management decision, made on the basis of various factors including the structure of the industry, the rarity and confidentiality of the knowledge, and the organisation's policies ... factors that are all considered in either Binney's knowledge management spectrum or Boisot's I-Space model. It is therefore essential for those who wish to introduce knowledge-based support into their organisations to apply knowledge management principles before embarking on decisions about methods or approaches.

Bibliography

[1] Artale A., Franconi E., Guarino N., and L Pazzi. Part-Whole Relations in ObjectCentered Systems: an Overview. *Data and Knowledge Engineering*, 20(3):347– 383, 1996.

[2] M. Aben. *Formal methods in Knowledge Engineering*. PhD thesis, SWI, University of Amsterdam, 1994. The relevant chapter is also available as CommonKADS report KADS-II/T1.2/WP/UvA/040/1.0.

[3] S. Aitken, I. Filby, J. Kingston, and A. Tate. Capability descriptions for problemsolving methods, 1998.

[4] H. Akkermans, B. Wielinga, and G. Schreiber. Steps in constructing problem solving methods. In *Proceedings of the European Knowledge Acquisition Workshop (EKAW'93)*. Springer Verlag, 1993. Also available as chapter 5 of the CommonKADS Expertise Model Definition Document, ed. Wielinga *et al*, June 1993.

[5] H. Akkermans, B.J. Wielinga, and G. Schreiber. Refinement: Competence directed. In B.J. Wielinga, editor, *Expertise model definition document*, pages 117–135. University of Amsterdam, 1994. Technical Report ESPRIT Project P5248, KADS-II/M2/UvA/026.5.0.

[6] H. Alani, S. Harris, and B. O'Neil. Ontology Winnowing: A Case Study on the AKT Reference Ontology. In *Proceedings of IEEE International Conference on Intelligent Agents, Web Technology and Internet Commerce*, 2005.

[7] M. Asimow. *Introduction to Design*. Prentice Hall, 1962.

[8] L. Barros, A. Valente, and R. Benjamins. Modelling planning tasks. In B. Drabble, editor, *Proceedings of 3rd International Conference on AI Planning Systems, AIPS-96*, Edinburgh, Scotland, 29-31 May 1996. AAAI Press.

[9] V.R. Benjamins. *Problem Solving Methods for Diagnosis*. PhD thesis, University of Amsterdam, Amsterdam, The Netherlands, 1993.

[10] J. Bicard-Mandel and X. Tong. ICT: Integrity Checking Task - A Generic Task for Design under Constraints. In

Proceedings of the 2nd KADS User Meeting, Siemens AG, Munich, 17-18 Feb 1992. European KADS User Group.

[11]   B. Boehm. A Spiral Model of Software Development and Enhancement. *Software Engineering Project Management*, 1987.

[12]   M.H. Boisot. *Knowledge Assets: Securing Competitive Advantage in the Information Economy*. Oxford University Press, 1998.

[13]   J. Boose and B. Gaines. *Knowledge Based Systems*. Academic Press, 1988. Vol 1: Knowledge Acquisition for Knowledge-based Systems Vol 2: Knowledge Acquisition Tools for Expert Systems.

[14]   J. H. Boose and J. M. Bradshaw. Expertise transfer and complex problems: Using aquinas as a knowledge-acquisition workbench for knowledge-based systems. *Int. Journal of Man-Machine Studies*, 26:3–28, 1987.

[15]   J.H. Boose. A survey of knowledge acquisition techniques and tools. *Knowledge Acquisition*, 1(1), 1989.

[16]   J.M. Bradshaw, J.H. Boose, S.P. Covington, and P.J. Russo. How To Do With Grids What People Say You Can't. In *Proceedings of Knowledge Acquisition Workshop*, 1989.

[17]   B. Bredeweg. Model-based diagnosis and prediction of behaviour. In J.A. Breuker and W. Van de Velde, editors, *Expertise model document part II: The CommonKADS library*, pages 113–148. KADS-II consortium, 1994.

[18]   J. Breuker. Problems in indexing problem-solving methods. In R. Benjamins, editor, *Proceedings of the Workshop on Problem Solving Methods*, Nagoya, Japan, 23 August 1997. IJCAI-97.

[19]   J. Breuker and W. van de Velde. *The CommonKADS Library: reusable components for artificial problem solving*. IOS Press, Amsterdam, Tokyo, 1994.

[20]   J. A. Breuker. *Model-driven Knowledge Acquisition*. University of Amsterdam and STL, 1987. ESPRIT project 1098, Deliverable A1.

[21]   D.C. Brown and B. Chandrasekaran. *Design Problem Solving: Knowledge Structures and Control Strategies*. Research Notes in Artificial Intelligence. Morgan Kaufman, 1989.

[22]   D.C.   Brown   and   B.   Chandrasekaran. Investigating routine design problem solving. In C. Tong and D. Sriram, editors, *AI in Engineering Design, Vol. 1*. Addison-Wesley, 1992.

[23]   A.M. Burton, N.R. Shadbolt, A.P. Hedgecock, and G. Rugg. A Formal Evaluation of Knowledge Elicitation Techniques for Expert Systems: Domain 1. In S. Moralee, editor, *Research and Development in Expert Systems IV*. Cambridge University Press, 1987.

[24]   A.M. Burton, N.R. Shadbolt, G. Rugg, and A.P. Hedgecock. Knowledge Elicitation Techniques in Classification Domains. In *Proceedings of ECAI-88: The 8th European Conference on Artificial Intelligence*, 1988.

[25]   A. N. Campbell, V. F. Hollister, R. O. Duda, and P. E. Hart. Recognition of a Hidden Mineral Deposit by an Artificial Intelligence Program. *Science*, 217(4563):927–929, 3 September 1982.

[26]   A. Casson. PLINTH: Integrating Hypertext, Semantic Nets and Rule-Based Systems in an Expertext Shell for Authors and Readers of Regulatory Information. In *Proceedings of CIKM'93 Workshop on Intelligent Hypertext*, Arlington, Virginia, 1993. Also available as AIAI-TR-142, http://www.aiai.ed.ac.uk/.

[27]   B. Chandrasekaran. Generic tasks as building blocks for knowledge based systems: The diagnosis and routine design examples. *The Knowledge Engineering Review*, 3(3):183–210, 1988.

[28]   B. Chandrasekaran. Design problem solving: A task analysis. *AI Magazine*, 11:59–71, 1990.

[29]   Y.H. Chen-Burger. Knowledge sharing and inconsistency checking on multiple enterprise models. In *Proceedings of the IJCAI'01 Workshop on Knowledge Management and Organizational Memories*, Seattle, WA, USA, August 2001.

[30]   S.H. Chu and C.L. Tai. Animating Chinese Landscape Paintings and Panorama Using Multi-Perspective Modelling. In *Proceedings of the CGI 2001 Conference*, City University of Hong Kong, Hong Kong, July 3-6 2001.

[31]   W. Clancey. Heuristic Classification. *Artificial Intelligence*, 27, 1985.

[32]   P. Coad and E. Yourdon. *Object-Oriented Analysis*. Prentice Hall, Englewood Cliffs, New Jersey, 1991.

[33]   L. Console, J. de Kleer, and W. Hamscher. *Readings in Model-based Diagnosis*. Morgan Kaufmann, 1992.

[34]   M.A. Cook. *Building Enterprise Information Architectures: Reengineering Information Systems*. Prentice Hall PTR, New Jersey, 1996.

[35]   R. Corazzon. Descriptive and Formal Ontology, 2000. Available at http://www.formalontology.it.

[36]   Olivier Corby and Rose Dieng. Cokace: A Centaur-based environment for CommonKADS Conceptual Modelling Language. In *ECAI*, pages 418–422, 1996.

[37]   H. Cottam, N. Shadbolt, J. Kingston, H. Beck, and A. Tate. Knowledge Level Planning in the Search and Rescue Domain. In M.A. Bramer, J.L. Nealon, and R. Milne, editors, *Research and Development in Expert Systems XII*, pages 309– 326. SGES Publications, 11-13 December 1995.

[38]   K.W. Currie and A Tate. O-Plan: the Open Planning Architecture. *Artificial Intelligence*, 51(1), Autumn 1991. Also available as aiai-tr-67.

[39]   Binney D. The knowledge management spectrum - understanding the KM landscape. *Journal of Knowledge Management*, 5(1):33–42, 2001.

[40]   Waltz D. Scientific Datalink's Artificial Intelligence Classification Scheme. *AI Magazine*, pages 58–63, Spring 1985.

[41]   T.H. Davenport and L. Prusak. *Working Knowledge: How Organizations Manage What They Know*. Harvard Business School Press, 1998.

[42]   H.P. de Greef and J. Breuker. Analysing system-user cooperation in KADS. *Knowledge Acquisition*, 4(1):89–108, March 1992.

[43]   R. de Hoog, B. Benus, C. Metselaar, et al. Applying the CommonKADS organisational model. Restricted circulation KADS-II/T1.1/UvA/RR/004/4.1, ESPRIT project P5248 KADS-II, Jan 1993.

[44] R. de Hoog, B. Benus, C. Metselaar, and M. Vogler. The Common KADS Organisational Model. ESPRIT Project P5248 KADS-II CK-UvA-41b, University of Amsterdam, 1993.

[45] R. de Hoog, B. Benus, C. Metselaar, M. Vogler, and W. Menezes. Applying the CommonKADS Organizational Model. Technical Report KADS-II project technical report KADS-II/T1.1/UvA/RR/004/4.1, 1994.

[46] R. de Hoog, R. Martil, B. Wielinga, R. Taylor, C. Bright, and W. van de Velde. The Common KADS model set. ESPRIT Project P5248 KADS-II KADS-II/M1/DM1.1b/UvA/018/6.0, University of Amsterdam and others, 1993. http://swi.psy.uva.nl/ projects/CommonKADS/Reports.html.

[47] D. Diaper, editor. *Knowledge Elicitation: Principles, Techniques and Applications*. Ellis Horwood, 1989.

[48] S. Dirks. Development of a knowledge-based system for personal financial planning. Master's thesis, Dept of Artificial Intelligence, University of Edinburgh, Sept 1993.

[49] J. Dobson and R. Strens. Organisational Requirements Definition for Information Technology Systems. In *ACM International Conference on Requirements Engineering, Denver, USA, 1994*. ACM, 1994.

[50] J.E. Dobson, A.J.C. Blyth, J. Chudge, et al. The ORDIT Approach to Requirements Identification. Technical Report 394, Computing Laboratory, University of Newcastle upon Tyne, 1992.

[51] J. Domingue, E. Motta, and S. Watt. The Emerging VITAL Workbench. In *Knowledge Acquisition for Knowledge-based Systems: 7th European Workshop EKAW '93*, pages 320–339, Toulouse and Caylus, France, September 1993. Springer-Verlag.

[52] Jon Doyle, Isaac Kohane, William Long, and Peter Szolovits. The Architecture of MAITA A Tool For Monitoring, Analysis, and Interpretation.

[53] B. Drabble, R.B. Kirby, and A. Tate. O-Plan2: the Open Planning Architecture. In *Working Notes of the AAAI Spring Symposium on Practical Approaches to Scheduling and Planning*, Stanford University, California, 25 - 27 March 1992. American Association for Artificial Intelligence. http://www.aiai.ed.ac.uk/ oplan/oplan/oplan-doc.html.

[54]   K. Dudman. *Jackson Structured Programming for Practical Program Design*. Springer Verlag, November 1996.

[55]   C. Duursma. Task Model definition and Task Analysis process. ESPRIT Project P5248 KADS-II CK-VUB-04, Vrije Universiteit Brussel, 1993.

[56]   Finkelstein A. (ed). Proceedings of Viewpoints 96: An International Workshop on Multiple Perspectives in Software Development. In *ACM Symposium on Foundations of Software Engineering*, San Francisco, Oct 14-15 1996. http://www.soi.city.ac.uk/ gespan/vptoc.html.

[57]   L. Eshelman, D. Ehret, J. McDermott, and M. Tan. Mole: A tenacious knowledge-aquisition tool. *Int. Journal of Man-Machine Studies*, 26:41–54, 1987.

[58]   F. Heylighen. Epistemological Constructivism. http://pespmc1.vub.ac.be/EPISTEMI.html.

[59]   D. Fensel and R. Benjamins. Assumptions in Model-Based Diagnosis. In L. Steels, G. Schreiber, and W. van de Velde, editors, *Proceedings of KAW-96*, 1996. http://ksi.cpsc.ucalgary.ca/KAW/KAW96/fensel/ambd.html.

[60]   N. Fenton. Representativeness. http://www.dcs.qmul.ac.uk/norman/BBNs/Representativeness.htm.

[61]   I. Filby. Recommendations on standardisation of conceptual-level knowledge modelling formalisms. Technical Report EuroK/T/010496-1/AIAI, ESPRIT Project 9806 (EuroKnowledge), November 1996.

[62]   I. Filby and E. Rodriguez-Camarena. A Rule Based Consistency Checker, CONCOR. In M. Ali P. Chun and G. Lovegrove, editors, *Proceedings of the 6th International Conference on Industrial and Engineering Applications of Artificial Intelligence and Expert Systems*, 1993.

[63]   K.M. Ford and J.M. Bradshaw. *Knowledge Acquisition as Modelling*, chapter 1. John Wiley, 1993.

[64]   J. Fox, N. Johns, and A. Rahmanzadeh. Disseminating medical knowledge: the ProFORMA approach. *Artificial Intelligence in Medicine*, 14(1-2):157–182, 1998.

[65]   J. Fox, C.D. Myers, M.F. Greaves, and S. Pegram. A systematic study of knowledge base refinement in the diagnosis

of leukemia. In A.L. Kidd, editor, *Knowledge Acquisition for Expert Systems: A Practical Handbook*, chapter 4, pages 73–90. Plenum Press, 1987.

[66]   U. Frank. Multi-Perspective Enterprise Models as a Conceptual Foundation for Knowledge Management. In *Proceedings of Hawaii International Conference on System Science*, Honolulu, 2000.

[67]   E. Friedman-Hill. JESS: The Java Expert System Shell.   Technical   report,   2001. http://herzberg.ca.sandia.gov/jess/.

[68]   B. Gaines, editor. *International Journal of Human Computer Studies Special Issue: Sisyphus: Models of Problem Solving*, volume 40, 2. Elsevier, 1994.

[69]   Erich Gamma, Richard Helm, Ralph Johnson, and John Vlissides. Design Patterns: Abstraction and Reuse of Object-Oriented Design. *Lecture Notes in Computer Science*, 707:406–431, 1993.

[70]   P. Gerstl and S. Pribbenow. Midwinters, End Games, and Bodyparts. In N. Guarino and R. Poli, editors, *Formal Ontology in Conceptual Analysis and Knowledge Representation*, Dordrecht, 1994. Kluwer.

[71]   A. K. Goel, K. S. Ali, M. W. Donellan, A. G. de Silva Garza, and T. J. Callantine. Multistrategy Adaptive Path Planning. *IEEE Expert*, pages 57–65, Dec 1994.

[72]   J. D. Gould, S. Boies, S. Levy, J. T. Richards, and J. Schoonard. The 1984 Olympic message system: A test of behavioural principles of system design. *Communications of the ACM*, 30:758–769, 1987.

[73]   J. D. Gould and C. Lewis. Designing for usability: key principles and what designers think. *Communications of the ACM*, 28:300–311, 1985.

[74]   I. Graham. *Object Oriented Methods*. Addison Wesley, 1991.

[75]   T. Gruber. A translation approach to portable ontologies. *Knowledge Acquisition*, 5(2):199–220, 1993.

[76]   N. Guarino. Concepts, attributes and arbitrary relations. *Data & Knowledge Engineering*, 8:249–261, 1992. North-Holland.

[77]   N. Guarino and P. Giaretta. Ontologies and Knowledge Bases: Towards a Terminological Clarification. In N. Mars, editor, *Towards Very Large Knowledge Bases: Knowledge Building and Knowledge Sharing*, pages 25–32, Amsterdam, 1995. IOS Press.

[78]   K.H. Haggie and J.K.C. Kingston. Choosing your Knowledge Management Strategy. *Journal of Knowledge Management Practice*, 2003.

[79]   U. Hahn and M.J.A. Ramscar. *Similarity and Categorization.* Oxford University Press, Oxford, 2001.

[80]   A. Hart. *Expert Systems: An Introduction for Managers.* Kogan Page, 1988.

[81]   T. Heycke. Historical projects. HTML document http://wwwcamis.stanford.edu/research/history.html, Center for Advanced Medical Informatics at Stanford, January 1995.

[82]   F. Hickman, J. Killin, L. Land, et al. *Analysis for knowledge-based systems: A practical introduction to the KADS methodology.* Ellis Horwood, Chichester, 1989.

[83]   V. Hubka. *Principles of Engineering Design.* Butterworth Scientific, Guildford, 1982. trans. W. E. Eder.

[84]   R. Inder. Experience of constructing a fault localisation expert system using an AI toolkit. In *Proceedings of the 1st International Conference on Industrial and Engineering Applications of Artificial Intelligence and Expert Systems - Volume 1*, pages 229–239, 1988.

[85]   R. Inder and I.M. Filby. A Survey of Knowledge Engineering Methods and Supporting Tools. In *KBS Methodologies Workshop.* BCS Specialist Group on Expert Systems, December 1992.

[86]   R. Inder, E. Goodfellow, and M. Uschold. Knowledge Engineering without Knowledge Elicitation. In P. Chung, G. Lovegrove and M. Ali, editor, *Proceedings of the Sixth International Conference on Industrial and Engineering Applications of AI and Expert Systems*, City Chambers, Edinburgh, June 1-4 1993. Gordon and Breach. Also available as AIAI-TR-126.

[87]   J. Kingston. Merging top level ontologies for scientific knowledge management. In *Proceedings of the AAAI*

workshop on Ontologies and the Semantic Web, AAAI-02 conference, Edmonton, Canada, 29 July 2002.

[88]   W.   Jansweijer.   Recommendations   to EuroKnowledge. KACTUS Deliverable KACTUS-DO1f.1-UvA-V0.2, University of Amsterdam, September 23 1996.

[89]   L. Johnson and N.E. Johnson. Knowledge elicitation involving teachback interviewing. In A.L. Kidd, editor, *Knowledge Acquisition for Expert Systems: A Practical Handbook*, chapter 5, pages 91–108. Plenum Press, 1987.

[90]   L. Johnson and E. Keravnou. *Expert Systems Technology: A Guide*. Abacus Press, Cambridge, Mass. 02139, 1985.

[91]   G. S. Kahn, E. H. Breaux, P. DeKlerk, and R. L. Joseph. A mixed-initiative workbench for knowledge acquisition. *Int. Journal of Man-Machine Studies*, 27:167–179, 1987.

[92]   KBSI. IDEF3 Process Flow and Object State Description   Capture   Method   Overview. http://www.idef.com/idef3.html.

[93]   A. Kidd, editor. *Knowledge Acquisition for Expert Systems: A Practical Handbook*. Plenum Press, 1987.

[94]   J. K. C. Kingston. KBS Methodology as a framework for Co-operative Working. In *Research and Development in Expert Systems IX*. British Computer Society, Cambridge University Press, 16-17 Dec 1992. Also available from AIAI as AIAITR-130.

[95]   J.K.C. Kingston. X-MATE: Creating an interpretation model for credit risk assessment. In *Expert Systems 91*. British Computer Society, Cambridge University Press, 17-18 Sep 1991. Also available from AIAI as AIAI-TR-98.

[96]   J.K.C. Kingston. Pragmatic KADS 1.0. Technical Report AIAI-IR-13, AIAI, University of Edinburgh, 1993.

[97]   J.K.C. Kingston. Re-engineering IMPRESS and X-MATE using CommonKADS. In *Research and Development in Expert Systems X*, pages 17–42. Cambridge University Press, 1993. http://www.aiai.ed.ac.uk/~jkk/publications.html.

[98]   J.K.C. Kingston. Design by Exploration: A Proposed CommonKADS Inference Structure. *Submitted to 'Knowledge Acquisition'*, 1994.

[99]   J.K.C. Kingston. Developing a reference ontology for scientific knowledge management. In *Proceedings of AAAI-02 Workshop on Ontologies and the Semantic Web, AAAI-02, Edmonton, Canada*, 29 July 2002.

[100]   J.K.C. Kingston. Modelling Agents and Communication using CommonKADS. In *Research and Development in Expert Systems XVII Proceedings of the BCS SGES ES'00 conference*, Churchill College, Cambridge, December 2000.

[101]   J.K.C. Kingston, J. Doheny, and I. Filby. Evaluation of workbenches which support the CommonKADS methodology. *Knowledge Engineering Review*,
          10(3):269–300, 1995.

[102]   J.K.C. Kingston, T.J. Lydiard, and A. Griffith. Multi-Perspective Modelling of Air Campaign Planning. In *Proceedings of AAAI-96*, Portland, Oregon, 1996. AAAI Press.

[103]   J.K.C. Kingston and A.L. Macintosh. Knowledge Management through Multi-Perspective Modelling: Representing and Distributing Organizational Memory. *Knowledge Based Systems Journal*, 13(2-3):121–131, 2000.

[104]   P. J. Kline and S. B. Dolins. *Designing expert systems : a guide to selecting implementation techniques*. Wiley, 1989.

[105]   P.J. Kline and S.B. Dolins. *Choosing Architectures for Expert Systems*. Rome Air Development Centre, Griffiss AFB, New York 13441-5700. RADC-TR-85192, 1985. Contains "forty-seven probing questions" to help select the correct knowledge representation(s) and inference strategy(ies) for building a knowledge-based system.

[106]   G. Klinker, J. Bentolila, S. Genetet, M. Grimes, and J. McDermott. Knack: Report-driven knowledge acquisition. *Int. Journal of Man-Machine Studies*, 26:65–79, 1987.

[107]   M. Kolp. Tropos - Requirement-Driven Software Development for Agents, 2002. http://www.cs.toronto.edu/km/tropos/.

[108]   A Krueger. Classification of Expert Tasks: the SEXTANT system. Master's thesis, Dept of Artificial Intelligence, University of Edinburgh, Sept 1992.

[109] C. Kruger and B. Wielinga. A KADS model for the industrial design task. In C. L¨ockenhoff, editor, *Proceedings of the 3rd KADS Meeting*, pages 131–141, ZFGE BT SE 21, Otto-Hahn-Ring 6, D8000 Munich 83, Germany, 1993. Siemens AG.

[110] B. Kuipers and J.P. Kassirer. Knowledge acquisition by analysis of verbatim protocols. In A.L. Kidd, editor, *Knowledge Acquisition for Expert Systems: A Practical Handbook*, chapter 3, pages 45–71. Plenum Press, 1987.

[111] B. Lawson. *How Designers Think*. The Architectural Press Ltd: London, 1980.

[112] B.R. Lawson. *Problem solving in architectural design*. PhD thesis, University of Aston, Birmingham, 1972.

[113] D. Lenat. The Dimensions of Context Space, 1998. http://www.ai.mit.edu/people/phw/6xxx/lenat2.pdf.

[114] D. Lenat and R. V. Guha. *Building Large Knowledge-Based Systems: Representation and Inference in the Cyc Project*. Addison-Wesley, 1990. 0201517523.

[115] J. Liebowitz. An Interactive Multimedia Tool for Learning Knowledge Acquisition Methods. In G. Lovegrove P. Chung and M. Ali, editors, *Proceedings of the 6th International Conference on Industrial and Engineering Applications of AI and Expert Systems*, pages 184–187, City Chambers, Edinburgh, June 1993. Gordon and Breach.

[116] C. Löckenhoff and A. Valente. A Library of Assessment Modelling Components. In *Proceedings of 3rd European KADS User Group Meeting*, pages 289–303. Siemens, Munich, March 1993.

[117] Musen M.A., Fagan L.M., Combs D.M., and Shortliffe E.H. Use of a domain model to drive an interactive knowledge-editing tool. *International Journal of Man-Machine Studies*, 26:105–121, 1987.

[118] A. Macintosh, I. Filby, and J. Kingston. Knowledge Management Techniques: Teaching & Dissemination Concepts. *International Journal of Human Computer Studies, Special Issue on Organisational Memories & Knowledge Management*, September/October 1999.

[119]   A. Maclean, R. Young, V. Bellotti, et al. Design Space Analysis: Bridging from theory to practice via design rationale. In *Proceedings of Esprit '91*, pages 720– 730, Brussels, November 1991.

[120]   C MacNee. PDQ: A knowledge-based system to help knowledge-based system designers to select knowledge representation and inference techniques. Master's thesis, Dept of Artificial Intelligence, University of Edinburgh, September 1992.

[121]   M. L. Maher. Process Models for Design Synthesis. *AI Magazine*, 11(4):49–58, 1990.

[122]   A.G. Maran, N.C. Molony, M.W.J. Armstrong, et al. Is there an evidence base for the practice of ENT surgery? *Clinical Otolaryngology*, 22:152–157, 1996.

[123]   S. Marcus. Taking Backtracking with a Grain of SALT. *Int. Journal of Man-Machine Studies*, 26:383–398, 1987.

[124]   J. McDermott. R1: A rule-based configurer of computer systems. *Artificial Intelligence*, 19, 1:39–88, 1982.

[125]   K.L. McGraw and K. Harbinson-Briggs. *Knowledge Acquisition: Principles and Guidelines*. Prentice-Hall International, 1989.

[126]   M. Musen. Protege-2000 Home Page. http://protege.stanford.edu/whatis.shtml.

[127]   N. Coulter et al. Report of the CCS Update Committee. Technical report, 1998. http://www.acm.org/class/1998/ccsup.pdf.

[128]   N. Guarino. Some Ontological Principles for Designing Upper Level Lexical Resources. In A. Rubio and N. Gallardo and R. Castro and A. Tejada, editor, *Proceedings of First International Conference on Language Resources and Evaluation. ELRA - European Language Resources Association, Granada, Spain*, pages 527–534, 1998.

[129]   B. Neumann. Towards libraries of problem-solving models - candidates for standardisation. Technical Report EuroK/T/960615-2/DTK, ESPRIT Project 9806 (EuroKnowledge), June 1996.

[130]   A. Newell. The knowledge level. *Artificial Intelligence*, 18:87–127, 1982.

[131]   Nguyen *et al.* Knowledge Base Verification. *AI Magazine*, 8(2):69–75, 1987.

[132]   I. Nonaka and H. Takeuchi. *The Knowledge-Creating Company: How Japanese Companies Create the Dynamics of Innovation*. Oxford University Press, New York, 1995.

[133]   Official Government Commerce. *Managing Successful Projects in PRINCE2*. Stationery Office Books, 2002.

[134]   R. Ostermayer, E. Meis, A. Bernaras and I. Laresgoiti. Guidelines on domain ontology building (version 2). KACTUS Deliverable KACTUS-DO1c2, RPK, Labein, 1996. http://www.swi.psy.uva.nl/projects/NewKACTUS/postscript/do1c2.ps.

[135]   M. Ould. Process Modelling with RADs. *IOPener: the newsletter of Praxis plc*, 1-5 to 2-2, 1992-1993.

[136]   S. Price and J.K.C. Kingston. KADESS: The KADS Approach to the Design of Steel Structures. In P. Chung, G. Lovegrove and M. Ali, editor, *Proceedings of the Sixth International Conference on Industrial and Engineering Applications of AI and Expert Systems*, pages 188–196, City Chambers, Edinburgh, June 1-4 1993. Gordon and Breach.

[137]   Rational Software. UML Resource Center. http://www.rational.com/uml/.

[138]   Y. Reich. Design knowledge acquisition: task analysis and a partial implementation. *Knowledge Acquisition*, 3:237–254, September 1991.

[139]   Han Reichgelt and Nigel Shadbolt. ProtoKEW: A knowledge based system for knowledge acquisition. In D. Sleeman and O. Bernsen, editors, *Recent Advances in Cognitive Science:*. Lawrence Earlbaum Associates, 1991.

[140]   R.I.B.A. *Royal Institution of British Architects' Architectural Practice and Management Handbook*. RIBA Publications, London, 1965.

[141]   S. Robertson. A KBS to advise on selection of KBS tools. Master's thesis, Dept of Artificial Intelligence, University of Edinburgh, September 1993.

[142]   Eleanor Rosch. Principles of categorization. In A. Collins and E. E. Smith, editors, *Readings in Cognitive Science: A*

Perspective from Psychology and Artificial Intelligence, pages 312–322. Kaufmann, San Mateo, CA, 1988.

[143]   W. W. Royce. Managing the Development of Large Systems: Concepts and Techniques. In *1970 WESCON Technical Papers, v. 14, Western Electronic Show and Convention*, pages A/1–1 – A/1–9, Los Angeles, 1970. WESCON. Reprinted in Proceedings of the Ninth International Conference on Software Engineering, Pittsburgh, PA, USA, ACM Press, pp.328–338.

[144]   J. Rumbaugh, M. Blaha, W. Premerlani, F. Eddy, and W. Lorensen. *ObjectOriented Modelling and Design*. Prentice Hall, Englewood Cliffs, New Jersey, 1991.

[145]   E.D. Sacerdoti. *A Structure for Plans and Behaviour*. Artificial Intelligence. Elsevier North Holland, 1977.

[146]   G. Schreiber, editor. *A KADS approach to KBS design*. University of Amsterdam, 1989. ESPRIT project 1098, Deliverable B6, UvA-B6-PR-010.

[147]   G. Schreiber, H. Akkermans, A. Anjewierden, R. de Hoog, N. Shadbolt, W. Van de Velde, and B. Wielinga. *Knowledge Engineering and Management: The CommonKADS Methodology*. The MIT Press, 1999.

[148]   G. Schreiber, B. Wielinga, H. Akkermans, and W. Van de Velde. CML: The CommonKADS Conceptual Modelling Language. In L. Steels, G. Schreiber, and W. van de Velde, editors, *A future for knowledge acquisition: Proceedings of EKAW-94*, Hoegaarden, Belgium, Sept 26-29 1994. Springer-Verlag.

[149]   G. Schreiber, B. Wielinga, R. de Hoog, H. Akkermans, and W. van de Velde. CommonKADS: A Comprehensive Methodology for KBS Development. *IEEE Expert*, pages 28–37, Dec 1994.

[150]   R. Schrooten. Sabena flight schedule case: an example of a design model. CommonKADS Deliverable D.M.7 KADS-II/M7/VUB/RR/064/2.1, Vrije Universiteit Brussel, 1993. This report has been included in the CommonKADS 'Design Model and Process' report, the number of which is given above.

[151]   R. Schrooten and C. Duursma. Configuration Support Environment: Functional Specification. CommonKADS Deliverable D.M.7.4 KADS-II/DM7.4/VUB/RR/004/1.0, Vrije

Universiteit Brussel, 1994. http://arti.vub.ac.be/previous_projects/kads/m7.4.ps.

[152] N. Shadbolt and A.M. Burton. Knowledge elicitation. In J. Wilson and N. Corlett, editor, *Evaluation of Human Work: A Practical Ergonomics Methodology*, pages 321–346. Taylor and Francis, 1990.

[153] M.L.G. Shaw and B.R. Gaines. KITTEN: Knowledge initiation and transfer tools for experts and novices. *International Journal of Man-Machine Studies*, 27:251–280, 1987.

[154] E. H. Shortliffe. *Computer-Based Medical Consultations: MYCIN*. Elsevier/North-Holland, Amsterdam, London, New York, 1976.

[155] J. Simpson, J. Kingston, and N. Molony. An Expert System for Best Practice in Medicine. *Knowledge Based Systems Journal*, 1999. Originally appeared in Proceedings of Expert Systems 98, SGES Press, Cambridge 1998.

[156] J. Smart. HARDY. *Airing*, 15:3–7, April 1993. AIAI, University of Edinburgh.

[157] B.C. Smith. *On the origin of objects*. MIT Press, Cambridge, MA, 1996.

[158] T. Smithers, A. Conkie, J. Doheny, B. Logan, K. Millington, and M. X. Tang. Design as intelligent behaviour: an AI in design research programme. *Artificial Intelligence in Engineering*, 5(2):78–109, 1990.

[159] J.F. Sowa and J.A. Zachman. Extending and Formalizing the Framework for Information Systems Architecture. *IBM Systems Journal*, 31(3):590–616, 1992.

[160] G. Spanoudakis, A. Finkelstein, and W. Emmerich. Viewpoints 96: Workshop Report, 1996. http://www.soi.city.ac.uk/ gespan/vprep.html.

[161] L. Steels. Components of Expertise. *AI Magazine*, 1990. Also available as: AI Memo 88-16, AI Lab, Free University of Brussels.

[162] D.G. Stork. The Open Mind initiative, 2007. http://www.openmind.org.

[163] E. Stroulia and A. Goel. Redesigning a problem-solver's operators to improve solution quality. In M. Pollack, editor, *Proceedings of the Fifteenth International Joint Conference*

on Artificial Intelligence (IJCAI '97), volume 1, pages 562–567, Nagoya, Japan, 1997. Morgan Kaufmann.

[164]   J.   Sundstrom.   Book   Burro,   2007. http://bookburro.org.

[165]   B. Swartout and Y. Gil. EXPECT: Explicit Representations for Flexible Acquisition, 1995.

[166]   D. S. W. Tansley and C. C. Hayball. *Knowledge-Based Systems Analysis and Design: A KADS Developers Handbook*. Prentice Hall, 1993.

[167]   A. Tate. Generating project networks. In *Proceedings of the Fifth International Joint Conference on Artificial Intelligence*, pages 888–893, Los Altos California, 1977. William Kaufmann Inc.

[168]   A. Tate. Characterising Plans as a Set of Constraints - the <I-N-OVA> Model - a Framework for Comparative Analysis. *ACM SIGART Bulletin: Special Issue on Evaluation of Plans, Planners, and Planning Agents*, 6(1), January 1995. A paper on this subject will also be presented at AIPS-96.

[169]   A. Tate, B. Drabble, and R. Kirby. O-Plan2: an Open Architecture for Command, Planning and Control. In M. Zweben and M. Fox, editors, *Intelligent Scheduling*, pages 213–239. Morgan-Kaufmann, 1994.

[170]   A. Tate, B. Drabble, and R. Kirby. O-Plan2: an Open Architecture for Command, Planning and Control. Technical report, AIAI, 1995.

[171]   Austin Tate. Roots of SPAR Shared Planning and Activity Representation. *Knowledge Engineering Review*, 13(1):121–128, 1998.

[172]   TEISS Fact Sheet. GRASP - Global Retrieval, Access and information System for Property items. http://www.ejeisa.com/nectar/teiss/6.1.3/fact-sheets/pdf/ grasp.pdf.

[173]   Teknowledge Corporation. Rapid Knowledge Formation project. http://www.reliant.teknowledge.com/ RKF, 2001.

[174]   A. ten Teije, F. van Harmelen, A.Th. Schreiber, and B.J. Wielinga. Construction of problem-solving methods as

parametric design. *International Journal of Human Computer Studies*, 1998.

[175]   T.J. Lydiard. A survey of verification and validation techniques for KBS. *Knowledge Engineering Review*, 7(2), June 1992.

[176]   A. Valente. Planning Models for the CommonKADS Library. In J. Breuker and W. van de Velde, editors, *The CommonKADS Library*, chapter 11. IOS Press, 1994.

[177]   A. Valente and C. L"ockenhoff. Assessment. In J. Breuker and W. van de Velde, editors, *The CommonKADS Library*, chapter 8. IOS Press, 1994.

[178]   A. van Beuzekom. Analysing Molecular Similarity using a KBS and CommonKADS. AIAI Visitor Project Report AIAI-PR-56, AIAI, University of Edinburgh, 1993. The author is employed at Unilever Research Laboratories, Vlaardingen, The Netherlands.

[179]   W. van de Velde, C. Duursma, and G. Schreiber. Design model and process. Unpublished KADS-II/M7/MM/VUB, Vrije Universiteit Brussel, 1993.

[180]   W. van de Velde et al. Design model and process. Unpublished KADSII/M7/VUB/RR/064/2.1, Vrije Universiteit Brussel, October 1994.

[181]   F. van Harmelen and J. R. Balder. (ML)^2: a formal language for KADS models of expertise. *Knowledge Acquisition*, 4(1), 1992. Special issue on 'The KADS approach to knowledge engineering'.

[182]   G. van Heijst and A. Th. Schreiber. CUE: Ontology-based knowledge acquisition. In L. Steels, A. Th. Schreiber, and W. Van de Velde, editors, *A Future for Knowledge Acquisition. Proceedings of the 8th European Knowledge Acquisition Workshop EKAW'94*, pages 178–199. Springer Verlag, Berlin/Heidelberg, September 1994. http://www.swi.psy.uva.nl/usr/gertjan/postscript/vanHeijst:94b.ps.gz.

[183]   Various. *Proceedings of the Third DARPA Workshop on Case-based Reasoning*. Morgan Kaufmann, 1989. Articles in this proceedings include "A Case-based tool for

Conceptual Design Problem Solving" and "Case Adaptation in Autoclave Layout Design".

[184]   S. Vere. Planning in time: Windows and durations for activities and goals. *IEEE Transactions on Pattern Analysis and Machine Intelligence*, 5:246–267, 1983.

[185]   W. Visser. Giving up a hierarchical plan in a design activity. Technical Report 814, Institut Nationale de Recherche en Informatique et en Automatique, Domaine de Voluceau Rocquencourt B.P. 105, 78153 Le Chesnay Cedex, France, March 1988. An English version of a paper presented in French at the COGNITIVA87 conference, Cesta, Paris 1987.

[186]   A. Waern and S. Gala. The CommonKADS Agent Model. ESPRIT Project P5248 KADS-II KADS-II/M4/TR/SICS, Swedish Institute of Computer Science, 1994.

[187]   A. Waern, K. Höök, R. Gustavsson, and P. Holm. The CommonKADS Communication Model. ESPRIT Project P5248 KADS-II KADS-II/M3/TR/SICS, Swedish Institute of Computer Science, 1994.

[188]   S.   Wells.   Data-Driven   Modelling.   In *CommonKADS Library for Expertise Modelling*. IOS Press, 1994.

[189]   S.A. Wells. Configuration Control. KADS-II Project Report KADSII/M2.2/TN/LR/0099/0.2, Lloyds Register, 1993.

[190]   J. Wielemaker and J-P. Billault. *A KADS analysis for configuration*. University of Amsterdam, 1988. ESPRIT project 1098, Deliverable F5, UvA-F5-PR-001.

[191]   B. Wielinga, W. Van de Velde, G. Schreiber, and H. Akkermans. The KADS Knowledge Modelling Approach. In *Proceedings of the Japanese Knowledge Acquisition Workshop (JKAW'92)*, 1992.

[192]   B. Wielinga, W. van de Velde, G. Schreiber, and H. Akkermans.   Expertise   Model   Definition   Document. CommonKADS Project Report, University of Amsterdam, Jun 1993.

[193]   Wielinga B.J., A.Th. Schreiber, J. Wieleimaker and J.C. Sandberg. From Thesaurus to Ontology. GRASP project publication,   University   of   Amsterdam.

http://www.swi.psy.uva.nl/usr/Schreiber/papers/Wielinga01a. pdf.

[194]   J. Wilkins.   Natural   and   artificial classification.   Technical   report,   1997.   http:// www.users.bigpond.com/thewilkins/papers/artifnat.html.

[195]   W.A. Woods. What's in a link: Foundations for semantic networks. In D.G. Bobrow and A.M. Collins, editors, *Representation and Understanding: Studies in Cognitive Science*, New York, 1975. Academic Press. Also in R. Brachman and H. Levesque, eds., *Readings in Knowledge Representation* (Morgan Kaufmann, Los Altos, CA, 1985).

[196]   R.M. Young and G.D. Abowd. Multi-perspective Modelling of Interface Design Issues: Undo in a Collaborative Editor. In G. Cockton, S.W. Draper, and G.R S. Weir, editors, *People and Computers IX: Proceedings of HCI 94*, pages 249–260. Cambridge University Press, 1994.

[197]   J. Zachman. A Framework for Information Systems Architecture. *IBM Systems Journal*, 26(3):276–292, 1987. Also published in the same journal, volume 38(2/3), 1999.

Part V: Appendices

A Library of generic inference structures

A.1 System Analysis

A.1.1 Assessment
Source: Adapted from [82]

In assessment, a case is interpreted in terms of a system model in order to classify it as belonging to one of the classes which are specified in advance as the decision classes. Assessment differs from simple classification because the correct classification is not 'given'; instead, it requires interpretation of the various attributes of an abstract case description against the system model. The resulting decision classes may lie on a continuum rather than being discrete. An example of an assessment task would be deciding whether the skills of a job applicant fulfil the requirements of the job.

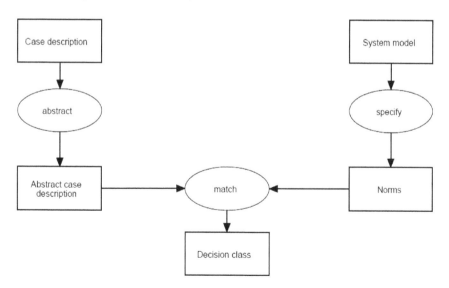

Figure A.1: Generic inference structure for Assessment

A.1.2 Heuristic Classification

Source: Adapted from Clancey, 'Heuristic Classification' [31]

Heuristic classification was claimed by Clancey to be the method of diagnosis in knowledge based systems [31]. It involves abstracting the problem and matching it against one or more solutions at a similar level of abstraction. The model can be followed from beginning to end, or from end to beginning (i.e. it is possible to abstract a solution, and then to see which problem(s) it solves); the choice of strategy will depend on the cost of obtaining data, and the need for a fully refined solution.

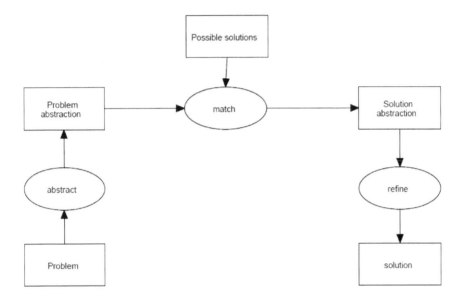

Figure A.2: Generic inference structure for Heuristic Classification

A.1.3 Monitoring

Source: [20] or [82]

Monitoring presupposes an existing system model and an actual running system. In monitoring, discrepancies (if any) are detected and decisions are made as to what kind of action(s) should be taken.

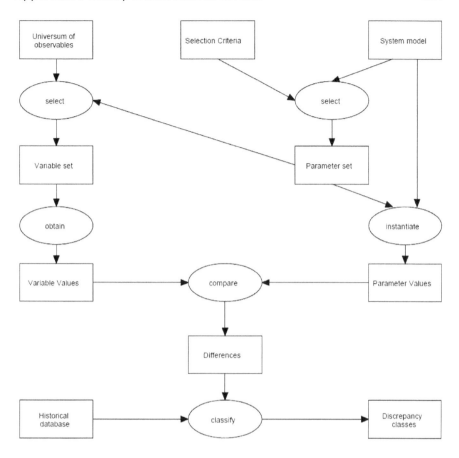

Figure A.3: Generic inference structure for Monitoring

A.1.4 Multiple fault diagnosis
Source: [82]. See Figure A.4

A.1.5 Simple Classification
Source: [82]
See Figure A.7

A.1.6 Prediction
Source: [20]

A prediction task can intuitively best be described as "determining what will happen next in a given situation". In a prediction task, there is always a description of a particular situation that specifies the objects and the processes that are involved; this description may need to be augmented with relevant common-sense knowledge before a prediction can be made. Solutions consist of (new) description(s) of processes and objects, although ideally prediction solutions should be limited to new descriptions which are relevant to the user's interests.

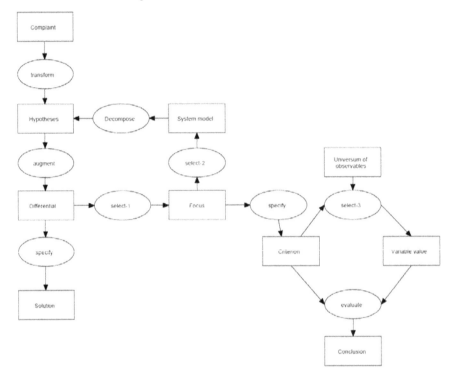

Figure A.4: Generic inference structure for Multiple fault diagnosis

A.1.7 Prediction of behaviour

Source: Simplified from [20]

Prediction of behaviour should not be taken literally. It may in fact involve postdiction, and may be used as part of causal tracing. It is accomplished by analysing the state description of a system and determining what behaviour the system will carry out next (or, for postdiction, what behaviour must have preceded the current state description). The state description describes what the system at the moment is like which can be done at various levels of abstraction.

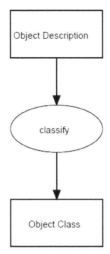

Figure A.5: Generic inference structure for Simple Classification

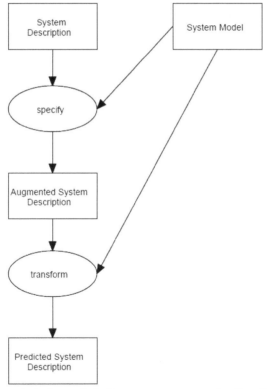

Figure A.6: Generic inference structure for Prediction

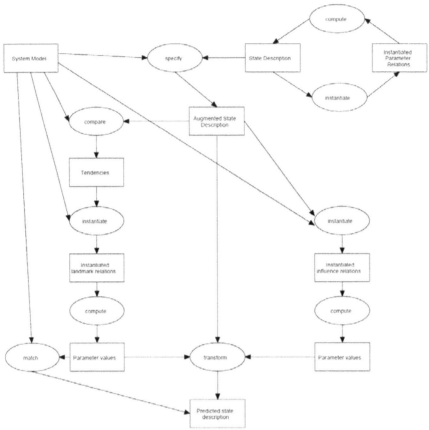

Figure A.7: Generic inference structure for Prediction of behaviour

A.1.8   Prediction of values
Source: [20]

The task is the prediction or identification of value(s) of variable(s) of a system at a certain point in time. The values are in general quantitative ones which are derived from some formal or mathematical model of the system.

A.1.9   Systematic Diagnosis
Source: Adapted from [82]

This model can be used for both causal tracing and diagnosis by localisation. The former requires a description of the system in terms of

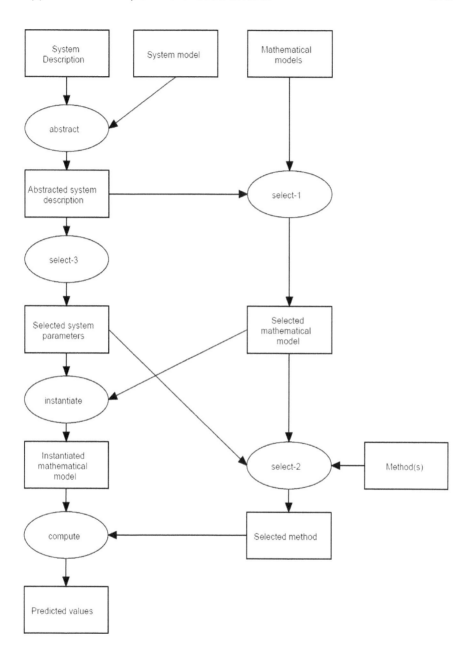

Figure A.8: Generic inference structure for Prediction of values

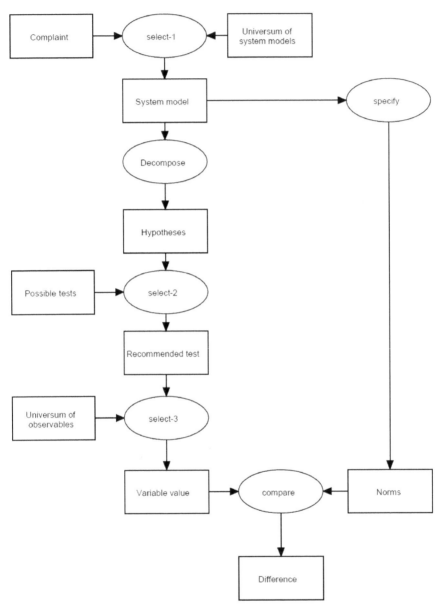

Figure A.9: Generic inference structure for Systematic Diagnosis

causal relations; the latter requires a description of the system in terms of PART-OF relations.

A.2 System Synthesis

A.2.1 Configuration
Source: [82]

Configuration is a simple form of design. The general structure of the artefact is given beforehand, only the specific components have to be filled in.

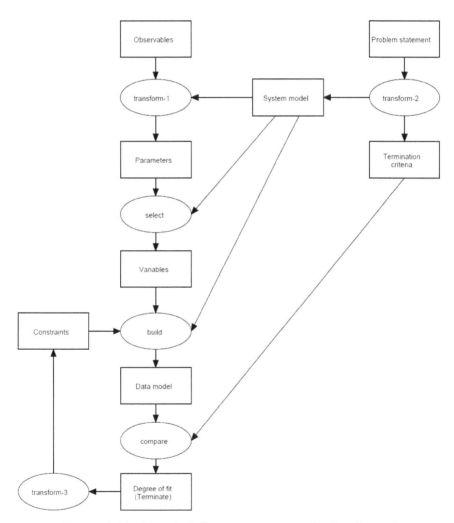

Figure A.10: Generic inference structure for Configuration

A.2.2 Propose-and-revise design

Propose-and-revise design occurs in tasks where a design is prepared, presented to the client for criticism, and then any criticisms are used as further constraints on a redesign. Propose-and-revise design will often start from a model of a previous design; on occasions, this model may produce no acceptable solutions, and so a new model may have to be selected.

Source: Chapter 10

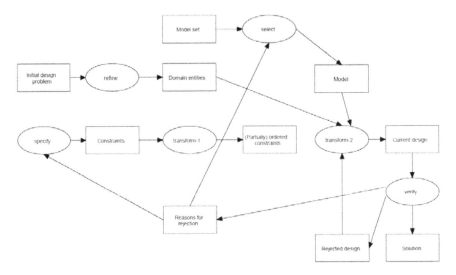

Figure A.11: Generic inference structure for propose-and-revise design

A.2.3 Hierarchical design

Source: [82]

The basic characteristic of hierarchical design is that at some stage in the design process, a model is created of the artefact to be designed, and that model is subsequently refined to yield the final result.

A.2.4 Single stream refinement design

Source: [20]

In refinement design (or "incremental design"), there is no straightforward transformation of the conceptual model to the detailed

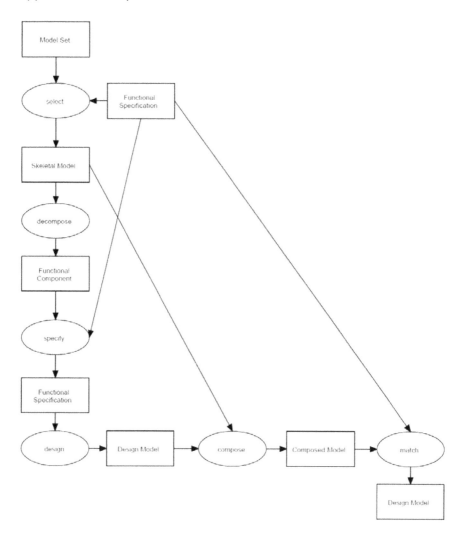

Figure A.12: Generic inference structure for Hierarchical design

design model, but rather elements of the conceptual model are transformed individually, while the structure of the design is constructed from constraints and/or skeletal models.

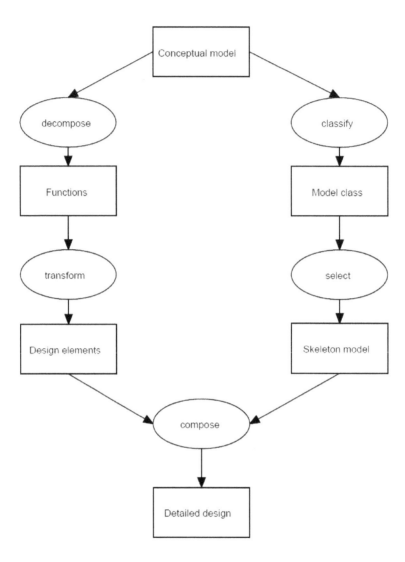

Figure A.13: Generic inference structure for Single stream
refinement design

B Semantics of Inference steps

Abstract: Abstraction produces an output concept with fewer attributes than the input concept; 'irrelevant' attributes are abstracted. What is relevant and what is irrelevant depends on a point of view. Many structures of static relations (e.g. is-a, consists-of) have fixed points of view, and enable abstract inferences.

Assemble: All assemble inferences take as their input a number of elements and produce a part-of structure. Essentially, there are two ways to construct an assembly (e.g. plan, configuration, design). First, bottom up by combining elements in such a way that they satisfy constraints. A second way is top down and consists of the selection of appropriate, constraint satisfying structures, in which the elements can be inserted.

Assign Value: Knowledge sources of this type derive values for attributes of concepts and assign them to those attributes. An example is the use of default values.

Classify: See *Identify*.

Compare: The values of (the attributes of) concepts are compared. In general, this refers to simple concepts which have few attributes. The output is a class (equal, not equal) or a difference value. The output of 'compare' may not be used as the input for some other knowledge source, but rather for control purposes.

Compute: On the basis of some structure of concepts and their instances, the value of some dependent factor is calculated. Note that computation may involve any form of value assignment on the basis of interdependencies of concepts: for example, computing whether a bathtub is 'overflowing' or 'not overflowing' ... COMPUTE is not strictly a primitive knowledge source, since it typically includes either a value assignment, or the instantiation of a new concept.

Generalise: In generalisation, one focuses on common features in the set of instances and tries either to map these onto an existing concept or to develop a new concept. The former resembles 'identify'; the latter is generally known as induction.

Decompose: 'Decompose' is the inverse of 'assemble'. The input is some composite structure and the output is a set of components.

Instantiate: This type of knowledge source creates an instance of a generic concept, or structure. It often involves assignment of values.

Identify: 'Identify' (also called 'classify') is the inverse of 'instantiate'. 'Identify' associates instances with descriptions, by matching the attributes of an instance (and the structure of these attributes) with a concept.

Match: 'Match' compares two structures; the output is a description of the respects in which the two structures are different. The description of the difference can be used to focus a task on particular issues. For instance, the description of the difference can be used to restrict or provide goals for further inferencing.

Parse: 'Parse' is a subtype of 'transform'. It transforms a linear structure of elements into a hierarchical structure.

Refine: see *Specify*.

Select: see *Specify*.

Specify: Specification is the inverse of abstraction. It produces a concept with at least one more specific attribute than the input concept. A good example of specification is descending a taxonomy of concepts ... Specification is the same as 'refinement', although the latter is often used to denote some complex trajectory of inferences that involve specifications ... A degraded form of specify is 'select', in which a specific concept is singled out.

Sort: 'Sort' can be viewed as a subtype of 'assemble' (sequencing elements according to some principle), or as a subtype of 'transform' (changing one structure into another).

Transform: Transform converts an input structure into another structure, either by reordering elements within a structure, or by assigning new structural descriptions to the elements. The latter often appears as translations from one description or formalism into another description or formalism. This may require abstraction steps as well, because the elements in the input description may not be sufficiently abstract to allow the transformation procedures to apply.

In addition, Pragmatic KADS suggests the following "activities" which are activities that are not knowledge based but are an integral part of many problem solving processes.

Add: Add an item to a set or a list.

Compute: The definition of this inference step is extended to permit basic arithmetic computations which are not based on "some structure of concepts and their instances".

Execute: Carry out any task which is not part of the inference process. This typically refers to tasks carried out by a user, such as performing a diagnostic test.

Identify: *Identify* is used not only to refer to linking an object with its correct category, but also to represent obtaining data, by table look-up or through some other external interface function.

Perform: see *Execute*.

Remove: Remove items from a set or a list.

Update: Add items to or remove items from a set or a list.

C   Probing Questions

C.1   AI Architectural Paradigms questions

C.1.1 Knowledge   Structure: Domain   Objects   &   Relationships

1.   if you want the KBS to reason on the basis of an explicit model of processes, in the world (as distinct from representing an expert's problem-solving behaviour in relation to them) then use model-based reasoning `weighting: 3`

2.   if the system can be adequately described by a procedural representation of the problem-solving behaviour of an expert: i.e. by representing the expert's inference steps then use shallow reasoning `weighting: 3`

3.   if the knowledge domain consists of objects which can be thought of as separate entities and domain objects have well-defined interactive behaviours not sensitive to global influences then use model-based reasoning `weighting: 1` and use object-oriented programming `weighting: 4` and don't use shallow reasoning `weighting: -3` **because** Objects are autonomous and communicate with each other; control is within the KR structures, i.e. local control; behaviour is emergent

4.   if the knowledge domain consists of objects which can be thought of as separate entities and control of the processes which significantly affect the objects in the knowledge domain is global rather than local then use model-based reasoning `weighting: 4` and use objects `weighting: 5` OR rules `weighting: 2` and don't use object-oriented programming `weighting: -2` and don't use shallow reasoning `weighting: -3`

5.   if you use model-based reasoning and attribute values in the domain can be adequately expressed by selection from a small set of standard 'qualitative' values (e.g. hi/med/lo, -ve/steadystate/+ve) and qualitative values can be combined by operators in a well-described and semantically valid way then use qualitative simulation `weighting: 3`

C.1.2 Knowledge Structure: Inferences and Generic Tasks

6.   if the problem space is shallow: i.e. if most of the items of data/evidence can be converted into a solution in a single inference step then use shallow reasoning `weighting: 4` and use a spreadsheet `weighting: 2` and don't use model-based reasoning `weighting: -4`

7.   if the problem to be solved is very large – say, more than 10 modules (where a module performs a distinct operation and most of them require more than one inference step) and problem-solving modules are independent of each other and problem-solving modules interact (as opposed to being sequential) and the interaction of problem-solving modules can be scheduled successfully then use a blackboard architecture `weighting: 4`

8.   if few/some/many previous examples of problem solving are available then use case-based reasoning (if few examples then `weighting: 1`; if some examples then `weighting: 2`; if many examples then `weighting: 3`) OR a neural network (if few examples then `weighting: 1`; if some examples then `weighting: 3`; if many examples then `weighting: 3`)

9.   if key factors affecting problem solving in previous cases can be identified then use rule induction for rule acquisition `weighting: 1`

10.   if previous examples of problem solving are described in text then use case-based reasoning `weighting: 1` and don't use a neural network `weighting: -1`

11.   if previous examples of problem solving are numerical then use a neural network `weighting: 1` and don't use case-based reasoning `weighting: -1`

C.1.3 Dialogue & Explanation

12.   if the *generation* of explanations of the KBS's reasoning in terms of cause and effect is important (as distinct from merely *presenting* explanations, e.g. as 'canned text') then use model-based reasoning `weighting: 5`

C.2   AI Programming Techniques questions

C.2.1 Knowledge   Structure: Domain   Objects   & Relationships

13.   if domain knowledge is structured in a taxonomic hierarchy (i.e. where objects can be grouped into classes and the classes recursively divided into subclasses, and where membership is a transitive relationship from subclasses to classes) then use an inheritance technique `weighting: 5`

14.   if default values are to be used for unknown values of properties of domain objects then use an inheritance technique `weighting: 4`

15.   if simple, binary, transitive relationships (e.g. connected-to, close-to) between domain objects can be defined, other than those which give rise to a hierarchy (e.g. subclass-of, contains) then use a semantic network `weighting: 4` use and use user-defined relations `weighting: 5`

16.   if domain knowledge is structured in a taxonomic hierarchy (i.e. where objects can be grouped into classes and the classes recursively divided into subclasses, and where membership is a transitive relationship from subclasses to classes) and you want to represent, with rules, the interactive behaviour of the objects in the hierarchy and you want to give priority to representing the

interactive behaviours rather than the objects then use order-sorted logic `weighting: 3`

17. if an inference structure for the analysed knowledge has been modelled in terms of inference actions and knowledge roles (types of domain object) and a 'match' inference action is to be implemented which matches 3 or more variables or a 'match' inference action is to be implemented for which a complete set of mappings is not available then use rule-based programming `weighting: 3`

18. if knowledge can be naturally described in terms of 'if certain conditions are true then certain conclusions follow' then use rule-based programming `weighting: 5`

C.2.2 Knowledge Structure: Inferences and Generic Tasks

19. if not KBS task is diagnosis then don't use confirmation by exclusion `weighting: -5`

20. if there is a possibility of infinitely long paths in the search space then don't use depth-first search `weighting: -1` and don't use data-driven reasoning `weighting: -1`

21. if not search can be constrained so that it recognizes irrelevant intermediate conclusions and does not pursue lines of reasoning therefrom then don't use data-driven reasoning `weighting: -2`

22. if a decision made at one stage of problem solving may violate a constraint which will be necessary at a later stage then use constraint propagation `weighting: 3`

23. if KBS task is single-fault diagnosis and it is easier to confirm that something is working than that it is faulty then use confirmation by exclusion `weighting: 4`

24. if problem solving requires choosing between alternative courses of action and choices between alternative courses of action have to be dynamically determined from domain knowledge during problem solving then use meta-reasoning `weighting: 5`

25.   if you want to represent time explicitly then use temporal logic `weighting: 3`

C.2.3 Uncertainty in Knowledge

These rules encompass two possible approaches to explicit representation of uncertainty: (a) attach uncertainty to particular axioms in system (rules and facts in a rule-based system) (b) cope with uncertainty in the way one performs the inference – non-monotonic reasoning, e.g. TMSs

26.   if there is significant uncertainty in the knowledge that the system will use – the data/evidence that it will acquire or the inferences it will make and it is possible to estimate uncertainty in knowledge, either by calculation or by ad-hoc assignment of values then attach uncertainty measures to axioms (e.g. rules and facts in a rule-based system) `weighting: 4`

27.   if the problem-solving task which the system has to perform entails the formulation of hypotheses which may later be falsified by the acquisition of further data/evidence or by further inference making then use a truth maintenance system `weighting: 5`

28.   if you use numerical representation of uncertainty and statistical measures are available from which the validity of inferences can be calculated in terms of the probabilities of conclusions given conditions and the domain objects/relationships about which uncertainty is to be represented meet strong conditions of independence then use Bayesian probability for numerical representation of uncertainty `weighting: 5` and don't use ad-hoc subjective certainty factors for representation of uncertainty `weighting: -5`

29.   if you use numerical representation of uncertainty and uncertainty is to be represented in terms of confidence in belief, rather than in terms of probabilities and the domain objects/relationships about which uncertainty is to be represented meet strong conditions of independence then use Dempster-Shafer theory `weighting:   5` and don't use ad-hoc

subjective certainty factors for representation of uncertainty `weighting: -5`

30.   if you use numerical representation of uncertainty and membership of classes by objects is important but classification on a true-or-false basis is difficult or impossible then use fuzzy logic for representation of uncertainty `weighting: 4` and don't use ad-hoc subjective certainty factors for representation of uncertainty `weighting: -5`

31.   if you use uncertainty measures attached to axioms and not Bayesian probability for representation of uncertainty and not Dempster-Shafer theory for representation of uncertainty and not fuzzy logic for representation of uncertainty then use ad-hoc subjective certainty factors for representation of uncertainty `weighting: 5`

32.   if you use uncertainty measures attached to axioms and it is important that explicit information about how uncertainty measures for solution(s) were calculated be output with the solutions (as distinct from being implicitly derivable from an explanation system) then use symbolic representation of uncertainty `weighting: 4` else use numerical representation of uncertainty `weighting: 3`

33.   if you use a TMS and hypotheses can be falsified on multiple grounds (e.g. a timetabling problem – multiple clashes) then use a TMS which records grounds for rejecting rather than accepting hypotheses `weighting: 4`

C.2.4 Solutions

34.   if the problem-solving task is such that a pre-enumerated set of solutions can be established (as distinct from the type of task in which solutions are constructed as a result of the satisfaction of constraints) then use goal-driven reasoning `weighting: 1` ELSE use data-driven reasoning `weighting: 5` and don't use goal-driven reasoning `weighting: -5`

35.   if ratio of number of items of potentially relevant data to number of solutions is high (e.g. where data will be obtained from large files, only some items of which will be relevant, and

a fairly small pre-enumerated set of solutions is known) then use goal-driven reasoning `weighting: 3`

36.   if ratio of number of items of potentially relevant data to number of solutions is low then use data-driven reasoning `weighting: 3`

37.   if NOT solutions are mutually exclusive (Examples of tasks where solutions are mutually exclusive are: constructive tasks, scheduling, single-fault diagnosis. Examples where solutions are not mutually exclusive are: monitoring, multiplefault diagnosis) then use data-driven reasoning `weighting: 3`

38.   if solutions are mutually exclusive (Examples of tasks where solutions are mutually exclusive are: constructive tasks, scheduling, single-fault diagnosis. Examples where solutions are not mutually exclusive are: monitoring, multiple-fault diagnosis) and the user will seek all possible solutions (as distinct from a single solution) then use data-driven reasoning `weighting: 3`

39.   if NOT the user will seek all possible solutions (as distinct from a single solution) and the user will seek the best solution (as distinct from the first available solution)

    a.   and the best solution can be represented as that with the lowest-cost solution path through a search space (which may, or may not, be the shortest path) and the best solution can be represented as that with the shortest solution path through a search space and not the problem space is deep then use breadth-first search `weighting:   4`   OR heuristically informed search `weighting: 4`

40.   if NOT the user will seek all possible solutions (as distinct from a single solution) and the user will seek the best solution (as distinct from the first available solution)

    b.   and the best solution can be represented as that with the lowest-cost solution path through a search space (which may, or may not, be the shortest path) and the best solution can be represented as that with the shortest solution path through a search space and the problem

space is deep then use heuristically informed search
weighting: 4   OR   use   breadth-first   search
weighting: 2

41.   if NOT the user will seek all possible solutions (as
distinct from a single solution) and the user will seek the best
solution (as distinct from the first available solution) and the
best solution can be represented as that with the lowest-cost
solution path through a search space (which may, or may not,
be the shortest path) then use heuristically informed search
weighting: 4 OR breadth-first search weighting: 2

42.   if NOT the user will seek all possible solutions (as
distinct from a single solution) and the user will seek the best
solution (as distinct from the first available solution) and the
best solution can be represented as that with the lowest-cost
path through a search space to a goal (which may, or may not,
be the shortest path) and not the best solution can be
represented as that with the shortest solution path through a
search   space   then   use   heuristically   informed   search
weighting: 4 OR use breadth-first search weighting: 1

43.   if NOT the user will seek all possible solutions (as
distinct from a single solution) and the first solution is likely to
be found at great depth in the search space then use depth-first
search weighting: 2   OR heuristically informed search
weighting: 2

44.   if solutions can obviously be decomposed into sub-
solutions then use goal-driven reasoning weighting: 3

45.   if NOT the user will seek all possible solutions (as
distinct from a single solution) and the first solution is likely to
be found at shallow depth in the search space and the search
space is deep – say, more than 3 levels then use breadth-first
search for a single-fault diagnostic task. weighting: 4

C.2.5 Data

46.   if NOT time of arrival of data is exclusively under the
control of the user (e.g. a plant monitoring system) then use
opportunistic data-driven reasoning weighting: 3   and

don't use goal-driven reasoning `weighting: 5` because if you don't know when input is arriving then goal-driven reasoning is problematic: e.g. you might get halfway through proving that something is false, when data arrive to prove it true

47.   if data have to be gathered by eliciting questions from the user THEN use goal-driven reasoning `weighting: 2` and don't use data-driven reasoning `weighting: -1`

48.   if data have to be gathered by eliciting questions from the user and you use data-driven reasoning then use a multiple-selection menu to elicit data `weighting: 1`

49.   if data are already available (e.g. on file) then use data-driven reasoning user (as distinct from, e.g., a plant-monitoring system, where it is not) `weighting: 4`

C.2.6 Dialogue & Explanation

50.   if the presentation of explanations of the KBS's reasoning is important and not the *generation* of explanations of the KBS's reasoning in terms of cause and effect is important (as distinct from merely *presenting* explanations, e.g. as 'canned text') then use goal-driven reasoning `weighting: 2` OR canned text `weighting: 4` OR rules `weighting: 2`

51.   if data are to be obtained from the user and the natural dialogue is to ask detailed questions about one subject before general questions about another subject then use depth-first search `weighting: 4` because it is the best way to get coherent conversation

52.   if data are to be obtained from the user and not the natural dialogue is to ask detailed questions about one subject before general questions about another subject then use breadth-first search `weighting: 3`

C.3   Knowledge Representation & Inference questions

C.3.1 Knowledge Structure: Domain Objects & Relationships

53.   if you use an inheritance technique then use objects `weighting: 5` OR rules `weighting: 1`

54.   if the ratio of number of attributes to be represented per knowledge role (type of domain object) to number of relationships to be represented per knowledge role is high then use objects (ratio up to 4 then `weighting: 2`; ratio between 5 and 7 then `weighting: 3`; ratio 8 or more then `weighting: 4`)

55.   if the domain knowledge includes knowledge in tabular form and these tables need to be updated frequently then use a spreadsheet `weighting: 4` OR use a programming language representation `weighting: 2`

56.   if the domain knowledge includes knowledge in tabular form and efficiency of the KBS is important and the tables are large – say, more than 100 cells then use a spreadsheet `weighting: 3` OR use a programming language representation `weighting: 2`

57.   if the domain knowledge includes knowledge in tabular form and the tables are large – say, more than 100 cells and not efficiency of the KBS is important then use a spreadsheet `weighting: 1`

58.   if the domain knowledge includes knowledge in tabular form and the tables are 2-dimensional and not the tables are large and not the tables are updated frequently then use facts `weighting: 2` OR use objects `weighting: 2`

59.   if the domain knowledge includes knowledge in tabular form and not the tables are 2-dimensional then use facts `weighting:  5` OR use objects `weighting:  4`

60.   if many lists are to be implemented then use facts `weighting:  3` OR objects `weighting:  2`

C.3.2 Knowledge Structure: Inferences and Generic Tasks

61.   if the problem to be solved is very large – say, more than 10 modules (where a module performs a distinct operation and most of them require more than one inference step) then partition knowledge base into components that are loaded separately `weighting:  3`

62.   if regulations are to be represented then use rules `weighting:  3`

63.   if knowledge is heuristic in nature (i.e. 'rules of thumb') then use rules `weighting:  3`

64.   if you use rules and problem to be solved is very large – say, more than 10 modules (where a module performs a distinct operation and most of them require more than one inference step) then use a declarative agenda `weighting:  1` and represent variable-free rules using facts `weighting:  1`

C.3.3 Uncertainty in Knowledge

65.   if you use a TMS and you design your own TMS then use facts `weighting:   3` OR use objects which permit nested lists as slot values `weighting:  3`

C.3.4 Computational Efficiency

66.   if NOT you use rules and you use meta-reasoning then use meta-functions for control `weighting:  3`

C.4 Definitions of terminology related to solutions

Goal: (1) An acceptable configuration – i.e. one that meets all constraints (e.g. all components fit on the PCB) (2) A correct diagnosis of a complaint.

Solution: an instantiation of the goal ('a way of achieving the goal') for a particular data set. The number of solutions for a goal varies from few to many. The number of solutions for a given data set can vary from none to many:

1. There may be zero or more acceptable configurations for a given set of components
2. There may be one solution for any given complete data set, but no solution for an incomplete data set.

Solution path: 'a way of achieving the solution' for any given solution – e.g. a sequence of operations which must be performed. This sequence may carry a measure of cost of achieving the solution. The cost may be in terms of (a) number of operations or (b) cost of operations. There may be more than one solution path to any solution (strictly speaking, the number may be infinite if looping is not eliminated). Note that while the solution path may carry a measure of cost, the measure of benefit is presumably implicit in constraints that have to be satisfied.

Outcome: solution-end leaf node of problem space. If an outcome is not a solution then there is a need to backtrack (i.e. search has hit a dead end). The number of outcomes is equal to or greater than the number of solutions.

D A User's Guide to Pragmatic KADS

D.1 Pragmatic KADS: Introduction

"Pragmatic KADS" is an attempt to provide an introductory version of CommonKADS for novice knowledge engineers. It has two main goals: one is to provide guidance on developing models and making decisions, and the other is to reduce the number of models that need to be developed. It is particularly recommended for small KBS projects where the overhead of using the whole of CommonKADS would overwhelm the project.

Pragmatic KADS was developed in response to my own experience of learning KADS and CommonKADS; initially I learned only a few models and their specific application, and only later did I understand the underlying context of these models. CommonKADS has also been criticised for being beyond the comprehension of mere mortals (or at least, those without a training in ontology or logic), though this is less common now that the CommonKADS book [147] has been published. Pragmatic KADS is intended to remedy this criticism by providing a "simplified" version of CommonKADS.

Pragmatic KADS assumes that a knowledge engineer knows what KBS he is going to produce; in other words, all the knowledge management and project feasibility activities have been completed, but little of the knowledge acquisition and none of the knowledge representation or other knowledge engineering activities have been completed. In the language of the Zachman framework, the Scope and Enterprise levels have been completed but the System and lower levels remain to be developed. This is a fairly common state of affairs for commercially active knowledge engineers.

D.2 Pragmatic KADS step by step

This chapter takes the reader through the main steps in the analysis and design of a KBS using Pragmatic KADS. These steps are:

1. Setting the context;

2. Initial knowledge acquisition;
3. Knowledge analysis:
    - Building an inference structure;
    - Modelling interaction;
    - Identifying procedural ordering using the task structure and the "strategy level".
4. KBS design:
    - Selecting knowledge representation & KBS implementation techniques using Probing Questions;
    - Design the KBS as a number of 'modules';
    - Produce a 'physical design' for each module.

D.3 Setting the context

Because Pragmatic KADS assumes that the top two levels of the Zachman framework have been completed, there is little need for development of the Organisational, Task, Agent and (high level) Communication Models. However, there are some benefits to be obtained from developing fragments of these models in order to set the context of the KBS development. It's often helpful, for example, to consider how the KBS will fit with the organisation's wider business goals. It's also instructive to consider how responsibilities and roles might change due to the introduction of the system; more than one KBS project has succeeded technically but failed to be used because it required too great an organisational change.

If context-setting is important, therefore, Pragmatic KADS recommends that two diagrams should be drawn:

- At the Scoping level (i.e. the high level goals of the business), a process diagram should be drawn. This will provide a high level overview of the KBS' contribution to business goals.
- At the Enterprise level (i.e. the details of a single business process in which the KBS will play a part), a Role Activity Diagram (or Dialogue Diagram) is recommended (cf. Figure 6.5). This captures a large part of the information from the Task, Agent and Communication Models in a single diagram. It might also be advisable to develop a second RAD in which the KBS is introduced as an agent to show how responsibilities will change when the KBS is introduced.

D.4 Initial knowledge acquisition

Knowledge acquisition and analysis are closely intertwined in Pragmatic KADS. It is suggested that the first step should be to perform some initial knowledge acquisition – either by interviews, telephone conversations, or literature reviews – in order to obtain an overview of the problem which the KBS is trying to solve. It is particularly important to obtain an overview of the problem solving process at this stage. Once this knowledge has been acquired, *knowledge analysis* can begin which will both require and direct further knowledge acquisition.

D.5 Knowledge Analysis

The knowledge analysis process in Pragmatic KADS focuses on the development of the inference structure component of the Expertise model. This is carried out much as it is in full-blown CommonKADS (see chapter 8); the task type is identified, a generic inference structure is selected from the library, it may be adapted or configured, and then its knowledge roles are instantiated to the problem at hand.

It is possible to use the partially instantiated inference structure as an aid to knowledge acquisition, by showing the model to the expert, asking for constructive criticism, and then revising the model based on the expert's comments. This approach was used successfully by AIAI in the X-MATE project (see chapter 8).

It may be that the entities in the domain will have numerous inter-relationships. In this case, it is wise to document those relationships in a CommonKADS domain model (see section 8.3) or in a report.

D.5.1 Modelling agents and communication

Once an inference structure has been developed, Pragmatic KADS recommends the development of a **system-level** communication model – or to be precise, a dialogue diagram (see chapter 6) that summarises the tasks being carried out, the agents who perform it, and the communication that is needed to achieve this.

The dialogue diagram is a clear and concise way of representing agents and communication. However, it does not provide a great deal of support in making decisions about *assignment* of agents and communication to tasks. To remedy this, Pragmatic KADS recommends the development of a "model of interaction" that leads knowledge engineers through the process of making these decisions in three steps. Based on the original KADS "model of co-operation", this model can identify input-output, task dependencies and system & user roles. This model can even replace the dialogue diagram and become a "Pragmatic KADS communication model"; however, for reasons that will be explained in chapter 13, this is only viable for small KBS projects.

The model of interaction is explained further in section D.9.

D.5.2   Identifying procedural ordering

The last stage of the analysis of knowledge is to identify procedural ordering on the inferences. This requires determining the order in which inferences will be performed (if this has not already been done in the model of interaction), and identifying any iteration, recursion, or conditional ordering. It's worth inserting a reminder here that an inference structure can be implemented using several different procedural orderings of tasks.

The chosen ordering should normally be represented using the *task structure* which acts as a summary of the knowledge acquired in the analysis phase: it shows each inference step that the KBS will perform, identifying required inputs and outputs, iteration and conditional statements, and points at which external interaction is required. The task structure may be represented in a semi-formal language or in another written format, such as pseudocode. A diagrammatic format is not recommended, unless the task structure is fairly simple; in this case, the model of interaction is probably sufficient to represent the task structure as well as the communication model.

The ordering selected for the task structure may be influenced by the "strategy level". This is a fourth component of the Expertise model that was proposed in KADS but was removed by CommonKADS and replaced with the concept of problem solving methods. In Pragmatic KADS, however, "strategic" knowledge is less likely to consist of an overall strategy for approaching the problem (i.e. a problem solving method) and more likely to consist of a collection of factors and features that have specific influences on procedural ordering. Examples might include user requirements on particular knowledge roles, efficiency gains from doing one step before another, or multiple inputs and outputs from a single knowledge role. Since this knowledge is often useful to record, if only in text, and since it actually fulfils one of the 'missing' perspectives of the Zachman framework ('why' knowledge), it is included in Pragmatic KADS.

Once the following models have been completed:

- inference structure (possibly including low-level inference structures);
- domain model (optional);
- model of interaction;
- dialogue diagram (optional for small projects);
- task structure (optional for small projects);
- strategy level

the analysis phase of Pragmatic KADS is complete.

D.6 Knowledge-based system design

Pragmatic KADS strongly encourages *structure-preserving design*. This means that the structure of the knowledge, as represented in the models produced in the analysis phase, is reflected in the final design of the KBS. Since the inference structure and task structure have probably been developed in much more detail than the domain model(s), functional decomposition is the recommended decomposition paradigm.

A three-stage selection process should be carried out. This should be recorded, and the diagram format of the CommonKADS Design Model (see chapter 12) is recommended. A more compact format, based on the original KADS Design model, is available but is only suitable for the smallest projects; see chapter 13 for an example of this.

The recommended approach is as follows:

1.   Select appropriate KBS programming techniques for each of the inference steps that are to be performed by the KBS (as identified in the model of interaction and the task structure). The selection process is guided using "probing questions" which constitute the largest single piece of guidance provided by Pragmatic KADS. Probing questions are also used to select appropriate knowledge representations for knowledge roles. The probing questions technique is described further in section D.10.

2.   Design the KBS as a number of 'modules', where each module represents a particular inference step. The inputs and outputs between modules are specified by the inference structure. The inputs and

outputs to the user, or to other software, are specified in the dialogue diagram.

3.   Select a "platform design" for each module – i.e. specify where rules, objects, functions, methods, demons, algorithms etc. will be used. The physical design will also need to specify techniques for I/O with the user and other software – menus, pre-defined text, input boxes, SQL interfaces etc. The selection of platform design techniques will be based on the recommendations from the probing questions, and on the facilities available from the chosen KBS tool. If a choice of tools is available (which is rare), then the probing questions can be used as the major determinant of the platform design.

Once the platform design has been prepared, the Pragmatic KADS design phase is complete. Like CommonKADS, Pragmatic KADS currently offers no further assistance with implementation or validation & verification, although its models may be used as a guide for making later changes to the KBS. However, chapter 13 supplies a worked example of Pragmatic KADS, and does give some details of how it was implemented.

D.7 Guidance: Choosing a generic inference structure

This guidance is based on the hierarchy of tasks shown below, drawn from an early KADS report [20][48]. Most of the leaf nodes in this task hierarchy have an associated generic inference structure; few generic inference structures for other task types are known.

As a rule of thumb, task types that are classified as "System Analysis" are easier to solve using a KBS than tasks classified as "System Synthesis". Tasks that are classified as "System Modification" are the hardest of all, and few KBS have been successfully built which tackle these task types.

Diagrams of generic inference structures can be found in appendix A. Sources for this information include [20], [82], and [96].

---

[48] A couple of refinements have been made, notably the addition of "propose-and-revise design", an explanation of which can be found in chapter 10.

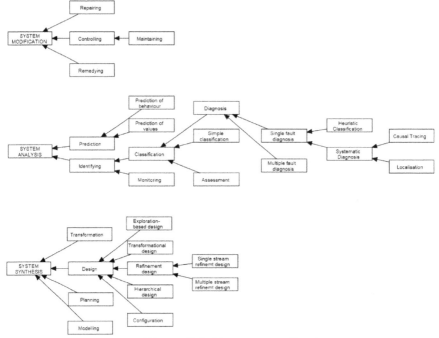

Figure D.1: Taxonomy of tasks

A small set of questions has been devised to assist in identification of the most appropriate generic inference structure [108]. These questions are given below: in each case, the words in bold type are the conclusion to be drawn from a positive answer to that question.

- Does the task involve
    1. Establishing unknown properties or behaviour of an object within the domain? : **System Analysis**
    2. Composing a new structural description of a possible object within the domain? : **System Synthesis**
    3. A combination of the above? : **System Modification**
- Can all possible solutions to the problem be enumerated?
    1. Yes : **System Analysis**
    2. No : **System Synthesis** or **System Modification**
- If the task is a System Analysis task then does the task involve
    1. Identifying a current property of a domain object : **Identification**
    2. Predicting a future state of a domain object : **Prediction**

- If the task is a Prediction task then does the task involve:
    1. Predicting behaviour? : **Prediction of behaviour**
    2. Predicting values? **Prediction of values**
    3. Predicting something else? : **Prediction**
- If the task is an Identification task then does the task involve
    1. Identifying a property of a domain object using various classification techniques? : **Classification**
    2. Comparing domain object properties against expectations and looking for anomalies, typically in a process? : **Monitoring**
- If the task is a Classification task then does the task involve:
    1. Classifying an object description into an object class? : **Simple-classification**
    2. Classifying a case description according to the terms of some system model? : **Assessment**
    3. Finding fault(s) in a system? : **Diagnosis**
- If the task is a Diagnosis task then does the task involve:
    1. Finding one fault in a system? : **Single-fault-diagnosis**
    2. Finding multiple faults in a system? (Same techniques as finding a single fault, only repeated application) : **Multiple-fault-diagnosis**
- If the task is a Single Fault Diagnosis task then does the task involve:
    1. Using heuristics to map from a problem space to a solution space? : **Heuristic Classification**
    2. Using systematic methods (e.g. eliminating impossible options) to diagnose a fault?: **Systematic Diagnosis**
- If the task is a Systematic Diagnosis task then does the task involve:
    1. Using a "part-of" model to represent the system model to be diagnosed? : **Localisation**
    2. Using a causal model to represent a system model to be diagnosed? : **Causal Tracing**

The next question has been added to the original set of questions, following Joost Breuker's more recent work [18]:

- If the task is a Systematic Diagnosis task then what type of solution is required?
    1. A faulty component – the solution of the original problem? : **Localisation**
    2. A single fault that is occurring – the cause of the original problem? : **Causal Tracing**

3. The argument that links the cause and solution of the original problem? **In this case, the reasoning process itself constitutes the desired solution. Choose the best inference structure according to other features and, if possible, choose an implementation tool that supports meta-reasoning**

- If the task is a System Synthesis task then does the task involve:
    1. Fitting one or more components into a constrained, pre-defined framework? : **Configuration**
    2. Designing an artefact which meets certain constraints, but without a pre-defined framework? : **Design**
    3. Determining a good step-by-step technique for solving a problem? : **Planning**
    4. Producing a good representation of a real world artefact or concept? : **Modelling**
- If the task is a Design task then does the task involve:
    1. Breaking down the design into subcomponents, and designing each subcomponent independently? : **Hierarchical design**
    2. Gradually transforming the design from one representation to another? : **Transformational Design**
    3. Suggesting a design, and using criticisms of that design to determine further constraints on the next design? : **Propose-and-revise design**
    4. Selecting a skeleton model, and fitting design elements into that model? : **Refinement design**

D.8 Guidance: Instantiating a generic inference structure

Instantiating an inference structure is a knowledge-based classification/design task. It involves deciding which domain entities (if any) match the knowledge roles suggested in the generic inference structure; this is a classification task. [49] If the model needs to be extended in order to accommodate important domain entities and concepts which are not represented in the generic inference structure,

---

[49] It's classification as opposed to assessment because assessment requires choices between competing alternatives, and there are few such alternatives in a typical knowledge based project.

then an element of design (not configuration, since there is no restriction on the size of the target model) is involved.

A good understanding of the generic inference structure is a requirement for the instantiation to be done well. This requires understanding the semantics of the inference steps. Pragmatic KADS uses the 22 "primitive" inference steps which were proposed at the start of the KADS project [20]; if these definitions are insufficient for a particular knowledge engineering problem, a more formal and more detailed description of CommonKADS' inference steps can be found in [2].

As for adapting inference structures, the following rules must be adhered to:

1. Each primitive inference step must have only one output. If the inference step is not primitive (i.e. it is decomposed into a lower level inference structure), this rule can be waived.

2. The definitions of the primitive inference steps must be followed. For example, the definition of *specify* is that it changes a structure into a similar structure with extra information added. The inputs and output of *specify* must therefore be structures of the same type.

In practice, Pragmatic KADS allows these rules to be 'bent' in the following ways:

• Pragmatic KADS includes definitions of "activities" that form part of the inference process but aren't strictly knowledge-based functions. These include arithmetic functions and functions that simply add or take away from a set or a list. It also includes "execute" (i.e. carry out some action) which broadly correlates with CommonKADS' concept of a "transfer function".

• Pragmatic KADS permits inference steps to have multiple outputs. This is used in situations such as in IMPRESS to allow the inference step that decomposes the set of hypotheses to have two alternative outputs – a hypothesis to test or a conclusion. Technically, this detail belongs in the task structure, but it makes the inference structure much more comprehensible to an expert if this is included.

D.9 Guidance: Building   the   model   of interaction

The purpose of the model of interaction is to specify input & output, and to make decisions about the respective roles of KBS and user explicit. The model is constructed by first creating a task hierarchy that represents every inference step from the inference structure. If some steps belong to a low level inference structure, then they appear at a lower level in this task hierarchy. This model is then annotated with dependencies, input/output requirements, and finally with role assignments. In more detail:

- Step 1 is to draw up an ordered list of the different subtasks which a KBS must perform in order to fulfil its problem-solving task. This list is derived from the inference structure, and may be partially or fully ordered; the knowledge engineer may choose to make decisions about ordering of inferences at this stage, or may delay the decision until the preparation of the task structure. Using IMPRESS (see chapters 7 and 8) as an example, the results of stage 1 would look like the diagram shown in figure D.2
- Step 2 is to identify the dependencies between subtasks i.e. the inputs and outputs of each subtask. The process of adding dependencies to the diagram often identifies requirements for I/O with external databases, files, the user, or other sources of information. All external I/O should be explicitly represented in the model – see figure D.3.
- Step 3 is to make design decisions about which subtasks will be performed by the KBS which by the user, and which by the KBS and user together. In the IMPRESS system, the main design decision was whether the selection of a **test to perform** should be done by the KBS and user in conjunction, or by the KBS alone; in other words, whether the user should be permitted to reject the system's recommendation of a test. It was decided that the user would indeed be allowed to reject the recommended test, and to ask for another test to be recommended. The inference step *select test to perform* was therefore assigned to **KBS & user**.

The assignments made are represented by shading the inference steps in figure D.4.

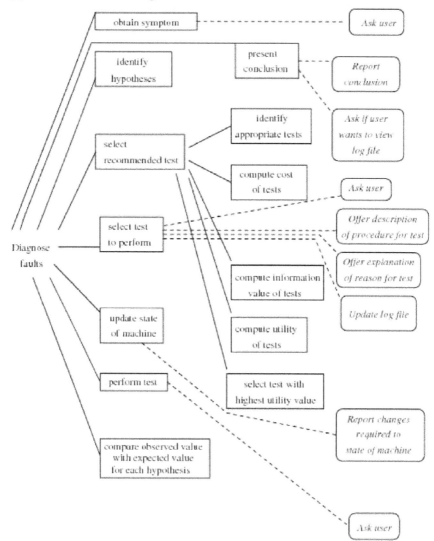

Figure D.2: IMPRESS Model of interaction: Step 1

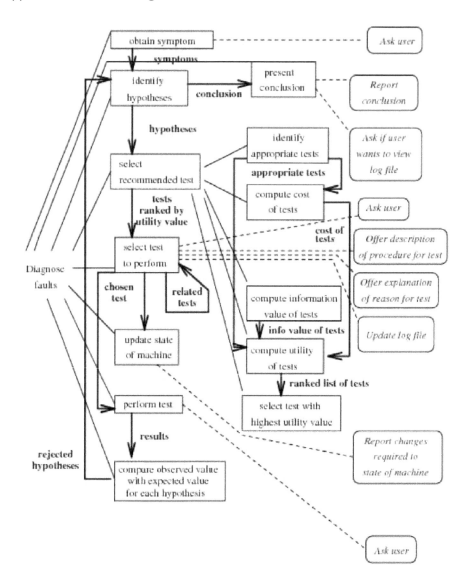

Figure D.3: IMPRESS Model of interaction: Step 2

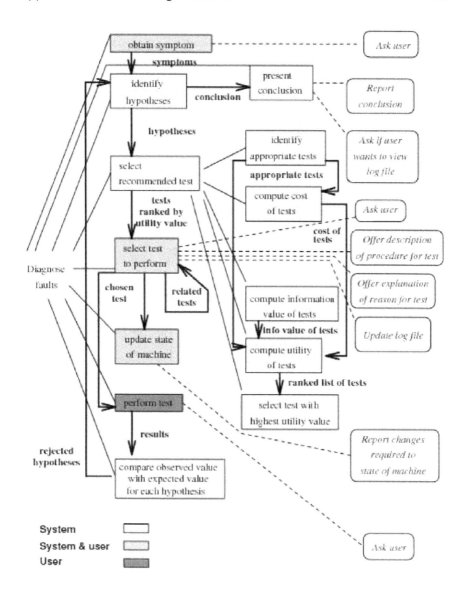

Figure D.4: IMPRESS Model of interaction: Step 3

The model of interaction can be based on the task structure instead of the inference structure. Here is an example, drawn from a KBS which helps civil engineers to check the design of a building against British standards: (see chapter 6 for details). The task structure is:

task assessing-building-against-British-standards
goal check that a building design conforms to British standards
task structure
assessing-building-against-British-standards(results of checks)
obtain(numerical description of building)
transform(numerical description → model of the building)
select(a check to perform)
obtain(any further information required for that check)
match(model of building + standards relevant to the chosen check
→ result of check)
report(results of check)

The resulting model of interaction is shown in Figure D.5.

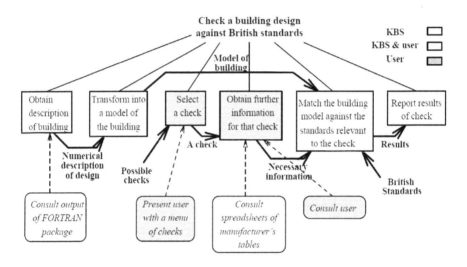

Figure D.5: Model of interaction for the KBS which checks the
design of a building against British standards

D.9.1 Benefits of the model of interaction

What are the benefits of the model of interaction? At the very least, it serves as a useful *aide memoire* for the designer of the I/O components of the KBS, both for the inputs & outputs of the KBS as a whole, and for any I/O which occurs within the KBS. The model of interaction is at its most useful when it is used to identify that one or more subtasks should be carried out by the user of the KBS; if this is so, the design of the KBS may be radically affected. An excellent example of this comes from a project carried out for an insurance company. The task of the KBS was to identify errors on forms; the task structure is shown below.

    task identify-errors-on-forms

    goal check each field on a form against its predicted value to identify errors made when filling in the form **control-terms** fields = set of all fields on the form

    task structure

        identify-errors-on-forms(classified-errors)

        decompose(form → fields)

            do for each field ∈ fields **specify**(expected value)

    read(actual value)

            match(actual value + expected value → mismatches)

            classify(errors → classified-errors)

Figure D.6: Task structure for form processing

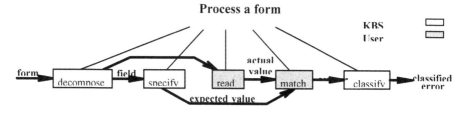

Figure D.7: Model of interaction for a form processing KBS

Each of the five tasks identified must be carried out by either the KBS or the user. Since knowledge based systems are typically good at performing matching tasks, it would be normal for the "match expected value against actual value" task to be allocated to the system. However, this would have required the user to type in many values from many different forms, and it also required the KBS to have considerable knowledge about the nature of the data, near-matches, etc.

It was decided that the forms would not actually be input into the KBS; instead, the KBS would advise the user on fields to check, and the user would perform the actual matching. The effects of assigning the matching task to the user were immense. KBS designers often use production rules to implement matching tasks; but, with the matching task being performed by the user, it was decided that the forms processing KBS could be developed entirely using object-oriented programming. In the terminology of the model of interaction, the *match* subtask would be carried out by the user, as shown in Figure D.6.

The biggest drawback of the model of interaction is its complexity. This is discussed further in chapter 13.

D.10 Guidance: Selecting techniques using Probing Questions

Probing questions are used to guide knowledge engineers in the selection of appropriate knowledge representation and KBS implementation techniques. This is accomplished by the knowledge engineer asking himself questions about the analysed knowledge. The questions are of the general form

if a certain feature exists in the analysed knowledge

then consider using a particular knowledge representation, or implementation technique.

The probing questions are intended to be heuristics to guide the design process.

In Pragmatic KADS, probing questions are divided into three categories:

1. "Application design" questions that suggest **AI paradigms** – ways of approaching the design as a whole. Examples of AI paradigms might be
   - blackboard reasoning;
   - constraint-based reasoning;
   - case-based reasoning;
   - model-based reasoning.

The use of an architectural paradigm will greatly restrict other design choices, and so the possibility of using paradigms is investigated first.

2. "Architectural design" questions which suggest **AI programming techniques**. Examples of AI programming techniques are:
   - depth-first search;
   - truth maintenance;
   - fuzzy reasoning;
   - data-driven reasoning.

Some of the suggestions at this level are based on the implementation of particular inference steps in particular task types;

for example: "if the task type is localisation then recommend using **Generate and Test** to implement the *select-1* inference step".

3. "Detailed architectural design" questions that suggest **AI representation & inference techniques**. Representation techniques include:

- rules;
- objects;
- user-defined relations;
- sorted logic.

Inference techniques include:

- forward chaining;
- slot daemons;
- meta-rules;
- using recency for conflict resolution.

The current list of probing questions which is based on knowledge acquired from three members of AIAI staff by Colin MacNee [120] [98], can be found in Appendix C. They are divided into the three categories, and are secondarily subdivided according to the following scheme:

- Knowledge Structure – (A): Domain Objects and Relationships;
- Knowledge Structure – (B): Inferences and Generic Task;
- Uncertainty in Knowledge;
- Solutions;
- Data;
- Dialogue & Explanation;
- Computational Efficiency.

Probing questions are intended for use as knowledge engineer's heuristics. The advice that they give is applicable in most situations, but it is expected that it any real life problem, there may be exceptional circumstances which override the recommendations of the probing questions. An obvious example of such a circumstance would be if the KBS is to be implemented in a shell which does not support any kind of object-oriented programming; then all recommendations regarding the use of objects would have to be ignored.

D.11   Summary

Pragmatic KADS is intended to support knowledge engineers on small KBS projects. It provides some guidance, much of which is in the form of heuristic rules; it seems sensible to practice what I preach. The model of interaction, although similar in form to the original KADS model of co-operation, is intended to support knowledge engineers in making agent and communication-related decisions, and the three-stage development of it supports that.

E List of John Kingston's publications

Listed below are all John Kingston's publications to date on knowledge management, knowledge engineering, or knowledge modelling. They are ordered by date, starting with the most recent.

John Kingston, Tacit Knowledge: Capture, Sharing and Unwritten Assumptions. *Journal of Knowledge Management Practice,* 13(3), Sep 2012. *http://www.tlainc.com/articl310.htm.* A response to the oft-asserted claim that tacit knowledge cannot be captured through knowledge acquisition. It classifies four types of 'tacit' knowledge – noting the irony that the nature of 'tacit' knowledge is often not made explicit by other authors – and argues that three of the four can indeed be captured.

John Kingston, Multi-perspective Ontologies: Resolving Common Ontology Problems. *Expert Systems with Applications*, 34(1), Jan 2008: 541-550. This paper looks at how a multi-perspective approach can help to resolve ontology problems such as IS-A overloading, inaccurate expert responses, dependence relations and particulars.

John Kingston, Multi-Perspective Modelling: A Framework for Knowledge Representation and Knowledge Management, Proceedings of AI-METH 2005, Gliwice, Poland, Nov 2005. The paper discusses in detail an approach to multi-perspective modelling based on the Zachman framework; applies this approach to key knowledge management approaches and modelling methods; and validates the approach by showing how meta-analysis of the framework can be used to derive well-known software development techniques.

John Tickner, Jeff Friar, Karen S. Creely, John W. Cherrie, D. Eric Pryde and John Kingston, The Development of the EASE Model, *Annals of Occupational Hygiene* 49(2), 2005:103-110, The creation and development of the EASE system for occupational hygienists from 1992 to 2002 is described.

John Kingston, Conducting Feasibility Studies for Knowledge Based Systems, Proceedings of BCS SGAI AI'03 conference, Peterhouse College, Cambridge, 15-17 December 2003. Also in the *Knowledge Based*

Systems Journal, 17, Elsevier Science, 2004. This paper describes how to carry out a feasibility study for a potential knowledge based system application under three headings: the business case, the technical feasibility, and stakeholder issues. It concludes with a case study of a feasibility study for a KBS to guide surgeons in diagnosis and treatment of thyroid conditions.

Knox Haggie and John Kingston, Choosing your Knowledge Management Strategy, *Journal of Knowledge Management Practice*, Volume 4, 2003. Applies and extends Binney's KM Spectrum to provide a guide to selecting a KM approach that matches organisational strategy.

John Kingston, Ontology, Knowledge Management, Knowledge Engineering and the ACM Classification Scheme. Proceedings of ES '02, the 22nd annual International Conference of the British Computer Society's Specialist Group on Artificial Intelligence, Peterhouse College, Cambridge, 10-12 December 2002. This paper tests the theory of multiple perspectives being necessary for completeness in ontologies by applying it to the task of placing "knowledge management" and "knowledge engineering" within the ACM classification scheme.

John Kingston, Merging Top Level Ontologies for Scientific Knowledge Management. Proceedings of the AAAI workshop on Ontologies and the Semantic Web, AAAI-02 conference, Edmonton, Canada, 29 July 2002. Describes the merging of four independently developed ontologies describing academics, their publications and research areas, etc.

John K.C. Kingston, High Performance Knowledge Bases: Four approaches to Knowledge Acquisition, Representation and Reasoning for Workaround Planning. *Expert Systems with Applications*, Volume 21, 4, November 2001. Describes and compares four solutions to the same "challenge problem" in knowledge acquisition and knowledge-based planning.

John K.C. Kingston, Ontologies, Multi-Perspective Modelling and Knowledge Auditing, In Proceedings of the Ontologies Workshop, German and Austrian Joint Conference on Artificial Intelligence (KI-2001), Vienna, 18 September 2001. A position paper on the use of ontologies in knowledge auditing, and the use of multi-perspective modelling principles in building adequate ontologies.

K. Nammuni, J. Levine and John K.C. Kingston, Skill-based Resource Allocation using Genetic Algorithms and an Ontology. In

Proceedings of the International Workshop on Intelligent Knowledge Management Techniques (I-KOMAT 2002) held at the 6th International Conference on Knowledge-Based Intelligent Information and Engineering Systems (KES 2002), September 2002, IOS Press, Amsterdam. Uses genetic algorithms and an ontology to make optimal allocations of resources (tutors with various skills) to tasks (tutorials requiring certain skills).

John K.C. Kingston, Modelling Agents and Communication using CommonKADS. In *Research and Development in Expert Systems XVII*, Proceedings of the ES'00 conference, Churchill College, Cambridge, December 2000. Details, worked examples, and proposals for extension of the CommonKADS Agent and Communication models

John K.C. Kingston, Knowledge based system development tools. In the Encyclopedia of Life Support Systems, pub. UNESCO, 2002. Describes categories and capabilities of KBS development tools

J. Kingston and A. Macintosh, Knowledge Management through Multi-Perspective Modelling: Representing and Distributing Organizational Memory. In *Research and Development in Expert Systems XVI*, proceedings of BCS SGES Expert Systems '99 conference, Churchill College, Cambridge, December 1999. Also in the Knowledge Based Systems Journal, 13 (2-3), Elsevier Science, 2000, pp. 121-131. The who, what, how, when, where and why of a medical procedure, expressed using complementary knowledge modelling techniques, also including a discussion of how a knowledge model can be used as a user interface.

A. Macintosh, I. Filby and J. Kingston, Knowledge Management Techniques: Teaching & Dissemination Concepts. *International Journal of Human Computer Studies (Special Issue on Organizational Memories: Knowledge Management)*, vol. 51, no. 3, Academic Press, September 1999. Brief description of a knowledge management methodology.

Jon Simpson, John K.C. Kingston and Neil R. Molony, Internet-Based Decision Support for Best Practice in Medicine. In *Applications and Innovations in Expert Systems VI*, proceedings of the 15th Annual Conference of the British Computer Society's Specialist Group on Expert Systems, Cambridge, 14-16 December 1998. Also in the Knowledge Based Systems Journal, 12 (5-6), Elsevier Science, 1999, pp. 247-255. Design and development of a prototype Internet-based decision support/ knowledge-based system for following clinical protocols, using knowledge models as part of the user interface.

M. Sideris, N. Kyrtatos, N. Parthenios and J. Kingston, A Computer based Application for Ship-Survey Reporting. *New Review of Applied Expert Systems*, volume 5, 1999, pp. 113-128. Design and development of VESSELL, a KBS for determining techniques and cost for repainting ship cargo holds.

R. Power, S. Reynolds, J. Kingston, I. Harrison, A. Macintosh and J. Tonberg, In *Applications and Innovations in Expert Systems V*, proceedings of BCS SGES Expert Systems '97 conference, Churchill College, Cambridge, 15-17 December 1997. Also in the Knowledge Based Systems Journal, 11 (5-6), Elsevier Science, 1998, pp. 339-344. Motivation, design and development of a knowledge-based decision support system which supports the reprovisioning of spare parts within the RAF.

John K.C. Kingston, Designing Knowledge-Based Systems: The CommonKADS Design Model, In *Research and Development in Expert Systems XIV*, Proceedings of BCS SGES Expert Systems'97, Cambridge, 15-17 December 1997. Also in the *Knowledge Based Systems Journal*, 11 (5-6), Elsevier Science, 1998, pp. 311-319. Worked examples of the CommonKADS Design Model, using IMPRESS and X-MATE as examples.

John K.C. Kingston, Anna Griffith and Terri J. Lydiard, Multi-perspective modelling of Air Campaign Planning. Proceedings of the International Joint Conference on Artificial Intelligence (IJCAI '97), Nagoya, Japan, 23-29 August 1997. Using the CommonKADS Organisational and Task models to represent the process of air campaign planning by the USAF.

Stefan Robertson and John K.C. Kingston, Selecting a KBS Tool using a knowledge based system. Proceedings of PACES/SPICIS '97, Singapore, 24-27 February 1997. Design and development of a prototype KBS for deciding on the best programming package for a KBS project.

J.K.C. Kingston, Building a KBS for Health and Safety Assessment. *Applications and Innovations in Expert Systems IV*, Proceedings of BCS Expert Systems'96, Cambridge, 16-18 December 1996. SGES Publications. Design, development and roll-out of EASE which is used by occupational hygienists from the Health and Safety Executive when assessing the safety of a new manufacturing process

J.K.C. Kingston, N. Shadbolt and A. Tate, CommonKADS Models for Knowledge Based Planning. Proceedings of AAAI-96, Portland, Oregon, 5-8 August 1996. Describes how a new "CommonKADS" model was developed based on the O-Plan system, and how the model was used in the Search and Rescue project.

H. Cottam, N. Shadbolt, J. Kingston, H. Beck and A. Tate, Knowledge Level Planning in the Search and Rescue Domain. In Proceedings of BCS Expert Systems'95, Cambridge, 11-13 December 1995. Motivation, design and development of a prototype system for planning the deployment of Search and Rescue helicopters.

J.K.C. Kingston, J.G. Doheny and I.M. Filby, Evaluation of workbenches which support the CommonKADS methodology. *Knowledge Engineering Review*, 10, 3, 1995. Comparison of KADSTool, Open KADS Tool and the CommonKADS Workbench.

S. Dirks, M. Haggith and J. Kingston, Development of a KBS for Personal Financial Planning Guided by Pragmatic KADS. *Expert Systems with Applications*, 9(2), 1995, pp. 91-101. Design and development of a prototype system for designing a personal financial portfolio (28 pages).

J.K.C. Kingston, Applying KADS to KADS: knowledge-based guidance for knowledge engineering. *Expert Systems: The International Journal of Knowledge Engineering*, 12, 1, Feb 1995. An overview of three KBS prototypes which advise on selecting models from the CommonKADS library, good KBS design, and good selection of a KBS tool

J.K.C. Kingston, Linking Knowledge Acquisition to CommonKADS Knowledge Representation. Proceedings of BCS SGES Expert Systems'94, Cambridge, 12-14 December 1994. Techniques for mapping the output of knowledge acquisition into CommonKADS, based on the TOPKAT system.

J. Kingston, Re-engineering IMPRESS and X-MATE into CommonKADS. BCS SGES Expert Systems '93, St. John's College, Cambridge, 13-15 December 1993. A detailed description of key components of the new CommonKADS methodology, using IMPRESS and X-MATE as examples.

S.J. Price and J. Kingston, The KADESS Knowledge-Based System: employing the KADS methodology in an engineering application. In Proceedings of the Sixth International Conference on Industrial and Engineering Applications of Artificial Intelligence and Expert Systems, Edinburgh, June 1-4 1993. Design and development of a prototype KBS for assessing whether portal frame buildings conform to regulations.

J. Kingston, KBS Methodology as a framework for Co-operative Working. Proceedings of Expert Systems 92, the 12th annual technical conference of the BCS Specialist Group on Expert Systems, Churchill College, Cambridge, 15-17 December 1992. Design and development of the IMPRESS system for diagnosing faults in plastic moulding machinery.

J. Kingston, Pragmatic KADS: A methodological approach to a small knowledge based systems project. In *Expert Systems: The International Journal of Knowledge Engineering*, 4, 4, November 1992. Design and development of the Course Selector system.

J. Kingston, Modelling interaction between a KBS and its users. Newsletter of the BCS SGES Methodologies Interest Group, volume 1, Spring 1992.

J. Kingston, How to build a knowledge-based system for credit risk assessment. Presented to the annual conference of the Institute of Mathematics and its Applications, Edinburgh, 25-27 September 1991. This paper is a revised version of the paper on X-MATE below.

J. Kingston, X-MATE: Creating an interpretation model for credit risk assessment. Proceedings of BCS SGES Expert Systems 91, London, 17-18 September 1991. Development of a knowledge based system for mortgage application underwriting.

www.ingramcontent.com/pod-product-compliance
Lightning Source LLC
Chambersburg PA
CBHW070931050326
40689CB00014B/3155